What the IRS
Doesn't Want
You to Know

A CPA Reveals the Tricks of the Trade

Ninth Edition

MARTIN S. KAPLAN, CPA

WILEY

John Wiley & Sons, Inc.

For general information on our other products and services, or technical support, please contact our Customer Care Department within the United States at 800-762-2974, outside the United States at 317-572-3993 or fax 317-572-4002.

Wiley also publishes its books in a variety of electronic formats. Some content that appears in print may not be available in electronic books.

For more information about Wiley products, visit our web site at www.wiley.com.

ISBN: 0-471-44972-5

Printed in the United States of America.

10 9 8 7 6 5 4 3 2 1

I would like to dedicate this book to Harriet, my wife and best friend,
for her love and unselfish support of all my endeavors,
and for always being there for me.
Also to Sharon, Jason, Hillary, Bruce, Brian, and Nancy—
children that any parent would be proud of.
A special note to my grandchildren, Lindsay and Dylan:
It's never too early to begin tax planning.

Contents

Acknowledgments

I would like to thank George K. Greene, CLU, for being such a good sounding board; Marvin Cohen, CPA, for his sound advice on technical matters; and Shelley Davis, former IRS historian.

I wish to thank David Burnham and Susan Long, cofounders of the Transactional Records Access Clearinghouse (TRAC) at Syracuse University (http://www.trac.syr.edu/tracirs/).

Also, I very much appreciate David Cay Johnston of the *New York Times* for his timely and comprehensive reporting on the IRS.

1

Why Every Taxpayer Must Read This Book

Each year hundreds of reputable books are written about taxes, audits, and the IRS. Unfortunately, the information taxpayers really need rarely, if ever, surfaces. No matter how much taxpayers read, hear, or research on the subject, they still remain easy targets for the IRS. We live in a megatechnology environment and hear promises about a more consumer-oriented IRS. This book tells you just how to approach the "new" IRS to maximize your tax return success.

It also includes the very latest information on the Jobs and Growth Tax Relief Reconciliation Act of 2003, the Job Creation and Worker Assistance Act of 2002 (JCWA) and the Economic Growth and Tax Relief Reconciliation Act of 2001. Throughout this book, the 2003 tax law will be referred to as the Tax Act of 2003, and the 2001 tax law will be referred to as the Tax Act of 2001; you'll learn what's in them for you and what you must know. To help you stay on top of your current financial situation, a detailed explanation of the most far-reaching provisions of this legislation is in Chapter 12, The Latest Tax Legislation.

So, welcome to the most important book you may read in 2003!

First, let's face some facts. Traditionally, the IRS has had a reputation for being all-knowing, all-powerful, and ruthless (many would say vicious). It is seen to have extensive manpower and technological resources, and the law seems to be on its side. Without actually knowing what the IRS is and how the organization really works—or, perhaps more important, how it doesn't work—the public remains in the grip of the IRS's reputation as the Big Bad Wolf.

Millions of taxpayers live with the fear that an IRS agent will single out an item from their tax return, initiate an audit, and come after them. In fact, the IRS is often referred to as an agency out of control—and with good reason. Once it selects its culprits, it chooses the punishment and proceeds to administer it with very little containment from any other governmental or nongovernmental agencies. It's not surprising that most taxpayers envision the IRS as harassing and abusive, using its power in an uncaring, even brutal way to potentially destroy their careers and families. Taxpayers are so fearful of dealing with the IRS that they rank an audit as an event as traumatic as divorce or losing their home, illustrating how enormously successful the IRS has been in creating its all-powerful-and-untouchable image.

Now let's look at those who know exactly what is going on and find out why they aren't talking. Any good Certified Public Accountant (CPA) or tax professional knows how to beat the IRS at its own game. But an unwritten law among tax professionals has traditionally prevented this vital information from being revealed publicly. What is this tacit agreement based on? It's based on their healthy fear that the IRS will turn against them, the tax professionals.

When filling out clients' returns, tax professionals use information they have gained as experts. But these very same professionals do not traditionally disclose information in three crucial areas. They don't tell the public

1. What the IRS really is and how it thinks, responds, and operates—or, more precisely, doesn't operate.
2. About endless loopholes in the tax laws that can be used in the preparation of an individual tax return.
3. How both of these can be used consistently to benefit taxpayers.

Tax professionals have made it a practice *not* to reveal such information—and with good reason: They've seen firsthand how people can be destroyed by both warranted and unwarranted IRS attacks. Why would CPAs, or any professionals in the tax field, put their lives, families, careers, and futures on the line? The answer traditionally prevents tax professionals from publicly explaining why the right kind of information never gets to the taxpaying public. It also keeps them from revealing that information on a broad scale.

To prevent an all-out personal conflagration and probably endless repercussions, tax professionals continue to offer whitewashed material that tells taxpayers how they can disappear from the IRS's view. In fact, much of this information is correct. It does work. But too much inside information that is critically important is left out, and no one knows this better than we do.

In 35 years as a CPA, I have repeatedly watched how the IRS can financially ruin all kinds of people: rich, middle-class, the average working family—people exactly like you.

A few years ago a fascinating case involving IRS wrongdoing hit the newspapers. It had begun simply enough.

Mrs. Carole Ward accompanied her son to an audit of their family business, three children's clothing stores in Colorado Springs. Because the audit was going poorly, Mrs. Ward spoke up to the female IRS revenue agent, saying, "Honey, from what I can see of your accounting skills, the country would be better served if you were dishing up chicken-fried steak on the interstate in West Texas, with all that clunky jewelry and big hair."

Four weeks later, IRS revenue agents raided the family's stores, padlocked all three of them, and posted notices in the windows that implied that Mrs. Ward, who was 49, was a drug smuggler. The IRS then imposed a tax bill in the amount of $324,000.

Mrs. Ward hired two attorneys and sought press coverage to publicize her plight. The IRS countered with a publicity campaign that included sending a letter to the editor of the local newspaper, giving details of Ward's case and providing a fact sheet about it to the TV show *Inside Edition*.

Three months after the raid, the government settled the tax dispute for $3,485, but a week later the IRS district director appeared on a radio show, detailing the IRS's position against Ward. He failed to mention that the bill had already been settled for little more than 1 percent of the original amount.

At this point, Ward sued the IRS for disclosing confidential information from her tax return. Until the case was brought to trial, Ward's daughter had to quit high school because the IRS statements led students to believe the family was engaged in drug smuggling. The family went from having no debts at the time of the raid to owing $75,000. The lease on one of the stores was lost. And only two-thirds of the goods and equipment seized in the raid was returned, much of that badly damaged.

During the nine-day trial the IRS and the Justice Department, which defended the lawsuit, denied any wrongdoing. In a harshly worded 17-page opinion, Judge William Downes of the federal district court in Denver found that one of the IRS agents had been "grossly negligent," had acted with "reckless disregard" for the law, and had made three false statements in a sworn declaration. The judge awarded Mrs. Ward $4,000 in damages for improper disclosures, $75,000 in damages for the emotional distress the IRS caused her to suffer, and $250,000 in punitive damages, giving "notice to the IRS that reprehensible abuse of authority by one of its employees cannot and will not be tolerated." The judge also criticized the IRS district director who had made the radio appearance.

"I never should have spoken condescendingly," Ward later said, "but what they did to me for mouthing off was criminal."

Never forget—the amount awarded by the judge, and the fact that such a case was settled in the taxpayer's favor, is the result of almost 20 years of private citizens fighting for retribution in thousands of similar cases but receiving nothing except bureaucratic doors slammed in their faces.

Here's another case that demonstrates the blatant and unmitigated arrogance of the IRS.

A high-level executive in a nationally known insurance company was the subject of an extensive IRS investigation. Allegedly he owed $3,500. The taxpayer agreed to admit to tax evasion, and the IRS promised, in a written agreement, to keep the matter out of the public eye. When the executive informed his employer of his tax problem, he was told that the one thing he must avoid was a public scandal. Since the agreement with the IRS seemed to preclude this, the matter should have ended there. But it didn't. About three months into the investigation, the IRS issued to more than 21 sources news releases that included the tax-payer's name, his address, and the name of his employer. The taxpayer promptly lost his job, had to move out of town, and never again regained his prominent position.

Why was the IRS so interested in pursuing a case in which the tax liability was only $3,500? The answer was revealed about two years later at a trial resulting from a suit the executive brought against the IRS. Here's what really happened:

Initially, when the taxpayer found out that the IRS was investigating him, he asked the agent assigned to the case what he had done wrong. He was told that his wife had made some bookkeeping errors in managing his records, resulting in the amount owed. But a transcript from the trial showed the real reason for the extensive investigation. "The only publicity that is good for the IRS is when it brings a big one down" were the agent's words. Since the taxpayer was a prominent figure in his area, he satisfied that need, although the agent admitted that he didn't think there was any real proof that the taxpayer even owed the IRS money. After a 20-year battle, the case was settled to the tune of $3 million for the much maligned insurance executive.

More recently, an IRS revenue agent informed a TV station that a search warrant was being served on a local company, and it was subsequently shown on the evening news. The reputation of the business was permanently damaged, even though the IRS never filed any formal tax charges. The company sued and was awarded $2 million from the IRS.[1]

I know many cases like these, but I have also come to understand which words, style, techniques, and knowledge can effectively make the IRS come to an abrupt standstill in a lot less time.

What is more heartening is tax legislation—the Taxpayer Relief Act of 1997 (TRA '97) and the Restructuring and Reform Act of 1998 (RRA '98)—that contains laws designed to limit the unbridled power of the IRS and restore certain rights to taxpayers.

In December 1994, an IRS collection agent entered the tax preparation office of Mr. Richard Gardner in Tulsa, Oklahoma, and demanded that he turn over $20,000 for nonpayment of income and Social Security taxes withheld from the paychecks of his seven employees. Mr. Gardner said that he would pay the amount in a few weeks, after receiving payment from his clients. The collection agent then threatened a "jeopardy assessment," in which cash, bank accounts, and property can be seized. To stall the IRS collection action, Mr. Gardner, who is the sixth-largest income tax preparer in Oklahoma, placed his two businesses, the second being a store selling used books and comics, in bankruptcy. Days later, he paid the overdue taxes and canceled the bankruptcy actions. Three months after that, armed agents raided Mr. Gardner's tax preparation office, seizing all the computers and files. That very night, Mr. Gardner purchased new computers, and the next morning he was back in business when an IRS agent from the Criminal Investigation Division telephoned. Hearing Mr. Gardner's voice, he said, "I'm surprised you're open. We thought we'd put you out of business."

In January 1998, the Justice Department withdrew the charges made against Mr. Gardner and, without admitting wrongdoing, paid $75,000 to Mr. Gardner's lawyer for the cost of the case. The two men had sought $102,000. This made Mr. Gardner the first person to have his legal defense fees paid by the Justice Department under a 1997 law intended to curb prosecutions that are "vexatious, frivolous, or in bad faith."

Mr. Gardner's lawyer has stated that the IRS took what were lawful, routine business actions on the part of his client as a personal affront and set out to destroy his client's business. Mr. Gardner believed that the charges made against him were essentially "unlawful actions" designed to punish him because he had the temerity to exercise his constitutional rights as a way of delaying payment of back taxes. What has made this case particularly extraordinary is that once an indictment is handed up in a tax matter, the Justice Department routinely insists on either going to trial or obtaining a guilty plea to at least one charge. It is inordinately rare for such a case to be withdrawn.[2]

Although examples such as this one, where a taxpayer wins out over the IRS, may occur more frequently these days, over the years, as I continued to witness the seemingly uncontrollable behavior of the IRS, I realized that I could no longer keep silent.

I have been collecting the information contained in this book for over 20 years. Am I afraid of repercussions from the IRS? Yes. But this information is too important not to be told. The value of the assistance it can bring to every U.S. taxpayer will, I hope, offset my risk.

In *What the IRS Doesn't Want You to Know* I will

- Tell taxpayers why they have been kept in the dark for so many years.
- Present a point of view that can make taxpayers more powerful than they ever thought possible.
- Give the taxpaying public new information, legal and legitimate, that is traditionally presented only by CPAs to clients in low voices and behind closed doors.
- Let taxpayers know in advance what they need to watch out for and how to protect themselves from new IRS onslaughts.

This information will allow taxpayers to

- View the IRS from an entirely new and realistic perspective.
- Learn how to use glitches, crevices, and loopholes in our tax laws to their benefit.
- Recognize the shortfalls of the IRS so that the scales of justice are tipped in the taxpayers' favor.

I have decided to make this information available so that you, the average taxpayer, can be armed with the same tools of the trade that I use every day. You will learn how to use these tools to

- Avoid an audit.
- Minimize your tax assessment.
- Dramatically improve your business and tax situation, especially if you are self-employed, a service provider, or an independent contractor.
- Increase your tax-deductible expenses without drawing attention to your return.
- Dramatically reduce your personal tax liabilities by learning little-known techniques used in the tax trade.
- Make the IRS consistently work for you, once and for all reversing a long-standing trend.
- Learn what to watch out for as the IRS undergoes its enormous reorganization.

These commonsense tools, rarely divulged to the average taxpayer, represent specific legal steps you can take to shield yourself from the far-reaching clutches of the IRS.

Furthermore, the idea that only wealthy individuals, those who hire expensive tax attorneys, or those in the know can avail themselves of aggressive tax information is false. Anyone has the right to receive the same kind of information and advice on how to best handle the demands of the IRS, particularly the average taxpayer. No one is too small to *deal successfully* with the long, powerful, and often ruthless and arbitrary arm of the IRS.

I intend to set taxpayers free by offering them a brand-new foundation from which they can deal with the IRS, one based on expert knowledge never before revealed publicly. For example, did you know that

- Despite spending billions of dollars, most of the technological advances the IRS predicted for the year 2000 and beyond have not happened?
- Each year the IRS loses files on which audits have commenced; the audit is then abruptly terminated?

- Travel and entertainment are still the first areas that are examined by an IRS auditor, because a partial disallowance of deductions is virtually certain?
- You should never represent yourself at an IRS audit? Such an ego trip usually ends up costing taxpayers dearly.
- In the past, the IRS has claimed responsibility for almost 50 percent more prosecutions than recorded by the Justice Department and more than twice the number of individuals sentenced to prison?
- You probably have a greater chance of being audited if you live in a certain part of the country?

With this information, and a great deal more like it, taxpayers will not only have a fighting chance in dealing with the IRS but can actually come out winners.

CPAs GRADE CLIENTS

Now, let's enter a CPA's inner sanctum, a place most taxpayers are not privy to.

Over time it has become customary for tax professionals to "grade" their clients. Clients who make the highest grade from the tax professional's view pay less in taxes, are rarely audited, and have more money in their pockets. I would venture to say that in our profession we deal with three types of clients. Let's call them Type A, Type B, and Type C. Here's how this works.

Type A are the "good" clients. A good client is a person who heeds the professional's advice most of the time, but especially when the professional presents the advice in the form of a strong recommendation. The ideas presented in this book are strong recommendations, and nothing irks a tax professional more than when a client doesn't follow strong recommendations and ends up paying higher taxes or, worse, is audited.

Let's skip Type B clients for a moment and discuss Type C. Type C clients, because of their difficult behavior and negative attitudes, are at the bottom of the totem pole. The fee that they are charged is never commensurate with the time that is spent with them, both at face-to-face meetings and on the telephone. They are usually terrible listeners who refuse to hear much-needed information, which must therefore be continually repeated. Type Cs often argue against the recommended course of action because they usually have a know-it-all mentality. Type Cs also receive the greatest number of notices from the IRS, simply because they do not follow the tax professional's instructions. In short, a Type C client causes the professional the greatest amount of aggravation, the professional earns the lowest hourly rate, and Type Cs are usually the first to complain that the bill is too high.

Type B represents all the clients who don't fit into Type A or C categories. As you might suspect, the majority of people are Type Bs. Although Type Bs aggravate you once in a while, they may overcome this by paying bills promptly. They may complain a lot, but they may also be a source of client referrals.

The dilemma faced by tax professionals concerning their client base should be becoming clear to you: Wouldn't it be great if we could drop Type Cs from our client roll, and have Type Bs gradually mend their ways and work themselves up to Type As? But, alas, this is a tax professional's fantasy. In reality, clients drop down from Type A or B to become a Type C, but a Type B or C rarely moves up to become a Type A.

Now that you are aware of this aspect of the tax business, I'd like you to benefit from it as fully as possible by incorporating these discoveries into your own thinking and behavior from this moment on, while you are reading this book. Here's how.

Most of the advice, recommendations, and tips contained in *What the IRS Doesn't Want You to Know* has not been made available to the average taxpayer before. Therefore, to receive the full value of what I am revealing, you need to respond like a Type A client. In fact, I'd like each of you to become a Type A client by the time you have completed this book. The closer you come to being a Type A client, the easier it will be for you to understand how your own thinking and behavior can positively or negatively affect how your return will ultimately be handled by the IRS. Behaving like a Type A or B instead of a Type C client can actually make the difference between an unnoticed return and an audit. Here's what I mean:

A Type C client, Mr. Richards, came to me with a problem. He had received a fee of $35,000, for which the payer issued a 1099-Misc form (Miscellaneous Income) listing him as the recipient. Mr. Richards claimed that the fee was actually earned by his son. I suggested that he contact the payer of the fee and obtain a revised 1099 in his son's name. Without any further explanation, Mr. Richards instead asked me if he should prepare a 1099 in his son's name showing that he paid the $35,000, acting as the boy's agent. I strongly advised against this course of action. If this was noticed and subsequently questioned, the IRS would ask for full documentation, including a contractual agreement and canceled checks. But Mr. Richards, acting like the perfect Type C, insisted that he knew better and refused to heed my advice. I knew it would be useless to argue further. He prepared the 1099 form showing the $35,000 payment to his son.

Six months later, when the IRS detected the existence of two apparently related 1099 forms, both belonging to Mr. Richards, they contacted him and, not satisfied with his explanation, proceeded with a full-scale audit. The audit encompassed all of Mr. Richards's personal and corporate activities, which were substantial, since he was a highly paid executive. An audit lasting more than three years culminated in Mr. Richards paying the IRS $140,000 in tax, interest, and penalties, plus $25,000 in accounting and legal fees. To this day, Mr. Richards still insists that he knows best, and his behavior has not changed one iota, despite the fact that if he had listened to me in the first place, it would have made his life a lot easier and saved him thousands of dollars.

Finally, the most crucial ability for taxpayers to have, which they cannot acquire on their own, is the ability to understand how the IRS thinks, operates, and responds. This is definitely something you as a tax-payer want to learn about and put into practice, yet it is rarely, if ever, made available.

In my interactions with countless clients and with the IRS, a great deal of unofficial information surfaces that is often more important than a specific tax law. In fact, quite often what is most important is not what a tax law says, but how the IRS interprets and acts on it. This knowl-edge, which tax pros gain from years of working in the field and inter-acting at all levels with the IRS, is what enables them to complete your return and know how the IRS will respond to each individual item recorded. This is the kind of information I will be revealing in this book. Here is a typical case:

Early in 2000, a Mr. Graham, who owned an interior design business, came to me for the preparation of his 1999 tax return. In reviewing his file, I saw that both his 1997 and 1998 returns had been audited. On the basis of what I knew about how the IRS thinks, it seemed to me that the audits were triggered by two items: First, Mr. Graham's gross income for each year was over $150,000, which in itself in-creases the chances of an audit. Second, in both years Mr. Graham claimed about 30 percent of his gross income, an unusually large amount, for entertainment, auto expenses, and travel, as reported on his Schedule C, Profit or Loss from Business (Sole Proprietorship). IRS regulations require anyone who is an unincorporated sole proprietor to file this schedule.

I knew that my approach would have to be based on presenting Mr. Graham's expenses from one perspective: in case he was audited. Any good CPA employs this kind of thinking automatically, but in this case it was more crucial because of the two previous audits. In addition, I had to eliminate, or reframe, whatever I could that had been previously questioned.

When my client and I set to work examining his business diary for 1999, one thing consistently kept showing up: Meal expenses on most days were for breakfast, lunch, and dinner. There is a rather obscure IRS regulation that some meals must be considered personal in nature. In other words, the IRS does not take kindly to three meals a day taken as a business expense. Mr. Graham was operating under the illusion that because these meals were business expenses, he would be able to reduce his overall tax bill by listing them that way. But he did not know that he was treading upon a favorite IRS attention getter: enter-tainment expenses.

I told my client about this regulation and promptly reduced Mr. Graham's business-related meals to two a day. To offset this loss, I also told him of another IRS regulation that would allow him to expense meals under $75 without a receipt if his business diary noted the person, place, and date of the meal, along with a brief description of what was discussed. With these additional diary entries, entertainment expense was back to its previous total, but because of the way it was presented on his return (and in backup material), I knew he would be safe if he was audited. I also insisted that my client substantiate every entertainment item above $75 with a receipt or canceled check, a practice he had previously been lax about.

Next, Mr. Graham's business diary showed $16,000 for out-of-pocket expenses but only $7,000 worth of checks made payable to himself. With his history, I knew the IRS would grab this in a flash. With a little investigation, I uncovered the source of the missing $9,000—cash gifts from his parents made during the year. In this case I used as documentation a section from the Internal Revenue Code (IR Code) that allows each taxpayer to personally give $10,000 (now $11,000) annually to any other person without filing a gift tax return. Now we could prove the source of the $9,000, and best of all, gifts of this nature are nontaxable. However, to clear him even further, I advised my client to have his parents write and sign a one-sentence letter that documented the fact that they had given him the money during the year as a gift.

Finally, to save Mr. Graham from ever again filing a Schedule C that would place his entertainment, automobile, and travel expenses under scrutiny, I strongly recommended that he change his business from a sole proprietorship to a new small business corporation, an S corporation. By doing this, Mr. Graham accomplished the following: He substantially reduced his chances of being audited (i.e., his $150,000 in personal income would not light up the IRS computers); as an S corporation, he had available to him new techniques for reducing Social Security costs that he didn't have as a sole proprietor; and he had all the other advantages of being incorporated (e.g., limited liability to creditors). The end result was exactly what I had hoped for: Mr. Graham's personal and business tax returns since 1999 have not been selected for audit by the IRS.

YOUR TAX-SAVING STRATEGY

Although the IRS no longer requires receipts for business transportation and entertainment unless the expense exceeds $75, detailed entries in your business diary are a must. Expenses for lodging require detailed receipts regardless of the amount. See Chapter 8 for more on S corporations.

Now, I have two requests of all taxpayers who read this book. First, I would like you to extract from the material all the points that have some personal relevance. Bring these points to the attention of your tax professional and ask for comments. If your tax professional says, for example, that you are too small to become an S corporation, ask for specific reasons to support that conclusion. If you are not satisfied with the response, get a second opinion.

My second request applies only after you have finished the book. When that time arrives, go back to your tax professional. Ask what it will take to make you a Type A client. Encourage your tax pro to let you know how successful you have been in following his or her advice. I'm sure he or she can pull some specific examples out of the files. Walk through one or two together to assess how your behavior held up. Were you cooperative? Did you listen carefully? Follow instructions? As a result of your way of responding to your tax professional's advice, did you gain a stronger tax position, or did you end up with a loss that could have been avoided?

If your tax professional claims not to know what a Type A client is, suggest he or she read this book.

2

The IRS Personality:
Playing It to Your Advantage

Every taxpayer is involved in a relationship with the IRS. The good news is that we have choices for influencing how that relationship will turn out. We can behave like sheep, following IRS dictates and threats as if they were gospel. We can take a middle-of-the-road approach and, amidst our complaints, begin to ask why and how the IRS does what it does. Or we can choose to work with and beat the IRS from a sound foundation built upon experience, knowledge, and an understanding of who the IRS is and how it operates.

Imagine that you've just met someone new, and you're very interested in finding out what that person is like. Naturally, you're curious about family history, aspirations, career, and key incidents that have shaped that person's life. You can use the same principle of learning what you can about someone to become familiar with the IRS.

EVENTS THAT SHAPED THE IRS PERSONALITY

I believe it is time for taxpayers to recognize that the IRS is an entity with a distinct personality that affects you each time you fill out your tax return. The significant events that make the IRS what it is today are clear-cut and straightforward. Through these the IRS personality unfolds.

THE EVENT: Establishing the Right to Collect Taxes
THE PERSONALITY: Stubborn. Tenacious. Undaunted.

Significance to Taxpayers
The U.S. government's privilege to levy taxes was incorporated into the Constitution in 1787. The responsibility for creating the machinery for

collecting taxes was given to the Treasury Department (where it has remained ever since), under the supervision of the assistant to the secretary of the Treasury. In 1792 that position was replaced with the Office of the Commissioner of Revenue.

By 1817 the issue of taxes was abandoned because the government's revenue needs were met by customs duties (taxes on imports). The outbreak of the Civil War 45 years later and the government's need for massive financing led to President Lincoln's signing the Revenue Act of July 1, 1862, establishing the nation's first real income tax and reestablishing the Office of the Commissioner of Internal Revenue via a legislative act in which the commissioner was to be nominated by the president and approved by the Senate. The IRS was officially born.

Shortly after the war ended, Lincoln's wartime revenue system began to be dismantled and, as before, the government's fiscal needs were met by customs receipts collected on imported goods and taxes on alcohol and tobacco. With nearly 90 percent of internal revenue coming from these sources, by 1872 the income tax was again repealed until 1913, when the Sixteenth Amendment to the U.S. Constitution was enacted. We'll take a closer look at this shortly.

Table 2.1 charts tax revenues in key years, starting with the first year tax was collected on a formal basis and continuing until the present time. This two-century span shows a great deal more than numbers on a page.

TABLE 2.1   Tax Revenues in Key Years

Fiscal Year	Gross Revenue Collected
1792	$208,943
1814	$3,882,482
1866	$310,120,448
1900	$295,316,108
1918	$3,698,955,821
1932	$1,557,729,043
1941	$7,370,108,378
1944	$40,121,760,232
1965	$114,434,633,721
1980	$519,375,273,361
1990	$1,066,600,000,000
2001	$2,128,831,182,000
2002	$2,016,627,269,000

Source: Shelley L. Davis, *IRS Historical Fact Book: A Chronology, 1646–1992* (Washington, D.C.: U.S. Government Printing Office, 1992), Appendix 3, pp. 245–47; The IRS Data Book from 2001 and 2002.

Stretches of stability and the depths of a country's economic depression are reflected here. So, too, are the strife and nationalistic fervor of war years, the growing pangs of a new nation, and periodic transitions as the United States moved from an agriculture-based economy to an industrial one. When the government's need for more income suddenly escalated, usually as a result of a war, taxes on products and/or income were imposed. Probably most impressive are the enormous sums the IRS has collected during our own lifetimes.

How Taxes Are Raised Without Taxpayers Noticing

Tax Bracket Creep

Congress, together with the IRS, continues to introduce new taxation policies to keep up with changing times. One phenomenon that increases taxes without a change in tax law is known as *tax bracket creep*. Until 1986, there were 15 tax brackets into which taxpayers could fall on the basis of taxable income. The lowest bracket started at $2,390 and the highest was $85,130 and over. Each year, owing to inflation, our taxable income typically increases. This increase eventually puts us into a new, higher tax bracket, forcing us to pay higher taxes. Voilà! This takes place without any change whatsoever in the tax law. Although currently there are only 6 tax brackets instead of 15, the principles of bracket creep remain the same.

Softening the blow of tax bracket creep are cost-of-living increases in the bracket ranges, designed to prevent you from creeping upward into the next-higher bracket. For example, a married man with taxable income of $44,000 was in the 15 percent tax bracket in 2002. His taxable income increased to $47,000 in 2003, but he remained in the 15 percent bracket because the top of the 15 percent range was raised from $46,700 in 2002 to $47,450 in 2003.

But Congress has been selective, perhaps even manipulative, in other areas where taxpayers can use some relief. For example, the limit on 401(k) contributions was stuck at $9,500 for three years, reaching $10,000 only in 1998 and $10,500 in 2001. Similarly, for a long time anyone taking a deduction for entertainment and meal expenses needed to produce a written receipt when the expense reached $25. It took Congress about 35 years to increase that threshold to $75. As for IRAs, you and your working (or nonworking) spouse can generally contribute up to $3,000 each, annually. If the $3,000 were indexed for inflation (i.e., adjusted to reflect increases in the cost of living), the maximum contribution would have been raised to $4,000 or higher years ago, giving a much-needed break to taxpayers who want to save more money in a tax-deferred investment. (See 1997 Tax Legislation and 2001 legislation in Chapter 12.)

Alternative Minimum Tax Snares the Unwary

The alternative minimum tax (AMT) was designed in the late 1970s as a leveling device to ensure that everyone, especially in the upper income levels, ends up paying some tax no matter how savvy they may be in reducing their income through such devices as tax shelters and itemized deductions. In other words, the government wants your money no matter what—even if you are able to reduce your taxable income to zero.

But here's the problem. The AMT has only two tax brackets: the first for those whose AMT income (taxable income plus add-ons) is $175,000 or less, and the second for those with AMT income above $175,000. Furthermore, to make sure the government doesn't leave anyone out, when filling out the AMT Form 6251 (Alternative Minimum Tax—Individuals), you are required to add back to your taxable income certain "adjustments and preferences." These include many items listed on Schedule A (Itemized Deductions), such as some medical and dental expenses, miscellaneous deductions and all taxes, plus personal exemptions. Taxpayers must then compute their taxes using both the regular IRS tax table and the AMT rates, and pay the higher of the two.

Minor but temporary relief was made to the AMT in the Tax Act of 2001 and the Tax Act of 2003. However, the number of taxpayers affected by the AMT will rise faster than before because the Tax Act of 2003 has accelerated the reduction in ordinary tax rates to 2003, disregarding its effect on the AMT. (See misconception 6 in Chapter 9 and rule 5 in Chapter 11.) According to the IRS, 1.5 million individual returns were hit by the AMT for 2001, up 100 percent from 1998, representing in excess of $5 billion. By 2010, the AMT is expected to snare up to 35 million unsuspecting middle-class taxpayers, a group never intended to be caught up in this trap.[1] These taxpayers are guilty of nothing more than having high deductions for such routine items as state income tax and unreimbursed business expenses, or simply because they have large families.

Stock Options and the AMT

There are two types of stock options, nonqualified stock options (NQSOs) and incentive stock options (ISOs). For NQSOs, you are taxed at ordinary income tax rates immediately after you exercise the options, on the difference between the price you pay and the market value of the stock. The price of NQSOs can be any value, and they are often issued at 10 to 15 percent below market value. Companies prefer this type of option because the company gets a tax deduction for the same amount that you must report as income.

To qualify as an ISO, at the time the option is granted, the market value cannot exceed $100,000 and the option price cannot be less than the stock's fair market value. No tax is due when the option is issued or granted, and no tax is due upon exercising the option. Tax is deferred until you sell the shares, and if you wait more than one year after exercise to sell and more than two years after the ISO is granted, you will qualify for long-term capital gain rates. Problem: The difference between the price you pay and the market value at the exercise date is includable in the computation of AMT income, which is often a significant amount for middle and upper management.[2]

YOUR TAX-SAVING STRATEGY

My advice is that you should run different tax scenarios for various numbers of shares and exercise just enough ISOs each year to keep you from paying the AMT. In this scenario, the money you spend for the services of a tax professional will be well worth the expense.

Phasing Out Itemized Deductions and Personal Exemptions

Itemized *deductions*, listed on Schedule A, Form 1040, are a group of expenditures you are entitled to deduct from your adjusted gross income that reduce your taxable income. Some examples are home mortgage interest, real estate taxes, state and local taxes, and charitable contributions. An *exemption* is not an expenditure but a portion of your income not subject to taxation at all—for example, a certain amount of income for each dependent. The effect of exemptions is also to reduce taxable income.

In a nifty way to pick taxpayers' pockets that generally slips by unnoticed, itemized deductions can be phased out. (Excluded from this are medical expenses, investment interest, and casualty and theft losses, which each have their own unique limitations.)

It begins with your adjusted gross income (AGI), which is a collection of all income items less a small number of adjustments to income, such as the deductions for self-employed pension contributions (Keogh plans) and alimony. AGI is typically the last line of page 1 of Form 1040 (U.S. Individual Income Tax Return).

If your AGI is more than $139,500 (married, filing jointly, or single), the IRS can disallow, or increase your taxable income by, as much as 80 percent of your total itemized deductions, at the worst leaving you just 20 percent. Working in real numbers, things might look like this. For the year 2003, Jay and Nancy Jennings have these itemized deductions:

Real estate and state income taxes	$15,000
Contributions to charities	2,000
Mortgage interest on their home	15,000
Total	$32,000

If their combined AGI for 2003 is $189,500, it means that $1,500 of their deductions is lost ($189,500 − $139,500 × .03), leaving net deductions on Schedule A of $30,500.

If they had a combined AGI of $289,500 and the same starting deductions, then they would lose $4,500 of their deductions ($289,500 − $139,500 × .03), leaving net deductions on Schedule A of $27,500.

In short, the more you earn, the more you lose in itemized deductions. Where does the money from this loss on itemized deductions go? It goes out of the taxpayers' pockets into the government's hands. In 2001, five million taxpayers were unable to deduct almost $25 billion. What better way to disguise a tax increase!

The Tax Act of 2001 recognizes this inequity, and the phaseout of itemized deductions is itself being eliminated from 2006 to 2009.

At the same time as the phaseouts for itemized deductions were initiated, a new barrage of phaseouts involving personal exemptions was introduced.

A personal exemption is a deduction, determined annually by law, that reduces your taxable income. Personal exemptions are taken on Form 1040 and usually include the taxpayer, the taxpayer's spouse, and anyone else who meets the Internal Revenue Code dependency and support requirements. These phaseouts start at $209,250 for married couples filing jointly and $139,500 for singles. When the AGI exceeds the threshold level, the taxpayer loses 2 percent of the total exemption amount for every $2,500 or fraction thereof for AGI that exceeds the threshold.

Thus, for example, when your AGI reaches $125,000 more than your AGI threshold of $209,250 (or $139,500), you lose 100 percent of your personal exemptions.

Mathematically it works like this: $125,000 ÷ $2,500 = 50. Then 50 × 2 percent = 100 percent of lost exemptions. This is clearly a three-Excedrin explanation, so let's look at it again.

Dan and Lorrie Jimson file jointly and their AGI for 2003 is $271,750. They have three children and claim five exemptions, each one worth $3,050. Subtracting the $209,250 threshold from the $271,750 leaves $62,500. Dividing $62,500 by $2,500 equals 25. Multiplying 2 percent by 25 gives a 50 percent loss of exemptions. Because of the phaseout, the Jimsons' deduction for their five exemptions will be slashed in half—from $15,250 to $7,625.

But wait—it could be worse. Suppose the Jimsons had $5 more added onto their AGI. Under the phaseouts, they would lose another 2 percent of their total exemptions, or an extra $305 down the drain. The Tax Act of 2001 recognizes this inequity, and the phaseout of personal exemptions is itself being eliminated from 2006 to 2009.

Despite the current IRS reorganization and its emphasis on customer service, taxation policy will continue to get more intricate, more sly, and more creative as it subtly reduces the amount of income it lets you keep.

THE EVENT: Income Tax Becomes a Favorite Child

THE PERSONALITY: As stubborn, tenacious, and unmoving as the government's right to levy and collect taxes. Also highly effective. You'll find it shifty, unfair, and subject to changing times. But be aware that it can be flexible and workable as well.

Significance to Taxpayers

The Sixteenth Amendment, which was passed on February 3, 1913, states:

The Congress shall have the power to lay and collect taxes on incomes, from whatever source derived, without apportionment among the several states, and without regard to any census or enumeration.

This amendment made it legal for Congress to impose a direct tax on the net incomes of both individuals and corporations, overriding an 1895 Supreme Court ruling that asserted that the income tax was unconstitutional because it was a direct tax rather than one apportioned among the states on the basis of population.

The right of Congress to levy an income tax, and the right of the IRS, as part of the U.S. Treasury Department, to collect taxes, periodically comes under fire from people who believe, mistakenly, that these functions are illegal or who fall prey to tax evasion schemes.

Don't be fooled by the latest: a variety of "tax kits," many available on the Internet, costing anywhere from $900 to $2,000, that promote the bogus philosophy that individuals are not part of the United States or aren't taxpayers, as defined by the federal tax code, but sovereign entities.[3] A sovereign entity is someone who exercises supreme authority within a limited sphere. Have no doubt, no matter how many dependents these kits recommend you claim (often up to 98), or how many W-4 forms (Withholding Exemption Certificate), W-8 forms (Certificate of Foreign Status), "Affidavits of Citizenship and Domicile," or "Affidavits of Claims for Exemption and Exclusion from Gross Income of Remuneration, Wages, and Withholding" they include, any sucker who tries will eventually discover that the IRS is much more sovereign than you or I. A U.S. citizen is subject to U.S. law, and that includes paying taxes.

Following the amendment's passage, the income tax very quickly became the favorite of the federal government, producing more revenue than anyone could ever have thought possible, surpassing all other sources of revenue.

Despite its past and current inequalities, the goal of the income tax is to establish a close connection between a person's income and his or her ability to pay taxes. In theory, a progressive income tax aims to ensure that those with a greater income pay more taxes than those who earn less. In reality, things don't work that way. The rich hire the best tax lawyers and accountants, which works to shift the taxpaying burden downward. Since the poor have little ability to pay any taxes at all, the tax burden tends to fall on the middle class, thus undermining the theory.

As Americans, we are allowed to express opinions about the income tax. Once we express them, however, the numbers speak for themselves. Twenty years ago, out of a total of over $519 billion in federal revenues collected (gross dollars), 55.4 percent, or over $287 billion, came from individual income taxes.[4]

By 1990, that figure rose to almost $540 billion, and in 2001 it was $1.2 trillion.[5] Income tax dollars continue to represent 50 percent or more of federal revenues collected—the largest piece of the pie.

But don't give up completely on finding a way to use the income tax to your advantage. Because income tax continues to be a function of who you are and how you earn your money, there is room within its bounds to determine how you report that income.

In 2001, the IRS reported that out of the 129.5 million individual tax returns, about 106 million indicated salaries or wages earned. Taxpayers in this group are typically more limited in how they report income than the 8 million who filed as sole proprietorships and the 2.2 million who filed as partnerships during the same year. (Choices regarding income tax reporting for straight wage earners do exist, and will be discussed further on.)

The basis of our system of taxation lies in something the IRS likes to call compliance. I'd like you to view compliance as having two components. One part of compliance relies on the honor system, and the other part relies on knowing how to report what you earn so that your return goes unnoticed by the IRS. Accomplishing this goal will render your return audit-proof, and that's the goal you want to achieve. You'll learn how as you read on.

THE EVENT: Rise of Lobbying and Special Interest Groups
THE PERSONALITY: Highly focused, egotistical, frenzied, calculating, and determined to the point of being obnoxious. Can also be vociferous, well connected, and generally very organized.

Significance to Taxpayers

Politics and tax-making policy were intricately and inseparably intertwined when reviving the income tax became a cause célèbre at the turn of the century. Immediately after the income tax law became official in 1913, affecting both individuals and corporations, the IRS scurried to organize a Personal Income Tax Division and create a structure to handle the instant rush of telephone calls and correspondence. Simultaneously, virtually every business trade association set up a tax committee or hired a full-time person to keep abreast of tax changes.[6]

Although one likes to believe that there are some principles left in the tax-making process, there is no doubt that organized interests are at the origin of most tax provisions. There is some pluralism here, some interest group bargaining there, some special versus general interest over here, some politics of principle over there, some sacred cow pleading its cause to attentive ears in that corner, some politics of indignation in another one, some strange bedfellows over there, someone tuning his political antenna over here, and so on.[7]

Today it is the norm for Congress to be consistently bombarded with hordes of lobbyists representing individuals, corporations, and foreign governments, and trade associations representing diverse industries (agriculture, oil, banking, real estate, dairy), all demonstrating why tax laws should be structured to accommodate their special needs.

Although this might sound like a more modern, democratic way of having the American people influence the voting, unfortunately it usually isn't. What happens is that the groups with the greatest financial resources, who are well connected, have greater access to the media, and are savvy in the communications process, are the more powerful, and they win out over the rest. The end result doesn't usually benefit most taxpayers.

THE EVENT: Tax-Making Policy Permanently Changed
THE PERSONALITY: Capricious and easily swayed, leading to favoritism and inequities. Grows increasingly more complex each year but offers substantial rewards to those who can decipher and manipulate the ins and outs.

Significance to Taxpayers
The Constitution states that a tax or revenue bill must be introduced in the House of Representatives. In making this determination, our Founding Fathers created a direct link between the creation of tax laws and the American people who directly elect members of the House. The actual step-by-step process was a clear-cut, sound model. But the rise of interest groups, which created a new set of linkages between government and its citizens, altered that model by opening up and actually distorting the process. As concessions or exceptions became introduced into our tax law because of pressure from special interest groups, innocent taxpayers got caught in the cross fire. Now we are forced to reckon with three types of tax traps:

- Tax laws that favor one segment of the population over another.
- An increase in the complexity of our tax laws.
- A rapidly expanding number of loopholes for avoiding or manipulating tax laws.

Each of these has a tremendous impact on taxpayers and their pocketbooks.

Tax Laws Play Favorites

A tax shelter is a way to protect your money from being touched by the IRS. (The politically correct phrase for this is "reducing your tax liability.") Essentially the tax shelter generates tax benefits in the form of investment tax credits, depreciation, and business losses, which allow taxpayers to save more in taxes than they had invested in the shelter. A person investing in a tax shelter is called a passive investor, with no say in the management of the actual operation of the investment; the investments are known as passive investments; and losses are referred to as passive losses.

But the term *tax shelter* has become a dirty word, because thousands of people use them not as legitimate investments but as a device to reduce their taxes, in that they offered substantial write-offs or deductions. Through the 1970s and into the '80s, these forms of abusive tax shelters grew geometrically, from $5 billion to $10 billion to $25 billion in write-offs.

Eventually the IRS was successful in pressuring Congress to outlaw most tax shelters (passive investments) through tax legislation—with one exception: Taxpayers could continue to direct their money into tax shelters involving oil and gas investments.

Who or what was behind this exception? A well-organized, well-connected, and especially strong oil and gas lobby.

Although some sound reasons for allowing the exception were put forth—such as, if people stopped investing in this field, it would drastically reduce oil and gas exploration—the bottom line was indisputable: The two groups that made out well were the IRS, and oil and gas interests.

One of the largest groups to take advantage of tax shelters over the years was the real estate industry. But by the late 1980s, and through tax legislation, if a taxpayer was a participant or owner in an active business, losses were legitimately allowed, except in the field of real estate. No investments in real estate that threw off losses could be used to offset other income by passive investors, or even owners or others who were legitimately in the real estate business. (This does look like a clear-cut case of the IRS getting even.)

But the real estate lobby fought hard, eventually gaining an amendment to this tax law before its effective date that allows active owners in the real estate business to take the first $25,000 of operating losses as a deduction against other income if their adjusted gross income is less than $100,000.*

Yes, this was a minor compromise, considering the thousands of people

---

*This advantage is phased out as AGI exceeds $100,000. When AGI reaches $150,000, the benefit disappears entirely. Unused losses can be carried forward indefinitely. Deferred losses can be fully utilized on sale of the property.

legitimately engaged in the real estate business who did not fit into the under-$100,000 category. But look at what happened to this group because of the Revenue Reconciliation Act of 1993 (RRA '93). Instead of giving the real estate advantage back to everyone, it gave the tax breaks back to the real estate professionals who should not have been excluded to begin with. Beginning in 1994, taxpayers engaged full-time in real estate activities (not passive investors but those who spend more than 750 hours per year in the activity) were once again able to use real estate losses to offset other sources of income, but passive, inactive investors are still excluded.

People are quickly learning that real estate is again a great investment. Why? You can often make a relatively small cash investment that may produce enough tax write-offs to keep your current income taxes at a minimum while providing a good opportunity for long-term capital gain at favorable income tax rates. Here's an example:

You purchase a multifamily residential unit for $1 million, put $100,000 down, and obtain a 7 percent, 15-year mortgage for $900,000, which calls for payment of interest only for the first five years (many other variations of mortgages are available if you look hard enough). Annual income and expenses are assumed to be as follows:

Rental income	$160,000
Less:	
Mortgage interest	63,000
Real estate tax	25,000
Repairs and maintenance	39,000
	127,000
Net income before depreciation	33,000
Depreciation (building cost—$890,000)	
(27.5 years write-off)	32,360
Net income	$ 640

This is a tax shelter in its simplest form. The income is sheltered from current income tax by the depreciation. If the property is sold five years later at a gain of $200,000, the first $161,800 of gain (depreciation taken) is subject to a 25 percent maximum capital gains tax. The balance of the gain, $38,200, will be subject to a maximum capital gains tax of 15 percent. The investor will have received an annual tax-free cash flow of $33,000, which means he recovers his down payment in just three years and pays tax at low capital gain rates when the property is sold.

IRS officials have already caught on to the recent proliferation of tax shelter arrangements being taken by corporations, and they're not pleased! Efforts to combat them have thus far been on an ad hoc basis. (See Chapter 13.)

If you are engaged almost full time in a non–real estate occupation, there are severe restrictions on the amount of real estate losses you can deduct. However, if your spouse, for example, obtains a real estate broker's license and actively works at it, she or he is considered to be a real estate professional. This will generally entitle you to deduct your full real estate losses on your joint tax return.

Tax Laws Become Increasingly Complex

Creating exceptions for special groups has resulted in a steady stream of new and revised tax laws, which have lengthened the Internal Revenue Code to over 4,500 pages and rendered it virtually unreadable. Often one section can run up to several hundred pages. A special tax service used by tax professionals (there are many), which explains the meaning and application of each part of the code, is contained in another 12 volumes!

The end result is an increasingly complex tax code that tries to please everyone but pleases no one. It is barely understandable to even the most experienced tax professionals. The harder Congress tries to simplify it, the more complex it becomes.

What does all this mean for you, the taxpayer? Preparing your tax return, delving into a tax law, if you need to, and strategizing how to keep more of your hard-earned dollars in your pocket become increasingly difficult with each passing year.

Even tax professionals with years of experience—trained and steeped in tax preparation—must religiously attend tax seminars and read myriad journals, magazines, and monthly tax tips, among other things, to correctly interpret the tax code and gain the advantage over the IRS.

Finding and Using Tax Loopholes: An Industry in Itself

Exemptions created in the tax-making process have led to the birth of an entire industry dedicated to searching out tax loopholes and using them to the searchers' advantage. One of the most effective ways you can get the IRS before it gets you is to learn how to find and manipulate to your advantage loopholes in the tax law—before the IRS uses those same loopholes against you.

Loopholes in the Lump-Sum Distribution Laws

Ten years ago, the president tried to pay for the extension of unemployment benefits by instituting a 20 percent withholding tax on lump-sum distributions from corporate pension plans, which is still in effect today. Let's take a few minutes to examine the loopholes you can make use of that were created as a result of that seemingly insignificant gesture.

One loophole lets you out of paying the 20 percent if you arrange to have your distribution transferred from the financial institution that currently has your pension money directly to another financial institution (such as your own IRA). This procedure, known as a trustee-to-trustee transfer, in which you do not touch the money in any way, absolves you of paying the withholding tax and dispenses with the 60-day rollover period and the required one-year waiting period between rollovers from one IRA into another. Just make sure to follow up and verify that the transfer agent or financial institution handling the transfer has actually transferred the money to an equivalent retirement account within 60 days. If transferred to a regular, taxable account in error, the IRS will consider this a taxable distribution subject to penalty.

However, the IRS can waive the 60-day requirement where failure to do so would be against equity or good conscience, including errors by financial institutions, casualty, disaster, death, disability, hospitalization, or other events beyond the reasonable control of the individual. See Revenue Procedure 2003-16, IRB 2003-4,1 for full details.

Here's a loophole within a loophole for a taxpayer who wants to keep the distribution but does not want any money to be withheld. If you want to take the distribution early in, say, 2003 , and use the proceeds—not roll it over—you can be adequately covered by following these steps:

1. First transfer the lump sum from your pension plan to your traditional IRA via the trustee-to-trustee transfer.
2. After the transfer is complete, you can make a cash withdrawal from your traditional IRA, which will not be subject to a 20 percent withholding.

There are a few trade-offs: Although you have avoided withholding, you cannot avoid the fact that any proceeds you take from an IRA or retirement plan distribution are fully taxable, just like any other income. You are also subject to an additional 10 percent penalty if you take money out prematurely from a traditional IRA (before you reach the age of 59½). (See Chapter 12, Penalty-Free Withdrawals from IRAs and Corporate Plans.)

Let's examine this situation one step at a time.

In 2003 you are eligible to receive a $9,000 distribution from your employer's pension plan, and you need $7,500 to buy a new car. You arrange to have the $9,000 transferred directly to your traditional IRA account. You then withdraw the $7,500 you need for the purchase of the car. (Note: You can transfer an unlimited amount of money into your traditional IRA from another qualified plan, such as a pension. This is not to be confused with the $3,000 limit on new IRA contributions.)

YOUR TAX-SAVING STRATEGY
- Since the distribution was taken from your traditional IRA, there is no 20 percent withholding tax requirement.
- If you change your mind and decide not to buy the car, you have 60 days to put the money back into the IRA (to roll it over).
- In April 2004 you can withdraw the final $1,500 from your IRA and use it to help pay the extra income tax and the 10 percent penalty for the earlier withdrawal. You'll now be responsible for the income tax and penalty on the last $1,500 withdrawal, but this is a small amount and you should be able to handle it. You have a whole year to plan for it.

If you choose this ploy, you have gained an extra 12 months—from April 2003 to April 15, 2004—to use your money and to pay any possible additional tax caused by the inclusion of the pension distribution in your 2003 income.

If there is a balance due when you file your return, you might be charged a penalty. Even if no balance is due, you could still incur a penalty if you did not pay estimated taxes on the distribution taken in four equal installments. In other words, you cannot arbitrarily wait until you send in your return to pay a large balance due. The IRS wants the money throughout the year. The bottom line is, you can take your distribution, but you must be aware of some of the pitfalls, which actually aren't that terrible.

Of course, it is impossible to define and report on all the loopholes that occur in our tax laws, although many will be explored in this book. So my advice is this: Be aggressive. Ask your tax professional to advise you of any loopholes you can take advantage of to make your burden easier. If you do not assert yourself, your tax pro could mistakenly conclude that you don't know loopholes exist, or that you are too conservative in your thinking to use them to your advantage.

If you don't have a tax professional (or even if you do), it's a good idea to contact a local CPA firm, one that issues a monthly or quarterly tax newsletter and perhaps even a year-end tax tips letter. Ask to be added to the firm's mailing list; usually you'll find a great deal of valuable tax help here. You don't have to feel as if you're using the information without giving something back. Most firms expect that one day you'll become a client, or that at the very least you will give them free publicity by circulating their newsletters and telling others what you have learned.

THE EVENT: The IRS as a Criminal Watchdog
THE PERSONALITY: Macho, showy, tough. Glib yet dangerous.

Significance to Taxpayers

Back when the Criminal Investigation Division (CID) was created, it was the Roaring Twenties, a scene packed with notorious gangsters, mob violence, and organized crime. Just imagine it! The Office of the Commissioner of Internal Revenue, established by our Founding Fathers as a revenue producer to meet federal needs, had grown into a full-fledged criminal investigation arm of the government characterized by tough guys, shootings, and its own private war against organized crime. The IRS's bad-guy image was born.

Very few would question the validity of investigating and bringing to light tax fraud or criminal activities. These significantly affect our country's revenue. But the contrast between what the agency set out to do and what it did indicates an agency that is certainly out of bounds, if not out of control.

This part of the IRS personality hits taxpayers hard. First there is the initial training IRS personnel receive, which brands taxpayers as criminals and cheats. This us-against-them philosophy, reported on by IRS personnel who work there today as well as those who worked there over 20 years ago, allows the IRS to do its job with the requisite aggressive mind-set: If you're dealing each day with taxpayers labeled as lying, dishonest cheats, you need to be suspicious, unemotional, inflexible, ruthless, and determined.

THE EVENT: Tax Payment Act of 1943—Withholding and the W-2 Form
THE PERSONALITY: Efficient, slick, savvy, and extraordinarily dependable. It is also highly inflexible, unless you know the key.

Significance to Taxpayers

The next milestone to influence the personality of the IRS was the Tax Payment Act of 1943, which made the withholding of taxes from wages and salaries a permanent feature of our tax system. It also introduced the W-2 form (Wage and Tax Statement). Under this system, the employee files a W-4 form (Employee's Withholding Allowance Certificate) with his or her employer that indicates name, address, Social Security number, marital status, and the number of exemptions claimed. By law, the employer then withholds specified amounts from each employee's salary, correlated to an income rate scale, and periodically remits these amounts to the IRS. Annually, employers must also report to the Social Security Administration the total annual amount withheld on a W-2 form (Wage and Tax Statement) and provide their employees with this information. Taxpayers fulfill their reporting obligations by attaching the W-2 to their 1040 (U.S. Individual Income Tax Return) and mailing both to the IRS, hopefully before April 15. This information reflects income for the preceding year.

People who are subject to withholding taxes work for a company or an organization and are paid a salary by that entity. According to the IRS Statistics of Income office, about 85 percent of those who mail in a 1040 form receive a salary from an employer.

Today, withholding continues to be lucrative for the IRS. In 2002, 72.4 percent of gross tax dollars collected by the IRS represented withholding by employers. The actual dollar amount collected was over $750 billion.

The collection process flows relatively easily; money comes into the government's coffers automatically from over six million employers across the United States. With this device, the IRS learns exactly how much employees are paid and how much is withheld from their earned income for federal, state, and Social Security taxes. Getting employers to do the dirty work was not only smart, it was also a real plus because it makes the IRS look terribly efficient. With good reason, withholding has been called the backbone of the individual income tax.

The attitude of taxpayers toward withholding is predictable. You never see it; it is a chunk that is taken out of each paycheck; there is nothing one can do about it. So most employees just accept it and forget it.

With the W-4's information from the employee and the W-2's wage and salary information submitted directly from the employer, the IRS figured that the government couldn't lose. But loopholes in tax laws weakened that position, providing opportunities for taxpayers to rescue tax dollars in the area of withholding.

YOUR TAX-SAVING STRATEGY

What happens if the company you worked for during the year went out of business and never prepared W-2 forms? Obtain Form 4852 (Substitute for Form W-2, Wage and Tax Statement) from the IRS, and by using your pay stubs and deposit slips, do the best job you can in stating your gross income and withheld taxes for the year. You can then attach Form 4852 to your tax return, which is acceptable by the IRS a majority of the time.

Loopholes in the Withholding Law and How to Benefit

There is one important loophole in the withholding law available to many taxpayers; unfortunately, many are not versed in how to manage it to their benefit.

An employee's paycheck reflects the amount of withholding taken out. However, if your deductions are high, and you know they will remain so—for example, you filed your 2002 tax return and will receive a ridiculously high refund—it makes sound tax sense to reduce the amount of your income withheld.

To accomplish this, you need to engage in a balancing act between your deductions and exemptions. If you know that your itemized dedu

tions (deductions that are allowable on a 1040 form) are going to be high for a given year, you should submit a revised W-4 form to your employer. The revised form should indicate a higher number of exemptions than you would ordinarily be entitled to. More exemptions will reduce your withholding, which in turn will result in your taking home more money each payday.

If, when you file your W-4, it turns out to be overly optimistic (for example, you closed on your new house six months later than anticipated and therefore estimated your itemized deductions too high), you can recoup. Just submit a revised W-4 to your employer, requesting larger withholding payments from your paychecks in the last few months of the year. The amount will be sent to the IRS with the fourth-quarter 941 form (Employer's Quarterly Federal Tax Return, the form used by companies to pay withholding) and will increase your "federal income tax withheld," box 2 on your W-2. The end result is that the W-2 system will record your withholding tax as being paid evenly throughout the year. In fact it wasn't, but you've made the system work for you.

(By the way, you do not want to overwithhold early in the year, because in effect you would be lending money to the IRS without collecting interest from them. This is a real no-no!)

How to Put More Money Back into Your Pocket Throughout the Year

A first-time homeowner exemplifies what happens when it's time to use this loophole to put more money back into your pocket. For the most part, first-time homeowners, who have never before had very high deductions, suddenly have enormous deductions for mortgage interest and real estate taxes. All new homeowners who are wage earners (both partners in a couple) should revise their W-4s immediately by balancing their exemptions to reduce their withholdings.

When you use this approach you may end up owing a few dollars, but don't worry. No penalties are involved as long as your total payment for the current year (withholding and estimated taxes) comes to at least 100 percent of the total tax liability for the previous year, 110 percent if your prior year's AGI exceeds $150,000, or 90 percent of the current year's tax. Here's how this one works:

Amy and Charles Lynfield had a joint 1997 income of $100,000 per year, $60,000 for Amy and $40,000 for Charles, and lived with their one child in an apartment that they purchased in January for $80,000. The purchase was financed with a $70,000 mortgage.

I determined their deductions to be $4,900 interest (7 percent mortgage), $6,200 real estate taxes, $5,900 state income tax, and $3,000 in contributions— a total of $20,000. Before they bought the apartment, the Lynfields were taking three exemptions (the husband one and the wife two). After revising both W-4s,

Amy could take six exemptions, and Charles could take four, a total of ten. This change reduced Amy's withholding and put $37 more per week in her paycheck, an increase of $1,924 for the year. And Charles saw a paycheck increase of $1,092 for the year, or $21 more per week.

As a result of rising real estate prices, the apartment doubled in value after four years, to $160,000, so the couple decided to buy a house. The new house cost $150,000, with a mortgage of $100,000. Based on the new itemized deductions (see Table 2.2), the Lynfields legitimately increased the number of their exemptions from 10 to 12. Their deductions now equaled $23,600, and they gained two extra exemptions. Since they bought their first home, the added exemptions provided Amy with $44 per week, or an extra $2,288 for the year, and Charles with an increase of $28 a week, or another $1,456 per year.

Computing the formula to fit individual needs should be performed on the worksheet on the back of the W-4 form. This advises taxpayers how many exemptions they are entitled to on the basis of their dollar level of itemized deductions. Additional help can be found in IRS Publication 505 *Tax Withholding and Estimated Tax*, and the online Withholding Calculator.

How to Use the Withholding Loophole If You Pay Estimated Taxes

Estimated taxes are paid by self-employed taxpayers who don't receive a W-2 and therefore can't use withholding to control their tax payments. Estimated taxes must also be paid by taxpayers who have the majority of their income reported on W-2s but also receive extra income not covered by withholding. This includes a mélange of miscellaneous money earned on anything from interest and dividend income to serving as a member of a board of directors, to prize and award money, to royalties or gambling winnings. In cases such as these, and there are many more, if federal tax amounts to more than $1,000 a year, quarterly estimated taxes must be filed to avoid penalties.

TABLE 2.2   Sample Increases in Deductions

	Apartment	House
Mortgage interest	$4,900	$7,000
Real estate tax	6,200	7,700
State taxes	5,900	5,900
Contributions	3,000	3,000
Total deductions	$20,000	$23,600
Total increase in itemized deductions: $3,600		

Estimated payments are made by people in this category for two reasons:

1. So they are not stuck with an unusually large amount of taxes to pay all at once with their returns.
2. To avoid penalties for failure to pay at least 90 percent of their 2003 tax or 100 percent of the previous year's total tax liability (110 percent if their prior year's AGI exceeded $150,000).

Determining the correct amount of estimated tax and working through whatever overruns or underruns result at year-end is a complex process. This is because anyone who uses the estimated tax method must generally calculate and pay the amounts in four equal installments to avoid penalties. However, this is only a general statement, a ground rule. In practice, often a taxpayer's itemized deductions and income will, like the Lynfields', vary during the year. When this occurs, although the required amount of estimated taxes will also vary, the taxpayer must still try to pay the four installments in equal amounts.

Regarding estimated taxes and filing an extension, if you miss the deadline (April 15), you may not have a clue as to the amount due with this first-quarter current year estimate. So you can intentionally overpay the amount you mail in with your extension. When you finally file the prior year's return, you can apply the overpayment (if any) to the following year, and you may completely eliminate penalties for failure to pay the estimated taxes in a timely manner. In effect, last year's overpayment becomes your required first and possibly second and third payments for the current year.

What if you forget to mail in the second or third estimated installment? Do not wait until the next installment is due to make up the shortfall. Unlike most IRS penalties, which are computed in 30-day cycles, interest on estimated tax shortfalls is computed on a weekly basis.

For example, if you should have paid $10,000 on September 15, but you do not send in the check until September 22, at 8 percent annual interest the charge will be around $2. My opinion is that there is even a two- or three-day informal grace period before any interest at all is charged.

This is an area best handled by a tax pro. The worksheet contained in the Form 1040-ES (Estimated Tax for Individuals) booklet also provides assistance.

YOUR TAX-SAVING STRATEGY

When applying part of this year's refund to next year's estimated taxes, try not to overestimate. If you are having a bad year and need the money from your applied estimates back quickly, you will have to wait until you file your next year's return.

How to Manage Withholding If You're an Employer

The concept of managing withholding also applies to small, closely held businesses that can massage withholding laws to their benefit. Here's how.

Small business owners often wait until the end of the year to take a bonus, since up until that point they're not certain about how much profit they'll have. As a small business owner, you can rely on your accountant to come in toward the end of the business year to determine your profit, which will in turn dictate your bonus.

True, this is manipulation of the withholding law because this same owner/taxpayer may have been taking loans from the business throughout the year in lieu of salary and paying no withholding to the IRS. (The payments are considered loans, not salary.)

If you continue to take these loans in the place of salary, the IRS will interpret this as a mechanism to avoid paying taxes. On an audit the IRS can easily see through this. However, during the year you can treat the money as a loan. When you, the owner/taxpayer, know the amount of salary you can take as a bonus at the end of the year, you convert the loans into salary—and "salary" is how it will be reported on your books. This technique is allowable as long as it is temporary.

One cannot continue to operate this way on a permanent basis, because in practice loans must be validated by having fully executed corporate minutes, and promissory notes that have stated maturity dates and bear federal statutory rates of interest. But the loan-to-salary conversion process is perfectly acceptable if performed within a time frame of one year.

In fact, the IRS does not normally question why withholding was or wasn't paid out during the year. To be sure, employers are required to report to the IRS any W-4s indicating more than 10 withholding allowances, as well as when any employee claims that he is exempt from withholding on wages that exceed $200 per week. The IRS always has the right to request W-4s. But the fact is, they don't.

Earned Income Credit

The Earned Income Credit (EIC) is a refundable credit for low-income working families. To qualify, a taxpayer must

- Have a job.
- Earn less than $30,201 if there is one qualifying child (essentially the child must live with you for more than six months of the year in a U.S. home).
- Earn less than $34,178 if there are two or more qualifying children.

- Earn less than $12,060 if there are no children, with an adjusted gross income of less than $12,060, and you or your spouse must be between 25 and 64 years old.
- Not have a filing status of Married filing Separate.

The best thing about the EIC is that it's the only credit the IRS makes available even if a taxpayer doesn't pay any tax. Moreover, if taxpayers have zero taxable income, they are still eligible to receive part or all of the EIC credit, which is granted as a refund. The requirements for the EIC credit are not affected by itemized deductions.

The EIC has had an interesting history: In 1991 the IRS sent out refunds on the basis of its assumption that some categories of low-income families were entitled to the EIC even though they had not filed a claim for it. In fact, a majority of these taxpayers did not even qualify. This error allowed 270,000 nonqualified filers to get the EIC credit, and it cost the government $175 million in erroneous refunds, an average of $650 per return.

The following year the IRS reached out to more than 300,000 taxpayers, notifying them that they had not taken the EIC, and suggested that they review their returns to include it.

Then the IRS had a change of heart. A study of returns filed between January and April 1995 showed that approximately $4.4 billion or 25.8 percent of total EIC claims were in error. EIC noncompliance was at unacceptably high levels, with over one-fourth of the amount paid out going to taxpayers who were not eligible to receive benefits. Based on noncompliance, the IRS continued to use new profiles of potentially erroneous EIC claimants to select for pre-refund audits. For the 2000 and 2001 filing seasons, the agency earmarked substantial resources for this intensified compliance effort.[8] This resulted in a 60 percent increase in the audit of individual low-income tax returns during 2001, as compared to 2000, while the overall audit rate for all individual returns remained the same. So it is no surprise that for the first time in many years, audits of low-income taxpayers exceeded those of high-income filers by a wide margin.

Most CPAs know that poor EIC compliance is the result of involved paperwork, confusing definitions, and the fact that EIC rules have been changed 10 times since 1976. Still, the number of taxpayers who take the EIC continues to rise, from 14.8 million in 1994 to 19.1 million in 2001, which represents $26.2 billion in refunds issued for 2001.[9]

Conclusions about the EIC

Clearly, Congress is tightening the reins on the money it had heretofore been almost happy to give away under the EIC. But watch out. If you recklessly, intentionally, or fraudulently claim the EIC, you become ineligible to claim it again for a period of 2 to 10 years. Make sure you qualify before you apply, and fill out the Earned Income Credit form, Schedule EIC, very carefully.

THE EVENT: The IRS Meets Corruption Head-on
THE PERSONALITY: Ever-present and inescapable. From its darkest self, the IRS can be sneaky, defiant, and too smart for its own good. But eventually everyone learns what's going on.

Significance to Taxpayers
The Founding Fathers were quite savvy in recognizing the potential for corruption in the tax collection process. Section 39 of the Public Statutes at Large for March 3, 1791, lists penalties for crimes that duplicate almost down to the letter those indulged in periodically since the inception of the IRS by its employees, public officials, and businesspeople. Although many IRS publications downplay or eliminate these crimes altogether, scandal built to volcanic proportions during the early 1950s. Unfortunately, the IRS was ripe for corruption.

Since its inception, the IRS had grown geometrically. Existing tax rates went up, new taxes were added, and the force of employees required to keep up with the workload jumped from 4,000 to 58,000 between 1913 and 1951.[10] A low point in the history of American tax collection came in the post–World War II period, when collections soared by 700 percent as the number of taxpayers rose from 8 million to 52 million.[11] By the early 1950s, the IRS was plagued with deplorable processing operations and a corrupt patronage system stemming from the presidential appointment of all 64 collectors of internal revenue. The system became so inbred that favor after favor was passed up and down the line, and bribe taking, influence peddling, and widespread defrauding of the government through payoffs, extortion, and embezzlement of government funds were endemic. Settling a large tax bill of $636,000 with a payment of $4,500 was commonplace.[12] So was having a case worth $2 million in tax claims somehow mysteriously disappear, preventing the government from collecting on it.[13]

After a three-year housecleaning, initiated in 1949, hundreds were let go at all levels, resulting in a major reorganization of the bureau in 1952, as recommended by President Harry Truman and incorporated into legislation passed by Congress.

In an effort to reduce the possibility of misconduct and corruption exerted through political influence, all employees except the commissioner of internal revenue would henceforth be under the civil service.

The bureau became a strongly decentralized organization in which a district office and its local branch offices were set up as self-contained operating units. Here taxpayers filed their returns, paid their taxes or got their refunds, and discussed and hopefully settled their tax problems. In short, the district offices became the focus in the organization where the primary work of the service was carried out. (Years later much of this work was taken over by IRS service centers.)

This new arrangement successfully reduced the power of IRS personnel in Washington, but it left regional commissioners and district staff, from directors to auditors and collections people, with considerable discretion to wield their powers. The situation eventually produced a new slew of problems. Instead of corruption being removed from the top and eliminated completely, it resurfaced at a new level. "While the data appears [sic] to indicate an increasing effectiveness and control of the integrity problem," writes one historian of the IRS, "IRS officials are the first to admit that internal criminal activity has by no means been wiped out."[14] Despite the vigilance of an internal inspection service independent of the rest of the bureau, the IRS is periodically consumed with corruption and scandals.

The task of keeping on top of the integrity problem in the IRS is compounded not only by the magnitude of its fiscal operations, but also by the fact that the daily work of employees consists of their making constant value judgments that can expose them to opportunities for graft. There is no easy way for someone reviewing a revenue agent's work to determine whether a monetary favor from a taxpayer influenced the agent's determination on certain issues.

The IRS's Internal Security Program typically uncovers a steady stream of corruption. For 1997, bribe payments received amounted to about $145,000, and embezzlement theft funds recovered totaled about $940,000.[15] In 2000, the IRS suspended eight employees in a criminal investigation tied to bribery and other offenses. Other employees were disciplined for simply failing to report efforts to bribe them. This was the first major corruption case involving IRS employees since the passage of the IRS Restructuring and Reform Act of 1998.[16]

THE EVENT: Information Gathering and the Matching Program
THE PERSONALITY: A technological whizbang that excels in some areas but fails in others. Shows unpredictable future potential because it is dependent on budget dollars and strong management skills.

Significance to Taxpayers
The final event to influence the personality of the IRS probably had its antecedents in that seemingly innocent W-2 form, a by-product of the withholding process, initiated in 1943.

The W-2 provided the IRS with a new source of information on how much money employers paid to employees. Comparing information submitted by the taxpayer with information reported by outside sources would put the IRS in a strong position to

- Catch taxpayers who have underreported or failed to report an amount.
- Catch nonfilers, taxpayers who have submitted no return.

The possibility of catching underreporters or nonfilers by matching information on individual tax returns to information received from a wide range of outside sources soon whetted the IRS's appetite for more of the same. Propelled by the information age and the introduction of new technologies, the IRS went full steam ahead to create a situation whereby increasing amounts of information must, by law, be reported to the IRS from an expanding range of sources for the sole purpose of verifying whether taxpayers, and those who should be taxpayers, are playing by its rules.

For tax year 2001, employers, banks, mortgage companies, and other financial institutions filed over 1.4 billion information documents, or third-party reports, with the IRS.[17] The magic of IRS technology matched these to the 124 million individual income tax returns filed. Through its document-matching program, in tax year 2001, the IRS contacted 3.5 million taxpayers because of *underreporting of income or nonfiling*. This generated $2 billion in additional taxes and penalties.[18]

But not all of the IRS's technology efforts are aimed at matching items of income. Because computers are an increasingly visible part of IRS operations, a separate chapter explores the subject. In Chapter 6 you will discover what very few will tell you about what the IRS can do and, much more important, what it can't do with its current technological capabilities.

NEVER FORGET!

Throughout this book I will be reiterating several themes. It is to your benefit to absorb these points until they become second nature:

- Don't be scared by the IRS image. Learn what's really behind it.
- You can become audit-proof. Managing and reporting income so that you reduce or eliminate your chances of being audited is a function of knowing certain tax information and techniques. These will be explained throughout this book.
- Our tax laws are enormously complex, with loopholes large and numerous enough so that taxpayers can understand and use them to their advantage.

- There are many reasons why the IRS may be unable to verify certain aspects of your income. It has operated and will continue to operate under budget and to be understaffed, disorganized, and mismanaged.
- Despite its technological successes, the IRS is still overburdened with paper and not technologically up to speed.

ACKNOWLEDGING DEDICATED IRS PERSONNEL

Many people working for the IRS are committed and hardworking and are concerned with doing their jobs properly, improving taxpayer service, and making the agency's operations more effective and responsive. But no matter how much we may want to view the agency employees as nice guys, inevitably the IRS can be counted on to go so far off course in the process of collecting the ubiquitous tax bill, that lives and families have been and continue to be severely disrupted, even destroyed, in the process. Peeking behind the scenes of the IRS and describing what really goes on there is my attempt to tip the scales in the taxpayers' favor.

3

Who Runs the Show:
What You're Up Against

THE IMAGE

How the IRS Gets You Where It Wants You

How much of the IRS's all-powerful and heartless reputation is truth and how much is fiction? The IRS's Public Affairs Department at the national office and IRS public affairs officers at local levels work hard to establish good relationships with print and broadcast media. Even state tax departments get into the act. It is no coincidence that a rash of articles publicizing IRS enforcement activities, investigations, and convictions typically begins to appear in January and February (to set the correct tone for the new year), and again in early April, before D day for taxes.

These cases tend to involve high-profile taxpayers: entertainment and sports figures like Willie Nelson, Pete Rose, and Darryl Strawberry; or attorneys, accountants, and political and religious figures like Lyndon LaRouche, Jr., and Jerry Falwell; and even John Gotti and Harry and Leona Helmsley, whose tax evasion charges hit newspapers just before April 15.

Then, as tax time approaches, in addition to the scare stories, the IRS becomes Mr. Nice Guy. "Trust us" is the message in Sunday tax supplements that appear in national newspapers during early March just as taxpayers are beginning to deal with the fact that tax season is upon them. These supplements usually contain valuable information about recent tax news, tax tips, and even human interest stories about how the people at the IRS are ready to help you.

Image creation is how chic Madison Avenue advertising firms make their money. But do taxpayers know that the IRS also secures the image it wants without incurring expensive advertising fees? How? By counting on taxpayers to spread the word, to tell their friends, neighbors, and business associates how an ordinary audit over something as simple as a padded expense account was turned into a horror story by the machinations of the IRS. An expensive public relations firm could not do nearly as good a job of getting the message out as taxpayers themselves.

So, which will it be? The good, the bad, or the ugly? Only time will tell, now that the winds of change have arrived.

The passage of the IRS Restructuring and Reform Act of 1998 (RRA '98) has resulted in the most significant changes to the structure and operations of the IRS in the past 40 years. It is predicted that anyone who comes in contact with the IRS, from professionals working in the field to taxpayers, will be directly affected by the ongoing changes.

Will this legislation rock the very foundation of the IRS, as alleged? Will a new, reorganized IRS ever be totally realized? And most important of all, will we be alive to see it?

To say that confusion and upheaval, mixed with a good dose of IRS resistance, abound is an understatement. Estimates are that the full payoff—better service, provided by a totally revamped IRS—may not come for another five years.

Meanwhile taxpayers need to know what's going on inside the IRS now.

WHAT IT LOOKS LIKE FROM THE INSIDE OUT

The IRS cares a great deal about how it is perceived by its own employees. By contrast, how many taxpayers do you think ever give a thought to what IRS employees think of U.S. taxpayers? They do not see us as hardworking, compliant citizens who are trying to scrape together annual tax dollars from a salary that never seems to be enough. In fact, if IRS employees are to do their jobs correctly, they must see taxpayers as cheaters and themselves as getting the government its due. Changing this view to one that makes the IRS responsible for informing taxpayers about their rights and options regarding tax compliance is already part of the new IRS agenda.

To the IRS employee, the image of us, the taxpayers, as the bad guys and them as the tough but strong and righteous good guys served as a motivational tool that won't be easily altered. A former attorney who worked for the IRS for over 10 years brazenly said to me, "During an audit we used to watch taxpayers squirm, and the more they squirmed and dug themselves into a deeper hole, the more we'd laugh at them later on."

THE ORGANIZATION

From its inception the IRS has operated under the U.S. Treasury Department. With over 99,000 employees during peak season and almost 83,000 the rest of the time, the IRS is the largest law-enforcement agency in the United States. The IRS has more employees than almost any major U.S. corporation.

IRS headquarters, in its national office in Washington, D.C., has about 7,900 administrators. From this base the organization reaches across the nation through its 4 regional and 33 district offices and 10 service centers. The IRS also has nine foreign posts open to the U.S. taxpayers living and working abroad, plus an office each in Puerto Rico and Guam. But that setup has recently shifted. Four new operating groups are intended to replace the IRS's four regional offices and much of the national office. Under the reorganization, wherein some IRS district offices have already been abolished, the concept of geography has been maintained since the new IRS divisions are now broken up by area and, within areas, territories. To the general public, these changes are not discernible. Accordingly, in this book, we will continue to refer to district and regional offices in our descriptions.

Regional offices execute broad nationwide plans and policies, tailor specific procedures to fit local needs, and evaluate the effectiveness of current programs. Each regional office also oversees a number of district offices and service centers.

Each district office, which is a self-contained unit that serves specific geographic areas, is responsible for four distinct operations: examination, collection, criminal investigation (tax fraud), and taxpayer services.

This three-tiered organizational setup has allowed IRS employees to wield extraordinary power in functions that dealt intimately with taxpayers. Furthermore, the decentralization makes it almost impossible to understand the real parameters of specific jobs. Confusion is one of the strategies the IRS uses to keep taxpayers at a distance.

The service centers serve as the local data-processing arm of the IRS. These offices are where the bulk of the work associated with the IRS occurs. Service centers across the United States receive individual and business returns, process them (open, sort, record the data, check the arithmetic, credit accounts), match returns with third-party reports, mail out refunds, and communicate with taxpayers regarding their tax situation by fax, letter, and/or telephone. Because of the range of work they do, service centers have areas or divisions (depending on their size) devoted to examination, collection, and criminal investigation.

One of the largest service centers is the Brookhaven Service Center (BSC) in Holtsville, New York, which processes tax returns for the five boroughs of New York City and nearby counties. Brookhaven employs about 6,400 people during peak filing season, January through April, and maintains a permanent workforce of about 4,000 including data transcribers, tax examiners, computer operators, technicians, and clerical workers. In 2001, Brookhaven received and processed 8 million tax returns.[1]

Where the Taxpayer Fits In

Taxpayer involvement begins and usually ends at the district level, where all of the four major IRS functions (examination, collection, criminal investigation, taxpayer services) are carried out. If you're going to stand your ground and deal with the IRS face-to-face, after becoming familiar with the IRS personality, the next skills you want to add to your repertoire are knowing where your district office is and learning about its main functions. Knowing what each function entails will give you a running start on when to call "halt" if somebody gets out of line.

WHAT YOU NEED TO KNOW ABOUT THE EXAMINATION DIVISION

What They Say They Do

Currently, the Examination Division has 18,931 employees, of whom 12,154 are revenue agents and 1,356 are tax auditors. The size of the division peaked in the late 1980s with nearly 32,000 employees, a decline of 40 percent compared with today.

The number of revenue agents and tax auditors also declined, about 32 percent, from a peak of just under 20,000 to 13,510 currently. Both of these declines reflect the shift of examination and other IRS staff to customer service areas in accordance with new tax laws passed in 1998, which emphasize taxpayer assistance. More than one-fifth of IRS employees are currently being used to shore up this area, which leaves fewer people to do other work, such as examining returns and collecting tax due.

Until the new IRS reorganization falls into place, the actual responsibility and authority for examining specific returns remains in the hands of IRS employees in the district offices in each state.

DIF Scores

The majority of returns selected for audit are picked by a computer program that uses mathematical parameters to identify returns that are most likely to generate additional revenue. The method of scoring, called the

Discriminate Information Function (DIF), is kept top secret by the IRS. No one outside the IRS and few insiders know how it really works.

We do know that every return filed receives a score in which a number of DIF points are assigned to key items included on or omitted from the return. The higher the DIF score, the greater the likelihood of an audit.

The DIF process that examines data from your tax returns is carried out at the Martinsburg Computing Center. Once selected, the score cards (cards representing tax returns whose scores fall into the audit range for one or more of the categories) are returned to the service center, where they are matched with the actual tax returns (hard copy). DIF selection represents the start of the audit selection process. (The actual step-by-step procedures of the audit selection process are discussed in Chapter 6.) In the final analysis, currently only 0.6 percent of all individual tax returns filed, or about 744,000, are actually audited.

Unreported Income

A close cousin of the DIF method is a new tool called Unreported Income Discriminant Index Formula (UI DIF), which is intended to identify returns with a high probability of having unreported income. Beginning with 2002, returns will receive a UI DIF score as well as a traditional DIF score. The IRS admits that until now it had no systematic method for selecting the returns at highest risk for unreported income.[2]

What's Behind the IRS Audit Strategy

Another very different type of audit is the Taxpayer Compliance Measurement Program (TCMP). Unlike the DIF system, TCMP chooses only about 50,000 returns for each audit year chosen. Although this is a comparatively small number for the IRS, the data collected is crucial. Here's why.

The TCMP has one major objective: to measure the effectiveness of the tax collection system by evaluating whether taxpayers are voluntarily complying with the law. To make this kind of determination, detailed data must be developed on selected groups of taxpayers, on the basis of which norms of all kinds are established. That's what the TCMP audits accomplish. TCMP information is gathered directly from one-on-one sessions with taxpayers whose responses are then compared to established national or regional norms or averages. As a result, the TCMP effectively shows the IRS where people are cheating and telling the truth on their tax returns. It also tells where voluntary compliance is at its highest and lowest levels in terms of income groups and other categories.

Gathering raw data from taxpayers across the nation through the TCMP is a crucial device used by the IRS to update the DIF scores.

Although we know that DIF and TCMP data are highly confidential, we can, by comparing tax returns that have been audited, identify some of the items within the DIF database that can trigger IRS computers to raise an audit flag. They probably include the following:

- Expenses that are inconsistently large when compared to income—for example, if a taxpayer shows $25,000 of expenses and only $15,000 of income on the Schedule C (Profit or Loss from Business). Other triggers could include itemized deductions (interest, taxes, contributions) that are much higher than average returns with the same level of income.
- Required schedules or forms that are missing.
- Reporting installment property sales (sales in which the seller receives the proceeds over more than one year, and interest for the unpaid balance accrues to the seller) but failing to report related interest income.
- Reporting the sale of a stock but failing to report dividend income from that stock.
- Married couples filing separate returns that contain large itemized deductions, perhaps with one or more duplications.

A TCMP audit is an all-encompassing, excruciatingly long (at least two times longer than an office audit), intense examination of your tax return, where every dollar and deduction must be documented. Because of the public outcry against TCMP audits, Congress has withheld funding for this type of audit for the past 13 years. The IRS could not wait any longer to feed fresh information into the DIF system. In its place, the IRS initiated in late 2002 its National Research Program, which it hopes will produce improvements in the examination selection process—which is exactly the same thing that TCMP audits were designed to do.

The IRS states that two of the main goals of the National Research Program are to "reduce burden on compliant taxpayers and ensure that all taxpayers pay their fair share."[3] "Unless the IRS can update its formulas for selecting returns for audit, it will unnecessarily audit an increasing number of already compliant taxpayers."[4] In fact, approximately 25 percent of present IRS audits result in no change.

The IRS has begun to select a random sample of 49,000 returns, but not all of these taxpayers will meet with the IRS. The IRS will check about 8,000 returns using information it already has and will not contact those taxpayers; 9,000 will be correspondence audits; 30,000 will be limited scope audits, testing selected items only, similar to an office audit; and, 2,000 will be line-by-line audits, similar to TCMP audits discussed earlier. For this last group, the IRS says that the substantiation requirement will be far more flexible than for TCMP audits, but it does refer to these 2,000 examinations as "calibration" audits.

What's really behind the IRS audit strategy? The primary reason a return is chosen for a face-to-face audit is the DIF formula. However, IRS data tapes show that DIF is playing a diminishing role in audits. In 1999, only one quarter of individual audits at an IRS district office were triggered by DIF.[5]

According to TRAC, the second reason a return might be selected is its connection to a second return that is already being audited. When the IRS finds a tax problem in a return filed by an individual in one year, it may go back and reexamine previous years. Correspondingly, if the IRS identifies a problem in the tax return of one partner, it often examines the filing of the other. This accounted for 18.6 percent of audits in 2000.

The third-largest reason for an audit is when someone decides not to file any tax return at all. In 1999, this factor was cited as the trigger in 8.7 percent of the face-to-face audits. The next likely returns selected are those the IRS believes may present certain compliance problems, such as those taking the Earned Income Credit, or those in the underground economy who might, for example, be involved in a cash-intensive business.

An interesting contrast is what triggers IRS audits of returns filed by corporations. Some of the country's largest corporations—nearly 30 percent—are automatically selected, along with those already being audited (23.7 percent). Then (22 percent) comes a DIF-like formula.[6]

What IRS Auditors Really Do

If you receive official notice that you are to appear for a formal audit, you need to know that examinations or tax audits are conducted on one of three levels: office, field, or correspondence. Recent auditing initiatives include economic reality or financial status audits and the Market Segment Specialization Program (see later section in this chapter).

A nonbusiness audit is generally conducted as an office audit by a tax auditor in an IRS district office. In addition, some small-business audits are done as office audits, but generally these involve few complex accounting or tax issues.

Tax auditors are generally trained by the IRS. They have no other special qualifications in tax law or accounting. As a result, they handle the less-complicated types of audits, which tend to be office audits.

Some tax auditors are pretty good. The nature of their work is highly repetitive, and the auditing routine is second nature to them. What they audit is very specific, and often the same, whereas in a field audit, any line of income or expense is open for exploration.

The IRS recognizes that this process of assigning tax auditors to repeatedly audit the same issues increases the effectiveness of the audit process. To ensure this, the IRS has devised a series of kits on different aspects of conducting a district office audit. These are presented in "Pro-Forma Audit Kits—Office Examination," in the Internal Revenue Manual—the IRS's bible—page 4231-11. Specific audit kits instruct what to look for, what questions to ask, and how to proceed on items regarding the following:

Miscellaneous
Taxes
Medical
Interest
Casualty loss
Moving expense
Contributions
Rental income and expenses
Employee business expense

Although the use of the pro-forma aids is mandatory for all office examinations, the Internal Revenue Manual stresses that the kits suggest the minimum amount of work to be completed and are not designed to include all possible audit procedures. Accordingly, the auditor is encouraged to use his or her judgment in deciding what extra steps should be taken in each case.

Now, while the repetitiveness of an office audit can make tax auditors more efficient, it can also make them unreasonably shortsighted by encouraging them to stick too closely to the rules while ignoring the bigger picture. Obviously, efficiency benefits the IRS, while shortsightedness benefits the taxpayer.

The field audit, or on-site examination, generally occurs at the taxpayer's place of business, where records pertinent to the examination are kept. It involves the examination of individual, partnership, and corporate tax returns. Corporate or partnership returns are audited only in the field. In addition, some individual returns are field-audited, especially those thought to involve complex accounting or tax issues.

In my experience the only individuals who are field-audited are

- Self-employed people who fill out a Schedule C and have significant income. Even a corporate wage earner who earns between $100,000 and $200,000 is not as great an attraction to the IRS as a self-employed person who earns over $100,000.
- Those with multiple rental properties, especially properties that throw off net losses that can be deducted in full by taxpayers who are involved full-time in real estate.

People who are self-employed in a service business (no product/inventory) can be assigned to either an office or a field audit. If a service business has a large gross income, over $100,000 annually, it will probably end up field-audited. However, sometimes the IRS makes mistakes in assignments and a case that should have been audited in the field may be assigned to an office audit, or vice versa.

An often overlooked benefit to having an IRS agent conduct an audit at your office is that you have the psychological advantage. Although agents are used to going to all sorts of locations to dig into all sorts of returns, as the business owner you will feel more comfortable in your own territory. A request for an on-site examination is often granted by the IRS if it is too difficult to bring the books, records, and other materials needed for the audit to the IRS district office. Also, the IRS usually considers a field audit if a taxpayer has other valid circumstances, such as someone being a one-man operation or being physically handicapped, that necessitate conducting the audit on-site.

Field audits are typically conducted by a revenue agent, also referred to as a field auditor. These are the most experienced of all audit personnel. The revenue agent will usually have a minimum of 24 credits of college-level accounting courses and will have received advanced audit training by the IRS.

With ongoing changes in our economy, the IRS continues to attract people to accept jobs as revenue agents who have college degrees in accounting and prior work experience in private industry. (See "There's a Varied Audit Mix" in Chapter 4.) This has introduced an interesting phenomenon into the examination function; if you are assigned an agent with this background, be prepared for the worst. Whereas someone from the "younger set" may overlook an issue, even a substantial one, a revenue agent with previous corporate experience, familiar with special accounting nuances, probably will not. I try to learn early on if the auditor assigned has had prior corporate or public accounting experience. I no longer assume that these people are lifetime civil service employees.

Correspondence audits are conducted primarily through the mail between taxpayers and the Correspondence Audit section of their service center. Although not technically audits, these are an attempt to resolve certain issues, or complete areas of your tax return, simply by having you mail specific information or documents requested. This type of audit is a recent attempt by the IRS to allow taxpayers to bypass bureaucracy.

Often a correspondence audit is generated through the Automated Correspondence Procedure, the most common one resulting from a mismatch between your W-2 or 1099, or on a third-party report, and what appears on your tax return. For example, if a third-party report indicates you received interest income of $1,000 and that amount did not appear on your return, you will receive a CP-2000, Notice of Proposed Changes to Your Tax Return. The taxpayer's reply may clear up the situation, or a bill may be sent for the amount due. The CP-2000 letter, often referred to as a "matching letter," is not a bill. It is a request for information that will resolve the mismatch. At this point, a taxpayer has the right to request an office audit, to be conducted at his or her local district office.

CP-2000 letters are used when a tax return cannot alone be used to make a determination of the tax due. CP-2000s are spit out by computers and sent to literally millions of taxpayers annually.

For the fiscal year 2001, 16 percent of all individual audits were done at the IRS district offices; 12 percent were conducted in the field, usually at a taxpayer's business or a tax professional's office; and 72 percent were done through correspondence audits at the service centers. The latter are conducted by clerks who often receive rudimentary training from the IRS and are required to have only a high school education.

The IRS places a tremendous emphasis on having the service centers examine returns, a more judicious use of manpower and technology. So if you disagree with the results you receive in the letter from the IRS about your case, and you feel the facts are on your side, fight the decision by providing full details in your first response and reasons for your position. When a final solution is arrived at, if you subsequently receive a bill, be sure to check the facts and figures because inaccuracies often occur.

Here's what the dollar amounts show:

Tax Dollars Collected by Type of Audit of Individual Returns, 1998–2000

- Office audits, conducted by tax auditors, averaged $3,337 in 2000, nearly the equivalent to 1998 and 1999.
- Field audits, conducted by revenue agents, averaged $20,520 per tax return, an increase of 2.3 percent.
- Correspondence audits generated on average additional monies of $2,602 per taxpayer, an increase of 25 percent over last year.[7] (For an explanation of the increase, see Audits at an All-Time Low, in Chapter 8.)

Total Dollars Recommended in Additional Taxes and Penalties

For audits that have been completed (individual, corporation, etc.), the IRS computes the total amount of additional taxes and penalties owed on the total number of returns audited. This has amounted to $30 billion for each of the past three years.[8] In the future, these figures may no longer be made available because of the intention of the IRS to draw attention away from any resemblance to a quota system, which could involve the tallying up of penalties, liens, seizures, and more.

Most recently, financial status auditing and the Market Segment Specialization Program have been used by the IRS to increase auditing dollars from its favorite place, the underground economy.

Financial Status Auditing

Financial status auditing, formerly known as economic reality or cost-of-living audits, is a new name for an old technique.

Whereas the standard method of uncovering unreported income and other possible taxpayer irregularities focused on verifying information on the tax return, the IRS's financial status audits training modules emphasize investigating the "whole taxpayer." This approach is supposed to provide revenue agents and tax auditors with an economic profile that will help them to reach certain assumptions regarding what is reflected on the return versus the taxpayer's actual lifestyle. How a taxpayer spends money can be a better indication of income than the tax return itself.

The program allows agents to use aggressive interviewing techniques that could include such questions as these: Do you own any large asset (over $10,000) besides autos and real estate? What is it and where is it kept? Is it paid for, and if not, what is the payment? Do you ever take cash advances from credit cards or lines of credit? How much and how often? What cash did you have on hand last year, personally or for business, not in a bank—at your home, safe-deposit box, hidden somewhere, and so on?

Whereas in the past these and similar questions might have been routinely asked in audits where fraud was suspected, many taxpayers have been facing barrages of this nature at the onset of an ordinary audit examination.

During an audit, if it soon appears that you're facing an inquisition with implications that fraud is suspected, there are some steps you should take. However, for the best preventive medicine, read Chapter 8, "How to Completely Avoid an Audit," so that you will be in the strongest position possible.

If you're already involved in an audit, and the auditor wants to interview you without an adviser, you can request a delay until you have a professional representative. My suggestion is, if you are alone, stop the audit immediately and postpone it for as long as possible. This way, the caseloads will pile up and the IRS may be forced to cut back on imposing economic reality audits, at least for a while.

If the notification of the audit arrives with Form 4822 (Statement of Annual Estimated Personal and Family Expenses), which requires you to estimate all personal living expenses paid during the audited tax year (the total cost of food, housing, vacations, clothing, etc.), you are in a no-win situation. An overestimate of expenses will possibly increase your taxable income, while a low estimate could possibly be rejected by the examiner. It's hard to figure out why the IRS requests this information to begin with, unless it is to use against you at a later time. Anyway, can you really remember off the top of your head what your annual expenditures were—two or three years ago—for such items as groceries, clothing, and vacation? Probably not. So remember that you are not required to fill out the form, and your refusal cannot be used against you during an audit. Consult with your representative. Be informed, however, that the tax examiner can search out additional data about you from external sources, such as social service agencies, motor vehicles databases, credit bureaus, trade associations, and court records. The examiner can also interview landlords, employers, and financial institutions. However, the IRS must notify you in advance if it intends to contact third parties for information about you.

Due to increased workloads, both tax auditors and revenue agents will try to extract evidence from the most direct source available, and that is *you*. Bring to the meeting supporting details only for items that were specifically requested. If a new issue is raised, state that you need time to consider your answer. It probably will not be brought up again. Also, do not engage in any small talk whatsoever. If the auditor is staring at the computer screen on his desk or laptop, he may be looking at a blank screen waiting for you to say something that he can use to possibly expand the audit.

Once you are working with a tax professional or attorney, you will need to proceed honestly. Ask your tax pro for a pre-audit evaluation to determine if a situation exists that might generate significant interest to an IRS tax examiner during an audit. Disclose as much as you can concerning what an examiner would be interested in. Consider your overall lifestyle, including your standard of living, overall yearly consumption versus costs, and method of accumulating wealth. What does your economic history look like? Do business profits or wages match your standard of living and wealth accumulation? Are your assets and liabilities consistent with your net worth? Also be prepared to answer questions about loans, large purchases (real estate, stock transactions, personal items), lender's source of funds, and possible cash hoards, gifts, or inheritances.

Ask your tax pro to request the IRS file on you, if this hasn't already been done, to assess the basis for the investigation and to send a message to the IRS that your tax pro intends to monitor the procedure.

During the audit, if the examiner asks financial status questions, your tax pro can challenge them by asking if there is any suspicion of unreported income.

Finally, remember that an examiner cannot conduct a civil examination as if it were a criminal fraud investigation. If indication of fraud is suspected, the audit must be suspended and a fraud referral report submitted through the ranks. The case then proceeds to the Criminal Investigation Division (CID).

Although the IRS has claimed that financial status audits came into play in only about 20 percent of all audits, the ensuing outcry, not only from bruised taxpayers but particularly from the American Institute of Certified Public Accountants (AICPA), has had a positive effect.

Congress has determined that the financial status audit technique is unreasonable and overintrusive. Accordingly, the IRS is now prohibited from using financial status or economic reality examination techniques to determine the existence of unreported income of any taxpayer unless the IRS already has a reasonable indication that there is unreported income.

Market Segment Specialization Program

Traditionally, revenue agents were trained to examine compliance problems within a particular geographic region, focusing on income ranges for individuals or asset ranges for corporations. Sometime in mid-1995, this technique was superseded by the Market Segment Specialization Program (MSSP), where the focus shifted to investigating taxpayers in specific industries.

With this initiative, the IRS believes it can significantly strengthen its audit capability as more of its examiners become trained industry experts able to uncover as yet undreamed-of sources of income. The IRS has isolated over 100 such industries and has kept quite busy developing and publishing a series of industry-specific guidebooks that address key issues and concerns, set guidelines for audits, and provide concrete, in-depth background information such as balance sheet accounting, components of sales and other income sources, costs of goods sold, and typical expenses. So, whereas tax auditors in the district offices are guided by the Pro-Forma Audit Kits contained in the Internal Revenue Manual, field auditors (revenue agents) are now guided by the material prepared for the MSSP. (For a more complete discussion of the industries targeted and what to do if you are in the line of fire, see Chapter 7.)

An Examiner's Personality

In general, the procedures that revenue agents and tax auditors are supposed to go through appear logical and well ordered when one reads them in the Internal Revenue Manual.

Under the heading "Research of Unfamiliar Items," the Manual (page 4231–10) advises revenue agents that "an examiner cannot perform adequately unless he is familiar with the issues on the return which scrutiny raises. . . . The tax law, regulations, Treasury decisions, rulings, court cases, the published services, and a myriad of other sources of information are the tools of the trade. No one can work without tools, and no one can improvise substitutes for such tools."

What really happens, however, is that this IRS bible can become virtually irrelevant as an agent's personality often supersedes, modifies, and even rewrites any procedures that should have been followed.

Often, I've walked into an audit genuinely concerned for my client, only to find that because of the personality of the agent assigned, not only does the audit go smoothly, but most of the information I was concerned about was never even touched upon. (Of course the reverse can also happen, as you will see in Chapter 4, when Mr. Fields, the IRS revenue agent, audited my client, an exporting agency.) Here's an example of how the revenue agent assigned to your case affects the course of the audit process.

Mrs. Price was the president of a closely held corporation dealing in wholesale medical supplies. After she received notice that her company's return would be audited, she called me to handle the audit and to review the tax work done by the company's corporate controller. I immediately saw several major audit issues that required more research. I secured additional backup data and prepared myself for some difficult negotiations. But I knew the final determining factor, the IRS revenue agent, could turn the whole thing around. In this case, he did.

The agent, Mr. Stores, was a pleasant young man who did not have much experience handling complicated audits. I determined this early on by his manner and the questions he began with.

On Day 1, Mr. Stores routinely inquired about how my client's corporation conducted business: who its customers and suppliers were, and the names and addresses of the banks the business used. He also went through the standard routine of examining paid bills for two random months and verifying them against cash disbursements journals. Then he verified two random months of sales invoices and traced them to cash receipts journals.

He worked so slowly that he didn't complete his work on a reconciliation of bank deposits until the close of Day 3.

At this point, I was waiting for him to raise a few of the larger issues that were part and parcel of this corporation's return, issues that would be quite evident to any trained professional, such as the following:

- *Officers' loans.* A balance of $400,000 was owed to the corporation by Mrs. Price. Although the money had been advanced over a six-year period, interest had been accrued only on the books; Mrs. Price had never actually paid any interest or principal. Moreover, the corporation's earnings were sufficient to pay Mrs. Price dividends, but she had never been paid any. Clearly, the IRS would strongly argue that some of the loans be reclassified as dividends, which are not deductible by the corporation. Therefore, they would be considered taxable income for Mrs. Price.
- *Officers' salaries.* In the corporation's year-end accounting journal entry, the corporate controller recorded $50,000 in officers' salaries, which was paid to Mrs. Price 45 days after the close of the corporate year. In a closely held

corporation, salaries are deductible only in the year paid, not in the year they are accrued or recorded on the books.

- *Officers' life insurance.* During the year, $30,000 of officers' life insurance was paid and was deducted as an expense on the corporate tax return. However, it was not listed as a separate item; it was buried in the category of "General Insurance." The problem with this is that officers' life insurance is not ever deductible.

Instead of stopping to discuss even one of these issues, the revenue agent made additional requests for more information to support bills paid for entertainment, travel, auto expense, and commissions. These areas are old standbys that revenue agents seem to fall back on especially when they have decided not to delve into other issues that are more complex. At the next meeting, Mr. Stores wasted half the day verifying the expense information he had previously requested. He also verified a schedule of bank interest that was nothing more than a reprise of two items per month that represented interest for two corporate bank loans. He pulled all 12 bank statements to verify that the interest was listed on our schedule accurately.

Why did Mr. Stores choose to engage in this painstakingly slow and practically redundant exercise? In my opinion, he was padding his work papers by including a schedule of bank interest to let his group chief know he hadn't omitted anything.

Toward the end of Day 4, he finally got around to insurance. I submitted paid bills for all ordinary insurance such as auto, worker's compensation, and health insurance, plus the bills for officers' life insurance totaling $30,000.

Finally he asked for promissory notes covering the officers' loans, which I gave him. He dropped the matter entirely without ever asking why interest had never been paid on the loans.

The audit was concluded with the agent disallowing the $30,000 in officers' life insurance. He also disallowed approximately $15,000 of travel and entertainment.

The issue of the officers' salaries paid in the wrong year was never discussed. This alone could have meant an additional tax liability of $25,000. Since the agent had my client's 1040s for several years, he could have traced the salaries if he had chosen to. He didn't.

If you're reading this and are awestruck, don't be. This kind of audit is not unusual. I know that Mr. Stores fully believed he was performing conscientiously. Revenue agents with more experience think and act differently (they get through the routine information more quickly) and stand a better chance of uncovering larger issues.

You can never predict how the audit process will go because so much depends on the kind of revenue agent assigned to your case. Even reading up on the subject probably won't help you much, although you can pick up a lot of very worthwhile and specific information. The key is to focus on preventive medicine: Make sure you never receive that audit notice—by following the advice in this book. If you do receive an audit notice, get the best professional you can find, one who has had plenty of experience facing IRS agents at audits, to represent you.

WHAT YOU NEED TO KNOW ABOUT THE COLLECTION DIVISION

What They Say They Do

In 1996, the Collection Division had over 17,500 employees. For that year, 6,500 people, nonrevenue officers, were shipped into a customer service area, along with another 4,000 others from Taxpayer Services. This boosted Customer Services from 1,777 people to 12,216 in one year! By 2000, 19,019 people were considered to be part of Customer Services.

This shift reflected one of the major directives of RRA '98—to better serve taxpayers. Using examination and collection people to help in the area of customer service is an ongoing effort. In 2001 and 2002, the number of revenue officers has held steady at approximately 5,400 people.

Collection deals with people who owe tax who say they cannot pay, those who never filed, and the innocent, victimized taxpayer who unfortunately falls into the IRS's "I made a mistake" category. IRS personnel from Collection are the ones who can wipe out your possessions and, until RRA '98, could do so with few limitations.

Collection has three major components: the service center, the Automated Collection System, and the district office.

What Collection Really Does

Since all tax returns are mailed to a taxpayer's appropriate service center, the actual collection process begins in the collection areas in each of the 10 service centers across the country.

To resolve balance due or delinquent tax matters, the service center routinely sends up to four "balance due" or "return delinquency" notices:

501 Reminder of Unpaid Tax
503 Urgent—Payment Required
504 Final Notice
523 Notice of Intent to Levy

In the past few years, the IRS often skips the 503 notice and goes directly to the 504 Final Notice.If you receive a 504 letter, this is really not the "final" notice, just the final notice from the service center. If you don't pay in full within 30 days of receiving this notice, the IRS can begin the enforced collection process. After this, the process can take on a life of its own. After the 523 notice is received, the IRS can seize your assets. So you must give this notice immediate attention.

In 1983, the amount collected from taxpayers on the first notice was close to $2 billion. In 2002, the average first notice from the IRS claiming money due brought in over $13.4 billion from taxpayers who were probably relieved to get the IRS off their backs simply by writing one check.[9] You can see the IRS's progress in this area alone.

The initial mailings of notices for tax due should include certain publications. "Your Rights as a Taxpayer," IRS Publication 1, commonly referred to as the "Taxpayer Bill of Rights," is usually mailed with the first notice, and "The IRS Collection Process," IRS Publication 594, is mailed prior to enforced-collection action. The latter will answer many of your questions and explain clearly and objectively what you need to do when you receive a bill from the IRS.

If a taxpayer has not responded after receiving the last notice, or if the situation looks as though it may not be easily resolved, the Automated Collection System (ACS) takes over.

Automated Collection System (ACS)

ACS has offices around the country, staffed with employees responsible for collecting unpaid taxes and securing tax returns from delinquent taxpayers who have not responded to previous service center notices. Their work is carried out strictly through the mail or over the telephone. Chances are, no matter how many people you speak to from ACS, you will never meet with any of them in person.

The work that goes on in the ACS offices is quite focused. Personnel trained to locate errant taxpayers are supported in their efforts by computer links to a range of information resources. These include state tax files and local offices as well as other records, such as the registry of motor vehicles, voter registration office, and membership in union, trade, professional, or other organizations. They also use telephone books and post office records and can easily obtain unlisted phone numbers. ACS employees also routinely write letters of inquiry to your employees, next-door neighbors, and schools that you or your family have attended.

Once the contact is made, the IRS says what will happen next:

When taxpayer contact is made, either through an outcall or in response to an ACS letter or enforcement action, the ACS employees will discuss how best to resolve the tax matter. Where there are unpaid taxes, the IRS has written guidelines for considering an installment agreement to pay the tax over a period of time, for adjusting incorrect tax bills and reducing or eliminating penalties, and for determining situations where the case should be reported currently not collectible.[10]

If and when ACS fails to get as far as it should and/or it looks as if the taxpayer is not cooperating, and/or it appears as if the situation is not easily going to be resolved, the service center sends the case to the district office for further investigation.

District Office Collection

When ACS has determined that nothing else has worked and that it's time to take enforcement action, you've reached the final step in the collection process.

What happens at the district level is the all-too-familiar nightmare of the surprise visit to your home or office, where the revenue officer will ask lots of questions and arrange for a more formal interview. During the formal meeting, the officer will fill out a detailed financial report on an IRS form with the information you supply. Then the two of you will work through the methods and means you will use to pay the money you owe. These might include certain routes the revenue officer decides you must take no matter what, such as producing immediate monies to pay the bill, selling specific assets, or paying a visit to your bank to secure a bank loan. Payment could also be made via a carefully detailed installment plan, Form 9465, which, compared to the other choices available, begins to sound good. But be wary of this. (For more information, see Chapter 13.)

If none of these are workable for you, the situation deteriorates before your eyes and things are, for the most part, taken out of your hands.

To fully realize the extent of authority vested in the Collection Division, each taxpayer should know the major steps Collections can take to, as the IRS says, "protect the government's interest in the tax matter, or if the taxpayer neglects or refuses to pay, or fails to help resolve a tax matter."[11]

A *summons* simply requires that you must appear at a given time and place and offer specific information as you are grilled by IRS revenue officers.

A *lien* is a much more dangerous weapon. First of all, it means that the IRS is going to publicly notify all your creditors and business associates that the IRS has a claim against your property and your rights to property, including property that you might acquire even after the lien is filed.

Second, you will, in effect, lose your credit rating because notice of a lien is filed with all the appropriate official and legislative channels, the secretary of state, and the county clerk. If this happens, it can take years to stabilize your financial standing, even if you have the best tax attorney on your side. IRS Publication 594, "The IRS Collection Process," makes this misleading statement under the heading "Releasing a Lien": "Usually 10 years after a tax is assessed, a lien releases automatically if we have not filed it again."

A lien is a notice to creditors that the government has a claim against your property for a tax debt. A *levy* gives the IRS control over your assets, so that it can literally, physically, take the property out of your possession to satisfy your debt. A levy encompasses property that you hold (home, boat, car) or property held for you by third parties (wages, savings accounts). The principle behind this is that your possessions are no longer yours but, rather, belong to the government.

The IRS must notify you in advance of all the steps it intends to take throughout the lien and levy process. The IRS must also allow you ample time to retain professional help and attempt to remedy the situation.

Under the levy (and seizure), you should be aware that the IRS is required to leave something behind. This includes unemployment benefits, workmen's compensation, fuel, provisions, furniture; personal effects for a head of household, with a total value of $6,780; books and tools used in your trade, business, or profession, worth up to $3,390; and a minimum weekly exemption for wages, salaries, and other income. Because the previous limits were so small, the IRS was able to take cars and other personal belongings from individuals with limited means. The present exemptions allow taxpayers at least to retain some of their belongings. All amounts are subject to inflation adjustments. The full list is in "The IRS Collection Process," IRS Publication 594. Use IRS Publication 1494, "Table of Figuring Amount Exempt From Levy on Wages, Salary and Other Income," to determine the amount of earned income exempt from levy.

Other collection techniques involve the IRS making a special arrangement with

- Your employer to collect money owed, by initiating payroll deductions from your wages.
- Anyone who pays you interest or dividends, to withhold income tax at the rate of 31 percent.
- The IRS's own Collection Department, to apply your annual tax refund to offset any balance due.

Let me emphasize that all of these actions, which have been part of the tax collection process and which occurred across our nation, used to be standard operating procedures. Before any other law enforcement agency so radically disturbs a citizen's peace and lifestyle, it must by law obtain a court order. The IRS Collection Division was exempt from this procedure until RRA '98. Taxpayers should now have a much better chance at due process when dealing with the once strong-arm tactics of the IRS Collection Division.

In fact, given shifting staffs, a decrease in the number of tax collectors, an increase in tax returns, and what appears to be a backlash against the 1998 laws that affect collection procedures, plus learning or not learning how the new laws need to be applied, collections in all areas—seizures, liens, and levies—have dropped significantly. (See Chapter 13.)

Forms and More Forms

Each of the procedures just described—and there are even more of them—consists of very specific steps that the taxpayer and the IRS are supposed to go through before an actual collection action can be made. Enter IRS forms, those things that have become second nature to the IRS since its inception: forms that tell taxpayers what is about to happen "unless"; forms that rescind the threats; forms that announce that the IRS is going to proceed with the action after all, no matter what; forms that give the taxpayer one last chance; forms that repeal or dismiss the action because the taxpayer is ready to settle the bill.

The paperwork, telephone calls, and correspondence required both to set these actions into motion and to stop them are unbelievably intricate, voluminous, even ridiculous. Add to this the tricks and techniques tax professionals extract from their "what-to-use-against-the-IRS-Collection-Division" repertoire to stall, delay, or reverse decisions already put into action via the forms, and we could go on forever. I prefer to focus first on how to deal with the human element in the IRS if you do get involved, and second, on how you need not get involved in these quagmires at all.

Collection People Mean Business

IRS collection staff mean business, and they have always had a great deal of power and substantial leeway to exercise it. Here's what I mean:

Anthony was the owner of a business with about 100 employees that contracted cutting clothes for the men's garment industry in New York City. Because of intense competition that resulted in small profit margins, Anthony made a dangerous mistake: In a six-month period, he fell behind in paying $58,000 of payroll taxes to the IRS.

When Anthony hired me to help him out of this mess, the first step I took was to make sure current payroll taxes were paid. To do this, Anthony borrowed $12,000 from relatives. Next, I called the telephone number shown on the collection notice to arrange an appointment with a revenue officer with the intention of settling the case by negotiating an installment agreement. One week later I met with a Mr. Michaels and explained that Anthony was in a position to pay off the existing $58,000 liability at the rate of $10,000 a month while continuing to pay current payroll tax obligations. I submitted Forms 433-A (Collection Information Statement for Individuals) and 433-B (Collection Information Statement for Businesses) to show the agent Anthony's current personal and business financial situation and to make clear his willingness to meet his IRS obligations. Though he had no assets of value or any equity in his business, Anthony wanted to clear his debt because he was only 40 years old and the company was his sole livelihood. Hoping I had set the stage for negotiation, I then listened to Mr. Michaels's reply, here verbatim:

"I don't care what your client's intentions are, and it doesn't matter to me that he's paying his current obligations promptly. Let me just close him down and put him out of his misery."

To counter any further steps in that direction, I immediately asked Mr. Michaels if he would bring his group chief to the negotiating table, which he did.

Only after I handed her a bank check for $10,000 as a down payment (more money that Anthony had borrowed from relatives) did she reluctantly agree to approve an installment agreement of $8,000 a month stretched over a period of six months.

If you think the objective of every IRS revenue officer is to maximize collections, think again. Collection people mistakenly rely on prior cases of delinquent and tardy taxpayers and then do their best to make life miserable for average people like Anthony. So be forewarned. (The IRS is clamping down on payroll tax abusers more harshly than ever before.)

In another collections case, the owner of a hardware store owed $22,000 in payroll taxes. Twice before he had broken agreements to pay on an installment basis. The revenue officer on the case obtained a warrant from the court, showed up in the store, seized the entire contents of the store, and sold it at an auction a short time later.

In both these cases, the taxpayer was in trouble and the revenue officers assigned were doing their jobs—it was brutal, but expected. In payroll tax cases, revenue officers are instructed to be especially forceful because the IRS holds employers to a greater degree of responsibility (they must pay employees' taxes) than an individual taxpayer who owes only his or her own taxes.

Often, in collections, the end does not so pointedly justify the means.

A new chief of collections appointed in the Manhattan district office immediately placed a great emphasis on raising the level of collection of old cases. The new chief met with the revenue officers assigned to the district and told them to go out and get the job done, no holds barred. One story came back from this group about a taxpayer who had just undergone brain surgery. He owned a dry-cleaning establishment and owed $14,000 in payroll taxes. After agreeing to an installment plan, he had paid the agreed-upon $600 per month right on time, until illness struck. The new chief approved the seizure of the man's business, which was liquidated within a few weeks while the taxpayer was in a coma and his wife and family literally stood by helplessly.

Revenue officers are out to get what they can from you because you owe the government. If they can get all you owe, that's great for them. But they will also settle for taking whatever they can get their hands on.

If this sounds brutal, I advise you that they and the process are supposed to be.

WHAT YOU NEED TO KNOW ABOUT THE CRIMINAL INVESTIGATION DIVISION

What They Say They Do

If you are the subject of a criminal investigation, you'll be involved with the IRS's Criminal Investigation Division (CID), also referred to as Tax Fraud and Financial Investigations. In 2002, this division had 2,907 special agents, out of just over 4,000 employees.

Although very powerful in its own right, CID does not have the power to determine tax liability. It does have the responsibility of scaring taxpayers into compliance with the tax laws, stopping criminal acts involving tax violations, and punishing violators.

The heaviest caseloads for CID vary between tax fraud; drugs and illegal activities involving money laundering; white-collar crime committed by stockbrokers, investment bankers, and money managers; and organized crime. As a general rule, the average amount of taxes owed by a taxpayer when the IRS files criminal charges is over $70,000. Because of the nature of their job and whom they deal with—organized-crime figures, very wealthy individuals, drug dealers, executives, professionals—special agents have a certain untouchable aura about them that goes back to CID's establishment in the 1920s.

Where CID Receives Its Leads

Cases in which criminal activity is indicated or suspected are sent to CID from various sources:

- Revenue agents and other auditors refer cases while conducting routine audits. This is usually the most common way that criminal cases get started. Therefore, while you are involved in a regular audit, do not get caught in a lie that will arouse suspicion. It will increase the chances of your case being referred to the CID.
- CID employees search through newspapers, articles, broadcast media, and other public sources for specific circumstances, such as lifestyles that might indicate fraud, or items reported stolen (to see if they match up to a taxpayer's reported income).
- The Justice Department—refers primarily narcotics and organized-crime cases. The number of special agents who work on organized crime and narcotics cases is not publicized because it represents a very high percentage of the total cases handled by CID.

- Law enforcement agencies—FBI, DEA (Drug Enforcement Agency).
- Regulatory agencies—the Department of Consumer Affairs, Securities and Exchange Commission, Food and Drug Administration, Federal Communications Commission.
- Banks and other financial institutions—are required to report a cash transaction of $10,000 or more, as well as any other "suspicious" transactions, on Form 8300 (Report of Cash Payments over $10,000 Received in a Trade or Business).
- CID has its own staff of undercover agents who nab unsuspecting taxpayers. The undercover agent can even be part of illegal activity with the taxpayer, as long as the agent does not induce the taxpayer to commit a crime that he would not otherwise have committed. To prevent the taxpayer from using a victim of entrapment defense, the government's lawyer must show that the crime was the taxpayer's idea exclusively.
- Independent CID leads often come from paid informants. The Internal Revenue Code has a provision for paying informants 15 percent of tax that is recovered as a result of a tip (see Use of Informers in Chapter 7). CID also has people on its payroll who regularly provide tips about criminal activities.
- Voluntary informers—vindictive lovers, ex-wives or ex-husbands, former employees, and more—are very willing to tell all to the IRS. The best advice is not to brag about how you fooled the IRS. Don't make statements in public such as, "I live off cash and never file a return." You may regret saying it

If CID doesn't think a case will end up with a conviction, it will turn it back to the referring party. Special agents don't waste time. They are diligent, focused, and well trained, and they perform meticulous, detailed investigations.

A criminal investigation can be initiated by either the IRS, known as an administrative investigation, or by a grand jury. In an administrative investigation, a summons issued by the IRS is the vehicle that gets the taxpayer and any other witnesses to the investigation. Enforcement in this instance tends to be more difficult; long delays are common. In a grand jury investigation, which employs the subpoena, witnesses show up faster and the U.S. attorney immediately enters the picture. Subpoenas are easier to obtain, and the process is quicker and more effective compared to an administrative investigation.

Another difference is that in an administrative investigation CID is in charge, but with a grand jury, the U.S. attorney, who works for the Justice Department, is in charge and the IRS plays second fiddle. So although a grand jury investigation is quicker and more efficient and thus an easier task for CID and its agents, the IRS doesn't like taking orders from anyone.

But since a large percentage of cases are referred to CID from the Justice Department, CID doesn't have a choice. A case referred by the Justice Department automatically receives a grand jury investigation.

From a taxpayer's perspective, all I would say here is that an administrative investigation might be slightly more preferable (although being in a position of having to undergo a criminal investigation of any sort is completely not preferable), simply because it works much more slowly than a grand jury.

Once CID is convinced that prosecuting a citizen is in order, the case moves up through CID to the district counsel, then to the Department of Justice, Tax Division, Washington, D.C., and on to the U.S. District Court. The case must garner approval each step of the way, or it will be thrown out. This approval process normally takes two to six months.

After a criminal investigation is completed, the evidence and facts are compiled in the special agent's report. The examination auditor will probably use this report when imposing civil penalties. If you are the person under investigation, obtain a copy of the report by writing to the attention of the disclosure officer at the IRS district office where the criminal investigation took place and mention that your request is "pursuant to the Freedom of Information Act."

If at the conclusion of its investigation CID decides it doesn't have a case against the taxpayer, the case will be dropped. But that's not the end of it. The case then finds its way back to an auditor, who examines it for civil penalties, which can run as high as 75 percent of what is owed. Even when a person is prosecuted and found guilty, civil penalties are likely to be imposed as well.

When CID builds a case against a suspected tax criminal, the work it performs is very thorough and precise. By the time you, your friends, your family, or neighbors are contacted by a special agent, the case gathered against you will be pretty solid. The special agent will have already reconstructed approximately how much the suspect has spent during a given year and compared that amount with available cash from taxable and nontaxable sources, such as gifts and loans. The search will also include payments made with unreported income, such as cash used to pay off credit cards, college tuition, cars, newly insured jewelry, and more.

When a taxpayer falls into the criminal category, he or she stands to receive a fairer deal than a taxpayer caught up in the collections area. That's because in the Criminal Investigation Division, the burden of proof is on the government: The taxpayer is innocent until proven guilty. For every case handled by any other division of the IRS, the reverse is true. The only recent change comes from RRA '98 regarding noncriminal proceedings that reach the level of Tax Court or Federal Court. In these instances, the burden of proof may shift to the IRS if the taxpayer meets certain conditions. (See 1998 Tax Legislation in Chapter 12.)

In summary, putting people in jail is the job of the Justice Department. When it comes to tax violations, it's the IRS that gets Justice headed in the right direction.

In 2001, CID referred 2,056 cases for prosecution, resulting in 1,121 convictions; many of these received prison terms.[12] This represented a 39 percent decline in prosecuted cases compared to the prior year. What is significant is that

- The number of criminal tax cases the IRS gets involved with is relatively low, less than .001 percent of the total population of taxpayers sending in tax returns—for 2001, 2,056 CID investigations initiated out of almost 225 million returns filed.
- While CID has the smallest staff of all the four major district-level operations (examination, collection, criminal investigation, and taxpayer services), it has the best reputation because of its ability to secure convictions.

You see, the decision to launch an investigation is made by CID with great care. True, CID may not always have a choice: If a person is well known and the IRS wants to make an example of him, or if the U.S. attorney insists that CID pursue a specific case in the area of organized crime, CID must follow up. But given the time and expense it takes to reach the stage where the IRS recommends a case to the Justice Department for prosecution, you can be sure that that case will stand a good chance of winning.

What CID Really Does Regarding Fraud

The Internal Revenue Manual clearly defines what conditions must exist for fraud, a criminal offense, to be indicated:

Actual fraud is intentional fraud. Avoidance of tax is not a criminal offense. All taxpayers have the right to reduce, avoid, or minimize their taxes by legitimate means. The distinction between avoidance and evasion is fine, yet definite. One who avoids tax does not conceal or misrepresent, but shapes and preplans events to reduce or eliminate tax liability, then reports the transactions.

Evasion, on the other hand, involves deceit, subterfuge, camouflage, concealment, some attempt to color or obscure events, or making things seem other than they are.[13]

But here's the problem: Because the final determination is made by CID, the gap between what is criminal and what is civil allows for significant leeway, which can be and has been used against the taxpayer.

Let's say a taxpayer files Form 4868 (Application for Automatic Extension of Time to File U.S. Individual Income Tax Return), on which he underestimates his tax liability, and then does not file the completed return. CID could hold that this seemingly innocent action involved intent to commit fraud, or criminal behavior.

In another case, suppose a taxpayer willfully lies to a special agent. This is a clear indication of intent, is it not? This makes it criminal.

Don't for one second think that criminal violations involve only organized crime, narcotics violations, and money laundering. The majority of taxpayers would never even think about getting involved in these kinds of vice activities. But that's all right. The IRS gives you lots of chances to be charged as a criminal violator anyway.

How to Tell If Your Behavior Borders on Criminal

Taxpayers are at risk of criminal exposure when they

- Understate income, such as denying receipt of income and then not being able to offer a satisfactory explanation for the omission.
- Conceal accounts with a bank, brokerage firm, or other property.
- Repeatedly fail to deposit receipts to business accounts.
- Use fictitious names on bank accounts.
- Manipulate personal expenses to appear as business expenses.
- Take excessive religious and charitable contributions.
- Show substantial unexplained increases in net worth, especially over a period of years.
- Show substantial excess of personal expenditures over available resources.
- Fail to file a return, especially for a period of several years, while receiving substantial amounts of taxable income.

Are You Exhibiting Badges of Fraud?

If you are being examined for a civil or criminal violation, there are certain kinds of behaviors, referred to as "badges" of fraud, which according to the IRS could indicate fraud. As listed in the Internal Revenue Manual, some of the more common badges of fraud are as follows:

- False statements, especially if made under oath. For example, the taxpayer submits an affidavit stating that a claimed dependent lived in his household when the individual did not.
- Attempts to hinder the examination. For example, failure to answer pertinent questions or repeated cancellations of appointments.
- Testimony of employees concerning irregular business practices by the taxpayer.

- Destruction of books and records, especially if it's done just after an examination was started.
- Transfer of assets for purposes of concealment.

Are You Exhibiting "Willful Intent"?

The Internal Revenue Manual goes on to explain that in and of themselves, these actions by the taxpayer usually are not sufficient to establish fraud. However, when they are combined with other items, they may be taken to indicate a willful intent to evade tax. These other items include

- Refusal to make specific records available.
- Diversion of a portion of business income into a personal bank account.
- Filing the return in a different district.
- Submitting false invoices or other documents to support an item on the tax return.
- Lack of cooperation by the taxpayer.

In short, the most common areas of interest to CID are

- Tax evasion.
- Filing a false tax return.
- Failure to file a tax return.

These indicators are behaviors thousands of taxpayers exhibit with good reason during examination proceedings. Now that you know them, you realize that if you act in any of these ways, you could set off a lightbulb in some examiner's head that will then place you in the category of exhibiting a "badge" of fraud.

Attorneys strongly recommend that the moment taxpayers know a case is criminal they should stop talking and get a lawyer immediately. The lawyer should be a criminal attorney who is familiar with tax matters, and not a tax attorney who is familiar with criminal matters.

How a Tax Professional Spots an Audit Case Turned Criminal

Just as the IRS has defined certain taxpayer behaviors that indicate fraud, tax professionals have learned to stay finely tuned and spot corresponding "triggers" on the part of the IRS that could indicate that one of our audit cases is being considered as a criminal violation.

I have had several clients whose cases I suspected might be recommended to CID. As each new audit meeting arrived, I carefully watched the revenue agent to see if I could detect any change in his attitude: Was he being overly cooperative? Or, perhaps, suddenly very uncooperative by keeping a tight lid on his comments? Was he beginning to request new information unrelated to the issues we had been discussing all along? In the end, settlements of the cases in question were made either with the revenue agent or at an appeals conference. None were turned over for criminal action.

An important piece of information for taxpayers regarding the possible change in classification of a case from civil into criminal is this: During a regular audit proceeding, you can ask the revenue agent if your case is being considered as a criminal matter. The agent is required to answer truthfully. If, however, the case is subsequently deemed to be a criminal one, the agent is not obliged to voluntarily reveal this information, even though you previously asked that question. Of course, you are still in your rights to ask the same question again, but this could in itself be interpreted as a badge of fraud, especially if the agent has already decided that your case is criminal or has, in fact, turned it over to CID.

A CPA colleague described the case of a taxpayer, Mr. Lockwood, with a janitorial services business whose customers were primarily large corporations. Mr. Lockwood's business was a sole proprietorship. During an audit of his tax return (Form 1040, Schedule C), the revenue agent had a problem reconciling Mr. Lockwood's books with his tax return. The agent appropriately began to request additional backup data and to ask a lot of questions.

Immediately Mr. Lockwood berated the auditor for being a clock-watcher and accused him of being "just like all the other civil servants—people without real feelings or regard for the taxpayer." At the end of the day the auditor requested a list of items, including customer invoices and vendor-paid bills for a two-month period, to be brought in to the next audit session.

My colleague told his client not to do any talking. Even though he had an appalling filing system, he was also told to show up with every item the auditor requested. The auditor was only following a set routine of selecting several test months for closer scrutiny. But my colleague had a full-fledged Type C client on his hands, as described in Chapter 1. The fact that he was losing his audit seemed less important to him than being right.

Several days later, when Mr. Lockwood finally produced the information requested, almost half of the items were missing. During the session he looked the auditor straight in the eyes and told him that the other items had been misplaced.

Three weeks passed, which made my colleague uneasy. When an audit is in full swing as this one was, a sudden break without any apparent reason is cause for suspicion. The CPA telephoned the auditor to ask him if he could set up another date. It was then that the agent said he was turning the case over to CID.

Before the CID person began the investigation, she sent a letter to each of Mr. Lockwood's customers on CID letterhead. The letter stated that Mr. Lockwood was under criminal investigation for tax fraud and requested verification of payments from each customer made to the taxpayer during the year under audit. After this, the CID agent checked Mr. Lockwood's bank records, and guess what? Mr. Lockwood was able to clearly explain away all of the agent's questions. The investigation then ended—at least as far as the IRS was concerned.

Within six months of this rather minor debacle, Mr. Lockwood lost over 30 percent of his clients and half of his annual revenue. As a postscript, the IRS never did send a follow-up letter to his customers explaining that no criminal activity had occurred.

Now Mr. Lockwood decided to sue the IRS under Section 6103 of the Internal Revenue Code, which allows a taxpayer to bring suit if the IRS "wrongfully revealed confidential tax information," which Mr. Lockwood claimed did occur in the letter the IRS sent to his customers.

The case arrived in U.S. Tax Court, where the judge agreed with the taxpayer and added that the agent should have attempted to resolve the discrepancy by examining bank and other records before sending out a letter to parties not directly involved in the investigation.

Not satisfied with this decision, the IRS appealed the case to the circuit court of appeals, which, unfortunately for Mr. Lockwood, overruled the lower court's decision, stating that although the agent could have used better judgment, the IRS had caused no liability to the taxpayer.

In a farcical attempt to mitigate the harshness of the decision, the circuit court added that it did not want people to think that the IRS could investigate anyone it wanted to on a whim, since this kind of investigation could devastate a small business in a local community. Well, that's exactly what it had done. Mr. Lockwood ended up devastated by the ruling, which almost cost him his business plus attorney fees.

The Real Reason CID Contacts Third Parties

The three real reasons CID summons witnesses or third parties in an attempt to prove its case against taxpayers are

1. To obtain information that will incriminate the taxpayer.
2. To scare the very same people being contacted into never violating tax laws themselves (the deterrent mission).
3. To use the contact as an opportunity for the IRS to spread its tough-guy image.

Once CID discovers incriminating evidence, there are no statutes anywhere that prohibit the use this information against the taxpayer. Many careers and reputations have been destroyed because some of this stuff just happened to leak out.

Unspoken Problems in the Criminal Investigation Division

Despite the positive reports reflecting the level of CID work, there are problems with CID and the entire CID process that often go unspoken.

- Total federal tax prosecutions referred by CID have dropped to 512 cases for 2002, a 45 percent decrease from only five years ago.[14]

- Criminal prosecutions for nontax crimes led by CID, including drug offenses and money laundering, have dropped to 667 cases for 2002, a 52 percent decrease from only five years ago.[15]
- Even though tax criminals go to prison and are assessed a given amount of tax and penalties, the IRS has not been successful in collecting the full amount of tax dollars owed.

See Chapter 9 for a discussion on the major misconception taxpayers have regarding criminal cases and client-accountant confidentiality.

WHAT YOU NEED TO KNOW ABOUT THE TAXPAYER SERVICES DIVISION

What They Say They Do

According to the IRS, more than 18 percent of its overall staff time is devoted to taxpayer services. In 2002, the people in this division numbered 16,024. In general, Taxpayer Services provides guidance and assistance to taxpayers who write, telephone, or visit an IRS district office inquiring about their federal tax obligations. It also disseminates tax information, publications, films, and other educational materials, conducts tax workshops, and generally helps people untangle IRS red tape.

Taxpayer Services' toll-free assistance telephone numbers consist of various toll-free answering sites in all states as well as the District of Columbia and Puerto Rico. There has been a sharp increase in staff who answer these toll-free assistance telephones. According to TRAC, personnel assigned to this function jumped significantly. One of the most obvious results of this enlarged effort has been a great improvement in the ability of taxpayers to get through when they call IRS toll-free assistance lines. There's still a lengthy up-front waiting period until you do get through, and even then, you may not reach the person you wanted to talk to.

There is also a "TeleTax" service, which provides recorded tax information tapes on over 150 topics. A complete listing of the topics available, automated refund information, and the local telephone numbers for TeleTax are in IRS Publication 910, "Guide to Free Tax Services."[16]

Other programs provide free tax information and tax return preparation for taxpayers 60 years or older that assists taxpayers who would not normally obtain counsel in audit, appeals, and Tax Court cases.[17]

What Taxpayer Services Really Does

Taxpayer Services exists to service taxpayers' general tax needs and to educate people regarding U.S. taxes. This division is a good place to begin if you have a general tax question or need information that only the

IRS can provide. The fact is that the Taxpayer Services Division, like the rest of the IRS, is traditionally understaffed. Getting through to a live person over the telephone still requires time and persistence. Additionally, the answers you receive are sometimes misleading or inaccurate, especially for complex questions.

YOUR TAX-SAVING STRATEGY

For important issues, call two separate times to insure that the answers are identical or at least substantially alike. If you can get the answer in writing, you can use it later on to prove your position. However, most IRS employees do not have the time or inclination to provide a written response.

Through the "Taxpayer Information Program," a responsibility of this division, the IRS places information in the print and electronic media to assist taxpayers and increase voluntary compliance. If you were to conclude that a great deal of this material is image-sensitive, you would be correct. Thus, the news releases, fact sheets, and question-and-answer promotional pieces that the IRS prepares on diverse tax topics and offers to newspapers, local network and cable TV stations, radio stations, and others give the IRS the opportunity to spread its images—the omniscient IRS and the caring IRS helping befuddled taxpayers through another tax season.

In the theater, an empty stage slowly comes to life with scenery, lights, actors. Now that the background and the structure of the IRS are in place, let's bring up the curtain on the people who work there.

4

IRS People:
Whom You Need to Know;
What They're Really Like;
How to Work with Them;
Standard Operating Procedures

The IRS continues to face the second-largest overhaul since its inception. Still, things move slowly, and the new organizational structure will take years to put into place. (See Chapter 13.)

The existing organization keeps the IRS going until each new function is phased in. And this is what you need to know about people at the IRS.

THE IRS CHAIN OF COMMAND

At the top of the IRS organization chart are the commissioner and deputy counsel. Both are currently appointed by the president and report to the Treasury Department. The chief inspector, who is responsible for agency and employee honesty, is also at this level, along with the National Taxpayer Advocate and the National Treasury Employees Union (NTEU) Advisor. (See the new IRS organization chart in Appendix E.) Constant reorganization makes it difficult to analyze or keep track of the IRS organizational structure.

WHO RUNS THE SHOW?

What had been unique about the commissioner's job was the short term. This was generally because

- A new one was appointed every four to eight years, reflecting our political process.
- Offers from law and accounting firms often seduce them away.

—— The author David Burnham has calculated that "since the end of World War II, the average tenure at the top position has been only 37 months."[1] How much can a person really learn about the workings of the largest bureaucracy in the world in three years? More important, how much can that person ever really be held accountable for the agency's failures or successes? With RRA '98, the commissioner's term has been made permanent for a five-year period, with the possibility of reappointment to another five-year term. Unfortunately, at the end of 2002 former Commissioner Rossotti completed his first five-year term and chose not to seek another.

At the field organization level are the district directors and, on the same functional level, the service center directors, all of whom report to the regional commissioners.

THE EXAMINATION DIVISION

What People in the Examination Division Are Really Like

As I researched this book, I kept hearing, "Years ago there were better people in the IRS," or "Things were better in the old days," or "Things have really gone downhill." Such claims tend to be accurate.

Abusive Tax Shelters Monopolized the Audit Function

In the late 1970s and throughout the 1980s, when the IRS realized the extent to which people were using tax shelters, hundreds of auditors and revenue agents were assigned to ferret out and destroy tax shelters listed on individual and corporate returns. In fiscal year 1979, tax shelter exams accounted for only 1.7 percent of a revenue agent's workload, but by fiscal 1984 this percentage had grown to 19.1 percent.[2]

According to tax law, if an investment is not intended to make a profit, deductions and credits and certainly the huge write-offs generated by tax shelters are not allowable.

Here's what used to take place with a typical tax shelter. For $10,000 a taxpayer would purchase the rights to a well-known performer's unreleased record album that had been professionally appraised at $100,000. The balance of the acquisition costs, in this case $90,000, was regarded as a loan from the seller, to be paid down from earnings derived from sales of the record album.

What is the overall effect of this simple procedure? If the taxpayer was in the 50 percent tax bracket, the $10,000 investment would have allowed him to reduce his taxes in the first year by about $15,000, including the investment tax credit. In the second year, without the taxpayer investing any additional funds, that initial $10,000 investment would still have functioned as a vehicle for a major tax write-off of about $19,000. This system of gaining substantial tax reductions annually would continue until the asset was fully depreciated—in about six years in the case of a record album. By then, the initial investment would have saved the taxpayer an estimated $58,000 in taxes.

Tax shelters rob the government of money and divert investments into frivolous assets.

The Tax Reform Act of 1986 put an end to tax shelters by 1990 and made the rules retroactive as far back as 1980. Many of the cases involving audits of tax shelters took years to complete and lasted into the mid-1990s. At one point in 1985, about 24 percent of pending Tax Court cases involved tax shelters.[3] The impact of all this on the Examination Division was practically irreparable. The shift weakened the function so severely that the percentage of taxpayer audits dropped steadily for the next 10 years, from 1.77 percent in 1980 to about 1 percent in 1990. This drop translated to about 800,000 fewer individual tax returns audited each year. Just a few years ago, I was still working with several clients to settle their tax shelter cases. Abusive tax shelters are on the rise again, but this time the abusers seem to be coming from the corporate sector. (See Rise of Abusive Tax Shelters, Chapter 13.)

Outdated Management Practices Stymie Results

Typically, the turnover in entry-level positions at the IRS is quite high. This group usually stays two to three years and then leaves for a private accounting firm or tax law practice, where they are likely to double their salary. According to a former compliance officer, the absence of talented young agents has really frustrated the IRS because it takes from three to five years to adequately train a revenue agent to handle complex cases.[4]

At the other end of the spectrum are the IRS career professionals, those 20-year employees who really know how to slow down the quality of work. This group represents a sizable number who are not interested in moving up the career ladder. They want job security (it is very difficult to get fired from the IRS), they are content to follow orders without asking questions, and they want to get through the day with minimum amounts of aggravation, mental dexterity, and energy. They think in the way the IRS wants them to (middle-of the-road), they do what they have been trained to do (don't rock the boat, conform at any cost), and they try hard to maintain the status quo.

A good example of the 20-year professional is a friend of mine who was finally promoted from revenue officer to revenue agent. After four months on the job he requested a transfer back to being a revenue officer. Why? He specifically told me that the tax issues were just too complicated and he was mentally exhausted at the end of each day. As a revenue officer, life was much easier. You just chased after delinquent taxpayers. No new issues were involved, and you didn't have to "tax" (pardon the pun) your brain.

Now add two more ingredients: Advancement at the IRS is almost strictly limited to people within the organization, which strips the lower ranks bare as the talented people are moved into supervisory roles; and simultaneously, the overall level of supervision has dropped dramatically. According to a former IRS agent, revenue agents in the field used to review cases fairly thoroughly with their supervisors. These days, if something doesn't get resolved in the time it takes to have a brief conversation, it just doesn't get resolved. (The extended four-day audit of my client Mrs. Price, the president of the wholesale medical supplies corporation discussed in Chapter 3, proves my point.)

IRS Auditors Always Operate Two Years Behind the Times

Unbeknownst to the majority of taxpayers, the following scenario is the norm: Tax returns are selected for audit 12 to 18 months after the filing date. By the time you, the taxpayer, have received notice of an audit appointment, it is often a year and a half past the year that your tax return under question covers. What's wrong with this picture? The revenue agent you will be working with on your old return, prepared almost two years ago, is still auditing issues using the old laws while he is simultaneously trying to learn the new laws. For example, in 2002 the Examination Division was still auditing 2000 returns, whereas on January 1, 2002, sweeping changes enacted with the Tax Act of 2001 were put into effect.

In contrast, tax pros have already mastered the new laws. We have to because of the nature of our work. Our clients need us to advise them about how today's tax laws, as well as past laws, are affecting them, particularly if there's an audit.

This confusing situation translates into some important information for taxpayers:

- Given our complex tax laws, and the pressured situation of learning new tax laws while having to perform as an "expert" in past tax law, revenue agents tend to stick to the old standbys when conducting an audit. These include travel and entertainment, real estate, matching of income, and verification of cash and bank balances.

- From this we can infer that more complicated issues such as officers' loans, excessive compensation, aggressive inventory valuation methods, or accounting for the deferral of revenue from one year to another stand a good chance of not being scrutinized.

A revenue agent friend of mine admitted the following: In a good-sized IRS local office, there are usually only one or two people who are familiar with tax law involving capitalization of inventory costs or passive losses to an extent that they could teach it to other employees. Now just pause for one moment and look at the significance of this. Seventeen years later, after they were created by TRA '86, there are many complex issues involved in these aspects of that tax law still virtually undigested by IRS agents who work on the front lines with taxpayers.

There's a Varied Audit Mix

Today's auditors come from very different segments of the population. The first—these are in the majority—is the younger set with three years or less of auditing experience.

The next group is a constantly changing mix of people resulting from downsizing in the private sector where experienced people, in good positions (e.g., corporate controllers), 50 to 55 years old, who have been let go from corporations, are drawn to the IRS because they want to continue working. There are also college-educated women, some of whom are CPAs, who want a secure job, good benefits, and shorter working hours (agents in the field are usually freer), without feeling the need to put in overtime.

If one of these people is subsequently hired by the IRS as a revenue agent, his or her greatest asset is knowing what deserves further scrutiny on a return. This kind of business experience, as opposed to book learning and IRS training courses, dramatically improves someone's chances of being an effective IRS auditor.

But here's the rub. There aren't enough of these people to make a real difference in the quality of auditing at the IRS.

Finally, with the IRS push to educate its auditors about specific markets, an entire new group has become MSSP specialists (see Chapter 7).

In short, taxpayers often encounter the following when they become involved with the audit level in the Examination Division:

- IRS auditors are generally not thorough and certainly are not interested in opening a can of worms. They just want to get the job done, move caseloads off their desks, and go home.

- Some of the new IRS auditors have become experts on how to avoid answering a question.
- Some auditors have become especially efficient at shuffling tax-payers from one IRS person to another in an effort to push the work onto someone else.
- If you were to describe their work ethic, to say that auditors are clock-watchers is putting it mildly.
- During the transition from the old to the new IRS, some auditors can't wait to leave, some are accepting transfers to do the same job in a new location where auditing functions are being moved to, and others are volunteering for new assignments entirely.

How to Work with the Examination Mentality

The auditor, therefore, has become the biggest unknown factor when a taxpayer is facing an audit. Sometimes the most difficult cases have escaped scrutiny because the auditor was not experienced, was not interested, or did not care enough to do a thorough investigation, like Mr. Stores in Chapter 3. On the other hand, sometimes the easiest, most uncomplicated audit will turn into a nightmare.

A recent case of mine involved a corporation that exports foodstuffs, such as soybean oil and sugar, to Central and South American countries. Although this may sound intriguing, even complicated, the guts of the audit were straightforward. The revenue agent, Mr. Fields, was a typical IRS hire with only two years' experience. After Day 3, I knew I was in for a long haul.

Obviously Mr. Fields didn't read the part of the Internal Revenue Manual that tells him to become familiar with the issues of his assigned audits, because he quickly made it clear that he knew absolutely nothing about exporting foodstuffs, freight forwarding, letters of credit, or international banking transactions.

As the audit proceeded, a number of issues required documentary proof: documents from court cases and excerpts from published tax services. Although I did all the research and had the data ready, something most auditors would accept at face value, Mr. Fields disregarded them. He was also unfamiliar with the documentation we were dealing with.

Slowly, it also became apparent that this agent did not have a strong accounting background. My client, Mr. Grant, often buys goods from his customers and sells them other items. For practical reasons, my client's bookkeeper simply offsets the balances between accounts receivable and accounts payable so that only the new net balance owed to or by the person remains on the books. This simple accounting approach was completely unintelligible to Mr. Fields.

At the end of each day, Mr. Fields would hand me a list of items to have on hand for the next meeting. The list contained many items I had already showed him. In my opinion the agent was either too lazy, too inexperienced, or too frightened to go to his supervisor for some direction. It was clear that he was in way over his head.

The professional fees were mounting and I saw no end in sight, so I insisted that we use the next meeting to finalize things. We agreed on four routine issues—travel and entertainment, auto expenses, insurance, and bad debts—out of a total of six. This amounted to $50,000 of disallowed expenses, which translated to a tax assessment of $17,000 plus another $7,000 in penalties and interest. As a condition of the settlement, Mr. Fields agreed to discuss the offsetting of receivables and payables with his group chief.

Six weeks later, Mr. Fields got back to me. We settled on a disallowance covering the final issue amounting to $5,000, resulting in an additional assessment of $3,000 in tax, penalties, and interest. Considering Mr. Fields's inexperience, he most likely believed that he had done a good job, and my client also was satisfied.

Handling the Auditor

Friend or Foe?

I have read accounts by professionals in the tax field who recommend making the auditor your friend. I can't say that's a reality for me; everyone involved is fully aware that an audit implicitly involves an adversarial relationship. However, that shouldn't mean that anger or aggression has to be a part of the audit process.

The approach I use and recommend for working with examination staff, especially auditors, is to be polite, friendly, and cooperative. You don't have to go so far as to offer information or documents unless asked, but civility is de rigueur. Be focused on reading the auditor's personality (that's usually not too difficult to do) and providing the auditor with the information requested.

Be in Control

It is also very important for you and your representative to be extremely well prepared, neat, and precise. Receipts, cash register tapes, journals, bank files, and the like are better indications of integrity than dog-eared, discolored papers and containers of disorganized data. Know and look as if you are in full control. My friends in the IRS tell me this can put off the auditor, which usually works to the taxpayer's advantage. It also helps to appear relaxed.

Offer Direction

During an audit situation, things can go awry for various reasons. When an audit seems unfocused, presenting your position in a strong, clear, and affirmative way usually helps. With Mr. Fields, for example, I felt he needed a structure, since he couldn't create one for himself. Regarding the documentation that I submitted, which he kept refuting, I finally told him: "You can either accept what I am submitting or come up with new research yourself." That successfully worked to extinguish that part of his behavior. He knew that I knew I was right and he was floundering.

Handling a Clash

There may also be a clash of personalities. The auditor may become angry and challenge you. I have also known auditors to lie, bluff, and manipulate. Don't blow these things out of proportion. With all the pressure and heavy workloads that auditors face regularly, you may just be the one they've decided to take a stand against. It may pass if you stay calm.

Yes, there's a fine line between standing up for your rights and being pushed around, but it works to approach each situation individually. If you and the auditor are stuck on a few points, you can request to have the supervisor's input. I've gotten some positive responses using this method. Choices are available each step of the way, but they can and often do change at a moment's notice.

If an auditor is showing complete incompetence, the audit is getting nowhere, or the auditor is not agreeing to anything you say for reasons you may not be aware of, you have the right to request another auditor—a request not granted very often. Even if it is granted, it could all backfire, since you could end up with a competent person who may locate items that the disagreeable auditor never would have found.

If the point of disagreement is a large dollar amount and the auditor's supervisor doesn't agree with you, or if the auditor takes an entirely unreasonable position and the supervisor agrees, you can begin to move up the line to the IRS Appeals Office. (You could bring in a CPA or tax attorney at this point if you haven't already done so. To go it alone, see the discussion of the appeals process later in this chapter.) The argument could end there in your favor, or the case could continue to escalate, depending how far you choose to push.

Obtaining Your Tax File in a Disputed Case

Preparing an appeal takes time and can be costly if you are using a tax professional. Before you bother to take this step, be aware of the following: There is an often overlooked IRS policy regarding protested and disputed tax cases. Previously the IRS kept its enforcement strategies and litigation approaches secret and consistently maintained that this information should not be released to the public. As usual, the IRS didn't want to give away anything it didn't have to. In several cases, however, the federal court ordered the IRS to comply with individuals' Freedom of Information Act requests for all relevant documents in their tax files. (See the discussion of the Freedom of Information Act in Chapter 5.) Although the IRS does not like to admit giving way to pressure, the change in policy, as the IRS calls it, seems to have been a direct result of these cases. So a new precedent has been set: The Examination Division must now provide taxpayers with the IRS's rebuttal position regarding issues under conflict in cases that are being forwarded to Appeals.

The good news is, you get to see in black and white what positions the auditor has taken, and an idea of how much and what information is being sent to the appeals officer.

The bad news is the auditor's work papers are often incomplete, which could lead you to believe the auditor has a weak case. Don't assume. He may know more than he's written down. You can disregard any incompleteness, but be sure to review the auditor's assumptions and the accuracy of his calculations. If you uncover an error in your favor, you are not obligated to bring it to the auditor's attention. No matter what, prepare your best case for presentation at the appeals conference.

Explanation of Taxpayers' Rights in Interviews

The IRS is required to rewrite and to more clearly inform taxpayers of several audit safeguards. You can terminate an audit at any time by stating that you'd rather not continue, since it appears that nothing further can be accomplished. At this point, you should consider hiring someone authorized to practice before the IRS. Otherwise the auditor will write up the case as being "unagreed" and pass it up to the supervisor. Perhaps a new auditor or the Appeals Office will offer a solution.

The IRS is required to inform taxpayers of the methods used to select their tax returns for examination unless such information would be detrimental to law enforcement. Audit selection is based on criteria obtained from DIF scores, TCMP audits, and the income matching process, as discussed in Chapters 3 and 8. Disclosure of audit selection provides taxpayers with some genuine benefits. It offers clues regarding issues that the IRS might raise during their audit, and this, in turn, should help taxpayers and their representatives present a stronger defense.

THE COLLECTION DIVISION

What People in the Collection Division Are Really Like

IRS revenue officers, also referred to as collections officers, are traditionally focused, determined, and unemotional. They face taxpayers one-on-one to carry out the actual collection process, and they are trained to think and act quickly and efficiently. Though the latest statistics show dramatic decreases in collection activity due, to a large extent, to newly legislated taxpayer safeguards, it is the job of collection officers to get the equivalent of your house, your car, your savings, and more into the pockets of the federal government to pay your tax debt. (See Chapter 13.)

How Revenue Officers Differ from Auditors and Other IRS Employees

- First of all, revenue officers like what they do, or they wouldn't be in that division.
- Second, their personalities combine with their work to make a perfect fit. If people get into collection who don't belong there because they have too much heart, they leave. The ones who remain are die-hards.
- Revenue officers, at least the ones who go on-site to do the actual negotiations and confiscations, are unquestionably more ambitious than those in auditing or examination. They want to be noticed.
- Until recently, the IRS tradition was to reward employees with plaques, honors ceremonies, and rapid promotion to higher grade levels if they used their power to achieve the desired results.

How to Work with the Collection Mentality

Part of the collection mentality is formed and predicated on quotas, even though they may not be called that. This is something the IRS vehemently denies, but quotas nevertheless seem to exist, according to several former auditors and revenue officers I have spoken to. With the pressure to levy, place liens, seize property, and turn in a better weekly or monthly performance than those at desks to the left and right of them, how would you expect revenue officers to behave? (All of this is starting to change with RRA '98; see Chapter 12.)

The best way to work with collection people is to avoid ever having to deal with them. But if you get this far down the road and end up in a tax jam in which you have to face one or more collection officers, don't mess with them. Do what they say. Follow your part in the collection process. Answer their queries. Don't ignore the letters you keep receiving. Be clear. Stick to your story.

Because there are different stages in the collection process, you are likely to encounter different personality sets common to each stage. No one tells taxpayers that. For example, quite often a lot can be cleared up at the ACS (Automated Collection System) level just by dealing with a collection representative over the telephone. Sometimes things can even be sorted out with revenue officers before they visit your home or office. The point is, just because you find yourself under the jurisdiction of the collection department doesn't mean you have to panic.

Here's a fairly representative case involving the beginning stages of the collection process, what you're likely to encounter, and how to deal with it.

One day, I received a call out of the blue from one of my corporate clients, who told me that the securities firm he does business with had received a letter from the IRS notifying him that his brokerage account had a $2,500 levy placed on it.

My client, a medium-sized and very successful corporation, very much in the black, was and has always been an A client. The firm's brokerage account in question did a sizable amount of securities trading and at that time contained a portfolio of stocks and bonds valued at over $600,000. A levy placed on this brokerage account was very serious. It meant the corporation was unable to engage in any securities activities; the securities firm would in turn be highly fearful of doing business with them while their account had a levy placed on it by the IRS.

I knew my client had done nothing wrong and that the IRS had messed up. The challenge was to find out where the problem was, to get the IRS to recognize what they had done wrong, and to work with them to correct it. Gearing up for the utterly outrageous and unexpected, I telephoned the revenue officer from the local district office who had signed the letter.

Within two minutes things became clearer, at least from my end. "We never received any notices," I said.

"We sent all four of them [the 500 series, remember them?]," the revenue officer replied.

"Where to?" I asked.

"To ———," he said.

"The company moved from that address almost four years ago," I answered, rather blatantly disgusted.

"Well, you should have had the mail forwarded," he said.

"We did," I replied, "but the post office only forwards mail for one year. Why didn't you look on your computer for the 2000 file, which has the new address on the corporate return?" I asked.

"No returns were showing for that year," he said. "The corporation didn't file a return."

"Of course we filed a return," I said. Now I knew that this guy was too lazy to look for it.

"Look," the revenue officer replied, totally avoiding my points because he knew that I knew that he hadn't looked for the return, "you owe us $2,500 for 1998 payroll taxes."

"If you look on your computer, you'll see you owe us a $38,000 refund due from an overpayment on corporate income tax," I replied.

"That has nothing to do with it," he said. "You still owe us $2,500."

At this point I decided to go for a compromise and fight the $2,500 later. "Since the $38,000 is due to be received by us within the next few weeks, why don't you just deduct the $2,500 from the $38,000 credit and release the levy from the stock account?"

"We can't do that."

"Why not?"

"It's too much trouble. I don't have time to check into all the details. Pay us with a bank check and then we'll release the levy."

"We can't wait that long," I said. "You know that will take over a month, and my client can't leave that account dormant all that time."

"Hold on a minute. I'll be right back."

"O.K. Now," I thought, "maybe something will happen because he is obviously going to speak to his group chief."

Next I heard a new voice from the other end of the phone, obviously the group chief, although he didn't introduce himself as such. He did provide his name and badge number. Some IRS people don't always have the time, inclination, or awareness to recognize that it's helpful to know whom you're speaking to. "We don't have the facilities to arrange for the $2,500 to be offset against the $38,000. If you want the levy released, just pay the $2,500 with a bank check."

Although I could have continued to argue that my client in no way owes $2,500, I knew I was speaking to two people who would continue to parrot each other and the only solution was to agree to do it their way, at least that time.

So we sent the bank check the second week in April, and the levy was released two weeks later. The way this works is that the IRS sends a release of levy form to the brokerage firm so that the firm knows everything has been cleared up and activity begins again.

A brief analysis will clue in taxpayers about the collection mentality. (Note: Any perceptible overlaps with the Examination Division are actually common threads that link all IRS divisions to the IRS personality.)

- Collection staff are inflexible.
- Collection staff generally take the easy way out.
- Lying, bluffing, and deceiving are common practices.

Another entrée into the mentality of revenue officers in Collection is this: Most whom I have met are always worried about their jobs. (This is also true for many revenue agents in the Examination Division.) If they make too many mistakes, will they be fired? Or demoted? Or put last in line for a promotion? If they disagree with the tactics that are used and do not take an aggressive line of action, which is expected, will they fall from grace? The answer used to be yes.

In some ways, the situation regarding their concern remains the same, but now the reasons for dismissal stem from RRA '98 and the 10 deadly sins for which collection agents can be fired. (See Slowdown in IRS Collections in Chapter 13.) In no uncertain terms, these new laws, designed to modify unwieldy and often unjustified collection tactics, represent a step toward fairness in the collection process and a gain for taxpayers. Although collection agents may currently seem at a loss as to how to operate, or they may resent the changes they are faced with, in the long run the outcome should be positive, though it may take several years for this to be manifest.

Above and beyond all of this, revenue officers have been trained to provide answers for every question, and to fill in every blank on the preprinted IRS collection procedures forms. In this division, as in Examination, it's paperwork that counts.

Sometimes when I watch revenue officers filling in line after line, page after page of IRS forms, it just seems downright stupid under the circumstances. But my conclusions fall by the wayside as they follow some IRS voice inside their heads (which I certainly don't hear), which tells them to fill in the blanks, no matter what. Here's what I mean:

Similar to the tone of the last case describing the collection mentality (I know it sounds more like a bad dream), I received a notice from the IRS that a client of mine hadn't sent in the IRS federal payroll tax form for the first quarter of 2001, and that currently, with penalties and interest, the amount due had reached $30,000.

I knew this was not plausible. This client had sold her business to a big conglomerate and moved to New Mexico two years before. The revenue officer refused to hear any explanations over the telephone and insisted that I come to the local office to settle things.

At our cozy one-on-one, there sat the revenue officer with a pile of forms one inch thick on his desk. He explained that the 2001 quarterly payroll tax was missing. "But the company was sold in 2000. The last quarterly payroll tax you received was for 1999."

"It was," the revenue officer agreed, "and we've been sending notices ever since, but haven't heard anything."

There were obviously three irritants that prompted this situation. First, the client's bookkeeper who sent in the last form neglected my directions to properly notify the IRS that this would be the final quarterly payroll tax form.

Second, the notices were going to nowhere. Where was the post office in all of this? (Are you beginning to realize that given the nature of the tax collection process, the post office is a vital, albeit somewhat uncontrollable, link in the process?)

Finally, because the IRS did not know the company was extinguished, and because it did not receive the next quarterly payroll tax form, some clerk in the examination department checked the amount of the last payroll tax, entered a made-up figure based on the last amount entered on the quarterly form, and came up with $25,000.

Once this occurs, you are face-to-face with a problem that materializes out of the vacuum created from missing information the IRS expected to receive but didn't. Since there is no response, penalties and interest accrue, no matter what. By the time I was contacted, the amount due had reached $30,000.

Now let's return to the face-to-face meeting at the local office. I calmly repeated to the revenue officer that my client had sold her company and had been out of business for over two years. This is what happened next: Appearing to have heard every word, the revenue officer, staring at his topmost form, pen poised for action, responded by firing a string of questions at me. "What is the new location of the business? How many employees are there? What are the taxes owed in the current year?" To jolt him out of his fill-in-the-blank reverie, I grabbed his arm and said rather loudly, "I already told you, my client is out of business. This is a self-generated liability. The IRS computer created it."

"No," the officer said. "It's a tax due."

"No, it's not. It's an estimate."

At that point he got up and left the room, actually another good sign, probably a trip to his group chief.

When he returned, there was good news. The group chief agreed with me. The revenue officer was told to void the liability entirely. He assured me that he would fill out the necessary forms and send the credit. Approximately six months later, the credit was finally issued.

The fact that IRS employees are taught to leave no line blank has become a double-edged sword. Yes, there is the possibility for completeness on the one hand. But on the other, the revenue officer, diligently performing as he was taught, becomes so focused on the line information that he fails to ask for or recognize that there are a lot of other more important things going on. It appears that group chiefs will scold someone on their staff more easily for a piece of missing information because an empty line is particularly visible.

THE CRIMINAL INVESTIGATION DIVISION

What People in the Criminal Investigation Division Are Really Like

Special agents employed in the Criminal Investigation Division are involved in the kind of investigation work and chasing down the bad guys that we see depicted in the movies. Involvement at this level means possible criminal offenses levied against you, leaving you subject to a possible jury trial and imprisonment.

Special agents are highly skilled in locating hidden assets and unreported sources of income and in identifying false records and fraudulent tax returns. Working with a full array of the latest in police and crime detection technology, they interrogate, untangle intricate transactions, obtain corroborating statements, make third-party investigations, conduct raids, use electronic surveillance, and decide whom to summons.

The agents who work in this division are extraordinarily thorough, painstakingly patient, and tough. They have to be—it's their job to build a case against the unsuspecting taxpayer.

But they are also calm, at least initially, and have a way about them that says to the taxpayer, "You can trust me. I'm easy to talk to." Part of their job is to instill this feeling in taxpayers. But once you open up to a special agent, well, their case is made, and your fate could be sealed. That's why, if that special agent comes to your door, anything you say could be an open invitation or a recrimination. Neither does you any good. Reach for your phone and dial a good tax attorney.

While other areas of the IRS may be haphazardly run, the process involved in catching big- and small-time tax criminals is tedious and time-consuming. Completion of a good case in the space of a year is considered a satisfactory performance for a special agent. The work may be hazardous, and advancement is generally faster here than in other IRS divisions.

How to Work with the Criminal Investigation Mentality

Recently, I was a witness before a grand jury relating to a CID investigation of one of my clients. It was there that I learned how meticulous the CID can be.

The IRS typically has a great deal of trouble locating a taxpayer's past returns, especially returns that are five years old or older. When I was on the stand, the prosecutor showed me not only the last ten 1040s filed by my client, but the original ones at that!

After that, the CID subpoenaed all my client's books and records (he owned and operated several corporations). When the records were returned to the corporation, CID inadvertently also included a large portion of the work papers it had created and assembled for the case—an obvious mistake by CID but a golden opportunity to examine their work firsthand. No, it's not illegal. Their mistake was fair game to us.

The work papers showed a complete analysis of all corporate bank accounts and the client's personal bank accounts, including every deposit slip, canceled check, and debit and credit memo. In our profession, that level of work is highly impressive. Coming from the IRS, it is astounding!

In the end, my client wound up having no charges brought against him. Ultimately the grand jury investigation was terminated and my client was not brought to trial. Therefore, I concluded that no damaging evidence had been uncovered.

When you are working with CID, the message is clear: CID is thorough and determined. Don't underestimate them or their abilities.

THE UPPER ECHELONS

What People in the Upper Echelons Are Really Like

A large group that stands out and apart from IRS employees is the chief counsel's office. These are IRS attorneys, accountants, and specially trained people with advanced educational degrees. Their work exposes them to a very full range of legal matters, from appeals and criminal tax cases (including the kind that end up in the Supreme Court) to international tax matters. Never for a moment forget: Every time you get in the sights of the IRS, there is an enormous legal infrastructure ready to fire.

The chief counsel's office is separate and distinct from another IRS upper-echelon function, the Legislative Affairs Division, which is heavily focused on developing, coordinating, and monitoring plans to implement new or pending legislation; developing legislative proposals for the

IRS; and coordinating IRS responses to the General Accounting Office (GAO), the investigative arm of Congress.[5]

Many at this level stay an average of five to ten years before they go off to a specialized law or accounting firm, where they command larger salaries and are considered prized property, having come from the IRS.

How to Work with the Upper-Echelon Mentality

Taxpayers rarely, if ever, come in contact with this level of IRS personnel. If you do, what you'll find are highly educated professionals, many attorneys who know their stuff. They are hardworking, focused, and operate essentially like trial lawyers, doing research, interviewing, preparing legal papers, and appearing in court cases.

The only time taxpayers might meet someone from the IRS upper echelon is if they go to Tax Court or the Appeals Office. At both of these levels, your representative will talk to his or her person, and that's where you'll get some inkling of how these people operate.

You and the Appeals Process

The IRS Appeals Office has the authority to settle cases, partially or wholly, on the basis of its assessment of the IRS's chances of winning. In other words, the ultimate objective for an appeals officer (who may be a lawyer or someone trained by the IRS to handle appeals) is to prevent a case from going to Tax Court. The Tax Court calendar has a huge backlog of cases, and the process of going through it is extremely trying for both sides. Even after a case has left the audit level and is filed with the Tax Court, to avoid going to Tax Court the Appeals Office can intervene and offer the taxpayer an additional four-month period to settle the case in Appeals.

The Appeals Office categorizes the cases it hears into small cases and all others. Small case disputes involve $25,000 or less. For this simplified procedure, look at IRS Publication 1660, "Collection Appeal Rights," available at www.irs.gov. If you continue on to Tax Court and your dispute is not more than $50,000 (per tax year), here, too, are simplified procedures. Small cases are initiated by the taxpayer but must be concurred with by the Court. The trial for small cases is conducted informally, with taxpayers typically representing themselves, though they can also choose anyone admitted to practice before the Tax Court. Briefs, oral arguments, and rules of evidence are not applied. Furthermore, any decisions rendered in small case procedures may not be cited as precedent in future cases and may not be appealed to a higher court by the government or the taxpayer. The Court will usually agree to the taxpayer's election of a small case unless the dispute will exceed the small case dollar amount, or if justice requires that the case be heard by a regular division of the Court—that is, if the decision would have an impact on other cases. Then a full trial is preferable.

Note: Small cases are normally decided by a brief statement by the Court, often orally, with only a summary of the reasons for the decision.[6]

The settlement ratio that Appeals has with small cases is an impressive 98 percent and a success ratio of 90 percent of all docketed cases. Regarding all other cases, the IRS doesn't go to Tax Court unless it believes that it has a better than 50 percent chance of winning.

If the appeals officer in the Appeals Office determines that the IRS may have a tough time winning the case, he'll recommend coming to a settlement. To achieve this he will probably concede an issue to induce the taxpayer to settle without delay. Even if it looks as if the IRS would win, the appeals officer might still offer a small concession simply to avoid the time and expense of going to Tax Court. At this point it has always been wise for the taxpayer to settle, because if the case went further, the Tax Court automatically presumed that the IRS position was correct. Now that the burden of proof has shifted to the IRS in noncriminal court proceedings regarding a taxpayer's liability, the question of whether you should settle or fight still remains. (See 1998 Tax Legislation in Chapter 12.)

The IRS has in place a program to help taxpayers prepare and file protest letters in resolving undue delays in getting a case through the appeals process. To take advantage of this service, speak to an Appeals Office representative by calling the IRS at 877-457-5055. You can also send for IRS Publication 5, "Your Appeal Rights and How to Prepare a Protest If You Don't Agree." In any case, a filing must be made with the Tax Court no more than 90 days after the mailing date of a tax deficiency notice. Forms can be obtained from the Clerk of the Court, U.S. Tax Court, 400 Second Street NW, Washington, D.C. 20217. The Tax Court website is www.ustaxcourt.gov.

Mediating Your Tax Dispute

The IRS has recently introduced Fast Track Mediation to speed the settlement of tax disputes and reduce delays and litigation costs for both taxpayers and itself. Mediation is available for most tax disputes that haven't been filed in court yet, including those arising from audits, collection actions, and offers in compromise. During a one-year test of the program conducted in four IRS districts, 75 percent of cases were successfully resolved in an average of 40 days—a much better resolution rate than otherwise would be expected. The mediator is an IRS appeals officer who has no prior knowledge of the case, has received special training in mediation skills, and whose goal is to expedite a resolution of the dispute. The entire process is voluntary, so if you feel the mediation isn't working out for you, you can end it at any time while retaining your rights to contest your case through IRS Appeals and the courts under normal rules. To learn more, visit the "Fast Track Mediation" web page on the IRS web site. Go to www.irs.gov, then click on "Businesses," then "Small Bus/Self-Employed."

YOUR TAX SAVING STRATEGY

You can only win by using IRS mediation. At best you may reach a satisfactory settlement much more quickly and at less cost than otherwise. At worst, even of you don't reach an agreement, you will see the IRS spell out its arguments and its side of the case in detail during the mediation process—and learning its arguments in advance will help you prepare to meet them during the regular appeals process or in court.

OFFERING A BRIBE—WHAT ARE THE CONSEQUENCES?

Accepting bribes has been against the rules of conduct for anyone working in the IRS, at any level or division, from its inception, as the U.S. Constitution clearly states. That doesn't mean, however, that the practice doesn't exist.

A quiet bribe between a revenue officer (or even a revenue agent or tax auditor) and a taxpayer who owes tax money (or has obviously fiddled around on a tax return) is not and has never been unique. There are two primary issues to be considered here. What constitutes a bribe, and did you offer one?

Generally a bribe involves an offer to an IRS employee with the purpose of persuading or encouraging that person not to take a certain action against you, the taxpayer. The bribe can be anything from a fancy lunch to a gift, a flight to Santa Fe, money, and lots more. But essentially a bribe is anything that sounds as if it is a bribe to the IRS person whose mind and actions you are trying to bend your way.

The Office of Government Ethics issues Rules of Conduct that apply to all governmental agencies, including the IRS. Furthermore, there is a standard procedure regarding the taking of bribes that IRS collections officers, revenue agents, and anyone else having intimate contact with a taxpayer must follow. The procedure, which is drilled into the heads of these IRS personnel, is very precise, and goes something like this:

Procedure for Reporting Bribes

- If an IRS employee believes he or she has been offered a bribe, nothing is done or said at that time, while the taxpayer is present.
- As soon as the meeting with the taxpayer is over, the employee is to immediately notify the Inspection Division, whose job it is to keep tabs on corruption within the IRS.
- If the Inspection Division decides to take the next step, and in most cases it probably does because it accepts the employee's word, the taxpayer is set up with the same employee at another meeting—except this time the employee is wired and has been briefed so that he or she knows how to get the taxpayer to repeat the bribe offer.
- If this occurs, someone from the Inspection Division will appear at the right moment and the taxpayer will be placed under arrest.
- The worst scenario: The U.S. attorney's office will get involved and prosecute the case, and the taxpayer could face a jail sentence. The best scenario for the taxpayer is if the bribe offer proves to be inconclusive. However, the items under audit will surely be disallowed in full.

I would never advise any client of mine to offer a bribe or anything that sounds like a bribe to anyone employed by the IRS. You may feel bad about paying an enormous tax assessment—but compare that to a stay in prison.

STANDARD OPERATING PROCEDURES

If anyone in the tax field were given two minutes to come up with a handful of epithets to characterize the behaviors we often face at the IRS, I am certain the list would include the following:

- Out-and-out lying
- Bluffing
- Threatening
- Sheer incompetence
- System breakdown
- The "IRS shuffle"
- Offering misleading or erroneous information

Watch how the first three weave in and out of a client audit that began in 1997, covering 1995, and lasted over two years.

Some background: An IRS analysis of my client's 1998 checking account showed that out of a total of $500,000, only $100,000 was accounted for. My client attributed the other $400,000 to the sale of an art collection that he had accumulated over a 40-year period. The sale of the art was conducted by an auction house that had gone out of business about six months after completing the sale.

Things began to heat up as auditor number two entered the scene toward the end of 2000. The first auditor, assigned to us by the IRS for over nine months, had been in way over her head. Her replacement was a shrewd, middle-aged woman who told us she had 15 years with the IRS. She was also extremely busy, with a full workload at the IRS and college teaching besides. It became common for her to cancel meetings, be out of the office for weeks at a time, and be difficult to reach.

For the final meeting she promised to bring in an IRS "art expert" to refute the sales prices and/or costs we were submitting. She also said that the case would drag on unless my client accompanied me. Clearly she was hoping he would make some admission that she could use against him. How did I counter her threats? By showing her documented costs of the art, a 45-page inventory list packaged with canceled checks and receipts (vendors' bills) that were from 1 to 30 years old (some of the paper looked quite antique). The total of the checks and receipts came to $90,000.

Next I counseled my client so that he said nothing of use to her. I actually liked the idea of his being there because he was, in effect, the resident art expert.

Our auditor never did bring in that IRS expert (it was a big bluff) because, I believed then and still do, she was in an enormous hurry to finish with us (you'll see why), and requesting an expert can require a lot of lead time.

By the end of the day, we submitted the following data:

Total sales price	$400,000
Costs we claimed (total inventory list)	210,000
Taxable capital gain (profit)	$190,000

Since the inventory records were meticulous and authentic, the IRS auditor agreed to allow us all of the $90,000 plus half of the cost for which we had no paperwork—that is, half of $120,000, or $60,000. (In audits of this nature, actual receipts are requested but are not an absolute requirement to win your case.)

In summary, these were the figures:

Total gross proceeds		$400,000
Less allowable cost (justified with receipts)	$90,000	
Extra as agreed (our deal)	60,000	150,000
New capital gain		$250,000

Since the maximum long-term capital gains rate was only 20 percent, we argued long and hard for any unreported income to be considered from the art sale (capital gain) rather than being considered as ordinary income, since my client was in the highest tax bracket of 39.6 percent.

The proposed settlement was a tax liability of $50,000 plus approximately $5,000 of penalties and interest.

We decided to accept the proposal, and the auditor said she would write it up and, as is customary, submit it to her group chief for approval.

Four weeks later I called her to ask when we could expect the papers. At this point she informed me that she was allowing $90,000 for our costs (only the amount we could prove), but she did not mention the extra $60,000 she had agreed to. She insisted that she had never agreed to it and that as far as she was concerned, there was nothing more she could do.

I called her group chief and told him that she had lied to me and my client. He took it under advisement for a couple of days and called me back to say that he believed her story and that if we were not happy, we should take the case to the Appeals Office, so we did. As was her style, she managed to drag out the meeting with the appeals officer by not forwarding her work papers until six months later, which of course meant an additional six months of interest tacked on to the bill.

The Appeals Office will carefully examine the merits of a case. If they don't believe there will be a clear-cut victory in Tax Court, the IRS will strike a bargain, and that's exactly what happened after a two-hour meeting.

The appeals officer allowed the original cost of $90,000 plus $50,000 of the extra $60,000. This meant that my client had "regained" $10,000 (20 percent of $50,000 equals $10,000) plus accumulated penalties and interest.

P.S. Within two months after the conclusion of the audit, our shrewd auditor was promoted to the Appeals Office, a rather significant promotion for a revenue agent.

Many questions remain open: Was the revenue agent in a big rush because she expected a promotion? (In a friendlier moment, she did actually mention to me that she was expecting it.) After agreeing to allow us half of the $120,000, did she realize that she had given up too much, which was not her normal performance? Or, remembering that she was brought in as a relief quarterback, did she want to avoid showing weakness (giving a taxpayer too much), which would hurt her chances for that promotion to Appeals?

Now watch as the IRS easily and predictably produces the last few items of behavior that often show up during an audit.

In early September 1999, out of the blue, I received a copy of a check that a client received from the IRS in the amount of $40,000. As I scanned it, the particulars of her case came back to me.

On her 1040 form for 1998, we requested that the IRS carry over $40,000 to her 1999 return. The money represented an overpayment that would do my client more good if carried forward to the following year. This was because by the time her 1040 was expected to be filed, June 15, 1999, she already owed $40,000 in estimated taxes for 1999, so we proceeded as if the carryover had taken place. (As planned, her 1040 for 1998 was filed June 15, 1999.) Although we thought the IRS had honored our request, three months later, when we looked at the check in hand, we saw that obviously something had gone wrong.

The first question was, what should we do with the check? The problem was that now my client would begin to incur penalties for not paying the April and June 1999 quarterly estimated income taxes in a timely manner.

After mailing a power of attorney to the IRS district office, I called a revenue officer at the district office (taking the number directly from the letter in hand) and asked why the IRS had sent the check. The revenue officer's response was typical: "I don't know, and I can't tell you. The 1998 return is not showing up on the computer."

"Well, what about the 1999 return? Can you locate any estimated payments?" I asked.

"No, I can't. I'm too busy right now. I've got too much to get through. You'll have to call back later."

"But then I'll have to start all over again."

"Just call the same number," the revenue officer said. "You'll get someone to help you."

"Can't you just take a minute to look it up?"

"I have to go. Call back," he said and hung up.

A few hours later I called back and, surprisingly, ended up with the same revenue officer. Again I asked him to locate my client's 1998 return. Guess what? After a few minutes, he found it. "Oh, yes," he said. "Here it is. The income listed is $732,000, but no tax is due."

Now I was fully aware that my client's taxable income was $732,000. I was also aware that the tax paid on that return was $225,000. Here I was, faced with an IRS revenue officer in the Collection Division telling me that my client had no tax due. "How could there be no tax due on $732,000?" I asked, totally astonished.

"Well," the person replied, "maybe there were a lot of deductions." I actually held my breath wondering if in a few weeks my client would receive another refund, this time for $225,000. "Oh, wait a second," he said. "I've got another screen that says there is an assessment on this return of $225,000."

"That's not an assessment. That's the tax we paid on the account."

After a few more minutes of banter, the revenue officer became convinced that I was correct, and we proceeded to find an answer to the $40,000 check by going over the payments one by one. "The tax was entered in the wrong place," he said.

"That's impossible," I answered.

"Oh, not by you. On my screen." I guess an IRS entry clerk made the error.

Now a plan of action became clear. I would instruct my client to return the original $40,000 check to the IRS with a cover letter explaining that the money should have been credited to her 1999 estimated tax account.

The Secret to Finding Your Way Through the IRS

I am not interested in taxpayers understanding what each individual section of the IRS does in isolation. You have to be able to make connections, to see literally the whole of what the IRS does, so that things take on meaning within this framework. Those who have become experts in working with the IRS say one of the secrets to their success is the ability to grasp, even superficially, what goes on from one end of the agency to the other. Taxpayers who can afford it flock to these specialists, who know how to find their way through the IRS because of their ability to view the agency from a larger perspective.

Taxpayers also need to recognize where the power of the IRS comes from, above and beyond the never-ending process of collecting, enforcing, and processing billions of tax dollars. Dissecting this power into its component parts, then learning how to manage it, is the next hurdle to jump.

5

Neutralizing the IRS's Power

THE IRS POWER BASE

The IRS power base comes from several sources. The IRS has unique

- Information resources
- Legal standing
- Role as a law enforcement agency
- Legislation-originating authority
- Ability to make mistakes without consequences
- Freedom to do what it wants

POWER FROM INFORMATION RESOURCES

Information gathering, with state-of-the-art equipment, has imbued the IRS with more power than any other bureaucracy in the world. This fact goes hand in hand with other, more disturbing realities: IRS computer centers have questionable security; there is significant evidence of periodic leaks for political purposes; few, if any, independent private or governmental bodies review IRS operations or management processes. "Thus," comments David Burnham, "it has come to pass that the IRS has developed into the largest, most computerized, and least examined law enforcement agency in America."[1]

What Information Is Gathered about You?

Did you know that the IRS is legally entitled to collect information about you from the following sources:

- Your employer or anyone who pays you over $600 for services rendered
- Institutions that provide pensions and annuities to the elderly

- Casinos and racetracks
- Banks or corporations
- Barter deals or exchanges of property
- Real estate agents, when you buy or sell a property
- Any organization granting you a loan
- Your state unemployment office

In fact, the IRS receives information from such a wide range and number of sources that if it wanted to, it could easily discover what you earn, how you live, how many homes you own, the type of car you drive, where you spend your free time, where you go on vacation, and on and on.

Did you know that once it has the information, the IRS can do the following:

- Label you as a someone who owes the government money, never filed a return, earns above a certain dollar amount, has high audit potential, and more.
- Allow thousands of IRS agents across the country easy access to your tax return.
- Share the information on your tax return regularly with other states, cities, and federal agencies.

What Are Your Legal Rights against Misuse of the Information?

There is a body of law that protects private citizens by prohibiting misuse of financial information. One is the Privacy Act of 1974; another is the Computer Matching and Privacy Protection Act of 1988, Public Law 100-503.

Generally speaking, preventing misuse means making certain that only those who are allowed by law to access the information can in fact do so. It means using the information for its designated purpose—for example, to verify that someone's annual income can support a specific mortgage loan amount, or to answer taxpayers' questions about their tax returns. It means ensuring that the information used is up-to-date. The fact that someone has declared bankruptcy, for example, must be cleared from a person's record after a period of 10 years.

If these laws are broken, private citizens can legally seek redress. What if, for example, a seller accepted your bid to buy a new home, and an independent private agency that verifies credit standing notified all parties concerned that your credit was unacceptable? Suppose that wasn't true. Suppose your credit rating was fine. With a credit agency, you have the right to demand a printout of the information, or to follow specific procedures to update or correct it. With the IRS this is not possible.

Who Is Guarding Your Privacy?

Information protection for taxpayers regarding the information collected about them and overseen by the IRS must come from two sources: the technology, which stores and manipulates the information, and the people who have access to it.

Scrupulous and precise rules for accessing information should be in place in IRS data centers to protect your interests and prevent leaks and misuse. However, there really aren't such rules.

Part of the problem, according to the IRS, is lack of resources. It takes funding to track down what systems networks within the IRS are being linked to what other IRS systems networks, and to close any gaps through which information can be accessed or leaked. It takes time and effort to sweep each system clean of passwords used by former employees so that at least these entry points are locked. And, yes, it is expensive to install security-oriented software and to conduct periodic security audits.

Timely reports by the GAO continue to point out "serious weaknesses" in the controls used to safeguard IRS computer systems and protect taxpayer data. Here's some comforting news: In a 1997 report, after visiting five IRS facilities, the GAO said that some 6,400 computer tapes couldn't be properly accounted for and that some might contain thousands of taxpayer files. Three months later, an IRS spokesperson was quoted in *New York Newsday* as saying that 5,700 of the tapes had been located.

Why were the tapes lost? Where did they go? Who had access to them, where are the rest of them, and how much, if any, information about you leaked out?

To reveal or not to reveal information disclosed on an individual's tax return has been debated since President Lincoln signed the first income tax into law in 1862. Almost from the beginning there were two opposing camps.

Congress's position at that time required that tax returns be published in at least four public places and for at least 15 days. (Can you imagine it!) In this way it was hoped that everyone would be kept honest. In 1914 the Supreme Court ruled that returns of individuals shall not be subject to inspection by anyone except the proper officers and employees of the Treasury Department.[2]

The battle over confidentiality raged on. Each time a new revenue act was proposed, proponents of disclosure argued for the people's right to know, while the opposition argued that people have a right to privacy concerning their business affairs.

The real kicker came with the Nixon administration's abuses of individual privacy through misuse of IRS information during the early

1970s. Section 6103 of the Internal Revenue Code was eventually approved by Congress several years later to prevent political use of IRS-generated information by limiting the number of people and governmental agencies that could access tax information. But the IRS is still plagued by "snooping," or unauthorized inspection of tax returns by the agency's own employees.

The Taxpayer Browsing Protection Act (IR Code Section 7213A) imposes criminal penalties of up to $1,000 or imprisonment of not more than one year, or both, for the unauthorized inspection of tax returns and tax information by any federal employee or IRS contractor, as well as any state employee or other person who acquired the tax return or return information. The bill also provides that offended taxpayers may bring a civil action for damages against the government in a U.S. district court.

The IRS has defined its approach for implementing the Taxpayer Browsing Protection Act. The IRS is currently modernizing its automated systems, which will allow the IRS to restrict employees' access to taxpayer records that need to be looked at only if there is a work-related reason to do so, and to detect unauthorized access almost as soon as it happens. All IRS employees have been briefed about unauthorized access, and a new unit tracks proven access violations that would also help to administer penalties.

In a recent year the IRS identified more than 5,000 potential instances of unauthorized access, and has completed preliminary investigations of more than 4,000 of those. In 15 cases, the IRS has determined that employees had intentionally accessed taxpayer data without authorization. These employees either resigned or were fired.[3]

But programs that seem to ignore taxpayer privacy continue to be launched by the IRS. One of these programs, unofficially called "the lender project," was developed after a two-year test period and works like this:

When you apply for a home loan, the lender typically asks for copies of your income tax returns to verify your income. It is not uncommon for taxpayers to try to increase their chances of success by inflating their income on a 1040 specifically "revised" for the mortgage lender. In the new IRS program, participating lenders in California fax the income information to the IRS, and within 48 hours the IRS replies with tax data—typically the applicant's AGI for one or more years.

If the income on the application doesn't match the income on the tax return, not only may you be rejected for the loan, you also stand to face an audit, since the IRS assumes you either underpaid taxes or filed a false loan application.

The prime targets for this effort allegedly are self-employed borrowers who have a high degree of flexibility regarding how much income they report. Among 31,985 loans for which the IRS was asked to verify income, differences were found on 1,687, or 5.27 percent. Five hundred of these have been selected for audit.[4]

It seems as if the IRS has decided that mortgage lenders are a perfect vehicle to police taxpayers' returns, especially those of the self-employed.

If the IRS goes national with this program, lenders will e-mail authorizations by home-loan applicants to the IRS, and the agency will e-mail back the tax data as a matter of course.[5]

Now, we should always be accurate in reporting our income, but is this an issue of catching tax cheats, as the IRS claims, or is it a gross manipulation of privileged information? Although Section 6103 is on the books, given the IRS's controlling, secretive nature, the reality is that an elaborate set of barriers discourages taxpayers from seeking legal redress in the courts. The misapplication of the well-intentioned privacy law, says Burnham, has led to a situation where "lawyers are blocked from obtaining information they need to initiate suits challenging genuine IRS abuses. . . . A congressional committee empowered to investigate the IRS is partially blocked from investigating serious allegations of IRS corruption by a tortured application of the same law. The IRS has repeatedly initiated audits, leaked information, or otherwise harassed individual citizens, both in and out of government, who raised valid questions about its performance."[6]

POWER FROM THE IRS'S UNIQUE LEGAL STANDING

If you are a taxpayer suspected of violating our tax laws, you are guilty until you prove that you are not. No other area of our government operates upon this premise. In fact, the entire foundation of our civil law is based upon the assumption that one is innocent until proven guilty—except where the IRS is involved. The IRS can accuse taxpayers of an infringement, garnishee their paychecks, put a lien on their homes, and seize their cars and businesses, with minimal court approval. Unfortunately, the accused taxpayer is fully responsible for proving his or her innocence. Limited relief is now available if your case reaches the U.S. Tax Court. (See 1998 Tax Legislation in Chapter 12.)

POWER FROM ITS UNIQUE ROLE AS A LAW ENFORCEMENT AGENCY

A look, even a rather cursory one, at IRS operations since its reorganization in the early 1950s reveals an indisputable trend: the continuous expansion of the IRS's authority to penalize taxpayers for a growing laundry list of freshly created tax-related violations. In the early 1960s there were about six penalties that the IRS regularly imposed on taxpayers due to, for example, filing late, paying late, and underestimating income. Now the IRS has the authority to penalize taxpayers and business entities for some 150 types of violations. For example, taxpayers are penalized when they

- Write checks to the IRS that bounce.
- Don't provide a Social Security number for themselves, their dependents, or other persons.
- Don't file a complete return.
- Don't report their tips to their employer.
- Are considered negligent in the preparation of a tax return.
- Overvalue a deduction by more than 20 percent.

A slew of new violations and consequent penalties has been created by the phenomenon of information reporting—or, rather, inadequate information reporting. Who is liable? People or organizations that do not provide the IRS with information that Congress has deemed necessary for collecting taxes. This includes

- Tax preparers who fail to enter their federal ID number on a return they have prepared.
- Banks, real estate agencies, and securities houses that don't provide the IRS with accurate and timely information about money they are paying to taxpayers. (Fines can be stiff, up to $100,000.)
- Any business or organization that employs independent contractors or consultants and fails to file 1099 forms for payments of $600 or more per year.

Congress and the courts have also granted the IRS powers that have been specifically denied traditional enforcement agencies. For example, when the FBI investigates drug-related crimes or money laundering, its actions are rooted in strictly defined criminal laws. If it is proven that a person's civil rights have been violated, even if the target is a major drug offender, FBI agents involved suffer the consequences.

Too often with the IRS's Criminal Investigation Division, however, the laws guiding its special agents are what the IRS determines they should be.

The IRS and its employees are carefully protected in carrying out a range of activities that no others in the field of law enforcement would dare attempt for fear of losing their jobs or being jailed.

POWER FROM ITS UNIQUE LEGISLATION-CREATING AUTHORITY

The majority of taxpayers do not know that the IRS plays a major role in influencing and actually creating legislation through several distinct vehicles, including

- Technical advice memoranda
- Revenue rulings
- Private letter rulings
- Regulations

In addition, there are several not-so-well-known arenas in which the IRS has the ability to affect a tax bill before it becomes a law, and also literally to sponsor its own tax legislation.

As taxpayers, we should be cognizant of the IRS's capacity to affect and create legislation that has an impact on each of us. Most of these are powers that have been granted to the IRS by Congress and authorized by the Internal Revenue Code.

Technical Advice Memorandum

A technical advice memorandum arises from a request by an IRS district office or the Appeals Office concerning a technical or procedural question that can arise from several sources: during the examination of a taxpayer's return, in consideration of a taxpayer's claim for refund or credit; or in some other matter involving a specific taxpayer under the jurisdiction of the Examination Division or Appeals Office.[7]

A technical advice memo is highly specific in its focus and is binding only upon a particular issue in a given case. If the IRS feels it has unearthed an issue that could have broader appeal, it can be developed into a revenue ruling. (For an example, see "Securing a Tax-Advantaged Life" in Chapter 8.)

Since 1993, the IRS has made decisions on an average of 290 technical advice memoranda per year.[8]

Revenue Rulings

A revenue ruling is an official interpretation of the Internal Revenue Code, issued to provide guidance to taxpayers and the agency itself. The subjects of revenue rulings can originate in many areas, such as rulings to taxpayers, technical advice memos, court decisions, tax articles, news reports, and suggestions submitted by tax organizations and industry specialists.

Revenue rulings are published weekly in the *Internal Revenue Bulletin* (an IRS publication) and various other tax services. They also often show up in trade publications or monthly tax newsletters, where taxpayers can read about them. Specific rulings are selected for publication because

- They answer questions commonly asked by taxpayers on specific tax matters.
- The IRS believes the information presented has fairly widespread application to taxpayers in general.

Thus, without any congressional involvement, the IRS is freely empowered to interpret how a specific area of the tax law should be applied. The IRS decides, "This is the law. This is how we see it."

Since 1993, the IRS has made decisions on an average of 379 revenue rulings per year.[9]

Private Letter Rulings

Private letter rulings are written statements issued to a taxpayer that interpret and apply the tax laws to a taxpayer's specific set of circumstances.[10] These rulings are initiated because a company or individual is considering a specific action and needs to know how the IRS would treat any tax implications involved. A company, for instance, may need to know how substantial sums should be treated on its books—for example, as tax deductions, legitimate losses, or tax savings. The transaction in question is generally outside the normal range of categories described in the Internal Revenue Code.

Because they are elicited by a specific request, the rulings may be applied only by the taxpayer who receives the ruling. They cannot be relied on as precedents by other taxpayers or by IRS personnel in examining other returns.[11] How to request a private letter ruling is provided in "IRS Revenue Procedure 2001-1," which is contained in Internal Revenue Bulletin 2001-1. Go to the IRS web site at www.irs.gov and in the "IRS Guidance" section.

In reality, private letter rulings are well known to and mainly used by businesses, especially major companies that are advised by experienced and handsomely paid tax attorneys. They are often willing to take a chance by relying on another taxpayer's private letter ruling on circumstances similar to their own particular case. These attorneys also know that the IRS often gathers several private letter rulings on a similar subject and molds them into a revenue ruling.

The IRS states that with a few exceptions, all letter rulings are available for public inspection after the deletion of all data that could identify the taxpayer.[12] But since most people are not aware that private letter rulings exist, they are not likely to ask to see one, even though these rulings can affect broad segments of unsuspecting taxpayers. On those occasions when the IRS hands down a negative conclusion to a taxpayer's question in a private letter ruling, watch out. The IRS will warn the taxpayer when the unfavorable ruling is about to come out, and the taxpayer can change or withdraw the original request altogether. However, the IRS notifies the taxpayer's local district office to inform them that research on the ruling is available from the IRS National Office. Those who requested the ruling should not be surprised if their tax return is later audited.

Private letter rulings allow the IRS broad discretion in handing down final decisions related to tax law, often to function de facto like the Supreme Court. Sometimes Congress eventually gets involved in more important cases, but it is likely to be years after the impact of the letter has been felt.

Since 1993, the IRS has decided on an average of 3,157 private letter rulings per year.[13]

Regulations

Once a tax bill is signed into law by the president, the bill is passed to the IRS. In essence, Congress says, "Here's the law, IRS. Now work out how it's going to be administered."

Regulations ("regs") accompany about 80 percent of new tax laws. They are written by IRS attorneys and other staff who work directly with the chief counsel's office to interpret, clarify, and advise taxpayers and tax professionals about how to comply with the new law. Regs can appear soon after a revenue act is passed or, because the process of developing final regs is so complicated, years later. Since regulations are law, when they do appear they automatically become retroactive and taxpayers are required to file amended tax returns accordingly.

Because regulations can be hundreds of pages long for any given piece of tax law, they appear first as "proposed," then "permanent," then "final." Once issued in either temporary or final form, they are binding on all taxpayers and employees of the IRS.[14]

All regulations appear in the *Federal Register* (a daily publication of all governmental proceedings) and some commercial publications. Then they are thrown open for public comment. Most often CPAs and lobbyists send written replies to the IRS National Office suggesting how to reword or reframe them. The IRS also offers the opportunity for a public hearing on proposed regulations if a hearing is requested.[15] The IRS is supposed to consider the comments it receives before a final regulation is developed.

What do taxpayers and tax professionals use as a guide between the time when a reg is proposed and when it is finalized? They play a kind of guessing game during which they interpret the law and worry about the consequences later.

Sometimes an aspect of a new tax law may require a quick fix, especially if delaying the issuance of the final regulation(s) would mean a hardship to those affected by the new law. In this case, the IRS does not wait for the regulation process to be completed. Instead, it issues temporary regulations that short-circuit the usual opportunity for public comment.

Given the situation, wouldn't most taxpayers ask, "Isn't the system of creating tax laws and applying them to the taxpaying public a chaotic and virtually unregulated situation?" The answer is a definite no, because basic tax laws that affect the majority of taxpayers get fixed right away.

Waiting is the norm, however, in more complicated areas of the tax law—for example, allocations of partnership income and loss, distribution of money and property, or the intricate machinations involving how certain expenses can be recorded—where regulations have been in the process of being finalized for years. Numerous revisions of interpretations of the Taxpayer Relief Act of 1997 were issued in early 2003, and additional changes are still to come. The favorite statement from Congress at the end of a new tax bill is "Regulations to be promulgated by the IRS." Usually no timetable is attached.

I hope the present system regarding preparation of regulations by the IRS continues. Tax professionals usually enjoy trying to think how the IRS thinks, making decisions accordingly, and patting ourselves on the back when the outcomes are confirmed by final regs.

Since 1993, the IRS has made decisions on an average of 223 regulations per year.[16]

The Role of the IRS before a Bill Becomes Law

Many Americans are familiar with how a revenue bill becomes a law. But do they also know the extent to which the IRS is involved in shaping tax legislation *before* a bill becomes a law?

The IRS Legislative Affairs Division is brought in to analyze and contribute to the development of pending legislation long before it comes up for a vote in Congress, and to ensure effective implementation of new legislation after it is enacted. This is actually sound management practice. But taxpayers must learn to recognize the extent to which the IRS becomes involved with new tax legislation—especially legislation the IRS doesn't like—and more, the extent to which it can massage, refine, or downright change, oppose, or block legislation to protect its own point of view or maintain the status quo.

Here's a specific example of how this works:

In 1987, when Senator David Pryor (D-Arkansas) introduced the Omnibus Taxpayer Bill of Rights legislation, the first of its kind that describes the rights private citizens should have when dealing with the IRS, he knew what he would be up against: major opposition from the IRS. He has even gone on record saying it was very difficult indeed to find members of Congress to support the bill. "I saw real fear of the possible IRS retaliation among many members of the Senate and the House of Representatives," he said at the time.[17] In other words, other elected officials believed that if they supported his bill, the IRS would get after them in one way or another. (For more on the "Taxpayer Bill of Rights," see Chapter 7 and Appendix D.)

When it comes to shaping or even rejecting new legislation that it doesn't want to see enacted into law, the IRS is not shy. It labels the legislation as unnecessary, says it will interfere with the normal tax collection process, claims it would involve too great an imposition on the administration, and asserts it doesn't have the budget or staff to comply.

IRS-Sponsored Legislation

Ensuring even greater clout in the legislative arena is the IRS's ability to sponsor legislation and to lobby Congress for IRS-backed proposals to become law. Currently, this is the highest rung the IRS has reached in its ability to gain legislative powers almost equal to those of the U.S. Congress.

During the hearings on the Revenue Act of 1962, the IRS uncovered the phenomenon of companies claiming large deductions for vacations, club dues, theater tickets, sports activities, business gifts, and so on, from an audit of 38,000 returns. The IRS recommended remedial legislation to Congress, including substantial limitations on deductions for travel and entertainment expenses. Congress enacted the legislation, which became Section 274 of the Internal Revenue Code and ended up filling three pages of fine print.[18]

In another example, the IRS fought to make punitive damages taxable. Although some district courts ruled in favor of taxpayers (that proceeds of punitive damages were not taxable in some cases), the IRS continued to fight it until it got its way in the 1996 tax law.

In 1792, the Office of the Commissioner of Revenue was established to levy and collect taxes. Today, the IRS frequently goes head to head with Congress, creating and shaping tax legislation and challenging new and existing tax laws.

POWER TO MAKE MISTAKES WITHOUT CONSEQUENCES

When people find themselves chatting about the IRS, one remark that inevitably surfaces is the fact that the current audit rate for individual tax returns hovers between 0.5 and 1 percent. This remark is phrased to imply a certain comfort level, almost a gift to the American taxpaying public. Nothing could be further from the truth. The 0.6 percent of individual tax returns audited in 2001 translates into over 743,000 people. Now that percentage doesn't sound so small, does it?

Just extrapolate this same thought to the numbers of taxpayers affected each year by IRS mistakes. Let's say an IRS computer mistakenly sends out a past due tax notice to only 0.5 percent of the taxpayers in New York City. The letter charges them with penalties for failing to pay their quarterly estimated taxes in a timely manner. In fact, the computer program was malfunctioning, and most of these people did make their payments correctly.

Most taxpayers—imagine you are one of them—would naturally respond by calling their local service center, writing the necessary letter, even double-checking with their tax professional. Weeks go by, all to no avail. More letters and telephone calls later still haven't succeeded in short-circuiting the process, and now you are faced with a large collection of new IRS notices announcing dollars and penalties due.

No matter what you do, eventually your case reaches the Collection Division, where you personally fit the bill as the cheating taxpayer that the IRS teaches its employees about. You are trapped in IRS Problem City. The thing is, this is not happening only to you. It is simultaneously happening to 30,000 others, because that's 0.5 percent of the taxpayers in New York City!

The IRS does not keep records of how many taxpayers it has abused. IRS computers can be highly effective in catching a mismatch between 1099s and 1040s. But the same technology isn't at all interested in slowing down because of IRS mistakes made along the way.

POWER FROM THE FREEDOM TO DO WHAT IT WANTS

Another aspect of IRS power comes when it decides to ignore the federal government, our judicial system, Congress, individual rights of citizens, or its own job requirements and chooses, instead, to do just exactly what it wants.

The IRS Defies the Judicial System

Dr. Nader Soliman, an anesthesiologist who worked in three hospitals a total of 30 to 35 hours a week during the year, also set up a home office in his McLean, Virginia, apartment to maintain records, consult with doctors and patients, perform billing and scheduling activities, and study medical journals. The doctor entered the public's view when the IRS, during an audit, denied his $2,500 home office deduction (Section 280A of the Internal Revenue Code) on his 1040 form for the tax year 1983, alleging his home office wasn't his "principal place of business." Dr. Soliman appealed the IRS's decision in the U.S. Tax Court and won.

To say that the IRS was furious (because the decision was more lenient toward taxpayers than any previous home office interpretation in that it allowed taxpayers to deduct home office expenses even when they do not spend a majority of their time working at home) is an understatement. The IRS decided to fight, taking the case to the U.S. Court of Appeals for the Fourth Circuit in Richmond, Virginia, which upheld the Tax Court's decision.

Because this was a substantial expansion of the home office rule as it traditionally stood, it would automatically result in a large chunk of lost tax dollars. The IRS was going to fight this to the finish, and it did, right up to the Supreme Court.

On January 19, 1993, in *Commissioner v. Soliman*, the Supreme Court reversed the two lower-court rulings and strongly reinforced the long-held IRS position, established in the Tax Reform Act of 1976, that to take a home office deduction the site had to be used exclusively and regularly as the principal place of business, and that the relevance of the business activities performed in the home office was now the key criterion for determining whether the deduction could be taken, rather than the amount of time spent there. Immediately, this eliminated the home office deduction for those who spend most of their hours in another place (plumbers, gardeners) and who only use the home office for routine tasks such as record keeping.

Effective January 1, 1999, this narrow interpretation of the eligibility for the home office deduction was rolled back to the 1993 law, but this effort clearly illustrates how the power of the IRS can affect the tax laws itself. (See Chapter 7 for the latest home office rules.)

The IRS Defies the Federal Government

During the Watergate investigations, Senate Watergate Committee investigators accused the IRS of obstructing the panel's continuing inquiry by defying the Senate's resolution to provide tax returns and other data to the committee, and by refusing to provide tax data and investigative files on more than 30 individuals and corporations.[19] The IRS's underlying motivation, consistent since its inception, is tenacious and simple: When the IRS doesn't want to do something, no matter who or what is telling it what to do, the IRS will fight long and hard to get its way.

The IRS's ability to do what it wants despite directives from governmental bodies, individuals, and the law brings into play two particularly important laws specifically devised for and suited to the American way of life. These are the 1966 Freedom of Information Act (FOIA) and the 1974 Privacy Act, both enacted to formalize a citizen's right to request records from federal agencies.

Before enactment of the FOIA, the burden was on the individual to establish a right to examine these government records. There were no statutory guidelines or procedures to help a person seeking information, and there were no judicial remedies for those denied access.

With the passage of the FOIA, the burden of proof shifted from the individual to the government. According to a guide published by the House Committee on Government Operations, those seeking information are no longer required to show a need for information: "Instead, the 'need-to-know' standard has been replaced by a 'right-to-know' doctrine. The government now has to justify the need for secrecy."[20]

All taxpayers should know their rights in these matters, as explained in the "Citizen's Guide on Using the Freedom of Information Act and the Privacy Act of 1974 to Request Government Records," available from the U.S. Government Printing Office, Washington, D.C. Regarding what records can be requested under the FOIA:

The FOIA requires agencies to publish or make available for public inspection several types of information. This includes (1) descriptions of agency organization and office addresses; (2) statements of the general course and method of agency operation; (3) rules of procedure and descriptions of forms; (4) substantive rules of general applicability and general policy statements; (5) final opinions made in the adjudication of cases; and (6) administrative staff manuals that affect the public.[21]

The IRS Defies Private Citizens

The *Internal Revenue Manual* is a major weapon against the often ludicrous situations that the IRS is known to suck taxpayers into, yet it is something most taxpayers don't know a thing about—for very good reasons. It contains IRS policies, procedures, job descriptions, and more that explain what the agency is made of. This information is exactly what the IRS hopes you won't bother to read. You see, it is especially useful for verifying the functions of each division, for providing the parameters of specific jobs, or for spelling out specific instructions to employees on how a specific task is supposed to get done, such as seizing your assets.

The FOIA describes the *IR Manual* as the "administrative staff manual that affects the public." Until a few years ago it could be obtained by making a cumbersome, written request to the IRS Office of Disclosure, plus the payment of a fee.

As a CPA, I can access the *Internal Revenue Manual*, with commentary, published not by the IRS or Government Printing Office but by a tax service, in a professional library closed to the public. For you taxpayers, the IRS is now pushing its good guy image and simultaneously has dramatically improved its web site. A new version of the *Internal Revenue Manual* is now available at the IRS web site, www.irs.gov. Go to "Businesses/Tax Regulations/Internal Revenue Manual." I fully expected these excerpts of the *IR Manual* to contain what I consider the nuts and bolts of the behavior expected of tax auditors and revenue agents while conducting audits, or techniques used by revenue officers when trying to collect old tax debts from taxpayers. In this watered-down version available on the Web, which contains information from *four* years ago, IRS employees are reminded to be courteous and fair at all times and to continuously notify taxpayers of their rights, which they are mandated by law to do.

However, this revised version of the *Manual* does not contain the instructions (previously published) that are given to every trainee regarding such things as when taxpayers are exhibiting "badges of fraud" (which may indicate that the case is ready to be referred to the IRS Criminal Investigation Division), or techniques used during an audit, such as staring at a blank computer screen in silence, waiting for the taxpayer to say something that might lead to an expansion of the audit. Also missing is the instruction to revenue officers to ask the telephone number of the taxpayer the moment he calls one of the 800 numbers to obtain any information whatsoever about his old tax bill. And the IRS doesn't understand why so many people hang up immediately.

Some have made the difficult decision to legally battle whatever allegations the IRS has made against them, and some of these have made a real name for themselves and become recognized experts on how the IRS administratively and otherwise resists making any information available. Most people never get very far and are forced to give up.

Others do succeed in suing the IRS, winning a judgment, and getting charges against them dropped, but it takes an enormous toll in time, and often tens of thousands of dollars in legal fees.

WHY DOES THIS CONTINUE?

There are several reasons.

The IRS Manages to Get the Job Done

In 2002 the IRS collected $2.0 trillion in gross tax dollars. It also examined over 826,000 returns and recommended almost $21 billion in additional taxes.[22] All this at a cost of about only one half of 1 percent of the more than $2.0 trillion it brings in.

According to one account, "In the early 1940s, many people—even highly placed officials of the Internal Revenue Service—doubted that an income tax covering almost everyone could be administered effectively."[23] Although there are enormous problems up, down, and across the organization, the job is being done.

For 2003, the IRS was operating with a budget of $9.9 billion; the president's budget request for 2004 is $9.9 billion which includes an increase of $248 million for tax law enforcement.[24]

The IRS Is Backed by the Government—Usually

Congress and our legal system (the courts, judges, district attorneys) have consistently supported the IRS by

- Legitimizing or ignoring the growing powers of IRS personnel.
- Seeking to punish taxpayers through a growing list of tax violations.
- Demanding ever-increasing amounts of information from an ever-growing range of third-party sources.
- Ensuring that Americans obey the IRS or face stiff consequences and penalties.

In addition, Congress has repeatedly taken the IRS under its wing to

- Protect the IRS, despite repeated cases of wrongly abused citizens, valid findings about its poor performances, and corrupt misdealings.
- Ignore instances when the IRS has skirted and gone beyond the law into realms it has no business being in.
- Give the IRS more protection from citizen suits than any other federal agency.[25]

The IRS Has the American People's Support—Usually

Despite Americans' never-ending grumblings about, resistance to, and enormous fear of the IRS, the fact that federal taxes are an inescapable part of our lives is widely accepted. It is also true that the majority of Americans willingly complete and mail in their returns, and pay their taxes, giving the United States one of the highest tax compliance rates in the world—about 83 percent.

The Winds of Change Are Here

The level of disgust expressed by the media at the time of the Senate Finance Committee hearings in late 1997 came as no surprise to me, to anyone working in the tax field, to a great many taxpayers, or to those who have read past editions of this book. The following conclusion is what those witnessing the hearings on taxpayer abuses discovered:

"Many IRS foot soldiers are frequently rude, arrogant, dismissive of taxpayers, lazy, and mouthy—basically about as unprofessional as one encounters in government. Some are so high on the power granted them under the law that they violate or ignore taxpayer rights. And they do so with impunity—protected by a Treasury employees union unresponsive to the feelings of voters or taxpayers in this country, concerned only with its entrenched power, and seemingly unanswerable to no one."[26]

Following 1997 hearings and subsequent examination of the workings of the IRS, a change was due, and that is exactly what has been happening for the past five years.

Sizing Up the IRS as an Opponent

As a general rule, a taxpayer never wants to get antagonistic toward the IRS. What you do want to aim for is the ability to manipulate the power of the IRS through the income tax process. You have to take extreme care doing this. It cannot be accomplished haphazardly or without sufficient knowledge. In the martial arts a small person can bring down a much heavier, stronger one. By the same token, I and thousands of other tax professionals continue to witness taxpayers accomplishing similar feats when dealing with the IRS.

6

IRS Technology:
What Works,
What Doesn't Work

It hasn't been easy for the IRS to adapt to an ever-expanding workload and advancing technology. Until the mid-1980s a great deal of the work was still being done manually. Sacks of tax return information sat for years in IRS corridors; massive amounts of incorrect information were disseminated to taxpayers en masse; huge numbers of tax returns would disappear forever; annually thousands of letters from taxpayers remained unanswered because they couldn't be matched to their corresponding files.

Today the IRS computers housed in the National Computer Center (NCC) in Martinsburg, West Virginia, contain trillions of bits of information on millions of U.S. taxpayers. The current IRS technology behemoth, called the Tax Systems Modernization (TSM), was initiated in the early 1990s at a cost of $8.3 to 10 billion. (This was on top of a previous $11-plus billion technology project.) The system was, among other things, supposed to

- Execute the IRS's Information Returns Program, or matching program, in which information on all 1040 forms (Individual Tax Return) is matched up or compared with all W-2s (Wage and Tax Statement) and the full range of 1099 documents that are sent to the IRS by third parties (i.e., employers, banks, real estate agents, loan companies, and more). This process enables the IRS to isolate underreporters and nonfilers.
- Eliminate millions of unnecessary contacts with taxpayers.
- Provide copies of tax returns to taxpayers who have lost their copies and to IRS employees who are conducting audits in less than one day rather than the current 45-day average.

- Reduce by one quarter the time it takes to process cases.
- Tailor correspondence to the taxpayer's account rather than issue generic form letters.

These were strong indications that the IRS was serious regarding its efforts to build, manage, and employ technology. By now, however, it is clear that relatively few of the IRS's technology efforts have been successful. But that's something the IRS would rather taxpayers not know.

THE PROCESSING PIPELINE

What Happens to Your Return?

The IRS processing pipeline is a process your tax return goes through from the time it is dropped into the mail until a refund is issued.

Where does all the other stuff take place? Where are tax returns selected for audit? Where is the matching program run? Where are people targeted for a criminal investigation? These all take place in a vast IRS-land that has come to be called the "nonprocessing pipeline."

The problem is, for the most part this phase is not fully revealed to taxpayers. Even explanatory material sent out by the IRS labeled "nonprocessing pipeline" is not complete. By not telling the whole story, the IRS triumphs over the taxpayer, because what transpires in the nonprocessing pipeline holds tremendous importance for anyone who files a tax return.

First, let's take a brief look at what happens to your return in the normal processing pipeline.

Millions of mailed returns are delivered to the service centers, where they are fed into computerized equipment that reads the coding on the envelopes, opens the envelopes, and sorts them by type—married, single, business. (Uncoded envelopes take longer to open and sort; using a properly coded envelope will speed things up.) Next, clerks manually remove the contents of the envelopes and sort the returns further into those with or without remittances. Payments are credited to taxpayers' accounts and are separated from the returns, totals are balanced, and the checks are sent to the service center's bank for deposit, eventually to end up in the U.S. Treasury.

All returns are then verified for completeness of information (the filer's signature, Social Security number, the proper forms), and coded to assist in converting the raw data directly from the return into an electronic language for computer processing. IRS personnel transcribe the data directly from the tax returns to computer disks; then the computer analyzes the information and enters error-free returns onto magnetic tapes.

If errors are encountered, they are printed on a separate report and passed on to tax examiners in the service center, who check the error records against the appropriate returns and correct what errors they can. If the errors are not easily corrected, the error is coded, indicating that the taxpayer will be sent an error notice requesting clarification.

Now the magnetic tapes containing data from all the accurate tax returns are shipped to the National Computer Center and added to the master directory of all taxpayer accounts, and updated records are sent back to each service center for further processing.

Refund tapes are sent to the Treasury Department for issuance of refund checks directly to taxpayers, and the processing pipeline ends. The total time from mailing your return to receiving your refund generally runs about six to eight weeks.

Electronic Filing

The processing pipeline is speeded up considerably if you e-file your return (see Chapter 13 for full details). Before an e-filed return is accepted for transmission to the IRS, Social Security numbers are verified and the return is checked for mathematical accuracy. E-filing does not increase or decrease your chances of being audited.

THE NONPROCESSING PIPELINE

What Happens

Taxpayers are kept in the dark about many phases of the nonprocessing pipeline that are quite important for them to know.

- For paper returns, the first round of letters is cranked out by IRS computers only in cases of missing information. If someone forgot to sign a return, if a schedule is missing, if the W-2 is not attached, these issues are handled within the first month after the return is mailed in. (All of the time periods given in these examples are for tax season, February 1 to April 15. At other times of year the turnaround time is probably shorter.)
- The next round of letters is sent to correct purely arithmetical errors. For the past four years, there have been about 6 million of these errors each filing season. Letters of this nature are sent anywhere from two to three months after a taxpayer has mailed in his or her return.
- The Information Returns Program (IRP), or matching program, is not part of the normal tax-return-processing routine. It is run as part of the nonpipeline processing.

- The W-2, which taxpayers attach to the 1040, doesn't actually get matched to the 1040 until approximately one and one half years after it is submitted.
- Audit letters don't usually get sent out until six months to one year after the return is filed.
- No matter how spiffy the matching program sounds, the IRS itself admits that it is still a labor- and paper-intensive operation.
- In 1992, only 2 percent of the data maintained in tax accounts was readily available online. The other 98 percent was in paper files— returns filed in federal records centers or in databases without on-line retrieval capability.[1] There has been some, but not much, appreciable improvement in this area since then.

Here's the full story of what happens in the nonprocessing pipeline.

Enter W-2s
W-2s, from private and public entities that report employees' salaries, are due in to the IRS the last day of January, and 1099s, from business own-ers, are due February 28.

Enter Inquiry Letters
It's early July and tax season has been over for about three months. Initial inquiry letters are being sent out by the service centers, requesting that taxpayers send in information they inadvertently left out, and/or to cor-rect mathematical errors. Once these situations have been corrected, one to two months later, the service centers reenter the information and cre-ate a good tape, which is then fed into the Martinsburg computer system.

Enter Audit Selection
The initial process selects tax returns whose DIF scores (Discriminate In-formation Function, discussed in Chapter 3) fall in the audit range for one or more of the DIF items or categories. This amounts to about 10 per-cent of all individual returns, or about 12 million, that have potential dis-crepancies. These returns are sent by Martinsburg via tape back to the corresponding service centers, where the computer data is matched up with the hard copy, the actual tax return.

Staff in the Examination Division at the service centers manually re-view and select only returns that indicate the greatest potential mone-tary yield. As a result, at least another 90 percent of the original 10 percent are discarded, leaving approximately 1 million individual tax returns chosen for audit as a result of the DIF selection process. In 2001 only 732,000 returns were chosen for audit, close to the all-time low of 618,000. At this point, the tax returns targeted for correspondence audits are turned over to the Examination Division at the service centers. The balance of the tax returns are distributed to the district offices, which send out letters to taxpayers notifying them that they are being audited. This entire process takes from six months to one year after the tax return is filed.

While audit selection is taking place, so is another entire range of activities.

Enter the Social Security Administration

Did you know that the first link between you, your W-2s, and the matching process is the Social Security Administration (SSA)? Here's how this one works: The first copy of the W-2 is sent to the SSA by employers so that wages can be added to a taxpayer's lifetime earnings account. The SSA then forwards the W-2 information to the IRS on magnetic tape, where it is matched to the 1040 form and, along with the 1099s, initiates the nonprocessing pipeline.

Now the matching program can be run. The sequence of events goes something like this:

Enter Mismatches

On the basis of the data in Martinsburg, all 1040 forms (individual tax returns) are matched with W-2s and compared with over 1.4 billion 1099s and other third-party documents. All mismatches are downloaded onto a separate tape, which goes back to the service centers. The assigned sections in the service centers then analyze the data. When a discrepancy exists indicating a mismatch among 1099s, W-2s, and 1040 forms, the case enters the collection area at the service center level.

Enter Underreporter Notices

The service centers send out mismatch notices, underreporter notices, or CP-2000 letters, triggered when there is a disagreement between what a taxpayer reported on the 1040 and what was reported about that person's income by one or more third-party reports. The IRS classifies these notices as *correspondence audits* (see Chapter 3). These notices propose a change to income, payments, or credits and are sent to taxpayers about one and a half years after the tax return was filed. Apparently, the fact that the SSA uses the information first contributes to the enormous delay. In 1998 the IRS generated 1.1 million notices for underreporting. This was a drop of almost one million contacts over the previous year. The matching process is now much more efficient. The average recommended additional tax from correspondence audits for 2000 was $2,602 per return, a 25 percent increase over the prior year.

Enter the Collection Division

After this, depending on how the taxpayer does or does not respond to IRS correspondence, tax assessments are made or taxpayer explanations are accepted. In any case, the collection cycle is now triggered, and the case makes its way up through the collection process, as discussed in Chapter 4.

Enter the Criminal Investigation Division

At this point the Criminal Investigation Division (CID) takes center stage.

CID staff trains service center personnel to identify typical characteristics of false and fraudulent returns and potential criminal violations. If a return of this nature is recognized by someone in the service center, the case is brought to the attention of CID. From there it might head up the line, or be dismissed for lack of potential to produce big bucks and/or a conviction.

THE REST OF THE PROCESS

Individual taxpayers are not the sole focus of IRS processing, so if some of the delays that occur in both pipelines seem inordinately long, one of the major reasons involves the rest of the IRS tax return–processing pie.

In 2002, the 129 million individual tax returns the IRS processed represented 51.5 percent of total net dollars collected, the majority in the form of withholding. Employment taxes represented 34.1 percent, and corporation taxes were 10.5 percent of total dollars collected.[2]

The scope of the entire processing cycle is arduous, tedious, and enormous. But there is a major lesson for all taxpayers: There are so many levels the IRS must get involved with in processing tax returns that if you learn how to prepare an unobtrusive return, chances are in your favor that it will pass through the system unnoticed.

If you look at the three areas in the IRS that are responsible for bringing in tax dollars, you can get a good perspective on the agency's technological capability.

In 2001,

- Matching recommended $2.5 billion in additional taxes and penalties.
- The nonfiler program recommended $2.4 billion in additional taxes.
- Examination recommended almost $21 billion.
- Collection yielded over $24 billion on a combination of collections on *delinquent accounts* and assessments on delinquent returns.[3]

The matching program, which is dependent on technology, offers the IRS widespread coverage across the taxpayer base. Nevertheless, people-dependent Examination and Collection, where IRS staff do most of the work, actually bring in far more tax dollars because of their selectivity: They select only those cases with the greatest potential for tax dollars.

So just exactly where is IRS technology performing well, and what information is still sitting around or just completely unreachable, as in the old days?

WHERE THE IRS TECHNOLOGY WORKS

W-2s (Wage and Tax Statements) and 1099s (Third-Party Reports) Matched to the 1040 Form (Individual Income Tax Return)

As you know, the Information Returns Program (IRP), or matching program, allows the IRS to match up third-party information—wages, interest, dividends, and certain deductions—with the amounts taxpayers report on their 1040 forms. In addition, the IRS also uses the IRP to identify nonfilers, people who have received some income (as indicated by one or more third-party reports) but nevertheless did not file a return. The current estimate is that about 6 million people are nonfilers. (The reasons why this segment is so large are discussed in Chapter 7.

Mismatches result from a variety of factors: mathematical errors or negligence (taxpayers do make honest mistakes), unreported name and address changes, as well as downright cheating.

Taxpayer Implications

If you do not properly report your W-2 earnings, there is little doubt that the IRS computers will pick it up through the matching process. Therefore be honest here, to the letter.

Social Security Number Cheating Schemes

Several years ago a rash of taxpayers tried to avoid paying taxes by manipulating Social Security numbers. The incidence of fooling around with Social Security numbers increased to the point where the IRS was successful in having a law passed that requires all third-party payers to obtain corrected Social Security numbers from taxpayers when the IRS provides the payers with a list of mismatches that affects them. If a taxpayer does not comply with the third party's request for the corrected Social Security number, the institution or third party will be instructed by the IRS to begin to withhold tax from payments that person is receiving from business owners, as well as from any other third-party payments such as interest and dividends.

Among others, the requirement targets taxpayers who provide an erroneous Social Security number on their bank accounts to avoid including the sums as taxable income. This produces a mismatch on IRS computers and triggers the backup withholding mechanism.

Once the mismatch is identified, the IRS notifies the bank, and after a two-year period, if the taxpayer hasn't stepped up to resolve the issue or offer a corrected Social Security number, the bank will automatically take 31 percent out of the account in question. So if the account earns $3,000 in yearly interest, $930 will immediately be sent to the IRS as backup withholding.

Pension Plan Distributions

The IRS's matching program regarding pension plan distributions used to have some real holes in it. With approximately half a million pension plan distributions disbursed annually, the common practice is to roll over pension funds, or place them in a qualified investment that entitles the money to remain nontaxable according to IRS requirements. If the rollover isn't followed to the letter of the Internal Revenue Code, the distribution is considered taxable income and the taxpayer is generally subject to income tax and added penalties if the distribution is taken before the taxpayer reaches age $59\frac{1}{2}$.

Taxpayer Implications

According to the Internal Revenue Code, when the organization holding the distribution turns it over to the taxpayer it must issue a 1099-R (Distribution from Pensions, Annuities, Retirement or Profit-Sharing Plans, IRAs, Insurance Contracts, Etc.), which spells out the amount disbursed, and send this information to the IRS. For the most part, this reporting requirement is adhered to by companies making the pension distributions, especially since IRS computers are now fully capable of matching up the pension-plan distribution with the rollover amount. (For an update, see Chapter 12.)

Form 2119 (Sale of Your Home) and Schedule D (Capital Gains and Losses)

When you sell a house, you generally receive a 1099-S (Proceeds from Real Estate Transactions) from the real estate broker or attorney, which shows the gross sale price of your house. If no tax is due on the transaction, probably because your gain on the sale is $500,000 or less for married couples, or $250,000 or less for a single person, you are no longer required to file Form 2119. If your gain exceeds these limits, report the entire gain on schedule D (Capital Gains and Losses) and then subtract the exclusion.

YOUR TAX-SAVING STRATEGY

Even if no forms must be filed on your home sale, keep complete cost and sales records regarding your residence. Tax laws change. You never know when the current amount you are allowed to exclude from gain will be raised, affecting a future home sale. Or, conversely, Congress could scale back the amounts, leaving you with unforeseen tax to pay.

If you sell investment rental property, your return must include the sale on Schedule D (Capital Gains and Losses). Omitting this information could lead to an audit, because the IRS has increased its search capabilities of real estate transactions and is matching that data with sales shown on Schedule D. For planning opportunities, see Chapter 12.

Disposition of Investment and Schedule D

If you have been receiving dividends from an investment and the dividend income disappears, you must show a disposition of the investment on Schedule D or be ready to prove that the company ceased the payment of dividends.

Auditors are also instructed to account for investments appearing on the previous year's tax return that have suddenly disappeared, or are not accounted for on a subsequent Schedule D. If a rental property appears on a taxpayer's 1040 one year and does not appear on the subsequent year's 1040, the auditor will suspect that you sold it and did not report the taxable gain on your 1040.

Overreporting Income

When a taxpayer submits an overpayment of tax on a check enclosed with the 1040 form, the IRS is thoroughly honest and in almost all cases will return to the taxpayer the appropriate refund. But what happens to the thousands of taxpayers who innocently overreport income?

Taxpayer Implications

Just as underreporting income is easily detected through the matching program, so, now, is overreporting. However, when it comes to overreporting income, the IRS does not behave as honestly as when there is an overpayment of tax. When taxpayers overreport their income, and the IRS records it, the IRS doesn't tell taxpayers that they've made an error. If you pay more taxes than you owe, you will receive a refund from the IRS, but not when you overreport income.

Matching Form 941 (Employer's Quarterly Federal Tax Return) with Total Wages and Taxes Withheld on W-2s

The 941 form, filled out by employers and sent quarterly to the IRS, shows total wages, taxable Social Security wages, taxable Medicare wages, federal income tax withheld, and Social Security and Medicare taxes. Since these items all appear on each employee's W-2 at year-end, the totals reported on the employer's four quarterly 941s for the year must agree with the grand totals of all W-2s, also reported by the employer. The IRS meticulously matches the W-2 totals with the 941s to ensure that businesses have legitimately paid their tax liabilities to the government in a timely manner.

Discrepancies arise between W-2s and 941s for these reasons:

- Many 941s, year-end reconciliations, and W-2s are filled out by employers manually, not with a computer.
- Many employers do not fully understand the requirements for making payroll tax deposits.

Taxpayer Implications

This matching process is at once a safeguard for the taxpayer (your company is not allowed to play around with money it has deducted from your salary, such as Social Security and withholding), a deterrent for the employer, and also a deterrent for taxpayers who believe they can cheat the government on taxes withheld from wages earned.

It also prevents little games from being played—for example, creating a fictitious company and issuing oneself a false W-2. So why not send in a mathematically correct return with a phony W-2 from a fictitious company, which will result in a large refund, after which the taxpayer disappears fast? Forget it. It's a major criminal offense. No one gets away with it.

As for the genuine companies and employers, those who fail to make timely payments are subject to strictly enforced penalties. They are also held personally liable for any Social Security or federal withholding taken from employees' wages that are not transmitted to the IRS. If the tax liability and required payments as shown on the 941s do not match up with the actual payments made by the employer, the IRS contacts the employer immediately.

The IRS has completely revised the 941 requirements several times over the years to cut down on deposit errors. (There was a great deal of confusion about when to send in the money.) The goal was to make depositing easier for approximately 5 million employers and eliminate most of the deposit penalties. Errors on the 941 form probably accounted for more than 80 percent of IRS discrepancy letters received by employers.

Another benefit to how the IRS has managed Form 941 is this. The program places online account data in front of IRS employees. So when the tax professional or taxpayer calls, the problem is usually resolved then and there. In my experience, this is one program the IRS can be proud of.

YOUR TAX-SAVING STRATEGY

When a taxpayer is ready to collect retirement benefits, the Social Security Administration will use a specific formula to determine that person's monthly Social Security benefit, based on the total amount of earnings accumulated over the years.

My advice to all wage earners is to carefully examine that annual statement you receive from the SSA. Verify it with the entries from your W-2's. Errors are easier to correct this way than by waiting until an error is inadvertently discovered by the Social Security Administration.

WHERE MISTAKES ARE MADE IN THE IRS MATCHING PROGRAM

Just because the technology in these areas is impressive doesn't mean that mistakes can't be made. (By the way, these mistakes are separate from instances where the IRS technology falls short, discussed further on in this chapter.) Here are the most common mistakes:

Mismatching Information on W-2 Forms with Information on the 1040 because of Nonstandardized W-2s

A tax professional who prepares personal tax returns knows that it is standard operating procedure for W-2s to be in a nonstandardized format. But have taxpayers even noticed, much less asked themselves why, the W-2, a key player in the IRS's third-party reporting system, arrives in the taxpayers' hands in all varieties of forms? Here's the reason: Employers with 250 or more employees must submit W-2 information on magnetic tape, where it all appears in a standard IRS format. Almost all other employers submit the information on paper, in a format either prescribed or approved by the IRS but, unfortunately, not followed often enough. The end result for taxpayers was and still is a ludicrously simple situation of wrongly copied information: Even though some of the W-2 information has to be placed in predetermined positions, the rest of the information placement and the design of the forms still vary wildly. Surely the resulting error rate causes thousands of taxpayers to receive CP-2000 letters and collection notices each year because of IRS computer mismatches.

The goal of every taxpayer should be to stay out of the clutches of the

IRS; any minor recording error can in a flash destroy a taxpayer's ability to fulfill this mission.

Note: Corporations are still allowed to design and print their own W-2 forms, but regulations in effect require data for W-2s to be presented in the exact order as on the preprinted IRS form. However, many large and small companies still fail to print their W-2s in the prescribed manner.

YOUR TAX-SAVING STRATEGY

Take care when you transfer your wages information from your W-2s to the "Wages, Salaries" line of your 1040 form. Doing it incorrectly could mean problems; for example, by transposing FICA wages (Box 3 on the W-2) and gross wages (Box 1 on the W-2), you may be reporting more income than you should. This will attract unnecessary IRS scrutiny.

Mismatching Information on 1099 Forms with Information on the 1040

For self-employed persons who receive 1099s for income earned from a sole proprietorship and file Schedule C, it is inappropriate to list each 1099 separately on Schedule C. Some of my clients receive 50 or more 1099s. However, you must be absolutely sure that the total gross income from the self-employed business that you report on line 1 of Schedule C equals or exceeds the total dollar amount of the 1099s that you receive. Otherwise you will be flagged for underreporting income.

Mistakes Made through Social Security Numbers

An incorrect Social Security number will immediately trigger a mismatch. The error might come from someone who created a bogus Social Security number that turned out to be yours. When you opened your last bank account, did the bank employee ask for your Social Security card to prove the validity of the Social Security number you provided to him or her? Probably not, because this isn't common practice—so a person could quite easily give an erroneous Social Security number. If some devious person just happens to give a false Social Security number to a bank or elsewhere and it turns out to be yours, you will receive a mismatch notice. The IRS will eventually notify the bank (or source) to obtain a corrected Social Security number from the person who gave yours. Unfortunately, by then you've already been contacted by the bank or the IRS and been annoyed by unnecessary correspondence through no fault of your own.

Exempt Income Items

The IRS will sometimes select for a mismatch notice income items bearing your Social Security number that should have been excluded from your taxable income; such items might be interest earned on IRA's, interest on tax-exempt bonds, and transfers between your IRA and pension plan. An erroneous match of these exempt income items may occur if the third-party payer submitted the information on the wrong magnetic tape.

Keypunch Errors

Sometimes an error occurs simply because of one incorrect keypunch by an IRS operator: a misspelling of your name or address or one wrong digit in your Social Security number.

What to Do If You Receive an IRS Mismatch Letter

Promptly answer the IRS mismatch letter with full documentation in your first reply. Failure to do so keeps your return in front of an IRS employee unnecessarily. For example, if in the mismatch notice your income was increased by an IRA distribution that you properly rolled over within 60 days, document your answer with the statement from the financial institution that shows the receipt of the rollover money plus a copy of the canceled check, if you have it. Do not assume that the IRS employee understands the data you are sending. Include a cover letter stating all the facts.

Now that you know which areas of the IRS technology work, and also where the most common mistakes are made, let's focus on several of the IRS's sore points.

WHERE THE IRS TECHNOLOGY FALLS SHORT ON THE INCOME SIDE

We are first going to concentrate on items that show up as "income" on the 1040 form: distributions from partnerships, corporations, estates, and trusts; capital gains; and gifts and inheritances.

Schedule K-1

K-1s are schedules issued by partnerships (which report income on Form 1065), S corporations (Form 1120S), and estates and trusts (Form 1041), on which these entities show distributable amounts of income and expense that have been allocated to each partner, shareholder, or beneficiary. Information on K-1s must be reported on the partner's, shareholder's, or beneficiary's Form 1040. During the 2001 tax year, over 23 million K-1s were filed with the IRS.

Tax preparers for entities that issue K-1s are responsible for placing income and expense items on the proper line. This is not always straight-forward because of the factor of basis. Basis is a dollar amount that represents the cost of a taxpayer's investment in an entity. Because of continuous adjustments to each taxpayer's basis in that particular entity, the income or loss as shown on the K-1 may not reflect the true amount that must be recorded on the taxpayer's current-year Form 1040. If you are the recipient of a K-1 from an entity, you cannot take for granted that the income or expense as shown on the K-1 is ready to be transferred to Form 1040 as it is stated; you should rely on your tax pro to determine the correct information.

Once taxpayers are sure that they have the proper income or loss amount, they are then faced with the arduous task of transferring the K-1 information onto their Form 1040. Several lines on the K-1 are easy to comprehend, and their counterparts on Form 1040 and its schedules are easily located. These include interest income and dividend income, lines 4A and 4B, respectively, which transfer to Schedule B of Form 1040; and net short-term capital gain or loss and net long-term capital gain or loss, lines 4D and 4E respectively, which transfer to Schedule D (Capital Gains and Losses). But Schedule D remains as complex as ever.

Then there are complicated items that have their own deductibility limitations, such as Section 179, depreciation "Expense Deductions" (discussed in Chapter 7), investment interest, and low-income housing credit (Form 8586, Low-Income Housing Credit, discussed under Rule 5 in Chapter 11).

To prepare a proper return, taxpayers really have to dig deeply into K-1 form instructions—which are often 10 pages long—and also examine additional schedules that explain the more complicated items being reported. Imagine it! The K-1 has up to 48 lines, some of which baffle even tax professionals. When that information is transferred to a 1040, it can appear in a number of different places on various 1040 schedules besides Schedules B and D, such as Form 6251 (Alternative Minimum Tax—Individuals) and Form 8582 (Passive Activity Loss Limitations).

Taxpayer Implications

Clearly, Schedule K-1 is inherently complex. Add to this the necessity of transferring a great deal of detailed information to the 1040 in a variety of different places, and you can understand how difficult it would be even for computers to organize, digest, and store information from the K-1 and then match it properly to the 1040. I am aware of several specific cases that demonstrate this point.

On April 15, 1999, a colleague of mine received a call from a client who said that without fail her return had to be filed on time. He told her that he couldn't do that because it was missing a partnership K-1 form. "I don't care," the client said. "What was the amount from last year?"

"It was a three-thousand-dollar loss," he replied.

"Take the same loss," she said, "and file the return on time." He did. Four months later, the K-1 arrived from the partnership indicating a $1,000 loss. Her job was transferred overseas for the next few years, and she never filed an amended tax return. She has never heard a word from the IRS.

In another case, an elderly taxpayer filing on October 15, under the latest extension possible, was missing two S corporation K-1s. The return was filed as if it were complete, except it was not noticed that the information from the K-1s was totally omitted. Three months later, the two K-1s arrived showing several items of additional income. As was his way, the elderly taxpayer buried the forms in a pile of unopened mail. An amended return should have been filed but never was, and no inquiry was ever received from the IRS.

Before we leave the K-1, I'd like to inform readers about one more thing: K-1 reporting by the entities (the partnerships, corporations, estates, and trusts) that issue the K-1 forms is not standardized. K-1s issued by nationally syndicated partnerships are so complicated that they tend to be accompanied by a brochure generated by each partnership explaining how taxpayers should transfer K-1 information to their 1040. Although the explanations say precisely where on the 1040 specific information should be entered, the words "Consult your tax adviser" are almost always present. For taxpayers, this is a rather indisputable indication of the difficulty of the task at hand.

In early 2002 the IRS started matching K-1 information from partnerships, S corporations, and trusts to individual returns. By August 1, 2002, the operation was halted because some 50,000 errors occurred in a batch of only 65,000 letters sent to taxpayers. For example, the IRS picked up a negative amount on the K-1 as a positive amount, or matched the K-1 information to the wrong tax year. Of the $2 *trillion* of gross receipts covered by K-1s, the IRS thinks that 20 percent may not be reported. Accordingly, a new K-1 matching program is planned for 2003.

Capital Gains—Sales Price of a Stock Transaction

When a person sells a stock or any type of security, the broker who sold it is required to report the sale on a 1099-B form (Proceeds from Broker and Barter Exchange Transactions). The form contains pertinent information such as the broker's name, the recipient's name and Social Security number, the trade date, gross proceeds, and a brief description of the sold item—for example, "100 shares of XYZ Corporation stock." This information is reportable by the taxpayer on the 1040, Schedule D (Capital Gains and Losses).

There are billions of securities transactions annually, so taxpayers can understand how vital it is for the IRS to receive 1099-B information on

magnetic tape from the thousands of brokers who are members of securities and commodities exchanges. Once on magnetic tape, the information
is easily transferred to the IRS computer center.

There's the background. Now let's look at the reality.

The IRS requires that each security sold by a taxpayer be reported
on a separate 1099-B, but it allows a great deal of latitude in how the
information from the 1099-B is reported back to taxpayers. Although
the IRS does have its own standardized 1099-B form, the form is used
infrequently.

Essentially, reporting brokers create their own forms, so there is little
if any uniformity. It is not uncommon for brokers to issue substitute 1099-
Bs, which can be monstrous creations that list all the securities an individual taxpayer sold in a given year on letter-size paper. Sometimes up to
40 transactions are squeezed onto a single sheet, often excluding the
number of shares sold. This forces taxpayers who are looking for more
detailed information to search for their original trade confirmations from
their brokers. How are taxpayers to report the amount of money they receive from the sale of securities and transfer the proper information compiled by the financial institution onto Schedule D? With difficulty.

Further complications arise when a block of shares purchased as a
single lot is sold at different times, or when companies split their stocks
to take advantage of an opportunity to offer a lower market price to the
public. For example, how does one monitor the sale of 1,000 shares of
IBM purchased as a single lot, then sold on five different dates? Twenty
percent of the cost would have to be assigned to each sale of 200 shares.
Perhaps this sounds easy, but what if there were two or three stock splits
during the time you owned the stock? You could end up with a complex
math problem that might take a taxpayer hours to sort out.

Taxpayer Implications

The information that is now being reported to the IRS by the securities
industry is the sales proceeds of the transactions. Determination of the
cost basis, or matching what the taxpayer paid for the security, is another matter entirely. Because this task often requires intricate and complex record keeping, computers would have to monitor detailed cost
information for each taxpayer and deal with ongoing adjustments
caused by stock splits and dividend reinvestment plans. It is not a surprise, therefore, that taxpayers generally do not receive notices of mismatches originating from 1099-Bs. Any technology system would be
hard-pressed to sort out the quagmire of matching a 1099-B with the information on Schedule D.

During an audit, revenue agents do not always verify the buys and
sells of securities transactions. It is interesting to note that in the training
materials the IRS has developed for conducting office audits regarding

frequently examined items, there is no pro-forma audit kit on the verification of securities.

One reason for a seeming complacency by the IRS in its examination of securities transactions could be that it has discovered in its TCMP (Taxpayer Compliance Measurement Program) examinations (the ones used to compile the Discriminate Information Function scores) that the public has been generally honest in its reporting of securities transactions and further audit measures are therefore not required.

This isn't to say that the IRS doesn't use or can't access security transaction information. It certainly can and does. For example, if the Criminal Investigation Division is investigating a taxpayer, special agents will track down a list of any securities transactions made by that taxpayer and trace them accordingly. But this is done as part of another or secondary investigation. It is not normally done as part of the IRS matching program. Also, based on information from third-party reports, the IRS sends notices to taxpayers who haven't filed prior years' returns, reminding them that they have stock sales that must be more fully reported on Schedule D (Capital Gains and Losses).

To be perfectly frank, the entire area of securities transactions is too important a revenue source for the IRS to turn its back on. Years ago I said that the IRS will begin to solicit the assistance of financial institutions, brokerage firms, and other companies in the securities business on this issue. As of 2003, all of the major brokerage companies are matching cost data associated with securities transactions of their clients, but because there is no requirement to do so, they are not generally reporting it to the IRS.

I suppose readers next want to know when all this additional reporting is going to become a requirement. That I don't know. But I do know that what I just described is probably the strongest means by which the IRS could get a good, solid grip on securities transactions.

Estate and Gift Taxes/Lifetime Exclusions

Reporting inheritances and gifts—inheritances passed on through decedents' estates and assets received as gifts from living individuals—is another area difficult for the IRS to get its arms around. In addition to cash, the more common forms of inheritances and gifts are land, homes, jewelry, autos, and marketable securities, or stamp, art, and coin collections.

Reporting requirements for inheritances and gifts usually fall into three major categories:

1. If a decedent's estate exceeds $1 million in 2003, Form 706 (U.S. Estate Tax Return) is required.
2. Taxpayers who give gifts of more than $11,000 in one calendar year to one person must file Form 709 (U.S. Gift Tax Return). If a

married person gives a gift of $22,000, it can be treated as a split gift—that is, $11,000 from each spouse.

3. Taxpayers who receive gifts and inheritances and ultimately dispose of the items in a taxable transaction must report them as gains or losses on Form 1040, Schedule D (Capital Gains and Losses).

When taxpayers try to determine the value or cost of a gift or inheritance, they find themselves confronted with a complex problem. The following rules are used to determine the cost basis of inherited or gifted assets: In figuring gain or loss of an inherited asset, generally use the fair market value at the date of death of the decedent. For gifts disposed of at a gain, use the donor's original cost basis. For gifts disposed of at a loss, use the donor's original cost basis or the fair market value at the time of the gift, whichever is lower.

Taxpayer Implications

There is not a lot of information going into the IRS computers regarding the cost basis of gifts and inheritances. Therefore, in this area the IRS has to rely almost solely on taxpayer compliance. The situation has several rather far-reaching implications.

When a federal estate tax return, Form 706, is filed, the assets of the estate will be listed along with their fair market values. In this case a taxpayer could easily prove the cost of the inherited property, especially if these items are questioned during an audit, by producing the estate tax return of the decedent. Pay particular attention to stock splits and dividend reinvestment plans, which will make tracing individual stocks somewhat difficult.

YOUR TAX-SAVING STRATEGY

If you find yourself the recipient of an inheritance where there is no accompanying estate tax return, you should get an appraisal of the asset unless it is a marketable security whose value is readily obtainable. This will establish the fair market value of the item, which will allow you to properly compute gain or loss when you dispose of the asset.

Also, it is generally not wise for a relative to transfer assets just before passing away; rather, the assets should be in the will. This way, the cost basis of the assets you receive as a beneficiary of the estate will be valued at current fair market value, thereby reducing your tax bite when you sell.

If the transfer is made while the relative is still alive, it is classified as a gift, and upon the disposal of the asset, you will often be burdened with a significant taxable gain, since the cost basis of a gift when computing gain is the original cost to the donor and not the fair market value.

Mr. Davis's mother gifted her son a Florida condominium, which she had purchased for $25,000. One year later, Mr. Davis sold the apartment for $40,000. The cost basis for the gift is the original $25,000 and now results in a $15,000 taxable capital gain. On the other hand, if Mr. Davis had inherited the condo after his mother's death and then sold it a few months later for $40,000, his cost basis would be $40,000 (fair market value at date of death) and there would be no taxable gain or loss.

The question is, how can the IRS keep track of and catalog the value of bequests from an estate and gifts? For example, could the IRS require that every person, when asked to prove the cost of inherited property, produce the estate tax return of the decedent? Although this is requested during an audit, it is not feasible to include this step in routine practice because of the relative scarcity of estates with assets that are valued in excess of $1 million—hence of estate tax returns also. Sounds like another mission impossible.

It is up to the taxpayer to produce an appraisal or other proof to show fair market value, or to show a paid bill or canceled check to prove cost. Other than estate and gift tax returns, the IRS computer contains no information that will refute the documented proof that you are presenting.

To clear up a major misconception regarding tax implications of gifts and inheritances, see Chapter 9, and for newly enacted legislation, see Chapter 12.

WHERE THE IRS TECHNOLOGY FALLS SHORT— MORTGAGE INTEREST AND REAL ESTATE TAX

Mortgage interest and points paid in a mortgage transaction of $600 or more are reported to taxpayers by their mortgage lenders on Form 1098 (Mortgage Interest Statement). Others besides mortgage lenders who must file this form are taxpayers who pay out $600 or more of mortgage interest in the course of conducting their trade or business, even if the taxpayer is not in the business of lending money. At tax preparation time, the taxpayers must transfer this amount to line 10 of Form 1040, Schedule A (Itemized Deductions).

Taxpayers often make errors when entering or transferring information onto their 1040. In the area of mortgage interest the chances for error are extremely high. From the taxpayer's perspective, this is understandable. There are several reasons why this area has such a high error rate. Although home mortgage interest can be copied from Form 1098, most taxpayers copy both mortgage interest and real estate tax information from the annual mortgage expense statement that they receive from financial lending institutions, because Form 1098 does not contain real estate tax information. Besides information on mortgage interest and real estate taxes, other information found on annual expense statements is interest earned on tax escrows, homeowner's insurance, water charges, and late charges.

These annual statements, like the W-2 and K-1, are not standardized. Most are computer-generated by the reporting institutions. As a result, when taxpayers transfer the figures to their 1040s, they often transfer real estate taxes as mortgage interest and vice versa.

Another common error is to use homeowner's insurance and water charges as a valid deduction, which of course they are not. The end result is a mismatch between the figure(s) the taxpayer entered on Schedule A, and the figure(s) supplied by the third party reporting the mortgage interest and real estate tax information.

Sounds like a simple situation and a simple mistake, and indeed, this is a very common error. Of course things could be clarified and subsequently made easier for the taxpayer if the IRS were to revise the 1098 form to include a line for real estate taxes. Then these two figures would at least be broken out on the same sheet of paper, which would reduce or even eliminate this particular problem altogether.

Finally, there are the thousands of taxpayers who claim the mortgage interest deduction but who are not legally entitled to it. You must be the person who is legally liable to the bank for payment of the mortgage to qualify for the deduction. To be legally entitled to deduct real estate taxes you must appear as an owner on the property deed, making you liable for the real estate tax.

Reminder: You can deduct mortgage interest on only two homes, which for most people will be their primary residence plus a vacation home. If you own more than one vacation home, you can select one of them each year on which to deduct the mortgage interest, and change your choice annually. Property taxes can be deducted for any number of residences.

The tracking of real estate taxes is further complicated by the fact that real estate taxes are not reported only on the annual expense statement received from the lending institution. Consider these two examples:

1. A taxpayer with no mortgage on his home pays his real estate taxes directly to the municipalities. In this instance, no annual expense statement is received by the taxpayer. Furthermore, since the taxpayer now has four to six checks to sort through at tax time, he will often include in his total real estate tax deduction the payment for water charges or rubbish removal (nondeductible items), because they are paid to the same payee, the municipalities.

Many homeowners have been successful in having their real estate tax burdens reduced due to unequal or incorrect assessments in this way. If you receive a lump-sum check from your municipality, you should reduce your real estate tax deduction in the year you receive the check.

2. Mortgage interest for the short period, from the date of purchase to when the first new mortgage payment will be paid, is paid at the closing. Since this amount has been paid before the new account is set up, it is often not included on the annual expense statement or the 1098, both issued by the lending institution. The knowledgeable taxpayer will add up the total payments for the year, including interest and real estate taxes shown on the closing statement, and disregard the interest amount entered on the 1098. Too often, though, taxpayers forget to claim deductions for mortgage interest or real estate taxes that they are legitimately entitled to.

The IRS recognizes this problem and has tried to persuade Congress to change the law, to require lending institutions to include these adjustments on their annual expense statements. If this happens, taxpayers will receive more complete and understandable information from the lending institutions, which will help them claim their proper deductions.

Other possible sources of disagreement between mortgage interest as shown on Form 1098 and the deduction on Schedule A is the inclusion of late charges on the annual expense statements, incurred because the mortgage was paid after the usual 15-day grace period, and prepayment charges that accrue when a mortgage is paid off early. These charges are considered to be extra interest, not penalties. Accordingly, taxpayers can add the late and prepayment charges to the regular mortgage interest paid during the year.

Note that information regarding late and prepayment charges on mortgage payments is allotted two small paragraphs on page 4 of IRS Publication 936, "Home Mortgage Interest Deduction." Wouldn't you like to know how much revenue has been generated by the federal government because thousands of taxpayers did not realize that both of these charges were a valid deduction?

Taxpayer Implications

If you receive a mismatch notice on mortgage interest, don't panic. Often there is just as great a chance that the error comes from the reporting institution. Answer the inquiry promptly with full documentation, including copies of your original Form 1098 and, for new home buyers, the closing statement from the purchase of your home. This will show the IRS where the extra mortgage interest deduction can be found.

WHERE THE IRS TECHNOLOGY FALLS SHORT— NONFILERS AND UNDERREPORTERS

The General Accounting Office (GAO) does periodic studies of the IRS every two years and usually makes specific recommendations as to how the IRS can improve its performance. In 2002, the GAO studied IRS effectiveness in the area of nonfilers and underreporters, with these results:

- Nonfilers with incomes over $100,000 could more easily escape detection than those with lower incomes.
- When high-income nonfilers are pursued and they do file their returns, the IRS needs to scrutinize these late returns very carefully. It appears that the GAO made this very same suggestion in prior reports, but the IRS ignored it.
- The IRS should hire more employees to investigate high-income nonfilers.
- To reduce the time spent on reviewing underreporter cases that result from mistaken entries and not genuine underreporting, the IRS should change the matching program to search for reported income on as many different tax return lines as possible.
- The IRS should report to the Social Security Administration errors in wage data it finds in underreporter cases.

Taxpayer Implications

It does appear that the IRS is reducing the number of nonfilers. It remains to be seen how many of these delinquent taxpayers were contacted by the IRS because of its increased technological capabilities in the matching program versus how many voluntarily filed because they believed the IRS was on their trail; or how many were pulled in by the IRS nonfiler program, or the media hype regarding leniency and so-called taxpayer amnesty.

WHERE THE IRS TECHNOLOGY FALLS SHORT— LACK OF REPORTING REQUIREMENTS FOR CORPORATIONS

The biggest gap in the IRS technology infrastructure concerns payments to corporations of income, interest, dividends, rents, royalties, and capital gains. There is currently no requirement that any corporation receiving such payments be sent 1099s. (There are several limited exceptions, such as for companies performing legal services.) According to a 1991 IRS study, small corporations voluntarily reported 81 percent of the tax they owed on such payments in 1981, but by 1987 the compliance rate dropped to only 61 percent. The GAO and the House Government Operations Committee have consistently pushed for legislation that would require entities that pay dividends, interest, and other payments to corporations to file 1099s with the IRS. The IRS would then attempt to catch corporations that understated income or failed to file returns.

Note: There are no reporting requirements for financial institutions to send records of IRA payments to the IRS, according to an IRS spokesman.[4]

Taxpayer Implications

There are several valid reasons why the IRS has been dragging its feet on bringing in corporate recipients under the 1099 reporting umbrella:

- It would enormously increase the IRS processing burden of the already overworked IRS computers and staff. I estimate that more than 100 million new pieces of paper would be generated annually by payments to corporations. Also, the proponents of this arduous task have not considered the added cost to businesses, which may be as much as $1 billion annually.
- The IRS is going through an extremely difficult time strategizing, building, and managing its computer capabilities. The added burden of corporate reporting would set back the very much overexpensed and underperforming program even further.
- The task of matching bits of corporate income data to the multiple income line items that exist on Forms 1120 (Corporate Income Tax Return) and 1120S (U.S. Income Tax Return for an S Corporation) will be more formidable than matching individual income with lines on Form 1040.
- Many corporations base their books on years that end anytime between January 31 and November 30, while fiscal 1099 reporting is calculated on a calendar year. Thus, many 1099s will contain income that spans two corporate years. The only way to eliminate this problem is to require all corporations to convert to a calendar year. When Congress attempted exactly this procedure for S corporations in 1987, tax professionals revolted to an extent not seen since the Boston Tea Party. Being able to do fiscal year closings of books for corporations during off-peak times for accountants saves me (and no doubt countless numbers of other tax professionals) from an early death. Ultimately, Congress scaled back the calendar-year requirement just enough so that the revolt died down.

The House Government Operations Committee has repeatedly urged the IRS to initiate corporate document matching, saying that matching could bring in significant tax revenues and have a minimal impact on the payer community and corporations. Based on the points just made, you can see that whoever proposed this must have had no corporate experience or must not have been in touch with reality.

WHERE THE IRS TECHNOLOGY FALLS SHORT—THE AUDIT LEVEL

The IRS continues to have trouble accessing specific information from their own computers. Information retrieval for a given year, a given tax return, or a specific piece of information may be readily available, but one never knows what will happen once a request is made. Basic tax return information takes more than a year to reach IRS computers in a readable form, and IRS technology is still too slow to meet the needs of either IRS employees or taxpayers.

Taxpayer Implications

Despite state-of-the-art technology, there is still too much information and not enough people and/or systems to process it. In conclusion, it seems there are and probably always will be gaps and lags in IRS computer capabilities.

TECHNOLOGY OVERHAUL A FIASCO—STILL

Everyone agrees that modernization is vital "to bring in the trillions of dollars needed annually to pay for the government, to restore public confidence in the Service's ability to resolve taxpayers' problems quickly, and to increase the use of electronic filing of returns."[5] But no one seems to have the answers.

Over the past fifteen years, the IRS has spent in excess of $20 billion to overhaul its computer capabilities and has very little to show for it. What the IRS publicly admitted in 1997 is still true today: "The IRS must continue to work with dozens of antiquated computer systems that cannot trade information with one another."[6]

The biggest problems are the choices of software, security, and lack of integration across the IRS's vast computer network. With outdated equipment that prevents systems from sharing files—there are 70 different operating systems—the agency continues to rely on magnetic tapes transported between offices via trucks and planes. The basic tax and accounting systems were never designed for modern financial management. The failure of the technology effort means that taxpayers in a dispute with the IRS could face years of frustration. With records kept on two or more computer systems, being able to retrieve necessary information in a timely manner becomes difficult, if not impossible.

A part of the new system that is working, besides the matching program or Information Returns Program, is electronic filing and online filing (see Chapter 13).

Under Rossotti's charge, the IRS issued a request for a proposal for a prime systems integration services contractor to focus on the much-needed systems modernization. However, the Office of Management and Budget (OMB) has complained that too much was spent on customer service projects rather than on infrastructure and internal management improvement projects.

In early 2003, the OMB cut the IRS's 2004 request for business modernization funding from $450 million to $257 million, citing the IRS's continued inefficiency and waste. If this reduction stands, it will indirectly shield the tax cheaters and not protect aggrieved taxpayers who are continuing to pay their fair share of the overall tax burden. Although some of the newest systems ease processing, speed requests, and provide more across-the-board information on tax returns, I don't see the technology situation changing much for another three to four years, especially in the areas of audit rates and collection enforcement.

7

IRS Targets and What to Do If You're One of Them

The tax compliance rate—the rate at which taxpayers willingly (although perhaps not contentedly) pay their taxes in the United States—hovers around 85 percent.[1] Even so, only $83 of every $100 due in income tax is collected.[2] So despite the fact that the tax collection process brings in what seems like extraordinary sums ($2.0 trillion in gross collections for 2002), each year the federal government continues to be shortchanged an estimated $200 billion. (Even this is an understatement because it excludes an additional $300 billion or so of taxable income produced through drug sales, organized crime, and other illegal activities.) But really, who knows for sure?

In this realm of extraordinary tax evasion, very little has changed over the decades except the amounts owed and never paid, which continue to rise. Beginning in the late 1980s, however, the IRS seriously began to focus on breaking open the phenomenon that has come to be called the underground economy, whereby a substantial number of people, businesses, and organizations do not pay their proper share, or any share at all, of their taxes.

Without a doubt the underground economy is a serious problem—for the IRS, for our society, and for honest taxpayers. However, the IRS has taken such an aggressive position on exposing the underground economy that it is punishing innocent taxpayers and wiping out entire sectors of the independent business community. This chapter is written for the people who are being wrongly and often unlawfully pursued.

ARE YOU IN THE LINE OF FIRE?

Individuals are responsible for about 75 percent of each year's tax shortfall, while corporations account for only 25 percent. How does the IRS identify the groups who are not paying their fair share of taxes? These groups overlap, duplicate, and even meld as players in the underground economy glide through avenues that facilitate evading or avoiding taxes. Easiest for the IRS to identify are

- The self-employed
- People who work out of a home office
- Independent contractors
- Cash-intensive businesses
- Nonfilers
- Tax cheaters—omission of income
- Tax delinquents and tax scam artists

Within each group, the two primary methods for evading tax dollars are hiding income and overstating or manipulating expenses or deductions, or not filing tax returns at all.

TARGET: THE SELF-EMPLOYED

At the top of the IRS hit list for breaking open the underground economy are the self-employed, whether a sole proprietorship or a corporate entity. People who own a business and work full-time for themselves probably have the greatest opportunities not only to hide money but also to overstate deductions.

What makes matters even more embarrassing is that the IRS knows just exactly which segments of the self-employed are the worst offenders. According to the GAO, leading the list of underreporters are auto dealers, restaurateurs, and clothing store operators, who underreport nearly 40 percent of their taxable income. Telemarketers and traveling salespeople have a shortfall of about 30 percent. Then come doctors, lawyers, barbers, and accountants, who understate about 20 percent of their income.[3] In the Northeast, my recent experience strongly indicates that lawyers and doctors head the list of self-employed taxpayers who are being audited.

To more easily conquer this segment, as I see it, the IRS has subdivided the self-employed into three smaller groups:

- Sole proprietors
- Those who work out of a home office
- Independent contractors

Target: Sole Proprietors

A sole proprietor is defined as an unincorporated business or profession in which net income is reportable by only one person. The gamut of the self-employed runs from people who own a service business (beauticians, home services and repairs, tutors) to professionals (doctors, lawyers) to insurance agents and computer programmers and more.

How the IRS Attacks

Integral to the definition of sole proprietors is the necessity to file a Schedule C with a 1040 form. While Schedule C requires you to define the type of business you are in and/or your occupation, it also functions as a wonderful device for deducting business expenses dollar for dollar against business income (see also Rule 3, Chapter 11). As a sole proprietor, via Schedule C you have every opportunity to underreport your income and lots of other opportunities to convert personal expenses to business expenses.

For these two reasons, the IRS sees the sole proprietor as a double enemy: a cheat in the underground economy and a prime audit target.

What Sole Proprietors Can Do to Protect Themselves

Although Schedule C affords full deductibility of business expenses, a heavy concentration of expense items is a valuable indicator for the IRS, so the IRS is naturally going to focus on what you've listed. However, the IRS is not necessarily focusing on aggressive stances taken on expense items unless certain items jump out, such as travel being $25,000 out of a $50,000 income. The IRS is focusing on the type of business for which the Schedule C is filed, particularly if the business type falls into one of the IRS target areas: service providers, professionals, or cash-intensive businesses.

What will the auditor ask you to provide? A review of Form 4700 (IRS Examination Workpapers) indicates that the examiner will request the following information:

- A description of the business and the number of years you have been in business
- The number of employees and the bookkeeper's name
- The amount of cash in the business at the beginning and end of the year
- The name and address of your bank
- What method of accounting you use—cash or accrual
- Outstanding loans due to or from the owners of the business
- Business expenses verification
- Copy of tax return from prior year

This is the minimum information that the auditor will require. Make sure you review the data carefully before you hand the auditor anything.

Here's an amazing story, the sort of thing that pops up every once in a while in the tax field, about a taxpayer who without realizing it discovered the secret to resolving the double-enemy predicament—legally.

Sam grew up working in his father's hardware store, which was left to him after his father passed away. The normal tax procedure for this process would have been to close the estate by filing a final estate return, then to begin reporting the ongoing operations of the store on a Schedule C attached to Sam's 1040. However, the operations of the store were reported as part of a U.S. Fiduciary Income Tax Return (Form 1041), not on a 1040, and the store's net income was passed through to the son on a K-1 form (Beneficiary's Share of Income, Credits, Deductions, Etc.), which is a schedule of Form 1041.

Sam continued to report income from the store through the estate on the K-1 of Form 1041 until he retired. At no time did the IRS ever inquire why the operations of the store were included in the fiduciary income tax return. This unusual tax setup kept Sam's business virtually unnoticed by the IRS.

If you are a sole proprietor and are at a high risk for audit, the perfect solution, which Sam used without ever realizing it, involves the way you report your business activities to the IRS. By extracting yourself from the sole proprietorship/Schedule C category and transforming your business to, for example, a partnership or corporation, you can successfully remove yourself from the IRS hit list. However, in a surprising update, it seems the IRS has detected a sharp increase in the number of trust returns, using Form 1041 (U.S. Income Tax Return for Estates and Trusts) with a Schedule C attached. IRS officials fear that taxpayers are taking advantage of the low audit rate for Form 1041 returns by using this form to report and file their business taxes. IRS focus on this area is long overdue. What took them so long? Taxpayers, beware.

Because this subject is so closely linked to the audit component, the entire area will be discussed at length in Chapter 8.

Target: People Who Work Out of a Home Office

As many as 40 million people work at least part-time at home, with about 8,000 home-based businesses starting daily. Of these, in a recent year more than 1.5 million claimed home office deductions on their tax returns, their deductions amounting to over $3.8 billion.[4]

How the IRS Attacks People Who Take the Home Office Deduction

The IRS decided that taxpayers who take the home office deduction represented too large a segment of the underground economy. After all, a great many items taken as home office expenses that would ordinarily be for personal use, like telephone, utilities, repairs, maintenance, and depreciation of certain items in the home, were being transformed to deductible business expenses on the 1040 form. (Home office expenses are contrasted with out-of-pocket business expenses such as office supplies or postage, which would be incurred by a business whether it was located in a home or not.)

Home Office Rules

You can take a home office deduction if your principal place of business is where you perform administrative or management activities, provided there is no other fixed location to perform those activities. The home office must be used exclusively for business on a regular basis. If you are an employee, you can take the deduction only if such use is for the convenience of your employer.

Here's a case involving one of my clients affected by the home office rules:

Ellen Stedman is an employee of a corporation whose only office is in Chicago, Illinois. But she lives in Newark, New Jersey, and uses her apartment as a home office. There she arranges customer contacts, speaks with suppliers, and performs administrative functions such as writing up sales orders and expense reports, which she mails to her employer in Chicago. Her normal workday keeps her out of her home office and on the road from 9 A.M. to 4 P.M.

Ms. Stedman's home office qualifies as her principal place of business for deducting expenses for its use. It's where she conducts administrative activities, and she has no other fixed location where she performs these same functions.

Form 8829

Form 8829 is an IRS weapon for getting a grip on taxpayers taking the home office deduction. Anyone who chooses the deduction must submit the form with Schedule C, Profit or Loss from Business (Sole Proprietorship), together with the 1040.

Although the IRS consistently denies it, Form 8829 can single out your tax return for scrutiny. But just as with all other IRS forms, there are ways to interpret and fill this one out without quivering.

How to Solidify the Home Office Deduction and Avoid Audit Traps on Form 8829

First, make sure you maintain a separate telephone number for business purposes only. Also, make sure your business correspondence is sent to your home office address rather than to some other convenient place, like one of your biggest clients.

Finally, make sure you understand what benefits the home office deduction offers and how to make the best use of them. You can deduct depreciation on the business portion of your principal place of residence, depreciation on equipment and furniture, and the business portion of your transportation expenses; and you may be entitled to other related benefits. Here's what you need to know about each of these:

Percent of Home Space Used as an Office.   The percentage of expenses for business use of your home—insurance, utilities, repairs and maintenance, and rent, if you are a renter—that you can deduct is based on the total square footage of the residence that is used for business. Take a sensible approach in computing the percentage or you'll be caught in an audit trap. It is entirely acceptable for your business space to occupy 20 to 25 percent of your total home space, but a figure of 40 percent or more is unreasonable unless you store merchandise in your home.

Number of Square Feet.   Be sure to include space you use for storage shelves, file cabinets, and other equipment. The tax allowance that provides deductions for items pertaining to space allocated on a regular basis in the taxpayer's home office includes storage of product samples. This is particularly beneficial to businesses whose inventory and samples take up substantial space.

Note: Keep in mind that merchandise inventory is not always stacked up in neat piles. With all that tax auditors have to do, it's rare for one to visit your home to verify square footage information, so utilize the greatest amount sensibly available. Take pictures of the entire area used for your home office and keep them on file. If you move, an audit may take place two or three years later, and you can still show that your home was used for business.

Depreciation of the Home or Principal Place of Business.   Depreciation for the portion of your home used for business, referred to as "nonresidential rental property" on Form 4562 (Depreciation and Amortization)—Part Two, is based on a write-off period of 39 years. The basis for depreciation is the original cost of your residence (excluding land cost) plus additional costs for permanent improvements, or fair market value at the time of conversion to business use, whichever is less. If you use fair market value, a common mistake, your depreciation figure will show up as unnecessarily high because fair market value is generally much higher than original cost. This may attract IRS attention.

Depreciation on Equipment and Furniture.   You can depreciate the cost of new equipment and furniture over a five- or seven-year period (depending on the item as defined and explained in the instructions for Form 4562). In addition, anyone taking the home office deduction can also depreciate office machines, equipment, and furniture that have been converted from personal (not new) to business use. The basis for depreciation is original cost or fair market value at the time of conversion to business use, whichever is less. The IRS will not be surprised to see depreciation of this kind and will not hound you for bills covering original items purchased, since they assume you purchased them some time ago, probably as personal items.

You have several methods of depreciation to choose from:

- The straight line method allows you to ratably depreciate business capital assets evenly over the assets' useful life.
- The 200 percent declining balance method gives taxpayers twice the amount of depreciation in the earlier years. The process is described in IRS Publication 334, "Tax Guide for Small Business," and Publication 534, "Depreciation."
- Section 179 of the Internal Revenue Code allows taxpayers to write off current-year purchases of automobiles (with limitations) and business equipment and furniture up to $100,000 annually for 2003 regardless of the item's useful life (use Form 4562).* So if you experience high net taxable income and can make a major purchase of office equipment or furniture in the same year, utilizing Section 179 will increase your expenses and reduce your net taxable income. Say you purchase a $15,000 copier that is normally deductible over five years according to the Internal Revenue Code for depreciation on office equipment. Under Section 179, you can deduct the entire $15,000 in the current year. The benefit gained is an extra $13,500 of expenses in a year when you have high taxable income. In the 30 percent tax bracket, the savings is $4,050. Once you write off items under Section 179, you cannot depreciate them further.

Be aware that the election to use Section 179 can be made only on the originally filed tax return. You cannot use an amended return filed after the normal due date of the return to make or modify the election. Furthermore, the full extra depreciation of $100,000 for 2003 is available only if you purchase no more than $400,000 of eligible business assets. If your purchases exceed this amount, you lose part of the $100,000 depreciation,

*Bonus first-year depreciation deduction of 50 percent can be taken for new qualified property acquired between September 11, 2001, and September 10, 2004, but must be placed in service by December 31, 2004. The extra 50 percent or 30 percent (30 percent if the property was acquired prior to May 6, 2003) is in addition to any Section 179 expense that the business is entitled to deduct. Any leftover balance can be depreciated over the asset's normal useful life. See Chapter 11 for a comprehensive example.

dollar for dollar. Plan your purchases carefully. You might think about leasing some equipment instead of making an outright purchase in order not to exceed the $400,000 amount.

YOUR TAX-SAVING STRATEGY

The Section 179 deduction cannot be used to reduce your taxable income below zero (taxable income includes the aggregate net income or loss from all businesses you and your spouse conducted during the tax year, plus any wages earned as an employee). If a Section 179 deduction would reduce your taxable income below zero, your alternative would be to use normal depreciation methods. You must depreciate autos, typewriters, computers, copiers, calculators, and the like over five years. (Computers are subject to special dollar limitations, as described below. Automobile depreciation is discussed in Chapter 11.) The write-off period for office furniture (desks, files, and fixtures) and carpets is seven years.

Remember, when taking depreciation for home office equipment and furniture,

- You don't need a receipt for every last cent, since you might have purchased the items a while ago.
- An IRS auditor would not be surprised to see depreciation for a desk, chair, couch, and carpeting.
- Estimates, if they are reasonable, are acceptable by IRS auditors.

Transportation Expense Deduction. If your residence is your principal place of business, you may deduct daily transportation expenses incurred in going between your home and another work location in the same trade or business, regardless of the distance and whether or not the work location is regular or temporary. For various ways to report mileage expenses, see Chapter 11.

Other Tax-Related Benefits

Decreased Self-Employment Tax. Because the home office and transportation expense deduction usually reduce self-employment income, self-employed taxpayers receive a benefit of reducing their self-employment tax, which is computed at a rate of 15.3 percent of self-employed income (12.4 percent for FICA and 2.9 percent for Medicare). Even moonlighting taxpayers whose income exceeds the FICA maximum wage of $87,000 from a full-time job can obtain a reduction in the 2.9 percent Medicare portion of their self-employment tax.

Tax Benefits Corrrelated to Your Adjusted Gross Income. To the extent that deductions for home office and transportation expenses decrease your adjusted gross income, you may find that certain other tax benefits become available. For example, by taking these deductions, you may reduce your joint AGI below $150,000, which would make you eligible to make a full contribution to a Roth IRA.[5] By reducing your AGI, you can also benefit by an increase in a whole slew of other deductions and expenses that are subject to AGI limitations. These can include increased itemized deductions for medical expenses (see Chapter 11) and casualty and theft losses, along with exclusions for adoption expenses, Social Security benefits, deductions for rental expenses, student loan interest, the AMT exemption, eligibility for traditional IRAs, and more.

Reduced Computer Record-Keeping Requirements. A computer is generally considered "listed property" and is subject to more stringent rules than other office equipment in order to claim any part of its cost as depreciation on a business return. To be eligible for depreciation, business use must exceed 50 percent, and only that attained portion can be expensed. Where some personal usage is involved, use of a daily log to substantiate the business use is required by the IRS. However, if the computer is kept and used in your home office, it is assumed to be business property and therefore not subject to the special rules.

Disadvantage of the Home Office Deduction

For depreciation taken on your residence after May 6, 1997, you are subject to a maximum capital gains tax of 25 percent, even though the balance of gain on your residence will probably not be subject to tax because of the available $250,000/$500,000 exclusions.

If you are an employee and are taking a deduction for the home office, do not use Form 8829, which is meant for self-employed individuals. Instead, use the work sheet contained in IRS Publication 587, "Business Use of Your Home." You then transfer the total home office deduction from line 34 to Form 2106 (Employee Business Expenses) or Form 2106-EZ (Unreimbursed Employee Business Expenses). The employee business expenses end up as miscellaneous expenses on Schedule A (Itemized Deductions) and are subject to a deductible equal to 2 percent of your adjusted gross income.

Here is a final comment on Form 8829. At an American Institute of Certified Public Accountants (AICPA) seminar, an IRS presenter told the crowd that it would take an hour and a quarter to fill out Form 8829 and seven minutes to study the rules. This was followed by an outburst of laughter.[6]

I say there isn't a person alive who could learn anything useful about the Internal Revenue Code provision that governs this form in that time period. It more likely would take an entire day at a minimum.

Loopholes in the Home Office Deduction

The biggest loophole regarding the home office deduction is available to anyone who owns an S corporation, is a member of a limited liability company or a partner in a partnership, and uses a home office.

Owners of S corporations report income and expenses on Form 1120S (U.S. Income Tax Return for an S Corporation) whereas LLCs and partnerships report income and expenses on Form 1065 (U.S. Partnership Return of Income). There is no special form to identify the home office deduction. This means that you can be the owner of an S corporation, operating fully out of your home, and there is no distinction made between your home office expenses and any other business expenses. You avoid the home office IRS hit list altogether. This is more fully explained in the discussion of S corporations in Chapter 8.

Target: Independent Contractors

What began with millions of laid-off workers refashioning their experience and marketing themselves as one-person operations to be hired out on an as-needed basis spawned a new way to earn a living—being an independent contractor. To the IRS, the nature of how independent contractors are paid is evidence enough that some of them have joined the ranks of the underground economy. Their tax impact is an estimated shortfall of $10 billion a year.

Reclassification of Independent Contractors

By law, the IRS is entitled to receive from employers the following taxes for each employee:

- FICA tax (Social Security and Medicare), which comes to 15.3 percent of the employee's salary up to $87,000, covered equally by the employer and the employee, 7.65 percent each, 1.45 percent each on salary above $87,000.
- Federal withholding tax or the amount deducted from your gross wages on the basis of income level and exemptions.
- Federal unemployment insurance tax of 0.8 percent of only the first $7,000 in wages, paid by the employer. The federal unemployment insurance tax rate can be as high as 6.2 percent, which may vary according to the amount of state unemployment insurance tax paid by the employer. The rate differs in each state.

When employers hire independent contractors, these requirements and others disappear. Employers

- Are not required to include the contractor on the quarterly payroll tax reports. So business owners save at a minimum the employer portion of the FICA tax, or 7.65 percent of each independent contractor's gross earnings (1.45 percent on earnings above $87,000).

- Are not subject to state unemployment insurance premiums or even increases in these premiums when a contractor is let go, since business owners who hire independent contractors are not subject to state unemployment laws. This alone represents a major consideration when deciding whether to hire an employee versus an independent contractor.
- Reduce their compliance costs, since the federal Age Discrimination in Employment Act and the Americans with Disabilities Act of 1990 do not apply to independent contractors.
- Are not required by law to cover an independent contractor for worker's compensation insurance (accidents or sickness on the job) or disability insurance (accidents or sickness away from the job).
- Do not include independent contractors in the company's pension plan (this item alone is often as high as 10 percent of an employee's gross wages), sick leave or vacation benefits, medical coverage, or stock options.

All the business owner is required to do is file a 1099-MISC and send it to the IRS at the end of the year.

When workers choose to be classified as independent contractors, and/or employers choose to get rid of employees and instead hire independent contractors, the IRS is shortchanged in two ways because independent contractors can

- Deduct on their tax return many items that would otherwise be considered personal: travel, entertainment, office supplies, insurance, and home office expenses (subject to the key tests discussed earlier in this chapter). This could reasonably amount to 20 percent of one's net income.
- Set up their own pension plan, which is deductible against their income.

In turn, independent contractors must fulfill these obligations to the IRS:

- Pay their own FICA tax, which is about 15.3 percent of their net taxable income up to $87,000 and 2.9 percent above that, on Form 1040, Schedule SE (Self-Employment Tax).
- Pay withholding tax on their net taxable income.

The growing numbers of independent contractors surging through our economy present many opportunities for workers not to pay the IRS all the money it is legislated to receive.

Are you beginning to get the picture? Every additional worker classified as an independent contractor means the IRS loses tax dollars through unpaid FICA, withholding, and unemployment taxes, and through income tax deductions as well.

The IRS would be delighted if all workers became classified as employees and the category of independent contractor disappeared. In its attempt to make this a reality, the IRS has initiated an all-out nationwide attack on independent contractors. One of its claims is that 92 percent of the companies it called in for a worker classification review during one recent period were assessed a higher Social Security tax, with an average assessment of $67,000 per audit.[7]

The GAO has reported that between 1988 and 1995, the latest study available, 12,983 employment tax audits resulted in $830 million of proposed assessments and reclassifications of 527,000 workers as employees.[8] With the IRS paying so much attention to misclassified employees, it is more crucial than ever for businesses and independent contractors to recognize the IRS's aggressive tactics and how to stand protected.

IRS Attack Methods against Independent Contractors

Reclassifying Independent Contractors.   To determine whether a worker is an employee or an independent contractor, the IRS offers a general rule that gives the greatest weight to the degree of control exercised by the employer in three specific areas:

- Control of behavior (instructions and directions—what to do and how to do it)
- Control of finances (financial risks of the worker and opportunities for profit)
- Relationship of employer and worker (how they view each other in their written contract)

Employee or Independent Contractor?   The current IRS official guidance is contained in Publication 15-A, "Employer's Supplemental Tax Guide— Supplement to Circular E." Generally, an individual is an independent contractor if the business person for whom the service is performed has the right to direct or control only the result of the work and not the methods and means of accomplishing the result. The relationship of the two parties must be thoroughly examined by considering all evidence of control and independence.

Behavioral Control   Does the business have the right to control and direct the worker in the completion of the task for which he was hired? This could include what tools or equipment to use, where to purchase supplies and services, and even assigning tasks to specific individuals. This includes the type and degree of the following:

Instructions the business gives the worker. An employee is generally subject to the business's instructions about when, where, and how to work. Even with no instructions, sufficient behavioral control may exist if the business owner has the *right* to control how the work results are achieved.

Training the business gives the worker. An employee may be trained to perform services in a particular manner. However, independent contractors usually utilize their own methods.

Financial Control Does the business have the right to control the business aspects of the worker's job? This includes the following:

Unreimbursed business expenses for the worker. Independent contractors are more likely to request unreimbursed expenses than are employees. Fixed continuous costs that are incurred regardless of whether work is currently being performed are especially important.

Extent of the worker's investment. An independent contractor often has a significant investment in the facilities that he uses in the performance of services for others, but this is not mandatory for independent contractor status.

Extent to which the worker makes services available to the relevant market. An independent contractor usually advertises and is available to work in the relevant market, whereas an employee tends to work for a single business.

How the business pays the worker. An employee is usually paid a guaranteed wage for an hourly or weekly period of time, even if the wage is supplemented by a commission. However, an independent contractor usually receives a flat fee for a job although some professions, such as law, often pay independent contractors on an hourly basis.

Extent to which the worker can realize a profit or a loss. An independent contractor can make a profit or loss.

Type of Relationship What is the relationship between the business and the worker? This includes the following:

Benefits provided by the business. Employee-type benefits provided to a worker might include medical insurance and a pension plan.

Permanency of the relationship. If a business engages a worker with the expectation that the relationship will continue for an indefinite period, this is clear evidence that the business intended to create an employer-employee relationship.

Extent to which services performed by the worker are a key aspect of the regular business of the company. If the services performed are this important, then it is likely that the business will have the right to direct and control the worker's activities. This is indicative of an employer-employee relationship.

Written contracts describing the type of relationship the parties intended to create. The IRS publication contains no further details about the content of the written contract between the parties. There are, however, measures a business owner and an independent contractor can take to strengthen their respective positions.

The contract created between the business owner and the independent contractor is regarded by the IRS as a key item in assessing classification. When drawing up the contract, business owners can take several precautions.

YOUR TAX-SAVINGS STRATEGY
Under no circumstances should the business owner or the worker file IRS form SS-8, Determination of Worker Status for Purposes of Federal Employment Taxes and Income Tax Withholding, which often is provided to you by the IRS. See Chapter 11.

How to Draw Up a Foolproof Independent Contractor Contract

- Specify the services to be rendered.
- Insert a starting and completion date.
- Make sure that the independent contractor is controlling the procedures necessary to accomplish the agreed-upon services. This would mean that the contractor hires additional employees of his or her own choosing to carry out the job, provides work tools, and sets payment schedules on the basis of the completion of the work, not simply on the passage of time.
- Make it clear that the independent contractor is in complete charge of supervising and directing how the work will be performed.
- Indicate that all insurance—liability, fire and theft, worker's compensation, and disability—will be provided by the independent contractor.
- Payment methods should be sporadic and vary over time, to justify treating the worker as an independent contractor.

- Do not separately state an allowance for overhead costs, such as meals and transportation; these should be included in the contract price.
- Spell out that training of workers is the full responsibility of the independent contractor.
- Do not include a provision that grants the independent contractor office or working space on the business owner's premises. This implies an employer-employee relationship. If the contractor needs office space, he'll use it. There is no need to put it in black and white.
- Avoid paying a bonus or any fringe benefits such as vacation pay or medical insurance, since that isn't the nature of an independent contractor's arrangement.
- Tell the contractor that if things slow down, he will not be given other work to do. The business owner's obligation is only for the work originally assigned and agreed upon.

In addition to the contract, business owners should make it clear to independent contractors that their responsibility is to complete the contract; they can't be fired, nor can they quit the job, without being at risk of a lawsuit for nonperformance of the contract.

Business owners should consider these three actions:

- Do not fill out both 1099s and W-2s for anyone working for you. An independent contractor must have payments reported by the business owner on the 1099—Miscellaneous Income—while an employee has wages filed on a W-2. Each business owner must make the decision up front as to how the payments for the worker are to be filed.
- Do not give even limited benefits to an independent contractor. It's a sure indicator that the worker is more an employee.
- Have all independent contractors fill out Form W-9, Request for Taxpayer Identification Number and Certification. By signing this, the worker agrees to be responsible for paying required taxes. If the worker later says he was an employee and is suing for benefits, the existence of a Form W-9 may protect you.

In a recent corporate audit of a client's return, IRS auditors uncovered workers who were treated as both employees and independent contractors within the same calendar year. This occurred because the employer was "trying out" the employees, so for the first three months they were treated as independent contractors, to keep paperwork to a minimum and to allow for the possibility that they might not work out.

After the unofficial trial period was over, the workers were given employee status. This is a no-no! The workers should have been classified as employees from the first day they began working.

The results of the audit were expensive: The employer had to pay FICA, Medicare, and Federal Unemployment taxes of approximately 16 percent of the wages earned during the first three months, plus penalties and interest.

In a case that was decided by the Ninth Circuit Court of Appeals (*Microsoft v. Vizcaino*, 1999), the court ruled that Microsoft cannot withhold benefits from workers it had classified as independent contractors. Workers classified by Microsoft as independent contractors are entitled to participate in the company's Employee Stock Purchase and 401(k) plans. These workers had worked at the company for years and performed the same work as permanent employees. The court used the phrase "common law employees" in referring to this group of independent contractors employed by Microsoft.

How to Strengthen Your Status If You Are an Independent Contractor

- Independent contractors should always be able to take on assignments from other companies.
- The contract drawn up should never appear to be an exclusive agreement.
- Independent contractors should be able to prove that they receive income from other sources. This will help to legitimately determine their tax status as a self-employed person filing a Schedule C.
- Incorporate yourself. There is no obligation to issue a 1099 form to a corporation. As the IRS homes in on independent contractors by reviewing 1099 forms, you will no longer be included in this group.

In addition to using their guidelines, other techniques used by the IRS to turn independent contractors into employees include the following:

- Third-party leads (nothing more or less than informers)
- A shift in IRS Examination Division resources
- Unannounced audit blitzes by the Collection Department

Use of Informers. The IRS encourages both disgruntled workers and companies that use employees rather than independent contractors to tattle on companies that use independent contractors, via a snitch sheet. This snitch sheet was distributed by an IRS official at a taxpayer association meeting in California. The official reportedly asked technical service firms to act as snitches by filling out the sheet and returning it anonymously in a plain envelope. The official promised that all such leads would be followed up.[9]

The revenue officers whom the IRS turns loose for these snitch assignments are from the Collection Division. They come on as sincere and act as though they're on your side. They may promise that if you help them by providing the right information, they'll help you by allowing you to retain the classification of independent contractor or by allowing your company to continue to employ independent contractors.

Once you give in, and the case is open for audit, don't be surprised if these agents tell you they have acquired new information that they didn't have at the beginning of the audit and that is being used against you. The case could conclude with the agent's saying, "Even though you did as we suggested, all of your independent contractors have been reclassified as employees, and you owe $50,000 in additional FICA, withholding, and federal unemployment taxes."

Another information pool is large national firms that have actively and aggressively cooperated with the IRS in going after local firms in the same industry that treat workers as independent contractors. One national health-care agency has regularly contacted the IRS National Office regarding what it considers to be withholding-tax abuses involving the use of independent contractors in the supplemental nurse staffing industry.[10]

Now, however, larger businesses are hiring independent contractors with the same regularity (and gaining the same benefits) as smaller firms. For example, it is not unusual for large multinationals to hire new computer workers as independent contractors.

Despite the shift, the IRS continues to seek out independent tattletales. According to the agency, outside tips brought in over $167 million in 1999, representing almost $8 million paid to informers. Form No. 211 (Application for Reward for Original Information) allows you as an informer a maximum reward of $2 million and keeps your identity secret. The reward for informing is 15 percent of the amount collected. In the past 10 years, the IRS collected $1.56 billion on approximately 89,000 tips and paid out $35.6 million, which represents a pretty good return on their investment. For more information, see IRS Publication 733, "Rewards and Information Provided by Individuals to the Internal Revenue Service."[11]

Warning: The IRS is not legally required to pay fees to informers. In several recent cases, the IRS has gone back on its word by refusing to pay promised rewards. In fact, 19 informants who have sued the IRS to obtain reward money have all lost. The IRS offers reasons for not paying informers, which the courts go along with:

- The IRS already had the information. (How could you refute that?)
- The information was not valuable.
- The informer was a party to the criminal activity.
- The informer was a government employee and was just performing his normal duties.

What to Do If You're Pressured to Inform.   If you are involved in a reclassification audit and you have every reason to believe your involvement was the result of undue pressure from a revenue agent, and the agent begins to pile up new information that could have been gained only through other snitches, you have every right to cease the audit and gain professional advice. If you already have a professional on your side, your best bet is not to discuss the case any further with the auditor. Let your professional do it.

If you feel the auditor has lied in addition to applying pressure on you to inform, you can request that the auditor's group chief review the case. You can then ask the group chief to replace the auditor.

From here, you can move up the line in the appeals process. If you and your professional feel that you have a strong case, go for it. Taxpayers tend to do better at the appeals level, where they face more level-headed, educated people.

Shift in Examination Resources.   In the Examination Division, the IRS has instructed revenue agents to look for misclassifications in the course of regular audits and has developed special training programs and audit techniques to help them do this.[12] In 2001, IRS tax auditors started using the newest Market Segment Specialization Program guide entitled "Business Consultants." The guide instructs IRS employees in the fine art of auditing independent businesspeople who call themselves consultants, some of whom are engaged by the same company that previously employed them. See later on in this chapter for more information about this new audit guide and how to obtain it. In addition, the IRS admits to assigning several hundred revenue officers from the Collection Division to run special audits for the purpose of uncovering misclassifications. The focus of this group is businesses with assets of less than $3 million.

These investigations are nothing more than employment tax audits that are being carried out by the Collection Division instead of the audit personnel from Examination—who are supposed to be assigned to these tasks. Reports of incidents in the business world suggest that the way the IRS collection staff is handling these tax audits is nothing short of illegal. Restrictions have been placed on revenue officers from Collection, such as prohibiting them from acting without supervisory authority. Hopefully, this will keep revenue officers in check, along with "Your Rights as a Taxpayer," IRS Publication 1, or, as it is generally called, the Taxpayer Bill of Rights.

The Taxpayer Bill of Rights.   The goal of this bill is that taxpayers be treated fairly, professionally, promptly, and courteously by Internal Revenue Service employees.

Part of this fair treatment involves being handed "Your Rights as a Taxpayer" upon initial contact by Examination, Collection, or any other IRS personnel, as required by law. Sometimes these pamphlets are given out. But too often they are handed to the taxpayer, particularly independent contractors or employers who hire them, at the end of a collection agent's visit, when it's too late to know which of your rights the IRS has abused.

"Your Rights as a Taxpayer" (see Appendix D) is now available at www.irs.gov under "Individual," "MoreTopics," "Taxpayer Rights."

The Audit Blitz.   Once the IRS revamped its audit and collection resources, it came up with a new attack technique: an unannounced visit from the Collection Division. Often these officers do not explain the purpose of their visit or what they are looking for. If they do provide an explanation, be wary. The real reasons for the visit are to uncover people who are legitimately working as independent contractors but whom the IRS would like to classify as employees; to verify the level of compliance regarding a specific reporting requirement; or to gather incriminating information on a particular industry or individual organization. The blitz is an all-purpose weapon used by the IRS to audit whichever businesses or organizations strike its fancy.

What would you do if an IRS officer came into your company unannounced and demanded information from you, such as how the company distinguishes individual contractors from employees? This act in and of itself is against the law and in full violation of a taxpayer's rights.

Don't try to handle the audit blitz yourself. When revenue officers know you are afraid, they will use that fear to get as much information out of you as they can. You have the right to ask them to leave and not to answer any of their questions. When asked, they generally do leave. They are, after all, trespassing.

Then call your tax professional, CPA, or attorney immediately. I tell my clients that the definition of an emergency is when the IRS is at your door, or inside, ready to close your business down. An unannounced audit is an emergency. In my entire career I have had only two such calls, and in both cases they were triggered by revenue officers from Collection.

Long-Awaited Relief—Real or Not?

With continued pressure from the business community, and a congressional subcommittee examining the independent contractor issue at a White House Conference on Small Businesses, here's the result.

First, the Classification Settlement Program (CSP) was initiated by the IRS to help businesses currently being examined to settle their employee classification issues by offering deals based on a graduated settlement scale ranging from a 25 to 100 percent discount on a single year's back payroll tax liability. The offer is made using a standard closing agreement, and participation is voluntary. A company can decline to accept a settlement and still have the right to appeal an IRS ruling. The CSP was originally tried for a two-year test period and was so successful, it's been extended indefinitely.

Second, an early referral of employment tax issues to the Appeals Office allows a business to hasten settlement and will cut short the prohibitive penalties that can build up while a case is being disputed.

Third, a new training manual has been published to provide explicit guidance to field agents on the difference between an employee and an independent contractor. The manual does not preempt the material in Publication 15-A. Instead, it is designed to simplify and explain it, and, in so doing, introduces areas that the IRS has conceded for the independent contractor.

Revised IRS Stance on Independent Contractor Status
The new training manual presents these new IRS positions:

- Changes over time: The IRS admits that factors in determining worker status change over time. For example, uniforms previously indicated an employer-employee relationship. Today the IRS concedes that a uniform may be necessary for an independent contractor to perform the job.
- Control: The IRS admits that even in the clearest cases, an independent contractor is not totally without control, and conversely, employees may have autonomy, previously deemed a clear indicator of independent contractor status.
- Home offices: The manual strikes a blow at using a home office as a characteristic to prove independent contractor status. Renting an office is viewed as more concrete proof because it indicates a "significant investment."
- Financial dependence: The manual points out that Congress and the Supreme Court have rejected the argument that focuses on whether or not the worker is economically dependent on or inde-

pendent of the business for which services are performed and warns agents not to apply this standard.

- Hours and location: Given the current environment, the IRS no longer considers part-time versus full-time, temporary or short-term work, on- or off-site locations, or flexible hours as indicative of a worker's status.[13]

The manual also reinforces the importance of Section 530 of the Revenue Act of 1978, often referred to as a "safe harbor."

Safe Harbor—Section 530

An employer whose workers are under scrutiny by the IRS for reclassification from independent contractors to employees can apply Section 530 if the employer has

- Not treated the workers as employees in the past.
- Consistently treated the workers as independent contractors on all returns filed (including Form 1099).
- A reasonable basis (reliance on judicial authority, prior IRS audit, a long-standing industry practice, or advice from an accountant or attorney) for treating the workers as independent contractors.
- Not treated anyone else holding a substantially similar position as an employee.[14]

Any company meeting these provisions cannot be held liable for taxes not withheld after a worker is found to have been an employee rather than an independent contractor. The IRS often uses Section 530 as a bargaining tool, agreeing to its applicability only if a business reclassifies a worker.[15] In a 2002 case, an employer qualified for safe harbor protection even though it had not filed required 1099s for its workers in prior years. In Legal Memorandum 2002-11037, the IRS held that filing 1099s for the year under examination was sufficient to gain a safe harbor.

If you strongly disagree with the IRS, you can now take your case to the Tax Court. Within 90 days after the IRS has notified you of reclassification of your workers, you must file a petition with the Tax Court. You do not have to prepay any taxes or penalties and then sue for a refund, which was the previous method before 2001, and collection action by the IRS is suspended while your case is before the court. For $50,000 or less of total employment taxes, you can use the small-case division of the Tax Court, a simplified process for which no attorney is required. Many cases are settled before the judge hears them. Go to www.ustaxcourt.gov for further information.

Other Safe Harbor Rules for Treatment of Employees and Independent Contractors.

IRS revenue agents must advise taxpayers undergoing a worker classification audit (independent contractor or employee) that the safe harbor rules exist.

In a recent case, a used-car dealer who established that a significant segment of the used-car sales business treated salespeople as independent contractors, rather than as employees, demonstrated a reasonable basis for such treatment. Thus he was entitled to safe harbor relief under Section 530.[16]

If an employer has established a reasonable basis for treating a worker as an independent contractor, the burden of proof shifts to the IRS to prove otherwise.

A company that employed direct sellers on a contract basis scrupulously followed the rules to qualify the sellers as independent contractors. When the IRS stepped in to prove that the workers were employees, it conceded that the company provided all of its workers with the required 1099s and that its treatment of similar workers was consistent, thereby meeting the first two tests of Section 530. Furthermore, the workers' status had been upheld in two prior audits and the use of contract workers in the business is an industry practice, proving double validation of the third test of Section 530.

Despite this, the IRS auditor claimed that the company could not shift the burden of proof to the IRS. Even after the CPA in the case showed the auditor the new law, and demonstrated that the company's requirements for relief were met, the auditor said, "I don't believe it."

When the CPA asked for the written audit report to see why the auditor did not find Section 530 applicable, the report stated that the IRS agreed that the taxpayer met the reporting and consistency requirements, but that it didn't have any basis for claiming independent contractor status.

Further proof of independent contractor status was presented via an Internal Revenue Code section that allows direct sellers of services, such as this company had, to statutorily qualify as independent contractors. However, the auditor turned down this argument as well.

Now the CPA spoke to the auditor's group manager. But guess what? The manager had not yet taken the new IRS training program on worker status cases, and besides, the manager considered the auditor to be an expert, since he had handled these cases for years. As a result the manager backed up every decision the auditor made.

Finally the CPA provided the manager with the relevant sections of the IRS's own training manual for employment tax audits. The manager's response was, "What is this? Where did you get it? Why did you give it to me?"

The CPA was confident that his client would eventually win its case after going to the IRS Appeals Division or into court, and the IRS will likely be tagged with some of the client's legal bills.

But the bottom line is, even though the laws are on the books, in the end you're up against the auditor and typical IRS behavior—stubborn, uninformed, and stymied thinking.[17]

What All This Means

Settlement options aren't terrific. The taxpayer still has to fork over a large sum of money just to end the annoyance, and the IRS is getting backlogged with cases.

Publication 15-A and Section 530 are rehashes of old concepts. If you qualify, you beat the rap and the IRS can't touch you even if you employ independent contractors who really appear to be employees. The safe harbor rules, however, appear to apply mainly to larger employers, and not to too many at that.

In short, there is still not enough reason for the IRS to do anything else but continue to employ its pay-up-or-else tactics. The steps taken thus far appear to be in line with the agency's usual attempt to offer some leniency in the face of mounting criticism.

TARGET: CASH-INTENSIVE BUSINESSES

No doubt businesses in which large amounts of cash are routinely handed from consumers to business owners present the greatest opportunities to underreport income. These include everything from automobile dealers, check-cashing operations, jewelers, travel agencies, brokerage houses, and real estate businesses to hair salons, bars, and restaurants. So targeting this segment of the underground economy is naturally on the IRS's agenda. But it's another thing to treat legitimate cash-intensive businesses as if they are engaging in criminal activity.

IRS Attack Method against Cash-Intensive Businesses—Form 8300

In a big push to enhance compliance, particularly among cash-intensive businesses, the IRS issued proposed regulations that expanded cash transaction reporting requirements. Using Form 8300 (Report of Cash Payments Over $10,000 Received in Trade or Business), anyone who in the course of trade or business receives cash (cashier's checks, traveler's checks, money orders, or bank drafts) in excess of $10,000 in one separate or two or more related transactions must report the transaction(s) to the IRS. The information must be reported within 15 days of the date the cash is received, and a statement must be supplied to the payer by January 31 of the following year. Owners or operators of any trade or business who do not file this form face civil and criminal penalties, including up to five years' imprisonment.

Here are some examples of how the legislation works:

Through two different branches of a brokerage company, a person purchases shares of stock for $6,000 and $5,500 cash on the same day. Each branch transmits the sales information to a central unit, which settles the transactions against the person's account. The brokerage company must report the transaction because it fits the definition of being a single receipt of over $10,000 from one person.

A man buys a Rolex watch from a retail jeweler for $12,000. He pays for it with a personal check for $4,000 and a cashier's check for $8,000. The personal check is not considered cash. Thus, the amount of cash received is not more than $10,000, and the jeweler does not have to report the transaction.

Using the audit blitz, IRS agents swooped unannounced into businesses across the country. The goal—to secure so-called delinquent 8300 forms and the penalties assessed for the unpaid sums.[18] To enhance its coverage the IRS next shifted responsibilities onto the taxpaying public by requiring that businesspeople must report cash payments of over $10,000 in certain situations:

For example, a travel agent receives $8,000 in cash from a customer for a trip, and the next day receives another $8,000 from the same customer to take a friend on the trip. If a customer makes two or more such purchases within a 24-hour period totaling more than $10,000, it is considered a related transaction and therefore reportable.

The IRS is also encouraging businesses to report transactions of less than $10,000 if they appear to be suspicious, and smaller related or multiple-cash payments that total over $10,000 in one year. Pause for a moment and think what this represents:

- The IRS is asking the private sector to do work that should be assigned to the Criminal Investigation Division.
- The business owner must now be a detective, a mind reader, and an expert administrator with systems that can track these kinds of multiple payments.
- Given the volume of business common to most of the companies that fall into this reporting category, it's probable that some transactions that should be reported would be missed, a fate not likely to be discovered until audit time, when the businessman gets hit full-force in the pocketbook.

What to Do If You're in a Cash-Intensive Business

While testifying in a recent tax case, an IRS employee admitted that there is a high noncompliance rate for Form 8300.[19] Even so, stay within the law and report to the IRS cash transactions that exceed $10,000. Use as guidelines the information outlined in the instructions to Form 8300. When the IRS carried out its audit blitzes, most of the violations uncovered were straight cash transactions that exceeded $10,000. In other words, they were blatant violations of the Internal Revenue Code for which the taxpayer had no defense.

Don't worry that you might miss some suspicious chain of transactions because of the volume of cash transactions in your day-to-day business operations. There is no case law that sets a precedent that you should or could know that a series of transactions are related or suspicious.

TARGET: INDUSTRIES IN THE MARKET SEGMENT SPECIALIZATION PROGRAM

The Market Segment Specialization Program (MSSP) (see Chapter 3) is used by the IRS to assist IRS revenue agents to shift from functioning as generalists to specialists when examining tax returns of a variety of unrelated businesses. The IRS claims that the objectives of the program are to "share MSSP expertise through educational efforts with taxpayers, involve representatives of key market segments who can deal with the underlying cause of noncompliance, and conduct tax audits using examiners skilled and knowledgeable in a particular market."[20] With the experience it provides, the program is also supposed to allow an agent to conduct audits more quickly and efficiently.

To support these goals, Audit Technique Guides are developed by the IRS with input from industry representatives, covering almost 100 industries identified so far.

What to Do If Your Industry Is Targeted

Let's be honest. The MSSP is designed to tell agents whether taxpayers are paying what they should. However, the agency does appear to be going about this in a spirit of cooperation.

The guides themselves can serve as valuable assets for taxpayers. So the first thing to do is to send for the guide appropriate for you. Then become familiar with it. The more familiar you are, the more you can be on the alert to assess the direction of the audit and to work successfully with your tax pro.

Table 7.1 gives the most current list of Market Segment Specialization Program (MSSP) guides available, including the stock numbers and prices, and where to send your order and check. Note that advance payment is required. You can also find many of the guides at www.irs.gov ("Tax Information for Businesses") and download them directly from the web site for free.

The guides are thorough and well researched. Here are several examples from already published guides to show you what to expect regarding specificity and completeness.

The Beauty & Barber Shops Guide states, "The [hairdressing] industry is cash intensive, . . . the majority of the workforce had a high school education and were graduates of a cosmetology school. . . . It

TABLE 7.1   Market Segment Specialization Program (MSSP) Guide Order Form

Guide	Stock No.	Price
Air Charters (See Aviation Tax)		
Alaskan Commercial Fishing: Catcher Vessels—Part I	02357-1	12.00
Alaskan Commercial Fishing: Processors & Brokers—Part II	02358-0	9.50
Alternative Minimum Tax For Individuals	02423-3	10.00
Architects	02350-4	4.25
Artists & Art Galleries	02388-1	6.00
Attorneys	Out of Stock 02375-0	9.50
Auto Body & Repair Industry	02363-6	15.00
Auto Dealerships	02434-9	24.00
Aviation Tax (former title: Air Charters)	02409-8	10.50
Bail Bond Industry	02387-3	6.50
Beauty & Barber Shops	02362-8	5.50
Bed & Breakfasts	02345-8	6.00
Business Consultants		Online
Car Wash Industry	02399-7	Online
Carpentry/Framing	02410-1	Online
Child Care Providers	02427-6	3.75
Coal Excise Tax	02393-8	10.50
Commercial Banking	02382-2	Online
Commercial Printing	02379-2	11.00
Computers, Electronics & High-Tech Industry	02394-6	10.00
Construction Industry	02398-9	Online
Drywallers	02402-1	7.00
Entertainment—Important 1040 Issues	02365-2	14.00
Entertainment—Music Industry	02364-4	9.00
Farm Hobby Losses		Online
Farming—Specific Income Issues & Farming Cooperative	02420-9	7.00
Furniture Manufacturing	02383-1	24.00
Garden Supplies	02426-8	8.50
Garment Contractors	02391-1	10.00
Garment Manufacturers	02378-4	12.00
Gas Retailers*		Online
General Livestock	02428-4	17.00
Grain Farmers	02359-8	34.00
Hardwood Timber Industry	02392-0	10.50
Independent Used Car Dealer	02371-7	21.00

TABLE 7.1 *(Continued)*

Guide	Stock No.	Price
The Laundromat Industry	02431-4	6.00
Lawsuits, Awards & Settlements	02437-3	9.50
Low-Income Housing	02421-7	29.00
Manufacturing Industry	02396-2	Online
Masonry & Concrete Industry	02400-4	Online
Ministers	02343-1	4.75
Mobile Food Vendors	02356-3	17.00
Mortuaries	02344-0	20.00
Net Operating Loss For Individuals	Out of Stock 02407-1	10.50
Oil and Gas Industry	02372-5	22.00
Partnerships*		Online
Passive Activity Losses	02354-7	28.00
Pizza Restaurants	02346-6	7.00
Placer Mining	02417-9	8.50
Poultry Industry*		Online
The Port Project	02360-1	17.00
Reforestation Industry	02361-0	17.00
Rehabilitation Tax Credit	02373-3	26.50
Restaurants and Bars	02355-5	10.50
Retail Gift Shop*		Online
Retail Liquor Industry	02389-0	9.50
Scrap Metal Industry	02408-0	9.00
Shareholder Loan		Online
Sports Franchises	02418-7	15.00
Swine Farm Industry*		Online
Taxicabs	02348-2	4.00
Tobacco Industry	02374-1	15.00
Tour Bus Industry	02390-3	4.75
Trucking Industry	02349-1	Online
Veterinary Medicine	02406-3	13.00
Wine Industry	02352-1	12.00

Advance payment is required, and some guides are not reprinted after the initial supply is exhausted.

Mail your order to: Superintendent of Documents
P.O. Box 371954
Pittsburgh, PA 15250-7954
Tel.: 202-512-1800
Fax: 202-512-2250

*New for 2003

was important to compare the type of services and the number of appointments to the income reported," and it provides a specific technique to calculate unreported tips.[21]

The Architects Guide gives a rule of thumb that architects "will generally be paid about 10 percent of the project cost for small jobs while for larger jobs, that may drop to 4 or 5 percent of the project cost." It points out that billings will generally be progressive rather than in lump-sum payments often tied to completion of various phases. It also notes that the plans "represent the only real leverage the architect has to secure payment of fees and, therefore, will normally have billed 80 to 90 percent of the fees by the start of the construction phase."[22]

The Attorneys Guide says, "The businesses with one person having the majority of internal control have the most audit potential, i.e., there is more opportunity to manipulate the books. . . . Furthermore, certain areas of attorney specialization are more productive than others. The personal injury area produces adjustments through the advanced client costs adjustment since, by nature of the specialty, significant client costs may be advanced prior to settlement. Criminal attorneys have more access to cash receipts than most other attorneys."[23] Accordingly, it is no surprise that attorneys are near the top of the IRS's audit hit list.

The Garment Manufacturers Guide focuses on problem areas such as inventory, write-downs, costing errors, improper purchase accruals, and unallowable reserves for sales discounts, returns, and allowances. Under the section "Related Entities," it says, "It is not uncommon for individuals to own interests in more than one garment manufacturing company. Sometimes these entities will have intercompany transactions or similar issues that require the examiner to open another examination."[24]

Under the "Contractors" section, it says, "A significant number of contractor returns have been spun off from examinations of a manufacturer's return, as potential unreported income cases." Further on it states that "cases can be developed using the canceled checks of the manufacturer under examination. Civil or criminal fraud penalties may be applicable and should be considered."[25]

The Bars & Restaurants Guide urges IRS auditors to "determine the number of seats in a restaurant, multiply that figure by how many times per day the seats are occupied, and multiply again by the average 'check per seat' to arrive at the average daily sales."[26] In a "probing first interview," the auditor will gather information about markup percentages and the cost of food and alcohol and then use indirect methods to ensure accuracy. The auditor may also obtain records of purchases from local wine and beer distributors.

Newest MSSP Guides

The MSSP guide for business consultants was released in March 2001. The more than 8.5 million people who are independent contractors or freelance workers should read this guide. An in-depth discussion of independent contractors appears earlier in this chapter.

Under "Audit Techniques," the Business Consultants' Guide reminds the tax auditor "to analyze the individual's answers to the interview, as well as the contract (written or oral) between the individual and his or her major client to see if an employee/employer relationship exists. The examiner will want to be alert to behavioral control, financial control and the relationship of the parties." The auditor is then prompted to ask such probing questions as "How often do you or your employees travel? How are reimbursed expenses run through your accounting records? Do your clients reimburse for meals and entertainment? How is the contract price determined? Who are your major clients? (Follow-up questions if you have only one major client)."[27]

The guide also attempts to provide some insight to examining auditors by pointing them in the direction of consultants who make little or no net income, or who are improperly writing off vacations disguised as business travel.

The IRS is worried about noncompliance by consultants, and that is why this guide was issued. The IRS states that the guide's main purpose is to keep the auditor focused on pertinent issues and to promote time efficiencies. An IRS spokesman went on to say that "the existence of the guide did not imply that the agency thought it has a significant problem with cheating by consultants."[28] Is this guy kidding, or what?

Recently a guide was issued covering Alternative Minimum Tax (AMT) for individuals. If you are one of the millions of taxpayers now subject to AMT, consult the guide for line-by-line guidance on the calculations involved on Form 6521 (Alternative Minimum Tax—Individuals), along with the various adjustments that go into the basic computation.[29] The most far-reaching MSSP guide to date is called *Partnerships* and was issued in 2003. If you operate as a partnership or LLC, all of the 330 pages contained in this guide are required reading. The guide starts with the formation of a partnership, ends with its dissolution, and covers everything in between. Included are capital contributions, distributions of cash and other property, allocations of income and losses, limitations on losses, and separate sections on real estate, bankruptcy, tax shelters, and family partnerships.

Will the MSSP snare more taxpayers into the audit net, or will the audit guides provide the right information for taxpayers to prepare their returns?

Coordinated Issue Papers

Similar to MSSP guides are Coordinated Issue Papers (CIP). Each of these papers focuses on a specific tax issue that may be relevant to one or more businesses. These tax issues may include meal allowances, employment contracts, and deductibility of illegal bribes and kickbacks—a total of about 80 papers. Each issue is examined in detail and explains how IRS auditors are to handle it. To help you better understand the audit process, check if your industry is mentioned and obtain a copy at www.irs.gov under "Businesses/More Topics."

TARGET: NONFILERS

An estimated 6 million people across the United States do not file any income tax returns whatsoever, down from the 9 to 10 million of about five years ago. About 64 percent of nonfilers are self-employed people who deal primarily in cash. They have been out of the system an average of four years, are in their peak earning years, and live affluently. On average, less than 25 percent of their total income is reported to the IRS by an employer, bank, or broker.

As a group, nonfilers account for almost $14 billion a year in lost revenue to the IRS and cost each of us at least $600 extra at tax time. The good news is that when it comes to the nonfiler, the IRS has for the most part proved itself to be rather trustworthy. (See also Chapter 11, Rule 2, and "How to Pay What You Owe," in Chapter 13.)

The IRS Approach for Bringing In Nonfilers

The IRS's overall thinking is that as many nonfilers as possible should be brought into the system not by threats but by cooperation. The IRS believes that once they take the first step, nonfilers will feel all the better for filing, since many are not really willful violators. It's just that they've been out of the tax collection loop for so long that they're afraid of the amounts they might owe.

The IRS has developed a nonfiler program based on this assumption. While taxpayers theoretically could be prosecuted for failing to file income tax returns, if they come forward under this program, the IRS promises

- Not to prosecute, but only to charge for back taxes and interest owed, and possibly penalties.
- To work out installment payments.

- To expand its "offer in compromise" terms, whereby the IRS settles for only a portion of back taxes owed, depending on the taxpayer's ability to pay.
- That the approximately 24 percent of nonfilers who are due refunds will get them if they come to their local IRS office to claim the money within three years after the due date of their tax return.

Catching Nonfilers

According to TRAC, one area of collection activity in 1999 and 2000 involved the issuance of Tax Delinquent Return Investigations (TDIs). A TDI signals the IRS's preliminary decision to investigate why no return was filed by a taxpayer who had income that was taxable. In 1992, there were 877,966 TDIs; in 1999, that number nearly doubled to 1.58 million. The IRS initiated an average of almost 2 million delinquency return investigations in 1999 and 2000 and disposed of an average of 1.6 million cases in 1999 and 2000, which is an 80 percent success rate. IRS officials have stated that this increase is a result of a policy decision to place more emphasis on tracking down nonfilers. It also helps that the IRS continues to receive billions of income reports from third-party payers such as employers and banks, which tip off the IRS as to who the delinquent filers are.

If you're a nonfiler and need some advice, see the next section.

Another often overlooked way to catch nonfilers is via Form 8300, submitted by financial institutions, as described earlier in this chapter. This document is used to report currency transactions over $10,000, and when this information is run through the IRS matching process, it has great potential to identify nonfilers and unreported income.[30]

What to Do If You're a Nonfiler

Nonfiler cases are often unique, simply because when a nonfiler walks into a tax professional's office, you never know what to expect. About 10 years ago a new client came to me with this story:

Mr. Frammer was a used-auto-parts dealer who also refurbished autos for resale. He worked out of a junkyard, was foreign born, and had come to the United States about 15 years before.

He had never filed an income tax return and sought my advice because he thought he was in trouble with the IRS. Mr. Frammer believed this was so because the previous year, a lawyer he knew had convinced him to set up a corporation so that he could limit his personal liability in selling used autos. Now the IRS was sending him notices that his corporate income tax return was past due. Incorporating had established a direct link between Mr. Frammer and IRS computers.

I filed the past-due return for him but then was curious. How could he have escaped detection for 15 years? He owned a business and he had eight children. The answer was easy.

Although Mr. and Mrs. Frammer had Social Security numbers, they never used them. They had no bank accounts, no charge cards, no bank loans, nothing that would put them within the scope of any type of third-party reporting whatsoever. His children's Social Security numbers were never used, since he didn't take them as dependents on a 1040 form.

Mr. Frammer maintained a business checking account through which he paid monthly overhead items such as telephone, electricity, and rent, but he paid all other personal and business expenses in cash. As far as the IRS was concerned, the Frammer family did not exist.

This scenario would be hard to duplicate today.

In another case, two nonfilers ended up surprisingly pleased; in the words of the IRS, they were permanently brought back into the fold.

A man and a woman, both professional lawyers, came into my office saying they hadn't filed income tax returns for the past three years and now were ready to do so. Using their tax data, I computed the balances owed and refund due. The couple were quite pleased when I told them that the second year resulted in a refund of $1,000, and in the first and third years, the balances due were only $2,500 for each year.

We filed the first two years immediately and the last year a month later. On the refund return, we instructed the IRS to carry the balance over to the following year. The reason we delayed the filing of the third year was to ensure that the tax return containing the $1,000 refund had already been processed into the IRS system. When we filed the last year, we remitted only $1,500 ($2,500 minus the $1,000 refund carried forward).

When the entire process was completed, I thought I'd never see this couple again. But they have been my clients ever since, and their returns are always filed on time.

If this sounds simple, it was because the clients were able to supply me with all the necessary information. With nonfilers this is generally not the case. Much information is usually missing, which too often serves as a great deterrent for the taxpayer. Nonfilers are often motivated to file again when they understand what is required:

- Go to a tax professional.
- The tax professional will contact your local IRS office and inform it that he or she has a case of a nonfiling taxpayer who wishes to file.
- The tax professional will explain that information for the past three (or whatever) years is missing or lost because of illness, divorce, natural disaster, etc.

- The revenue officer will probably cooperate by providing the professional with income data entered under the matching program from the IRS computer listed under the taxpayer's Social Security number. This would include W-2s; 1099s for miscellaneous, interest, and dividend income; and possibly information from 1098s showing mortgage interest paid by the taxpayer. Most important, the W-2 would show the amount of federal tax that was withheld each year.
- Next, the tax professional will reconstruct the 1040, enlisting the taxpayer's support to fill in information such as estimates of contributions, medical expenses, and other deductions. Revenue officers have been accepting reasonable estimates in cases like this.
- The entire process could take as little as a few weeks or as much as a few months, if items can't be found immediately.
- The IRS will add up to 25 percent in penalties plus interest to the balance due. That is to be expected. However, perhaps you will be one of the 25 percent of nonfilers who are due a refund.

The IRS continues to stress that nonfilers who do not come forward will be pursued to the point of criminal prosecution. All in all, the process of moving from being a nonfiler to a filer is not difficult. In my experience it is a great relief for taxpayers.

TARGET: TAX CHEATERS—OMISSION OF INCOME

Rise of Abusive Tax Shelters

Toward the end of the 1990s, the IRS believed it had conquered the power of abusive tax shelters, an effort that had severely weakened the examination function for at least 10 years. Well, the IRS did accomplish that, at least for individual tax shelters, but the ugly beast has raised its head again. This time corporations are the culprits.

American corporations, whose profits have been consistently increasing, are now paying less in taxes because of well-conceived tax shelters. According to the IRS, less than 70 cents of each dollar of profit reported to shareholders in 1998 was reported by companies as taxable income, down from 91 cents in 1991.[31]

According to Treasury Secretary Lawrence H. Summers, "Corporate tax shelters are our number one problem in enforcing the tax laws not just because they cost money, but because they breed disrespect for the tax system."[32] From a purely moral perspective, it appears that some of the largest companies have thrown their integrity out the window in their search for tax breaks that will enable them to hold on to greater profit. As discussed in Chapter 4, tax shelters are considered abusive because they are not intended to make a profit, as a solid investment would be, but are designed specifically to allow for huge write-offs that reduce the amount of tax due. Though corporate profits reported to the IRS were 252 percent higher in 1998, taxes rose just 191 percent. It is estimated that abusive corporate tax shelters cost the government more than $10 billion a year, and that's a conservative figure.[33]

The government and IRS officials are calling for new laws that would require early disclosure of tax shelters and provide for a penalty tax on the promoters and buyers of such shelters. Meanwhile, corporations are still taking aggressive postures in their ongoing attempts to increase profits, and the courts are allowing them to get away with it. In mid-2001, a federal appeals court ruled that United Parcel Service did not use a corporate shelter to avoid hundreds of millions of dollars in corporate income taxes. Another appeals court ruled in favor of Alliant Energy, concluding that it had not engaged in sham stock trading to avoid $100 million of taxes. Both judges held that the transactions had a business purpose, and combined with even the smallest prospect of profit or risk of loss, that was sufficient to render the transactions legitimate. With decisions like this, the IRS is facing an uphill battle to curb abusive corporate tax shelters.[34]

Offshore Tax Havens

The IRS has long suspected that foreign tax havens are a device for American taxpayers to avoid the reporting of at least $70 billion a year in personal taxable income. The IRS is now widening its inquiries into tax evasion that uses offshore banks. It has subpoenaed the credit card records of people with accounts in Antigua and Barbuda, the Bahamas, the Cayman Islands, Hong Kong, the Isle of Man, Liechtenstein, Luxembourg, and Switzerland. Based on the result of these subpoenas, the IRS now estimates that as many as two million Americans have been concealing their spending in these offshore locations.

Credit cards issued by these banks can be used anywhere in the world. After payment, there is no record of income or spending except from certain transaction reports, which are typically in the hands of those very same credit card companies.[35]

New Technology to Catch Cheaters

Besides checking for tax cheats using specific technology, top IRS officials have recently admitted that the Internet contains a lot of personal information about taxpayers that is useful to the IRS. IRS auditors are using search engines to verify such things as news stories about taxpayers being audited and to obtain specific industry practices and statistics to compare with information provided by businesses that are undergoing an audit. The emphasis is currently on business audits, but you can be sure the use of the Internet will soon be expanded to individual audits as well. Business owners should carefully review what information is available at their web sites that would prove useful to an IRS auditor.

TARGET: TAX DELINQUENTS AND TAX SCAM ARTISTS

Tax Delinquents Avoid Paying Tax Bills

Given the much publicized drop in IRS audits and collection activities, it appears that a growing number of tax cheats—individuals at high income levels and major corporations involved with abusive tax shelters (discussed earlier)—have established a new trend of tax delinquency. The IRS has stopped pursuing more than a million tax delinquents. In 2000 alone, the IRS wrote off $2.5 billion of old tax debts. The IRS Oversight Board insists that the IRS simply needs more money to fix its enforcement deficiencies. Several former IRS commissioners agree with the board and state that efforts need to be redirected from corporate to individual tax avoidance.[36] The first problem is insufficient IRS tax auditors to weed out the delinquents. The second is IRS tax collectors allegedly more worried about losing their jobs than going after known delinquents.

The situation has resulted in billions of dollars of unpaid taxes. In the past, the IRS typically collected what it could from a taxpayer, and when the statute of limitations on collecting the debt was near, revenue officers would choose from its battery of weapons—liens, levies, or seizures to further collect on what was owed. With RRA '98, the IRS is supposed to negotiate all terms of the tax collection agreement up front. "But what has been occurring is, if a taxpayer cannot agree to pay in full, collectors apply the label 'currently noncollectible,' which effectively closes the case."[37] Since the performance of revenue officers is no longer judged by the amount of penalties they collect (although the IRS has consistently denied use of quotas), but by the efficiency with which they close cases, you can see the problem.

Furthermore, if a taxpayer does not agree to an extension of the statute of limitations, or if regular payments would not cover 100 percent of the debt even with a five-year extension beyond the limitation on collecting the back taxes owed, the IRS is refusing to accept an installment agreement, and it will suspend its collection efforts.[38] Then the taxpayer simply waits until the period of payment expires and—voilà!—no tax is paid. If the taxpayer attracts no undue attention by continuing to file tax returns and shows no evidence of an increase in income, there is minimal chance that his case will be revived in the time allotted for its settlement.

Tax Scam Artists

The biggest source of tax dollars being left unpaid comes from thousands of cases of withheld taxes owed by small businesses. Most critics of the IRS cannot believe that the agency has not stepped up its campaign to close down businesses that have brazenly declared that they have stopped deducting withholding taxes from their employees' wages, or other organizations that have publicly announced that they will no longer file tax returns or pay any income tax.

These businesses claim that they are privy to a secret that allows them not to withhold taxes from your wages. I assure you that there is no such secret. Still other scams promise a special refund to Afro-Americans as reparation for slavery, delivery of an authenticated document proving that all income taxes are voluntary, or help in preparing a claim for a refund of Social Security taxes.[39]

As the IRS completes its training and adds new employees, seizures of property and all the rest of collection activity will resume, along with renewed attention to the tax scam artists.

8

How to Completely Avoid an Audit

Can your tax returns slide through IRS computers and past IRS scrutiny? It is possible, and it's also uncomplicated. You simply must know the correct way to approach the situation. In this chapter you are going to learn how to avoid an audit through a set of clearly defined actions that apply to all taxpayers.

First a word on audit rates and how the IRS plays with them.

DON'T FEAR AUDIT STATISTICS

The IRS selects its audits from 12 or so categories, including returns filed by individuals, corporations, and small businesses, as well as estate and gift tax returns. Individual and corporate returns typically receive the most media attention, as does the overall audit rate.

During most of its existence, the IRS audit rate for individual tax returns hovered between 1 and 2 percent. This may seem minuscule, but it isn't, especially if you take into account that currently 127 million personal returns are filed annually. Between 1980 and 1990, though, the audit rate for individual tax returns dropped rather steadily, from 1.77 percent, or 1.6 million individual returns, to 0.8 percent, or 883,140 individual returns.[1]

As of 1994, however, all of this changed because the IRS engaged in some substantial historical revisionism, as reported in the IRS 1993 Annual Report. Here's the significance of what was done:

All audit statistics were amended retroactively to include the service centers' correspondence audits. This increased the overall number of returns that the IRS claimed it audited. Imagine how this affects audit figures across the board, and think of how taxpayers, tax professionals, financial writers, and analysts have reacted. Sure does make the IRS look better than ever. Every year since 1993, the IRS has increased its reliance on the use of correspondence audits. In 2001, 72 percent of individual tax examinations were correspondence audits done at the service centers, and only 28 percent were carried out by revenue agents and tax auditors.

AUDITS AT AN ALL-TIME LOW

There continues to be a steady decline in the audit rate for both individual and all returns. For individuals, the audit rate dropped from 1.57 percent in 1988 to 0.57 percent in 2001. Similarly, the audit rate for all returns declined from 1.26 percent in 1988 to 0.48 percent in 2001.[2]

The audit rate for individuals is now 45 percent below what it was 10 years ago, a decrease of 36 percent just from 1999 to 2001. There also appears to be a change in the IRS's focus over time. Statistics show that from 1988 to 2000, audit rates for the poor increased by a third, from 1.03 to 1.36 percent, while falling 94 percent for the wealthier Americans, from 11.4 to 0.7 percent.[3] Have audit rates really shifted from individuals with incomes of $100,000 and over to those earning less than $25,000? One reason for this might be that higher-income returns, especially over $200,000, have increased dramatically.

The IRS has said that the only reason for the audit rates focusing on the working poor while the rate for wealthy taxpayers has declined was a mandate from the White House and Congress to closely monitor the Earned Income Credit. But this, too, may be questionable, since most of these audits are correspondence audits sent through the mail. And remember that all audits have declined across the board. Some reasons are as follows: There's been a decline in the IRS staff, some purely by attrition, some by the shift of examination and collection people to customer service areas. The current IRS staff numbers about 83,000, a drop of 28 percent from 1990, when that number was over 116,000. That means fewer IRS examiners to conduct audits for increasing numbers of tax returns—227 million in 2002, compared to 201 million in 1990, a 13 percent increase. Furthermore, according to the Transactional Records Clearing House (TRAC), the IRS continues to rely on data from TCMP audits that are at least 12 years old on which to base its current audit selection. In so doing, the IRS ignores such recent phenomena as companies offering their employees stock options instead of cash, and taxpayers deducting interest on home equity loans and margin debt on stock purchases, which reduces the effectiveness of using TCMP data for discovering unreported income.

For 2000, IRS auditors spent an average of 16 percent less time per case. Similarly, individuals with income over $100,000 incurred 39 percent fewer audits compared to two years prior.

For 1999, fewer than 1 in 300 individual returns underwent a face-to-face audit with a revenue agent in the field or a tax auditor at an IRS district office, and in 2001, the chances of audit were one in 628.

The IRS does continue to get the biggest bang for its bucks with correspondence audits. When the service centers' correspondence audits are included in the audit selection, the audit rate more than doubles, which means that approximately one out of 240 individual returns will probably be audited either through the mail or face-to-face.

Despite the steady decline in audit figures, the IRS still generates about $3.64 billion a year in additional taxes and penalties on individual returns.[4]

"LIVE" AUDITS ARE AIMED AT CORPORATIONS

The IRS had traditionally aimed its resources at corporate returns, those with the highest dollar potential. Corporations with $250 million or more in assets have consistently been hit the hardest. In 1999, the IRS examined more than 34 percent of these; through 2002, this group continues to show the highest percentage of returns audited, despite the fact that the percentage of all corporations audited shows a steady decline. By comparison, the highest audit rate ever for individual returns was 2.3 percent in 1975.[5]

As Table 8.1 shows, the audit rate for small corporations ($1 million to $5 million) was almost 5 percent in 1999 but has dropped dramatically in 2002 to 2.08 percent. In fact, the audit rate for all corporations has dropped consistently over the past four years. This much-publicized drop, which currently also holds true for individual and all returns, can be attributed to RRA '98 and its focus on customer service. According to TRAC, in recent years, personnel assigned to the phones in a taxpayer services capacity rose 27 percent. Fewer auditors and revenue officers means fewer people left to examine returns and collect taxes owed.

But for individual returns, particularly those of the self-employed, audit risk is a function not only of income level but also of the type of return filed. Self-employed taxpayers who own small businesses and report their income on Form 1040, Schedule C, have consistently attracted greater IRS attention.

Each year since 1999, the IRS has maintained its audit focus on the under-$25,000 group of "C filers," whereas the audit rate for the over-$100,000 group has experienced a 40 percent decrease (see Table 8.1). This could be caused by the IRS emphasis on returns that contain both the Earned Income Credit and a small amount of Schedule C net income or, possibly, the under-$25,000 group produces high DIF scores.

Audit rates for partnerships, S corporations, and small C corporations, and what they tell taxpayers, are discussed later in this chapter.

TABLE 8.1 Audit Percentages

	Percent Audited			
Corporations' Balance Sheet Assets	1999	2000	2001	2002
$1–5 million	4.86	2.96	2.04	2.08
$5–10 million	10.09	6.99	5.33	4.63
$10–50 million	14.75	11.67	9.66	7.80
$50–100 million	16.05	14.69	12.32	10.74
$100–250 million	18.51	17.42	17.55	15.98
$250 million and over	34.55	31.41	32.09	34.37

	Percent Audited			
Individuals' Income as Shown on 1040	1999	2000	2001	2002
TPI under $25,000	1.18	.55	.40	.64
$25,000–$50,000	.36	.21	.22	.23
$50,000–$100,000	.37	.23	.23	.28
$100,000 and over	1.15	.84	.69	.75

	Percent Audited			
Income of Taxpayers Filing Schedule C	1999	2000	2001	2002
All filers	2.03	1.55	1.61	1.72
Under $25,000	2.69	2.43	2.72	2.67
$25,000–$100,000	1.30	.93	1.02	1.18
Over $100,000	2.40	1.48	1.20	1.45

Source: Advance draft of the IRS 2000 Data Book, Table 10, and the TRAC web site, www.trac.syr.edu/tracirs/.

AUDITS OF ESTATE AND GIFT TAX RETURNS

The IRS reports that cheating on estate tax returns is more prevalent than on individual tax returns. It is estimated that the shortfall from unreported income on estate tax returns exceeds $4 billion annually and that some of the biggest offenders are estates valued at $20 million or more. A study also found that underreporting increases if an attorney prepares the estate return. I agree that pressure from the client to cheat increases when a tax professional is on the job, because a client is usually a beneficiary of the estate.

To identify potential audit candidates, the IRS uses the same technique it uses for individual returns, the DIF score, Discriminate Information Function (see Chapter 3). The chance of audit increases when large discounts are taken for family-owned businesses, documents are sloppy, or when property appraisals look skimpy.

In 2001, 122,412 estate tax returns were filed, of which 7,151 were audited (5.8 percent). This is a much higher audit rate than that for individual returns. Included were 5,938 filings for estates valued at $5 million or more, of which 1,545 were audited (a lofty 27 percent). All of the audited estate tax returns owed additional tax amounting to a little over $1.4 billion, an overall average of $200,264 per return. However, $976 million (68 percent) of the $1.4 billion came from the 1,545 estates valued at $5 million or more, an average of $631,800. So, only 22 percent of the audited returns produced 68 percent of the additional tax recommended. In 2001, 303,800 gift tax returns were filed, of which only 1,899 were audited (0.63 percent). The audited returns owed a whopping $405 million in additional tax, an average of $213,257 per return.[6]

You would think that the IRS would devote more time and manpower to auditing estate and gift tax returns, but it has not done so. There are ways to minimize your audit risk, no matter what schedule you file, how much you earn, or even if you are on the IRS underground-economy hit list. Part of the answer comes from taking the proper preventive measures.

HOW TO PREVENT AUDIT PROBLEMS BEFORE THEY OCCUR

The first contact between your 1040 and the IRS is a computer. You can't reason with computers, so long before you get ready to fill out your 1040 or business tax return, there are certain steps to take so that your return is prepped to escape selection by the IRS's first technology go-around. Preventive medicine up front, or "covering your books" (CYB), can help you avoid an audit. Here's a rundown of the most effective measures for avoiding an audit and for reducing its scope if you are selected.

1. Make sure that any third-party income and reports agree with your records. Verify that

- W-2s from all employers match your declared salary.
- Interest and dividend reports from your banks and securities firms match the actual interest and dividends you have received and entered on your return.
- Mortgage interest statements from your bank or lender match your mortgage interest deduction.
- Income from 1099 forms matches the appropriate income items on your return.
- If you discover an error on any of these forms, you should contact the issuer and request a corrected version immediately. If possible, try to get the information corrected before the IRS receives the incorrect version.

2. Make sure you have selected the correct forms and schedules to fill out. Ask yourself these questions: Do the forms apply? Am I stretching the situation? Are there other credits that I am entitled to whose forms I haven't included but need to?

3. Make sure you have recorded all payments on your return. This is especially important for taxpayers who make estimated payments during the year.

4. Keep track of bank deposits so that all items will be easy to trace. Write the source of the check directly on each deposit slip, especially transfers between accounts, so that these are not inadvertently counted as income. The first things tax auditors request are your checking, savings, and investment accounts. They then proceed to do a total cash receipts analysis, comparing the total to the gross income shown on your tax return. By marking every deposit slip, you know where to look for further documentation to support your notation, and the auditor will have the trail in front of him or her for the source of unusual nontaxable receipts such as insurance recoveries, loans, gifts, and inheritances. It's not that much work.

Deposits into personal checking or savings accounts usually consist of one or two items, and most small- to medium-size businesses deposit a manageable number of checks on a daily basis. You would be amazed at how forgetful people can be regarding large receipts after two or three years have passed. You also need to keep copies of incoming checks that are unusual or very large.

5. Always keep your checking and savings accounts free of irregularities. Be sure you can explain large bank deposits and increases (especially sudden ones) in your net worth. At a minimum, the auditor will ask for verification of information on your return that is derived from an institutional account, including every item of interest income, dividend income, and capital gains and losses.

I recently heard about an audit covering a three-year period where the taxpayer, an attorney, had great difficulty recalling the source of two large checks: a $14,000 inheritance received from the estate of an aunt, and $28,000 from the sale of her mother's condo, subsequently managed by her. Because this information was not available right away, the revenue agent scheduled another audit day so that these items and a few others could be resolved. During that extra day, the auditor uncovered travel deductions totaling more than $10,000 that could not be supported and a $3,000 payment for college tuition included in charitable deductions. The taxpayer was charged an additional $5,000 in taxes, which could have been avoided if her records had been in better shape.

Warning: If you have unreported income of more than 25 percent of your adjusted gross income, the auditor may turn your case over to CID. If you suspect this may occur, do not provide any leads to the auditor regarding the sources of unexplained deposits. The burden of proof is on the IRS.

6. Keep business and personal bank accounts separate. Many taxpayers, especially those with sideline businesses, do not open a separate business checking account. This is a mistake. A business account should be the depository for all business receipts and disbursements. Although there is no prohibition against paying for items that are strictly personal, they should be charged to your loan or drawing account as personal items. If you use your business account to pay for personal items on a consistent basis, an auditor will suspect that other personal items have been inadvertently, or purposely, charged to business categories. This could lead to an expanded audit, which can easily be avoided. Although it may take some discipline, the reward for keeping your business account strictly business will be to dramatically eliminate hassles in case of an audit.

7. If you know that you're going to take a business deduction, pay for it by check. Although taxpayers can pay for these things in cash, why arouse the suspicions of an auditor who is going to ask you to prove the source of all that cash? Also, it is wiser to pay for routine personal items such as bills for electricity, telephone, rent, and clothing with a check or credit cards. If these payments do not appear, the auditor assumes you used cash to pay for them and you've opened yourself up to an expanded audit.

HOW LONG SHOULD TAXPAYERS KEEP RECORDS?

Generally the IRS has only three years from the date you filed to come after you for extra tax. These are the exceptions:

*   If your return omits more than 25 percent of your income, the IRS has six years to audit you.
*   If you file a false and fraudulent return with intent to evade tax, there is no time limit on your being audited.

However, from a practical viewpoint, this is how long I recommend that you hold on to your records:

Business Records

> Four years
> > Sales invoices
> > Purchases and expense bills
> > Routine office correspondence

Six years
     Bank statements and canceled checks
     Accounting journals and books

Ten years
     Payroll tax returns
     Business income tax returns

Personal Records

Four years
     Receipts, bills, and canceled checks that support all deductions on Form 1040
     Records that support receipts of income (e.g., 1099s and K-1's)

Until four years after an asset is sold
     Brokerage records showing purchases or sales of investments
     Records relating to IRA contributions and withdrawals; home ownership (buying and selling), including home office depreciation and deductions; receipts for improvements, repairs, appliances, and landscaping
     For multiple home sales, keep records including Form 2119 (Sale of Your Home) for all homes until four years after the last home is sold

Six years
     Bank statements and canceled checks

Forever
     Personal income tax returns and W-2 forms

For more information, check out IRS Publication 552, "Recordkeeping for Individuals," available at the IRS web site, www.irs.gov.

HOW TO COMPLETELY AVOID AN AUDIT

The majority of taxpayers believe that the way to reduce taxable income safely is to exaggerate deductions. Wrong! Increased deductions can act as triggers that raise a taxpayer's risk for an audit.

The most important and essential step you can take to make yourself audit-proof, and the central theme of this chapter, is to remove as much information as possible from your 1040 to another place where the chances of audit are greatly diminished.

Wage earners receive their earnings primarily from W-2 income. If, in addition, they report only interest and dividend income and follow the recommendations throughout this book, they will successfully place themselves in a low-audit-risk category because by definition they are not on any of the IRS hit lists.

However, self-employed people are generally open to greater audit risk. If this group is to become audit-proof, taxpayers must choose a business entity that allows them other reporting options than, for example, a Schedule C, used by a sole proprietorship. The most common choices of business entities available are an S corporation, a partnership, a C corporation, and a limited liability company.

Before we discuss the best form of business entity to choose, however, I would like you to review Tables 8.2 and 8.3 at the end of this chapter. They compare tax and legal ramifications for five of the most common types of business organizations: sole proprietorship, partnership, limited liability company, S corporation, and C corporation. Pick out several items that are most relevant to your own operations. This should give you a good head start in deciding which business form will offer you the most favorable tax position. Then read the discussion on S corporations, partnerships, and limited liability companies to see why these are the most preferred way of doing business for small to medium businesses; larger businesses that have many owners and greater potential liability typically become C corporations.

SMALL BUSINESS CORPORATIONS (S CORPORATIONS)

An S corporation is an organization that offers its owner the advantages of a corporation along with the favorable tax treatment of the sole proprietorship or partnership.

First introduced in 1958, the S corporation's original intention was to give mom-and-pop operations the ability to gain the advantages of incorporation (limited liability, perpetual life) while enabling them to avoid the double taxation of a corporation. Then the TRA '86 repealed the long-standing doctrine that a C corporation would have only one tax to be paid by its shareholders when it distributes property in a complete liquidation of the corporation. The new law imposed a double tax on a liquidating sale and distribution of assets (one tax upon the corporation and a second on its shareholders) for C corporations but not for S corporations. From that time, C corporations flocked to S status as a way to ensure that only one tax would be imposed on their shareholders.

For many years, I've observed that, from a tax perspective, the S corporation is the best because it offers the many advantages of a corporation along with the favorable tax treatment afforded the sole proprietorship, partnership, or limited liability company.

Avoiding an Audit by Setting Up an S Corporation

You are a prime candidate to be an S corporation if you

- Do not have to infuse large sums of capital into your business.
- Are a service business with modest requirements for investment in equipment.
- Invest in real estate or other rapidly appreciating assets.
- Expect to incur losses in the first year or two of operations.

Information No One Dares Tell Taxpayers: What They Can Gain by Operating an S Corporation

- The annual net income or loss of an S corporation passes through to each shareholder's 1040 on one line, which appears on Schedule E. Accordingly, no income or expense detail shows up on the 1040. You immediately avoid all the targets, triggers, and special programs that the IRS currently has in place to bring attention to taxpayers who file Schedule Cs.
- There is no disclosure of home office expenses. Although S corporations are subject to the rules regarding home office expenses, there is no special IRS form designed for an S corporation to list them. By contrast, a sole proprietor who operates out of a home office and files a 1040 must file Form 8829 along with Schedule C. You already know that Form 8829 is an audit trigger. S corporations report expenses incurred in home office operations on the 1120S (U.S. Income Tax Return for an S Corporation). The appropriate allocations are combined with all other expenses and placed on their appropriate lines.
- The IRS does a good job of matching personal income, but corporate income reporting requirements are entirely different. If a payment for goods purchased or services performed is made to a corporation, the entity making the payment is not legally required to file a 1099-MISC form reporting the payment. A major exception is for payments made to any entity that performs legal services. Accordingly, when the IRS uses 1099s to audit independent contractors, you can avoid all this as an S corporation.
- Chances are that expenses that are typical audit triggers (travel, entertainment, automobile) will receive less attention on an S corporation simply because the audit rate for S corporations is con-

siderably lower than for individuals. (See Table 8.3 at the end of this chapter.)

- There has never been a better time to own a small corporation because the IRS audit function is paying the least attention to small corporations, partnerships, and LLCs. Currently, the potential for the IRS to extract tax dollars through the audit process is immeasurably greater with large corporations because of the Coordinated Examination Program (CEP), which focuses on auditing the largest corporate taxpayers in the country. But look what's happening to the rest of the business population. The lowest percentages of business returns audited are for partnerships[7], S corporations, and small C corporations. For 2001, the percentage of S corporations being audited declined to 0.39 percent, involving only 11,646 returns out of 3,022,589 filed. For the same year, partnerships had an audit rate of 0.26 percent and C corporations (with assets under $250,000) had the lowest audit rate, at 0.24 percent.[8] (See Table 8.3.)

- By controlling the amount of salary you take out of an S corporation, you can substantially reduce FICA taxes. For example, an S corporation with one owner-employee has a net income before salary of $50,000. If the owner takes a $50,000 salary reportable on a W-2, the combined FICA taxes for the corporation and employee will be 15.3 percent, or $7,650. But if the owner takes a reasonable salary of $30,000, the fica taxes will be only $4,590, a savings of $3,060 to the corporation. The remaining corporate net income of $20,000 ($50,000 minus $30,000) is passed through to the owner on a K-1 form. As a result, his personal income tax remains unchanged.

- Owners of an S corporation are immune to double tax on an audit. If a C corporation is undergoing an audit, and travel, entertainment, or auto deductions are disallowed because they were found to be personal, the IRS will assess a tax at both corporate and shareholder levels (i.e., the corporation will be charged one tax on the disallowed expense, and a second tax will be assessed upon the individual shareholder). In an S corporation, disallowed business expenses pass through to the 1040 and become taxable income to the recipients. But in this case, the IRS can levy only one tax—at the shareholder level. It is my belief that this inability to double-tax an S corporation is a major reason why the audit rate is so low on S corporations.

- There are some real advantages for S corporations that expect to incur losses in the first few years of operation. A new business usually experiences hard times initially. If you expect to incur losses in the first three months of operation, the best time to apply for or elect S corporation status would be the last three months of the calendar year. (S corporations must use the December 31 calendar year-end. There are a few exceptions but they are rarely granted.) In this way, losses pass through to the shareholders in the current year and shelter income from other sources. This is a common scenario for a taxpayer who was an employee for the first nine months of the year, and then incorporates as an S corporation, using his losses to shelter W-2 earnings.

- It is easier for the owners of an S corporation to sell the business because, unlike a C corporation, there is no corporate-level tax when the assets are sold. Since most buyers are interested only in the assets, not a corporation's potential liabilities, this makes for a preferred sale.

Requirements for an S Corporation

- To have only individuals, estates, qualified pension and profit-sharing plans, and certain types of trusts used in estate planning as shareholders; no partnerships, corporations, or nonresident aliens.
- To have no more than 75 shareholders. This facilitates ownership in an S corporation by family members, employees, venture capitalists, and others.
- To have one class of stock.
- To be a "domestic corporation" created or organized pursuant to federal and state laws.

A corporation that decides to elect S status again, after not being one, can do so immediately, without the previous five-year waiting period.

An S corporation can also own 80 percent or more of a C corporation as well as become an owner of other kinds of business entities, including wholly owned S corporation subsidiaries. *Note:* The subsidiary does not have to file its own corporate tax return but can file a combined return with its parent S corporation. In other words, the parent S corporation can own a "qualified subchapter S subsidiary" that will not be treated as a separate corporation for tax purposes. This opens up the field tremendously for S corporation owners to place separate operations in subsidiary companies with significant tax advantages to boot.

New laws are constantly changing to make it more beneficial than ever to become an S corporation. An S corporation is not only more attractive for investment purposes, it also offers greater estate-planning opportunities to reduce estate taxes. This is not the right time to switch out of S corporation status.

Steps to Setting Up an S Corporation

1. Incorporate. Several choices are available. If you choose to use an attorney, the fees range from $600 to $1,000 depending on the size and location of the law firm. A second alternative allows you to incorporate yourself. The department of state in your home state will provide you with the required forms and fee schedule. Overall costs for this type of incorporation are approximately $400. For those who want a quick and more commercial route (without paying attorney's fees), there are incorporation services. At a very modest price, they offer step-by-step instructions and provide everything you need to know about legal aspects of forming your own corporation in any state of your choosing. (You can usually find these in the classified section of your Sunday newspaper.)

2. Either you or your tax professional can obtain a federal identification number by calling the IRS toll-free at 1-866-816-2065 during normal business hours. Or you can go to the IRS web site at www.irs.gov and obtain your new identification number immediately.

3. File Form 2553 (Election by a Small Business Corporation) with the IRS. Generally you must send in the S election within two months and 15 days after commencing operations. For existing C corporations, the election must be filed no later than two months and 15 days after the elected year has begun. For example, if you commence operations in 2004, the election deadline is March 15, 2004.

Once your papers are in order you should send Form 2553 to your IRS service center by certified mail, return receipt requested. This is the best proof of mailing acceptable by the IRS, although you can also use Federal Express, United Parcel Service, Airborne Express, and DHL Worldwide Express. It is important to file as early as possible to avoid missing the deadline and to avoid other hassles and delays.

In a recent year, 46,000 businesses could not file their Form 1120S (S corporation tax return) because the IRS did not have their S elections on file. Of these, 9,000 were processed as regular C corporations even after the taxpayers sent in proper verification that their S elections were filed.[9]

YOUR TAX-SAVING STRATEGY

These days, state and local taxes take a significant chunk of tax dollars. Therefore, for tax-planning purposes, all taxpayers, even S corporations, must be concerned about taxation at the state and local levels.

Currently, at least 40 states recognize some form of S corporation status. New York State imposes an annual fee of $100 for S corporations, while Florida doesn't impose any. California and Illinois impose a 1.5 percent corporate tax rate on an S corporation's taxable income, but these rates are considerably less than the regular rates for non–S corporations. In participating states, all the advantages that accrue to S corporations at the federal level are also recognized on the state and local levels.

New York City does not recognize S corporation status. Accordingly, the tax-planning opportunities for S corporations are limited within this jurisdiction. The optimum planning for states and localities that impose regular corporate rates is to reduce corporate net income of the S corporation to zero by increasing the salaries to the owners-employees whenever it is reasonable and proper. This results in minimal net corporate income subject to the regular corporate tax rates, and the increased salary is simply subject to individual income tax. If at all possible, try to locate the business in an area where the S election is available at the state and local levels of taxation so that you can receive maximum benefits.

However, the geographical location of your S corporation is just one part of your overall tax planning. Local personal income tax and sales tax are other parts of the tax planning puzzle. Alaska, Florida, Nevada, South Dakota, Texas, Washington, and Wyoming have no personal income tax, while Alaska, Delaware, Montana, New Hampshire, and Oregon have no sales tax.

Timing Loopholes of an S Election

Remember those myriad loopholes caused by our complex tax laws? Well, there are several that work to benefit owners of S corporations.

Let's say that you inadvertently let the 2½-month period pass, did not file the S election, and just made up your mind to actively operate as an S corporation. For the initial year of the corporation's existence *only*, the 2½-month period does not start until the earliest of the following:

- Date the corporation first had shareholders.
- Date the corporation first had assets.
- Date the corporation began doing business.

Therefore, to still elect S status, place a date that accurately represents the actual starting date of the corporation in Item H on Form 2553.

Let's say you recently incorporated and started doing business as a C corporation more than 2½ months ago. Generally, that means you are precluded from taking advantage of the first loophole unless you follow certain explicit instructions in Revenue Procedure 97-40, which can be obtained from the IRS. But what you can do is close off your C corporation year immediately and elect S status for the remainder of the year.

For example, the business was incorporated and started on January 5, 2003, and now, on May 10, 2003, you want S status. File the 2003 S election immediately and simply indicate in your S election, Form 2553, Item C, that the election is to be effective for the tax year beginning March 1, 2003. You will be able to operate as an S corporation beginning March 1, 2003, because you are filing within the first 2½ months of the new, short year, which began March 1, 2003. The only disadvantage to this ploy is that you must file a C corporation tax return for the short period from January 5, 2003, to February 28, 2003.

YOUR TAX-SAVING STRATEGY

As a new corporation, try to maximize the amount of C corporation short-year expenses as start-up expenses that can be amortized later on in S corporation years. Losses incurred while you are a C corporation will remain frozen as long as you are an S corporation.

Early Stage Loopholes in the S Corporation

Depreciation of Assets

New corporations usually purchase furniture and equipment at the outset. Under Section 179 of the Internal Revenue Code (see Chapter 7), you can elect to depreciate up to $100,000 of business furniture and equipment purchased anytime in 2003. Therefore, even if your initial S corporation year is but a few weeks in the current year, you can deduct the full Section 179 depreciation if the assets are purchased within that period.

YOUR TAX-SAVING STRATEGY

Section 179 deductions cannot reduce your taxable income below zero. If the S corporation's net income is approaching zero, utilize only the amount that you need to reach zero income. Or you can delay your asset purchases until the following year, when presumably there will be greater income to be offset with this deduction.

Loopholes in Reporting Income or Losses for an S Corporation

Shifting Losses

For S corporations, there is a unique way of shifting losses to a desired tax year. This brings the element of basis into play. Basis is a dollar amount that represents the cost of a taxpayer's investment in an entity. It can be adjusted upward or downward. S corporation losses can be used only by shareholders who have sufficient basis in the stock. If you need the losses in 2003, lend the corporation sufficient money to cover your share of the losses. If 2004 is the year you can make better use of the losses, make no additional loans until 2004. If need be, distribute loans to yourself before the end of 2003 so that your basis is minimized.

If you personally guarantee loans made to an S corporation, your basis is not increased. Therefore, borrow the money personally, and lend the proceeds to the S corporation. This will enable you to take greater losses if they become available. The key point is, S corporations provide many opportunities for the owner to handle losses.

YOUR TAX-SAVING STRATEGY
If you own two S corporations and one loses money and the other makes money, you should restructure them as a parent and a subsidiary and file a combined return. In this way, the loss of one corporation offsets the profit of the other, and you do not have to worry that the corporation with the loss does not have sufficient basis, as discussed above.

S Corporations: Now and Future

For the past 10 years the IRS has been giving the public a consistent message about S corporations: "S elections and S status are cumbersome and fraught with dangers. If you are a small business person, you will be better off filing as a sole proprietor on Schedule C." This is simply not true. The IRS is pushing this line because it can more easily watch over the activities of small businesses using Schedule Cs.

But in reality, there is a clear trend whereby existing laws and requirements pertaining to S corporations are consistently making it easier and wiser to choose this form of tax entity. For example, distributions of S corporation earnings are not and have never been subject to FICA or Medicare tax.

In 1997, the IRS issued Revenue Ruling 94–43, which frees up S corporations to be partners in partnerships. Even the Tax Act of 2001 has aided S corporations by permitting S corporation shareholders, partners in partnerships, and sole proprietors to borrow money from their retirement plans, beginning in 2002. Generally, an individual will be able to borrow $50,000 or half the value of the individual's vested interest in the plan, whichever is less. Loans for these classes of taxpayers were previously prohibited.

True, the top personal tax rate is 35 percent, which is something S corporation owners should keep in mind, because earnings from S corporations (unlike C corporations) must be included in your personal income, which could land you in a higher tax bracket. Does this mean that S corporations will flock to revoke their S elections in order to take advantage of lower C corporate tax rates? I would recommend against this course of action for several reasons.

First, for taxpayers who own S corporations with modest earnings, taxable income up to $174,700 on a joint return (up to $143,500 if single) is still taxed at 28 percent or less.

Second, you may be subject to the built-in gains tax if you revoke your S election and later decide to reelect to become an S corporation. This is a kind of corporate-level tax on appreciation of assets held by a former C corporation (such as merchandise inventory and real estate); it is imposed as these assets are disposed of during the first 10 years after you become an S corporation.

S corporations are more available and enticing than ever before, and the advantages being granted to S corporations are being accelerated on a regular basis.

LIMITED LIABILITY COMPANIES AND PARTNERSHIPS

Another type of entity, called a limited liability company (LLC), has emerged in the past few years. Each state now has an LLC statute.

An LLC combines two of the most important attributes that are important to business owners: pass-through taxation, where annual net income or losses pass through each shareholder's 1040 on one line, on Schedule E; and limited liability for business debts. Although these attributes are mentioned in this chapter in discussions of corporations and partnerships, for some types of businesses, setting up an LLC is more suitable. Here are some reasons why.

- Whereas an S corporation must allocate income or losses in proportion to stock ownership, in an LLC agreement you can vary the sharing percentages of income and losses and not have to worry about being subject to undue scrutiny by the IRS. An LLC can even allocate start-up losses to investors in order to attract capital.
- An LLC may have foreign investors, while an S corporation cannot.
- Most states allow single-member LLCs whereby the net income or loss of the business passes through to the owner's 1040 and there is no requirement for filing a business return.
- Separate LLCs can be created in each state in which you do business. You do not have to disclose operations in other states to the in-state tax authorities.

Furthermore, in a partnership, investors ordinarily become limited partners so that they are liable only for the amount of their investments. Because of this, they cannot take part in the active running of the business, which is left to the general partners, who are liable for all debts of the partnership. Under an LLP, all members can take an active part in the day-to-day operations of the partnership and not be subject to unlimited liability for the debts of the partnership.

In most respects, LLC members are treated for tax purposes like general partners and S corporation shareholders. For example, fringe benefits such as health insurance and group-term life insurance are generally not deductible. Additionally, LLC owners and general partners are at a disadvantage in that they are subject to self-employment tax (15.3 percent on the first $87,000 of earnings and 2.9 percent over that amount).

The trickiest part of forming an LLC or LLP is to make sure that the IRS does not classify the entity as a regular corporation, which would stop you from having a pass-through entity. To begin with, you must follow the guidelines of the LLC statutes in your state. Next, the operating agreement must contain everything that any corporate agreement would contain plus other sections that are specifically designed for an LLC agreement.

An LLC should use Form 1065 (U.S. Partnership Return of Income) to meet its annual filing requirements with the IRS. It is important to work with an attorney who is knowledgeable in this area to set up the LLC operating agreement so that it conforms with federal and state regulations.*

PARTNERSHIPS

A partnership is a good alternative to an S corporation.

This discussion focuses on only those general partnerships in which each partner is responsible for his or her share of partnership debts. It does not include a limited partnership, which is subject to its own rules and regulations beyond the scope of this discussion. (See also limited liability companies and partnerships, discussed earlier.)

Advantages of a Partnership

- A partnership is easier to create than an S corporation. Two or more people just agree to be in business together. This union is made evident by a written agreement best prepared by an attorney.

---

*Defined in the IR Code Section 7701-2(a)(1), and IRS Revenue Procedure 95–10.

- As with S corporations, a partnership has no double tax. Net income and other separately stated income and expense items, such as capital gains and contributions, are passed through to each partner via a K-1 form.
- If the partnership later decides to incorporate, the transfer will be tax-free as long as any property that is transferred to the corporation is exchanged for at least 80 percent of the corporate stock.
- It may be easier to obtain credit because one partner may provide expertise and additional net worth that could be used to guarantee partnership liabilities.
- Income or losses are allocated according to the partnership agreement, but the agreement can take into account the business efforts made by each partner. This means income can be allocated by a method that is not based on ownership percentages. But you cannot allocate income and loss merely to take advantage of the tax laws. Similarly, if you have a family partnership, you cannot allocate income to younger family members just to reduce taxes. The allocation must reflect the value of services rendered by each of the partners.
- As with S corporations, there is no special IRS form designed to list home office expenses.
- As with S corporation shareholders, a partner's tax losses cannot exceed his or her basis (see definition under "Small Business Corporations" earlier in this chapter).

A partner's basis

- Increases when he pays money or contributes property to the partnership.
- Increases by his share of income earned by the partnership.
- Can increase or decrease as his proportionate share of partnership liabilities changes.
- Decreases if the partnership reports losses, or if the partnership distributes money or property to the partners.

In an S corporation, basis is a more restrictive concept because it does not change as a function of the stockholder's share of general corporate liabilities.

Disadvantages of a Partnership

- A partner is personally liable for the debts of the partnership above and beyond his investment. This is characterized as unlimited liability, and it is the main reason why corporations are the preferred way of doing business. With a corporation or an LLC, generally you can lose only the money and property that you contributed to the corporation or LLC.

- Although a partnership is easy to form, it is also easily dissolved, such as when a general partner who owns more than 50 percent of the entity withdraws. Thus, there is no "continuity of life." With a corporation, a withdrawing shareholder simply sells his stock to a new shareholder and the corporation continues to operate.
- Similarly, it is difficult to withdraw from a partnership if the remaining partners refuse to purchase the withdrawing partner's interest. A buy-sell agreement drawn up when the partnership is formed is highly recommended to avoid this situation. The agreement should contain a formula to measure the amount that a withdrawing partner receives, or the amount to be paid to a partner or his or her beneficiary in case of death or permanent disability.

BUSINESS VENTURES AND THE HOBBY LOSS RULE

If you're in an existing business or considering starting up a new business, besides choosing which legal entity will work best from a tax perspective, you'll also need to be aware of Section 183 of the Internal Revenue Code, "Activities Not Engaged In for Profit," or the Hobby Loss Rule, as it is commonly called. Ignorance or mismanagement of the Hobby Loss Rule can easily increase the chances of an IRS audit.

In order not to be subject to the Hobby Loss Rule, taxpayers need to show a profit in any three out of five consecutive tax years ending with the current tax year. This rule covers sole proprietors, partnerships, S corporations, and estates and trusts. If the IRS determines that your business activity is "not engaged in for profit," according to the Hobby Loss Rule your losses will be considered personal expenses, and only expenses up to the amount of your hobby income will be deductible. Furthermore, these otherwise deductible hobby expenses will be transferred to Schedule A—Itemized Deductions (Other Miscellaneous Deductions), and be subject to a limit of 2 percent of your AGI.

What does this rule mean, and how does it affect the taxpayer? Many young businesses do, after all, legitimately experience operating losses in three out of five years. But the IRS created the Hobby Loss Rule to prevent taxpayers from using personal business ventures such as horse racing, farming, or stamp and coin collecting to throw off losses used to off-set other income (salaries, interest).

How to Strengthen Your Position Regarding the Hobby Loss Rule

If you are a taxpayer who could fall under the Hobby Loss Rule, you have to be ready to prove that you had an intention of earning a profit. Theoretically you could operate a business for many years and never actually earn a profit, but still be entitled to a deduction for the losses.

To strengthen your position in this direction, become familiar with these nine factors used by the IRS to determine whether a profit objective exists:

1. Conduct the activity in a businesslike manner. This includes keeping accurate books and records, printing business stationery and cards, keeping a separate bank account for the business, and obtaining a federal identification number.
2. Obtain sufficient knowledge to operate a successful business. This is an indication that you are trying to increase the profitability of the business. Read trade journals and books on the subject, attend professional seminars and the like to gain expertise, and be able to show proof of these activities within reason.
3. Spend a sufficient amount of time in the activity so that it doesn't look as though you're dabbling (as with a hobby). If you have another full-time occupation that produces income, and most of your time is spent there, your new venture would appear to be secondary. To counteract this, you could hire competent qualified people to run the new business for you or consult with experts in the same field.
4. If you expect the product that you're working on to appreciate in value, this is proof that you have a profit motive. For example, if you purchase antique cars and can show that their value has risen, that in itself is proof of the profit motive.
5. Your success or lack of it in prior business ventures is a consideration. If you have previously turned an unprofitable business into a profitable one, you have proved that your mode of operation involves having a profit motive in mind even though you are currently losing money. Try to write a business plan for your business and include in it how you expect to be profitable. The IRS looks favorably on a written business plan and how you have followed through with it, even though all the goals you may have outlined were not met.

6. The IRS will examine your income track record in the start-up business. If you had a string of successively profitable years more than five years ago, that is an indication that you have the ability and intention to turn your loss into a profit. Similarly, you may be able to show that your current losses are due to events beyond your control, such as depressed market conditions or natural disasters.

7. The IRS also looks at the existence of occasional profits, if any. Profits are compared to losses over the duration of the operation; how both relate to the value of assets invested in the business is examined.

8. The wealthier you are, the more likely that the activity will look like a hobby in the eyes of the IRS. If you don't have substantial income from other sources, the IRS will tend to look more favorably on your activity.

9. Does the business have a significant element of personal pleasure or recreation? This factor is probably the one that has caused the term *hobby loss* to come into being.

Sometimes, no matter what you do, the IRS will insist that your business is a hobby. For all of us who have seen pink Cadillacs cruising down the road, this next case reminds taxpayers that part-time salespeople seeking small returns and large deductions may soon be seeing red.

Mrs. Linde's business was selling cosmetics. In two consecutive tax years, she received the use of a luxury car and reported her activity on Schedule C, indicating losses in excess of $25,000 per year. These losses offset the substantial income earned by her husband on their joint returns.

Using the nine-factor test above, the Tax Court decided that the most important issue determining whether the business was a hobby was the manner in which the business was run. First, Mrs. Linde did very little to separate her personal and business activities. Although she presented mounds of records to prove the claimed expenses, some of the records proved that some of the deductions were taken for purely personal expenditures.

Mrs. Linde also produced summary sheets prepared by herself that the court called self-serving; it gave them no real weight. The actual books and records of her business were not organized well. After examining these, the court said it could not figure out how she computed the losses she claimed.

Lack of a profit motive was further evidenced by Mrs. Linde's failure to seek advice on how to run the business from people outside the cosmetics organization. This was particularly important because she had no prior experience in the business. The only evidence she cited to corroborate her time spent in the activity was her own testimony, which the court discounted.

Finally, the court observed that much of the time Mrs. Linde did spend in the activity involved taking people to restaurants and bars, which signified a substantial element of personal pleasure.

In summary, the court decided that Mrs. Linde's business was not a "for-profit" activity under Section 183, the Hobby Loss Rule. The result was that the taxpayer could deduct expenses only to the extent of the income from the hobby; expenses cannot reduce net operating income below zero (except for mortgage interest and real estate tax, which are deductible on Schedule A, Form 1040).

BUSINESSES THAT INCLUDE MERCHANDISE INVENTORY

If you file a business return and if you sell a product, as opposed to offering a service, one of the things the IRS computer (or audit reviewer) will focus on is the "Cost of Goods Sold" portion of the statement-of-income section found on all business income tax returns. Generally the IRS will devote greater attention to a return showing a smaller gross profit than industry norms. The IRS gathers this information and reaches its conclusions by trying to identify the cost of the product being sold, or how much gross profit (sales less cost of goods sold) a business earned in a year.

There are a number of avenues the IRS can take to scrutinize this and come up with how much money it thinks a business has made on the basis of the cost of goods sold. If the gross profit percentage that you report on the business return is found to deviate greatly from what other taxpayers report in the same industry, there are some acceptable explanations.

With acceptable proof, you may show that you experienced

- More than normal returns of merchandise, which you were forced to sell at cost price or lower.
- Normal increases in the cost of acquiring or manufacturing your products, but you were unable to pass them on to your customers in the form of price increases.

How to Prepare an Ending Inventory Schedule to Minimize Audit Risk

When a tax return showing a low gross profit is being examined, the IRS auditor will most likely ask for a detailed ending inventory schedule, or the inventory at the end of the company's fiscal year. In the Garment Manufacturer's Guide, it states: "The focus of the ending inventory examination is to determine whether the inventory is understated. In other words: Have certain costs been omitted? Have units of inventory been omitted?"[10] Taking a physical inventory is a time-consuming task, especially if you are trying to serve customers or sell products during the inventory process. On the basis of your past experience, you may be able to estimate some of the inventory quantities. In so doing, you must be aware of certain things:

- The method most widely used to value inventory is the "lower of cost or market." Use of this method allows you to assign below-normal values to inventory items that are collecting dust—or are obsolete, damaged, or unusable, or whose prices have dropped since you purchased them. Regarding write-downs, the MSSP Garment Manufacturers Guide states: "The most difficult write-down to locate in the audit is that which completely omits the item from the count and detail sheets. By doing so, the manufacturer is taking the position that the items are being written down to a zero value."[11]
- A majority of the items included in an inventory should be those purchased a short time before the closing date, generally not more than one year prior to the closing date. An exception would be hard goods, such as hardware, that can have a normal shelf life in excess of one year. The Garment Manufacturers Guide states: "The most recent purchases, that is, those made at year-end, are also commonly left out of the piece goods inventory. This omission is usually due to careless error."[12]
- The items included in the ending inventory should be traceable to subsequent period sales. For example, if December 31, 2002, is the closing inventory date, then a large percentage of items should have been sold in the first half of 2003.

Therefore, it is important that the closing inventory schedule be as current as possible and be based on gross profit percentages that are normal to your industry.

Audit Risk and Nonpayment of Payroll Taxes

If you own a business, here is something you should know regarding an audit triggered by nonpayment of payroll taxes. The IRS is required to notify a person it has identified as the "responsible person" (one who is responsible for paying certain FICA and withholding taxes in a timely manner to the IRS) at least 60 days before contacting that person for taxes and penalties owed. Previously, the IRS could contact a person without any notice and collect 100 percent from any "responsible person" without bothering to go after other guilty culprits. (This is similar to where the IRS chased an innocent spouse for all the tax and penalties incurred and owed by that spouse's guilty partner on a joint return; see Chapter

12.) The IRS must disclose the identity of others deemed responsible for not paying payroll taxes to those already identified as culpable. The IRS must also commence an action against the other responsible parties to pay their share of the amounts owed. This ensures, for example, that a low-salaried employee who was deemed by the IRS to be the "responsible person" doesn't take the fall for the head of a company who may be the real culprit.

SECURING A TAX-ADVANTAGED LIFE

The fact is that if you are self-employed and you incorporate, you will have a tax-advantaged life that will be sheltered within a corporate environment. A technical advice memorandum issued by the IRS puts an interesting slant on the importance of choosing the right business format.

After 40 years of operating their farm, a husband, his wife, and their son created a corporation, selling their house, automobile, crops, and farming equipment to the corporation in exchange for stock. They then became employees of the corporation. Given this situation, the family declared that providing food and shelter was not taxable income because it was required by the job.

The primary tax question that arose, therefore, was "Can the corporation deduct these as a legitimate business expense?" Normally a farmer cannot take the cost of his home and food as an expense against farm income.

The IRS agent examining the case declared that this was an example of avoiding income tax. However, in a technical advice memorandum involving a lengthy analysis, the IRS ruled that the taxpayers would have been entitled to the same deduction if a partnership and not a corporation had been formed. It was also decided that the taxpayers were not evading or avoiding federal income tax because they were only obtaining benefits otherwise permitted under specified statutes as outlined in the Internal Revenue Code.

Legally, technical advice memoranda are not supposed to set any kind of precedent; as with private letter rulings, they apply only to the taxpayer who receives them, as discussed in Chapter 5. But this case emphasizes the overriding principle that certain tax advantages can be gained by one's choice of a business format. The conclusions I offer taxpayers are these:

- If you want an environment in which most of your income is not reported to the IRS on a 1099 form, incorporate now.
- If you are self-employed, incorporate or form a partnership now.
- If you want to reduce IRS scrutiny of your business deductions, incorporate or form a partnership or LLC now.

- If you want to place your business income tax return in a category that is least susceptible to an IRS audit, incorporate or form a partnership or LLC now.

A Surefire Checklist for All Taxpayers Who Don't Want to Be Audited

- Know the proper time to file. You have learned that filing late is not the way to avoid an audit. IRS computers aren't programmed to review only those returns received on or before April 15. So who is to say that late returns, those filed after April 15, won't be audited, or will be audited less than returns mailed earlier? All returns, late or not, go through a secondary audit-potential selection process at the district level. All tax professionals have clients who filed late but were audited anyway. The days of thinking you're immune because you file late are over.
- Be thorough. Don't leave out any information that applies to you. Sign where you are supposed to.
- Be neat.
- Be sure your mathematics is correct.
- Be consistently accurate. Are the proper entries on the proper lines? Have you provided your complete address and Social Security number? Did you leave any lines blank that should be filled in?
- Balance out your total deductions with your income. Excessive and elaborate business expenses that add up to a substantial percentage of your income are an audit flag.
- Adjust your stated exemptions as shown on Form W-4, filed with your employer, so that you don't end up receiving large refunds. Remember, they only amount to a free loan of your money to the IRS (discussed in Chapter 2).

TABLE 8.2 Tax Considerations

	Sole Proprietorship	Partnership and LLC	S Corporation	C Corporation
Net operating income	Taxed directly to owner on 1040.	Passed through to partners'/members' 1040 via Form K-1 whether or not distributed.	Passed through to shareholders' 1040 via Form K-1 whether or not distributed.	Double tax: once on C corporation, again when paid to shareholder as dividends.
Net operating losses	Reduces Adjusted Gross Income. Can be carried back 2 years (5 years for 2001 and 2002) and then forward 20 years.	Passed through to partners'/members' 1040 via Form K-1. Losses cannot exceed partners'/members' basis in the partnership/LLC. Subject to at-risk rules and passive-loss limitations. Losses can be carried back or forward.	Passed through to shareholders' 1040 via Form K-1. Losses cannot exceed shareholders' basis in the corporation. Subject to at-risk rules and passive loss limitations. Losses can be carried back or forward.	Deductible only against net operating income. Losses can be carried back 2 years (5 years for 2001 and 2002) and then forward 20 years.
Capital gains	Taxed directly to owner or 1040.	Passed through to partners'/members' 1040 via Form K-1.	Passed through to shareholders' 1040 via Form K-1. Some gains are taxable under certain conditions for older S corporations.	Gains taxed at regular corporate rates.
Capital losses	Offset against capital gains + $3,000 per year. May be carried forward indefinitely.	Passed through to partners'/members' 1040 via Form K-1.	Passed through to shareholders' 1040 via Form K-1.	Deductible only against corporate capital gains. Can be carried back 3 years or forward 5 years as a short-term capital loss.

(Continued)

TABLE 8.2 *(Continued)*

	Sole Proprietorship	Partnership and LLC	S Corporation	C Corporation
Contributions to charities	Itemized deduction on 1040.	Passed through to partners'/members' 1040 via Form K-1.	Passed through to shareholders' 1040 via Form K-1.	Limited to 10% of corporate taxable income, as adjusted by special items. Unused can be carried forward for 5 years.
Dividends received	Taxed directly to owner on 1040.	Passed through to partners'/members 1040 via Form K-1.	Passed through to shareholders' 1040 via Form K-1.	Can deduct from income 70% of dividends received from domestic corporations.
Tax rates	Based on taxable income: 5%–33% on first $311,950; 35% on amounts over $311,950.	Each partner/member pays individual tax rate.	Each shareholder pays individual tax rate.	Based on taxable income: 15% of first $50,000; 25% of next $25,000; 34% of next $25,000. See instructions for amounts over $100,000.
Fringe benefits (e.g., health insurance and group term life insurance)	Partially deductible on 1040, subject to limitations.	All partners are not eligible to receive tax-free benefits	Cannot receive tax-free benefits if shareholder owns more than 2%.	No restrictions.

Retirement plans	Keogh, SEP, Defined Benefit, SIMPLE, or solo 401(k) is available. Loans are permitted up to half of your vested benefit or $50,000, whichever is less.	Keogh, SEP, Defined Benefit, SIMPLE, or solo 401(k) is available. Loans are permitted up to half of your vested benefit or $50,000, whichever is less.	Profit-sharing, SEP, defined contribution plan, Defined Benefit plan, SIMPLE, or solo 401(k) is available. Loans are permitted up to half your vested benefit or $50,000, whichever is less.	Profit-sharing, defined contribution plan, Defined Benefit plan, SIMPLE, or solo 401(k) is available. Loans permitted up to half your vested benefits or $50,000, whichever is less.
Sale of ownership interest	Capital gain.	May be part ordinary income and part capital gain. Special Section 754 election to step up basis of partnership's/LLC's assets for purchaser.	Capital gain.	Capital gain.
Liquidation	N/A.	Tax free.	Capital gain or loss to shareholder. Avoids double taxation. Exceptions if previously a C corporation.	Double taxation—first at corporate level, then at shareholder level.
Alternative Minimum Tax (AMT)	Subject to 26% or 28% AMT.	Partnership/LLC not subject. Preference items and adjustments passed through to partners'/members' 1040 via Form K-1.	S corporation not subject. Preference items and adjustments passed through to shareholders via Form K-1.	Applies at corporate level—at AMT rate of 20%. Certain small corporations are exempt from AMT.

(Continued)

TABLE 8.2 *(Continued)*

	Sole Proprietorship	Partnership and LLC	S Corporation	C Corporation
Payroll taxes	15.3% self-employment tax on first $87,000 of taxable income, 2.9% above that. Half of tax is deductible.	Partnership/LLC income not subject. Passed through to partners'/members 1040 via Form K-1 subject to self-employment tax.	Undistributed income is not subject. However, some part of distributions may be subject to payroll taxes if salary is deemed insufficient by IRS.	Corporation and its employees each pay 7.65% of FICA wages up to $87,000, 1.45% above that.
Items affecting basis	Not an issue.	(A) Income and gains increase partners'/members' basis in partnership/LLC; losses decrease basis. (B) Capital put into partnership/LLC increases basis; distributions decrease basis. (C) General partners' share of partnership liabilities increases basis. With some exceptions, members' share of LLC's liabilities do not increase basis.	(A) Income and gains increase shareholders' stock basis. (B) Capital put into S corporations increases basis; distributions decrease basis. (C) Loans put into S corporation by shareholder increase stock basis. Other corporate liabilities have no effect on shareholder basis.	Not an issue.
Cash vs. accrual method for preparing taxes	Cash or accrual method.	Cash or accrual method. Must use accrual method if inventory is a factor.	Cash or accrual—no limits on annual receipts. Must use accrual method if inventory is a factor.	Cannot use cash method if annual receipts are $5 million or more, or if inventory is a factor.

Profit allocation	Not an issue.	May be allocated by partners' agreement. LLC has more flexibility.	Allocated in proportion to number of shares owned.	Not an issue.
Tax year	Calendar year.	Must use same year as principal partners/members, which usually is calendar year.	New corporations must use calendar year (some limited exceptions).	Calendar or fiscal year.
Tax extension deadline	Form 4868 for four months; Form 2688 for an additional two months.	Form 8736 for three months; Form 8800 for an additional three months.	Form 7004 for six months.	Form 7004 for six months.
Accumulated earnings tax	Not subject.	Not subject.	Not subject unless S corporation was previously a C corporation	Unreasonable earnings above $250,000 ($150,000 for personal-service corporations) are hit with a special 15% tax.
Excessive compensation	Not subject.	Not subject.	Not subject.	If deemed excessive. Excess is deemed to be a nondeductible dividend.
Classes of stock	Not subject	For partnership not an issue. LLC can have more than one class.	Only one class allowed.	No limit.

(Continued)

TABLE 8.2 *(Continued)*

	Sole Proprietorship	Partnership and LLC	S Corporation	C Corporation
Disallowed personal expenses on audit	Individual tax rate.	Each partner/member pays own individual tax rate.	Each shareholder pays his individual tax rate.	Double taxation—first at corporate level, than at shareholder level.
Personal holding	Not subject.	Not subject.	Not subject.	Subject to a special 15% company tax* under certain conditions.
Home office expenses (Form 8829)	Required in order to deduct home office expenses.	Not required.	Not required.	Not required.
All Other Considerations				
Ease and cost of formation	No special actions.	No special actions. Usual arrangement is to prepare written partnership/LLC agreement.	Initial costs of $600 to $1000; $400 to $600 if you do yourself.	Same as S corporation.
Period of existence	Discretion of owner.	Termination if partners/members agree, on partner's/members death or retirement, or if 50% or more of capital and profit interests are sold or exchanged in a 12-month period.	Continues until dissolution. Not affected by sale of shares, unless sale is to ineligible shareholder.	Same as S corporation with no restriction on eligibility of shareholders.

Continuing costs	Minimal.	Annual federal and state partnership tax forms. Approximately 50% increase in tax preparation fees over sole proprietorship.	Annual federal and state S corporation tax forms subject to minimal taxes in some states. Approximately 50% increase in tax preparation fees over sole proprietorship.	Annual federal and state corporation tax forms plus payment of corporate-level income taxes. More tax planning is required. 50–100% increase in tax preparation fees over sole proprietorship.
Owners' exposure to business debts	Liable for all debts of business.	General partners are liable for all debts of business. LLC members are generally only at risk for their investment in the LLC.	Shareholders liable only for capital contributions and debts that are personally guaranteed.	Same as S corporation.
Effect on organization upon withdrawal of taxpayer	None.	Dissolution of partnership/LLC.	After stock is disposed of, corporation continues.	Same as S corporation.
Transfer of ownership interest	N/A.	Addition of new partner/member requires consent of others.	Easy to do—just transfer stock shares to new owner.	Same as S corporation.

*A corporation that is more than 50% owned by five or fewer individuals and 60% or more of whose ordinary gross income is derived from dividends, interest, royalties, and annuities.

(Continued)

TABLE 8.2 *(Continued)*

	Sole Proprietorship	Partnership and LLC	S Corporation	C Corporation
		All Other Considerations		
Limitations on ownership	N/A.	No limit on number of partners/members. Any type of entity can be a member of an LLC.	Limited to 75 eligible shareholders—no partnerships or corporations.	No limit on number and eligibility of shareholders.
Ownership control	N/A.	In a partnership, an owner serves as general partner. All others are limited partners. In an LLC, one member serves as manager.	Owner retains voting stock and transfers nonvoting stock to minority stockholders (generally those who own less than 50% of the stock).	N/A.

TABLE 8.3 Examination Coverage of Returns Filed

	Calendar Year 1999			Calendar Year 2000			Calendar Year 2001		
	Returns Filed	Returns Examined	Percent Examined	Returns Filed	Returns Examined	Percent Examined	Returns Filed	Returns Examined	Percent Examined
Partnerships	1,974,760	6,539	0.33	2,066,800	5,070	0.25	2,165,011	5,543	0.26
S corporations	2,767,000	15,200	0.55	2,887,100	12,437	0.43	3,022,589	11,646	0.39
C corporations (assets under $250,000)	1,484,300	4,371	0.29	1,432,500	3,576	0.25	1,395,497	3,343	0.24
Schedule C (all filers)	7,841,090	121,702	1.55	7,964,900	128,062	1.61	8,026,716	138,254	1.72
Schedule C (gross receipts $100,000 and over)	1,948,900	28,781	1.48	2,012,200	24,080	1.20	2,059,115	29,848	1.45
Individuals (TPI* $100,000 and over)	8,151,500	68,616	0.84	9,326,300	64,259	0.69	10,692,928	80,483	0.75
All individuals	124,887,140	617,765	0.49	127,097,400	731,756	0.58	129,444,947	743,881	0.57

*Total Positive Income (TPI) is the sum of all positive income that appears on a return, excluding losses.

9

The Twenty Greatest Taxpayer Misconceptions

1. "If I am in the 28 percent tax bracket, it means that my tax liability is 28 percent of my income."

Wrong! Here's What You Need to Know

Taxpayers in the 28 percent tax bracket operate almost across the board under the mistaken belief that because they are in that tax bracket, 28 percent of their income is being taxed. This is absolutely not true. A taxpayer in that tax bracket is actually getting taxed less than 28 percent. Even though you're in a 28 percent tax bracket, you pay less than that percentage because you get the benefit of being taxed at lower rates on the amounts you earn in the tax brackets that precede the bracket you are in.

Thus, a single taxpayer with $74,000 of taxable income, in the 28 percent bracket, is taxed this way: The first $7,000 of income is taxed at 10 percent, or $700. The next $21,400 of income is taxed at 15 percent, or $3,210. The next $40,400 is taxed at 25 percent, or $10,100. Only the remaining taxable income of $5,200 is taxed at 28 percent, or $1,456, and it is here, at this person's top income figure, that this taxpayer's tax bracket is determined. So even though this taxpayer is in the 28 percent tax bracket, the tax this person pays is actually just under 21 percent of $74,000, or $15,466.

You see, your total income tax bill accumulates as you climb up the tax rate ladder. While you are on the lower rungs, the rates being charged against your income are correspondingly lower.

The tax bracket that you finally fall into is also referred to as the marginal tax rate. Things would become much clearer to taxpayers if they viewed their top income figure as the outside margin, because it is this top percent that the government uses to fit the taxpayer into the tax bracket system. In no sense, however, is that percent the only one used to figure the actual amount of tax one pays.

2. *"When I transfer money from one mutual fund to another within the same family of funds to secure a stronger investment, or if I sell my tax-exempt municipal bonds, I don't have to worry about any tax consequences."*

Wrong! Here's What You Need to Know

Each time you move money around from one mutual fund to another, even if the funds are owned by the same company, it is a taxable event that requires the investment company to report your sales proceeds by sending a 1099-B to the IRS. The information on that form must subsequently be reported by you on Form 1040, Schedule D, whether it is a gain or a loss. So before you decide to transfer money within a fund family, be aware of the tax consequences.

Regarding tax-exempt municipal securities: These produce income that is generally not subject to being taxed at the federal level. However, when you sell tax-exempt securities, there is always a capital gain or loss that must be reported on Form 1040, Schedule D.

3. *"A company I invested in recently split its stock 2-for-1, and I am sure I will owe some tax. What form do I use to report it?"*

Wrong! Here's What You Need to Know

When a stock splits 2-for-1, your cost per share has not changed. It is simply now spread over twice as many shares. You will generally experience a taxable transaction only when you dispose of part or all of the stock. So it is important to keep track of the cost of each new share to report the correct gain or loss in the future. For example, if you initially paid $5,000 for 100 shares, each share has a cost of $50. After a 2-for-1 stock split, you now have 200 shares at a cost of $25 per share.

4. *"When I receive my inheritance from Uncle Leo, the IRS will take out a chunk of it."*

Wrong! Here's What You Need to Know

Many people mistakenly believe that when they receive a gift or an inheritance they have to pay tax on it. They don't. The provider does. Gifts and inheritances are not taxable to the recipient until the asset is disposed of, at which point taxes are due on any capital gain. The taxpayer should obtain documentation for the cost basis of the gift or inheritance so that when he sells the item he can determine how much tax he owes.

YOUR TAX-SAVING STRATEGY.

A parent or grandparent can make tuition payments for children or grandchildren directly to a college or private school and not be subject to the $11,000 per year gift tax limit. Although this exception applies to tuition only, there is no limit on the amount. They can also contribute a lump sum up to $55,000 into each child's or grandchild's 529 college savings plan, and the $55,000 will be spread out evenly ($11,000 each year) over a five-year period (see Chapter 12).

5. *"If I use the preprinted label that the IRS sends me on my tax return, my chances of being audited will be greatly increased."*

Wrong! Here's What You Need to Know

The purpose of the preprinted labels is to allow an IRS data transcriber to access an account and enter the data needed to process the return using one-third fewer keystrokes. According to the IRS, the preprinted label reduces the chance of error and saves time. Labels contain tax period information that is used to post remittances and return information to the IRS master file. As discussed in Chapter 8, the Discriminate Information Function (DIF) is the primary method the IRS uses to select the majority of returns chosen for audit, along with the ever-changing audit triggers. If the IRS were to use its preprinted labels for audit selection, the average tax assessment per audit would decrease dramatically due to the absence of audit criteria on the label. In other words, those labels offer absolutely no indication of a taxpayer's audit potential to the IRS. With over 226 million returns filed in 2002, the IRS must get the biggest bang for its buck. Those preprinted labels aren't even in the ballpark when the IRS considers audits.

6. *"I've heard about the increase in the number of people subject to the Alternative Minimum Tax (AMT). But since the AMT is supposed to prevent the very rich from getting away tax free, I don't have to worry about it."*

Wrong! Here's What You Need to Know

The AMT was originally designed to catch high-income taxpayers who were using loopholes to reduce their tax bills. (See Chapters 2 and 11). Although only 1 percent of all taxpayers are hit by this tax, the number of people being affected by it is rising at the rate of 50 percent a year, and it is predicted that by the year 2010, at least 35 million taxpayers will be subject to AMT.

My advice is that you should fill in Form 6251 (Alternative Minimum Tax—Individuals) to determine if you are subject to the AMT. If you don't, the IRS will, and you don't want that.

7. *"Isn't this great—I've just received a huge refund from the IRS. I sure know how to beat them at their own game."*

Wrong! Here's What You Need to Know

Many taxpayers prefer to overwithhold and go for a large refund as a means of forced savings, or to ensure that they do not have to make any additional payments to the IRS on or after April 15. The fact is, taxpayers who consistently receive large refunds are actually giving the IRS an interest-free loan, and the money the IRS is borrowing is yours.

The most likely candidates to be sucked into this trap of overwithholding are taxpayers with unusually high deductions (mortgage interest, contributions, taxes) who haven't properly assessed how these deductions will affect their final tax bill. These taxpayers would be better served if they reduced the amount of withholding taken out during the year and got more money each week, which adds up to the same amount as the refund check.

One final tip regarding large end-of-year refunds: Although the IRS continues to maintain that its audit selection criteria are top secret, in my opinion one of the things IRS computers look at is the size of a taxpayer's refund and how it was computed.

8. *"It doesn't matter in what part of the country I live. All areas are considered equal in audit selection."*

Wrong! Here's What You Need to Know

Sadly, this is so far from the truth that it has attracted increasing media coverage of late. Even the IRS admits huge variances in audit coverage and selection based on location; these are hard-to-explain differences in how the government treats taxpayers. Based on IRS data over the past four years, the Transactional Records Access Clearinghouse (TRAC) has ranked all 33 IRS districts from the most audited to the least. A selection of the figures shown in Table 9.1 demonstrates that the highest percentage of individual returns audited in the country was in the Los Angeles district.

From an auditing perspective, therefore, taxpayers would most likely

**TABLE 9.1   District Offices Ranked by Percent
of Individual Tax Returns Audited (1998–2000)**

IRS District	1998	1999	2000
Southern California	3	1	3
Los Angeles	2	2	1
Northern California	1	3	4
Central California	4	4	6
North Central	7	5	2
Manhattan	6	6	5
Brooklyn	16	13	7
New England	28	28	19
Pacific Northwest	21	22	24
New Jersey	24	30	33
Midwest	19	19	14
Upstate New York	26	32	22
North Texas (Houston)	10	5	8
Ohio	33	33	32

Source: Transactional Records Access Clearinghouse, Syracuse University.
Copyright 2002.

not consider California to be the "golden west." The IRS district offices in
California (Southern California, Los Angeles, Northern California) have
consistently been the most aggressive in auditing individual tax returns,
demonstrating an audit rate of 1 percent, roughly double the national average of 0.5 percent.

Conversely, district offices in the Northeast—including New Eng-
land, New Jersey, and upstate New York—and Ohio are the least aggressive regarding their audits of individual tax returns, with rates of about
half the national average.

In general, rankings by IRS district offices remain stable. What one
normally assumes are the money-center areas of the country—Los Angeles and Southern California, Houston, and Manhattan—tend to rank
high. But the Northeast and upper Midwest—Ohio and upstate New
York—tend to rank near the bottom.

Criminal enforcement of the tax laws generally follows the audit
rankings, based on 2000 and 2001 figures of IRS criminal convictions of
all kinds by location, per capita. (See Table 9.2.) Surprisingly, Honolulu
ranks the highest, with a high ranking also by Pittsburgh, Brooklyn and
Manhattan in New York City, Michigan, and Miami.

9. *"I can take more itemized deductions than I am entitled to (especially
contributions and medical expenses) and not be audited as long as I stay under
the national averages published by the IRS."*

**TABLE 9.2   IRS Criminal Convictions—
Ranked by District Office (2001–2002)**

Federal Judicial District	City	2001	2002
Hawaii	Honolulu	1	1
N.Y., S	Manhattan	9	2
N.Y., E	Brooklyn	11	14
Nevada	Las Vegas	5	3
Mich., W.	Grand Rapids	14	7
Penn., W.	Pittsburgh	4	9
Fla., S	Miami	8	20
N.J.	Newark	10	49
Cal. C	Los Angeles	58	35
Cal. S	San Diego	27	9

Source: Transactional Records Access Clearinghouse, Syracuse University. Copyright 2002.

Wrong! Here's What You Need to Know

Each year itemized deductions claimed by individuals on their tax returns, grouped by levels of adjusted gross income, are published by the Internal Revenue Service. These figures appear in Table 9.3. Play this game and you'll end up playing audit roulette. To take a tax deduction, follow this simple rule: If you pay for a tax-deductible item, you can use it on your return as long as you can prove it with a canceled check or an itemized bill or receipt.

Certainly, some reasonable exceptions are allowed. You don't have to prove the first $78 of cash contributions, and you don't need every last toll or taxi receipt if you are an outside salesperson. However, deductions for taxes and interest are straightforward—if you're lacking proof, you will owe money to the IRS when audited, no matter where you fall in the national averages.

TABLE 9.3   Average Itemized Deductions for 2000 by Adjusted Gross Income Ranges

Adjusted Gross Income Ranges	Taxes	Interest	Contributions
$20,000 to $30,000	$ 2,297	$ 6,317	$ 1,780
$30,000 to $50,000	3,093	6,595	1,829
$50,000 to $75,000	4,324	7,406	2,123
$75,000 to $100,000	5,896	8,578	2,604
$100,000 to $200,000	9,239	11,310	3,773
$200,000 +	39,691	26,144	21,301

Source: IRS Publication No. 1136, Statistics of Income Bulletin—Spring 2002.

10. *"Now that I have been audited by the IRS and had money due, I will be audited every year."*

Wrong! Here's What You Need to Know

As already mentioned, tax returns are most often selected for an audit based on computer-generated criteria. The selection process is done on a year-by-year basis, with each new year standing on its own.

YOUR TAX-SAVING STRATEGY
If one of the issues that caused a taxpayer to pay additional taxes resulted from an error, such as depreciation on a piece of office equipment, an auditor will know that this kind of error is often repeated. He or she will probably examine the prior year's return, if the statute of limitations has not expired, and/or the following year's return if it is already filed. However, since these steps will normally take place immediately after the current year's audit is completed, it helps to keep your current year's return on extension while the audit is in progress (extending the filing date to October 15), if at all possible.

If the same taxpayer's return for the following year contains another red flag, such as very high travel and entertainment expenses, that return is again at risk for having a higher than normal audit potential.

11. *"I'm in big trouble with the IRS, so I'd better hire an attorney because I can only obtain the right of privileged communication from an attorney who practices before the IRS."*

Wrong! Here's What You Need to Know

A taxpayer is now entitled to receive from advisers who are CPAs or enrolled agents the same confidentiality protection for tax advice as the taxpayer would have if the advising individual were an attorney. This coverage is for noncriminal tax proceedings before the IRS and federal courts. If you suspect that your case will become a criminal action, use only an attorney. (See Chapter 12.)

12. *"By filing a timely Form 4868 (Application for Automatic Extension of Time to File U.S. Individual Income Tax Return), I will be excused from all penalties and interest as long as I file my tax return within the extension period and pay the balance of tax that is due."*

Wrong! Here's What You Need to Know

By filing a timely Form 4868, the only penalty that you eliminate is for filing the return late (5 percent per month, 25 percent maximum). However, you do not eliminate the penalty on the tax that is paid late (0.5 percent per month) or interest on the late tax payment (currently 6 percent per annum). Therefore, even if you can't pay the full balance of tax due when the extension runs out, do not hold up filing your return,

YOUR TAX-SAVING STRATEGY
Here's a related matter regarding refunds. If your tax return results in a refund, you will be charged no penalties or interest for late filing because late-filing penalties and interest are based on the balance of tax due. In fact, you can file your refund return up to two years late and receive your refund while not being subject to penalties and interest. (Sorry, no interest is given on the refund for the length of time it takes you to file the return.)

13. *"I'm an outside salesman and my employer reimburses me for all my travel, meals, and entertainment expenses. Of course these amounts will be added to the gross earnings on my W-2 form at the end of the year."*

Maybe! Here's What You Need to Know

In most instances, not only will these amounts not be added to the employee's earnings and not be subject to FICA, there will be no accounting for them whatsoever on your Form 1040. If you document the entire outlay of expenses on an expense report for trips during a certain period, and a balance may be due either from you to your employer or vice versa, once this is met you have satisfied the requirements for what is known as an accountable plan, which is acceptable by the IRS.

YOUR TAX-SAVINGS STRATEGY
Commuting expenses: Your company can provide you with (1) up to $100 monthly for transit passes covering bus, subway or rail travel, or van pooling, and (2) up to $185 monthly for parking at the company site or the train or bus location used by the employee. These commuting costs are tax-free and exempt from FICA.

14. *"I didn't have any W-2 earnings this year, but at least I received unemployment compensation, which will allow me to make my $3,000 annual contribution to my IRA."*

Wrong! Here's What You Need to Know

Unlike W-2 earnings or net income from a self-employed business, unemployment compensation is not considered income from personal services. Therefore, no IRA deductions of any kind are permissible.

15. *"I must add to my taxable income all federal and state income tax re-funds that I received this year."*

Wrong! Here's What You Need to Know

First, federal refunds are never considered taxable income on federal income tax returns.

Second, state refunds are income on your 1040 only if you deducted state taxes paid in a prior year, thereby reducing your taxable income. Once you use state taxes as a deduction to reduce your income, then you must declare that year's state tax refund as income on your federal tax return. Here's an example: If you used a federal standard deduction—that is, one lump-sum amount, instead of itemizing deductions on your 2002 return, you do not have to include the state tax refund as income on your 2003 return. But if you took itemized deductions, and state taxes were listed, then you must report the state tax refund as income on your 2003 federal return—that is, if 2003 is the year you received the refund or if you applied the 2002 refund as payment against your 2003 state tax liability.

16. *"It doesn't pay to transfer income-producing assets to my child, who is under 14 years of age. The income will still be taxed at my top income tax rate."*

Wrong! Here's What You Need to Know

This statement is true only if the child's taxable investment income exceeds $1,500. The amount of tax charged is based on a three-tiered approach:

1. Zero to $750: Income produced at this level is wiped out, since the child is entitled to a standard deduction of $750. No tax is due and no tax form or return needs to be filed by the child.
2. $751 to $1,500: Investment income above $750 is not included in the parent's taxable income. However, it is taxed at a 10 percent rate using Form 8814 (Parents' Election to Report Child's Interest and Dividends). To report this, the child must file an individual tax return.
3. $1,501 and higher: After calculating the tax on the first $1,500 of investment income as outlined in 1 and 2 above, the balance of investment income is taxed at the parents' highest tax rate. The parents must fill out Form 8615 (Tax for Children Under 14 Who Have Investment Income of More Than $1,500) and attach it to their tax return. (See Chapter 11.)

YOUR TAX-SAVING STRATEGY

These rules cover investment income only. If your child earns other income, from salaries and wages, for example, that income is taxed at 10 percent of the first $7,000 and then at 15 percent to $28,400, which is the end of the 15 percent bracket for single taxpayers.

17. *"Since my wife is now eligible for a pension plan where she works, we are both prohibited from making a contribution to our traditional IRAs."*

Wrong! Here's What You Need to Know

You may still be eligible to make tax-deductible contributions to your traditional IRAs if you do not exceed certain income levels. In the above scenario, if the taxpayers' adjusted gross income is $60,000 or less ($40,000 or less for a single taxpayer), they could each contribute up to $3,000 to their traditional IRAs. They would be eligible for a partial contribution if their AGI is between $60,000 and $70,000 ($40,000 and $50,000 for singles). Above $70,000 AGI ($50,000 for singles), they would not be eligible. Furthermore, even if one spouse is in a pension plan at his or her job, the nonparticipating spouse can still contribute up to $3,000, subject to a phaseout at a joint AGI level of between $150,000 and $160,000.

YOUR TAX-SAVING STRATEGY

Even if you are ineligible to make a tax-deductible contribution to your traditional IRA, you might be eligible to make a nondeductible contribution up to $3,000 to a Roth IRA. (See Chapter 12.)

18. *"I'm glad that Congress changed the laws governing the sale of personal residences. Now I'll be able to deduct the loss from the sale of my house against other capital gains."*

Wrong! Here's What You Need to Know

Losses incurred on the disposition of personal assets not used for business, such as your home or car, are not deductible on your personal income tax return. Although the threshold on capital gains tax on the sale of your residence has been raised to $500,000 for married couples filing jointly, $250,000 for single filers, unfortunately losses are still not deductible.

19. *"I am happy to contribute to the campaign of my favorite political candidate, especially since my donation is tax deductible."*

Wrong! Here's What You Need to Know

We realize that money is the oil that runs the political machines, and contributing to your favorite candidate or political party is a nice thing to do. But do not expect any help from the U.S. government. You receive no deduction for any money that is paid directly or indirectly to a political candidate or party, personally or through your business. This ban includes payments to a political action committee, advertising in a political action committee, advertising in a political party's convention program or any other related publication, or tickets to dinners or events that benefit the candidate or political party.

20. *Now that the dividends and capital gains tax rates have been reduced to 15 percent, there is no doubt that the public will use this savings to stimulate the economy, and the reduced tax rate will also cause personal wealth to increase substantially.*

Not Necessarily. Here's What You Need to Know

There are ample reasons for skepticism that reducing tax rates on dividends and capital gains will stimulate individuals to consume. Most stocks held in taxable accounts are owned by upper-income taxpayers. Such taxpayers tend to reinvest tax savings rather than consume them. The most significant reductions in rates, to 5 percent, have been given to lower-income taxpayers who tend not to invest in stocks. Moreover, approximately 50 percent of stocks are held in qualified retirement accounts that currently pay no tax on dividends they receive.

The investors in qualified plans face another negative issue; that is, they will not see a direct benefit in the lower-income tax rate applicable to dividends because distributions from these retirement accounts will ultimately be subject to ordinary income rates. Nevertheless, the overall value of their holdings may rise based on the generally positive impact of the new dividend treatment on the value of the markets as a whole. Investors who are able to take full advantage of the current contribution limits on deferred retirement accounts and the lowered rates on dividends and capital gains must carefully compare all of the tax consequences of investments held in retirement accounts to those held outside of retirement accounts.

10

How to Hold On to More Money: Overlooked Credits and Deductions

SELLING SECURITIES FROM A DIVIDEND REINVESTMENT PLAN

When you sell a mutual fund or a security that had a dividend rein-vestment plan, taxpayers typically recall the original cost of the item plus periodic cash investments made along the way. But they frequently forget about those reinvested dividends used to purchase additional shares that were taxable each year as dividend income. Although notices of these are sent annually as paper transactions, taxpayers often overlook them, but they can represent more money in your pocket. Here's how: Add the costs of these dividends to your total cost basis when you sell a fund or security and you'll reduce your taxable gain, or increase your loss.

IDENTIFYING SPECIFIC SECURITIES THAT ARE SOLD

If you have purchased many shares or mutual funds over a period of time from the same company during a rising stock market, capital gain can be reduced if shares with the highest basis are sold first. (For a definition of *basis*, see Schedule K–1, Chapter 6.) To accomplish this, you must keep track of each specific lot of shares you purchased, plus any dividend reinvestments that were generated from the specific lots. This is something most taxpayers fail to do. You must also notify the fund manager or broker in writing as to which shares are to be sold, and request a written receipt. If you don't follow this procedure, you will be stuck with using other, less effective, methods for determining the cost of your purchase, such as average costing, which will result in higher capital gains subject to tax.

UNAMORTIZED POINTS ON A HOME MORTGAGE

With interest rates still very low, many taxpayers are refinancing their mortgages to obtain the lower rates. Points paid on an original home purchase can be deducted immediately, but points paid for a refinancing must be amortized over the life of the new loan, per IRS instructions. Often overlooked when doing a second (or more) refinancing is that the balance of the unamortized points from the previous closing is deductible in full when the mortgage for the previous financing is paid off.

DEDUCTIBLE INTEREST ON A HOME EQUITY LOAN

After you receive money from a home equity loan, the interest on the first $100,000 is fully deductible. But even if you reach that maximum amount allowed for deducting interest on a home equity loan, you may be able to go further. If the loan proceeds above $100,000 are used to run a business or for investment purposes, the interest on that portion of the loan can be deductible as well.

Note: Investment interest is deductible only to the extent that you have investment income such as dividend and interest income appearing on your 1040. Any unused deduction can be carried forward to the following year.

UNUSED LOSSES, EXPENSES, AND CREDITS

To prevent taxpayers from bunching up deductions in a single year, Form 1040 contains numerous limitations on losses, expenses, and tax credits. Some of these items are lost forever—for example, medical expenses that do not meet the 7.5 percent of AGI threshold cannot be added to next year's medical expenses. (For an exception, see next section.) However, many other deductions, losses, and tax credits can be carried forward from prior years and then be deducted on your current year's tax return. For example, the law allows taxpayers to deduct only $3,000 a year in capital losses (after offsetting your capital gains). So if you had net capital losses of $8,000 last year, the unused portion, or $5,000, can be utilized this year as a deduction against your income. Other often overlooked carry-forwards are investment interest and charitable donations, listed on Schedule A; home office expenses and Section 179 Depreciation (see Form 8829 in Chapter 7) on Schedule C (Profit or Loss From Business); and passive losses on Schedule E (Supplemental Income and Loss). So it pays to check last year's return for any unused losses or expenses that can be carried forward to this year's return and use them to put more money in your pocket. (There are also several tax credits available as carry-forwards, but it's best to ask a tax pro for assistance to know if you are eligible.)

SELF-EMPLOYED DEDUCTION FOR HEALTH INSURANCE

Self-employed taxpayers who file their taxes using Schedule C or 1120S (U.S. Income Tax Return for an S Corporation) can deduct 100 percent of the annual health insurance premiums (including long-term care) they have paid out in 2003 against their adjusted gross income. For example, if your AGI is $100,000 and your health insurance premiums are $6,000, you can deduct $6,000 on page 1, line 26, of your Form 1040, even though you fail to exceed the medical expense threshold of 7.5 percent of AGI on Schedule A. In effect, you are reducing your AGI and taxable income by $6,000 regardless of whether you meet the medical expense threshold.

CHARITABLE DONATIONS—SECURITIES

You can increase the amount of your charitable deductions listed on Schedule A (Itemized Deductions) by handing over to your favorite charity marketable securities that you have held for more than 12 months that have appreciated in value. You, in turn, can take a deduction for the securities' fair market value on the date of the gift. If you sell the securities first, and then contribute the net proceeds to charity, you'll be stuck for the tax on any capital gain. You can do the same thing with mutual fund shares, but advance planning is required because transfers of mutual fund shares can take two to three weeks to complete. Also, if you are not donating all of your shares, clearly identify the shares being transferred and make sure they have been held for more than 12 months to achieve the maximum tax savings.

If you held securities for 12 months or less, and they went down in value, you can either donate the stock to charity or sell the stock and donate the proceeds. There is no tax difference.

CHARITABLE DONATIONS—HOUSEHOLD ITEMS

The cartons of clothing, old furniture, and appliances you give away have residual value. Most charities will gladly give you a receipt each time you make a donation. If you're in the habit of making these kinds of donations regularly, check the list of used property values issued by the

Salvation Army, in Appendix A. The IRS should accept this list when determining the dollar value of secondhand items. The total of these receipts can translate into an unexpected windfall deduction on Schedule A, Form 1040, which can reduce your overall taxable income.

SOCIAL SECURITY TAX OVERPAYMENTS

Social Security tax paid by employees is deducted from gross wages up to $87,000. Therefore, if you worked at more than one job in 2003 and your combined W-2 earnings as shown in Box 3 of all your W-2s exceed $87,000, you probably overpaid Social Security taxes. You can check this by adding up the amounts of Social Security tax shown in Box 4 of all your W-2s. Anything above $5,394.00 is an overpayment. Put the excess amount on line 61 of Form 1040 and you'll receive a dollar-for-dollar reduction taken against your tax liability that will either increase your refund or reduce the amount you owe. If your gross wages are from only one source and your total wages exceeded that amount, chances are your company did not take more Social Security taxes than necessary, but you should verify it anyway.

JOB-HUNTING EXPENSES

Remember to add up all job-hunting expenses such as resume preparation, newspapers purchased, cabs and auto mileage taken, use of placement services, and even airline tickets, hotels, and meals if the interview was out of town and you were not reimbursed. Taxpayers typically lump these with other miscellaneous deductions on Schedule A, and together they are subject to a 2 percent deductible of your adjusted gross income. So do the computations and take what you are entitled to.

YOUR TAX-SAVING STRATEGY
For job-hunting expenses to be deductible, you have to be searching for a job that is in the same field as the one you currently hold. The expenses are valid even if you don't get the job you applied for. However, first-time job seekers, such as college graduates, cannot deduct expenses when searching for their first job.

STATE INCOME TAX DEDUCTIONS

If you pay estimated state taxes in four quarterly installments, the fourth scheduled payment is made around January 15 of the following year. This means that for calendar year 2002, you can deduct the January 2003 payment on your 2003 federal return as an itemized deduction on Schedule A. Another scenario, based on the same principle, is this: If the balance due on your 2002 state tax return was paid in 2003, usually around April 15, you can deduct this amount as an itemized deduction on Schedule A of your 2003 Form 1040. This gives you a solid deduction you might otherwise not be aware of.

PARENTAL OR GRANDPARENTAL SUPPORT

If you provide more than half the support for your parent or grandparent, you may be entitled to a dependency exemption of $3,050. Keep these conditions in mind:

- The dependent can't have more than $3,050 of reportable income.
- Social Security benefits do not count as reportable income.
- Medical expenses paid by you count toward providing support.

FEDERAL INCOME TAX WITHHELD ON FORM 1099

The largest amount of income tax paid to the IRS is withheld from employee salary and wage payments, both of which appear on Form W-2, issued at the end of the year. However, income taxes are also often withheld from nonwage sources such as backup withholding, or distributions from pension plans (Form 1099-R) (See Pension Plan Distributions in Chapter 6.) Make sure to attach a copy of the appropriate 1099 form(s) to your tax return along with copy B of your W-2 so that you receive full credit for all taxes withheld from 1099 payments as well as from salaries and wages. Because this is an often overlooked tax credit, whatever you gain is found money.

CLASSROOM EXPENSES FOR TEACHERS

For 2002 and 2003 only, teachers can take a $250 annual above-the-line deduction for classroom expenses. Qualifying are teachers from K to Grade 12, instructors, counselors, principals, or aides who work at least 900 hours during a school year. They may take a federal deduction for qualified classroom expenses directly from adjusted gross income on page one of Form 1040. This covers money they spent for out-of-pocket supplies including books, software, and computer equipment.

11

Ten Ground Rules Never to Break to Win with the IRS

Winning at taxes is not about finding the right piece of information. It is about knowing as much as possible about your own personal tax situation and moving beyond your fears to clearly see that the IRS is simply a group of people who have an enormous job to accomplish.

To continue to keep the scales between you and the IRS tipped in your favor, you must always follow these 10 ground rules for winning with the IRS.

RULE 1. ALWAYS REPORT INCOME ON YOUR TAX RETURN THAT IS BEING REPORTED TO THE IRS BY THIRD-PARTY PAYERS

The most common sources of information include W-2s, income items on K-1s, and the entire series of 1099 forms: distributions from pension plans and individual retirement accounts (IRAs); interest and dividend income; sales of stocks, bonds, and mutual funds; state income tax refunds; and Social Security and unemployment insurance benefits.

Some of the tax laws and requirements that govern third-party disclosures are

- Withholding law (Tax Payment Act of 1943)
- Requirement to report miscellaneous income totaling $600 or more in a year (1099-MISC)
- Requirement to report payments of interest and dividend income totaling $10 or more (1099-DIV, 1099-INT)
- Any of the other tax laws governing information reporting that bring into play the full series of 1099 forms, 15 in all

But as usual, when it comes to obeying the law, people don't always meet their legal obligations uniformly. Exceptions occur because people misinterpret, manipulate, or simply ignore what is requested. As a result, you must pay attention to more than the letter of these laws and be prepared for the following circumstances in adhering to this ground rule.

Some Employers Report All Payments

Be aware that many business owners report all payments on 1099-MISC to the IRS, even if they are less than $600. What implication does this have for taxpayers? To follow the letter of the law, taxpayers should report all income received, even if the amount is below $600 annually.

In fact, taxpayers should learn to assume responsibility for keeping track of all their own earnings. At least then they can be certain that a comparison between what they say they earn and the 1099s provided by payers will be accurate.

Payment Methods

A worker can be paid "on the books" or "off the books." Regular employees and independent contractors are paid on the books. Regular employees receive a salary from the entity they work for and have their income reported directly to the IRS by that entity on a W-2 form. Independent contractors' income is reported to the IRS by the entity that pays them on a 1099-MISC if their remuneration is $600 or more per year.

All payment methods—cash, checks, barter—are treated equally under the law. No matter what the form of payment, including barter, the business owner is legally bound to report the paid amount to the IRS on a W-2, on a 1099-MISC, or on any of the other fourteen 1099 forms. This information is carefully matched up on IRS computers, so if you don't report it, you place yourself at audit risk.

Workers who so choose or are talked into it are paid "off the books," in cash—and usually no reporting requirements are fulfilled by the entity to the IRS. This group usually believes they're getting a bargain. Not true.

When You Are Paid "Off the Books"

Fifteen or twenty years ago, "off the books" meant taking your earnings home with no taxes deducted. Today all of that has changed because of information technology and reporting requirements. Anyone who accepts this method of payment becomes an independent contractor in the eyes of the IRS and is liable for all of the taxes independent contractors must pay.

If your teenage daughter tells you she'll be working part-time, "off the books," what is really going on is probably not the classic definition just described, but something more like this: Mr. and Mrs. Owner are the only employees listed on the company's payroll records. All others whom they employ are issued 1099s at the end of the year. Since 1099s represent payments to nonemployees, no taxes are withheld from these payments, and the worker is treated like an independent contractor. Thus your daughter could earn $5,500 with no taxes withheld but end up being liable for paying FICA and Medicare taxes of $777.13. If she were instead treated as an employee, the FICA and Medicare tax deduction from her salary would be $420.75 (7.65 percent of $5,500), a net savings of $356.38. In both instances, she would owe no income tax because she would be earning below the $7,800 threshold for a single person. The $5,500 is wiped out by a personal exemption of $3,050 and a standard deduction for a single person amounting to $4,750.

In short, if you are a part-time or summer worker, insist you be paid "on the books," receiving full benefits, paying your share of taxes. A student is generally subject only to the withholding of FICA tax. If you are working full-time on a permanent basis and are not self-employed or are not inclined to file your tax return as a self-employed person, also insist that you be treated as a regular employee.

The Greed Factor

Dealing in cash presents temptations. Once you have been tempted, it's often difficult to overcome the greed factor. Problems arise when business owners pocket cash and fail to report it to the IRS, or get involved in schemes for hiding income. Why would a business owner report the full amount of cash payments made to workers on 1099s but report only part of the cash income to the IRS? To reduce the company's net taxable income. (If the income goes directly into the owner's pocket, the IRS can't tax it, right?) None of this is news to the IRS.

The only major reporting exception for business owners is something many tax professionals consider to be a major weakness in the IRS's reporting system: The IRS does not require business owners to prepare 1099-MISC forms for payments to corporations except for legal services. That means if you are an independent contractor or self-employed and you incorporate, anyone who pays you is not required to file a 1099-MISC with the IRS. (See "Avoiding an Audit by Setting Up an S Corporation" in Chapter 8.)

What Happens When You Don't Receive a 1099?

Some people actually believe that if they don't receive a Form 1099, it means that it was not mailed to the IRS and therefore they don't have to include that income on their tax return. Nothing could be further from the truth. It is vital that you follow Rule 1 even if you do not actually receive your 1099 form telling you how much income you received from a particular job.

Why Business Owners Don't Send 1099s

Occasionally business owners are unfamiliar with the rules governing payments for labor and services and fail to prepare the required 1099 paperwork. Or sometimes they inadvertently forget to mail the 1099 to the recipient. But the primary reasons business owners seemingly forget to prepare 1099s are these:

- They are fearful that the independent contractors they use will be reclassified by the IRS as employees. What better way to avoid reclassification than by not mailing the 1099s to the IRS?
- They believe that the less the IRS knows about their operation in general, the better off they are. If they do get audited and the IRS discovers that they didn't file 1099s, they would rather risk paying the penalties ($100 per nonfiling of a 1099) than reveal more of their business operations to the IRS.

An IRS auditor does not often impose a penalty for failure to file 1099s. Even if one does, though, the $100 per item nonfiling penalty is small compared to the possible costly reclassification of some or all of the business owner's workers as employees. However, if the IRS can prove intentional disregard of the filing rules by the business owner, there is no maximum penalty per information return.

The bottom line for workers is this: If you do not receive a 1099, ask the business owner if one is forthcoming. Upon receiving a late 1099, if you become paranoid about the unreported income, you can file an amended tax return. In a recent year the IRS received 2.2 million amended individual returns, most probably the result of late notifications of income plus guilty consciences. Remember, for small amounts of additional tax ($100 or less), it can cost double that in tax preparation fees.

RULE 2. NEVER INCLUDE OTHER FORMS THAT ARE NOT REQUIRED WITH YOUR TAX RETURN—DO NOT VOLUNTEER ADDITIONAL INFORMATION

This ground rule applies to a number of situations, some involving several specific IRS forms, some applying to cases in which taxpayers owe the IRS money and negotiations are a possibility, and some applying to audits.

Form 8275 (Disclosure Statement) and Form 8275-R
(Regulation Disclosure Statement)

The IRS would love it if all taxpayers used Forms 8275 and 8275-R more often, because they are supposed to be filed with a 1040 if a taxpayer knowingly takes a position on the return that is questionable. Both forms look extremely harmless and provide minimal direction. Form 8275 states, "Do not use this form to disclose items or positions that are contrary to Treasury regulations." Instead use Form 8275-R that states, "Use this form only to disclose items or positions that are contrary to Treasury regulations." Following each sentence is blank space.

The IRS designed Forms 8275 and 8275-R this way to give taxpayers enough rope to hang themselves. In 1995, the IRS admitted that your chance of being audited goes up if you file these two forms, and that position has not changed.

The instructions for Forms 8275 and 8275-R require that you support your position through revenue rulings, revenue procedures, tax court cases, and the like. This means that you need to locate, from thousands of pages in our current tax code, previous laws and decisions that support your position.

According to the IRS there is a plus side to all of this: If you attach Form 8275 or 8275-R to your return, and if the return is subsequently audited, and the issue is decided against you, you won't have to pay any penalties. However, you will still have to pay additional tax, plus interest.

Forms 8275 and 8275-R are nifty tools devised by the IRS to ease the burden of the Examination Department. Instead of IRS personnel manually sorting through thousands of returns to come up with questionable issues, with these forms, taxpayers are now flagging questionable items for the IRS of their own free will. Why should you be the one to start the ball rolling?

The fact is that you can disregard these forms entirely and still take the same position regarding income and expenses, and rely on the same rulings or procedures, which your tax professional may already be familiar with.

There's something else to consider when it comes to Forms 8275 and 8275-R. The consensus of tax pros regarding both of these forms is that the IRS wants to make it tougher on tax preparers if they take aggressive positions on their clients' tax returns. Existing IRS regulations say that when a tax preparer takes a questionable position on a return, one that stands less than one chance in three of being accepted by the IRS, the tax preparer must describe the position taken and then include support for it by using Form 8275. If the use of a borderline justification is not disclosed in this way, and the return is found unacceptable, the instructions to

Form 8275 indicate that the taxpayer is subject to additional tax, and the preparer can be charged with a $250 penalty as well.

Who's to judge whether the tax preparer has a one-in-three chance that the position taken on a client's 1040 will be accepted? The regulation goes on to say that the final decision will be based on a "reasonable and well-informed analysis by a person knowledgeable in tax law." If you were to bet on which position would win, the one taken by the IRS or the taxpayer, which would you choose?

My advice is that if your tax pro suggests including Form 8275 or Form 8275-R with your return, be sure that he or she justifies why the form is being used and convinces you that it is being used for your benefit and not just to cover your tax professional's own exposure.

Form SS-8 (Determination of Worker Status for Purposes of Federal Employment Taxes and Income Tax Withholding)

As explored in Chapter 7, the IRS is currently very focused on reclassifying independent contractors as employees. As you recall, reclassification enables the IRS to recoup huge amounts of tax dollars.

To file an SS-8 would be to admit that there is some doubt in your status as an independent contractor or, if the form is being filed by an employer, the status of your workers. Based on what you have already learned about the IRS, why would you want to place doubt on your own working status, or on the working status of your workers? It should not surprise you that 90 percent of the time, the IRS rules that a company submitting Form SS-8 has employees, not contractors, regardless of the information provided. The form is also quite complicated and cumbersome, even for professionals.

If you do not file Form SS-8, your status, or your workers' status, will probably come into question only during an audit.

Form 8082 (Notice of Inconsistent Treatment or Administrative Adjustment)

Schedule K-1 is an information form that reflects your shares of income and expenses that are passed through to your individual tax return by partnerships, S corporations, limited liability companies, and estates and trusts (see Schedule K-1, Chapter 6). If you do not agree with an amount or the way an issue has been shown on your K-1, you do not have the option of changing the form on your own and reporting it a different way on your Form 1040. In this situation, the IRS suggests that you use Form 8082, which contains adequate space to explain why you are taking a different position on your Form 1040.

Now, wait just a minute. Common sense tells you that informing the IRS in advance that you are taking a contrary position is tantamount to requesting an audit of your entire return. Here's what to do instead: If you're in a partnership, for example, discuss the situation immediately with the partner who handles tax matters and is responsible for the content of the tax return. If he agrees with you that a mistake was made, and the return has not yet been filed, he may be willing to make the necessary changes. If the return has been filed (which is likely), an amended partnership return could be prepared and filed. If the partner who handles tax matters does not agree with the changes that you believe are necessary, then using Form 8082 may be your only alternative, but be sure you have a convincing argument in favor of your position just in case you have to explain it to an IRS revenue agent.

Form 5213 (Election to Postpone Determination as to Whether the Presumption That an Activity Is Engaged in for Profit Applies)

If you file taxes as an individual, partnership, limited liability company, S corporation, or an estate or trust (pass-through entities) that has incurred or is expected to incur net operating losses for three out of five years, you can elect to file Form 5213.

If an activity is presumed to be engaged in for profit, the activity must show a net profit for three out of five years. Conversely, if you have net losses for three out of the first five years, your activity will be presumed to be a hobby, and on an audit, deductions will be allowed only to the extent of income reported from the activity. That is, you will be able to reduce the income to, but not below, zero. Here is a case that demonstrates the use of 5213 and the tax rulings associated with it:

During an audit, a client of mine, a producer of small documentary films, showed a string of losses for five years, amounting to approximately $15,000 per year. Although she had only small amounts of income and large expenses, she was still actively seeking distribution outlets for the films she produced. In her favor was the fact that three years prior to the five years showing losses, she showed a substantial profit in two out of three years.

During the past five years, however, she was living off her savings. Careful documentation provided to the tax auditor showed that she was making an honest attempt to sell her films. For example, many of the travel expenses charged to the business were in pursuit of this effort.

After a half-day audit that covered a two-year period, the agent concluded that my client had demonstrated an honest profit motive.

This goes to the heart of the Hobby Loss Provision. Losses in three out of five years merely indicate that you're not in it to make a profit. If you can prove the profit motive (time spent, investigation before starting, expertise, lack of other income to offset losses, etc.), then the losses will stand. (See Chapter 8.) The IRS would have loved my client to have filled out Form 5213 when she began producing films. This could have led the IRS to believe that this occupation was a hobby—which in reality it wasn't.

The IRS is trying to sell you on Form 5213 by attaching a bonus to it: If you file Form 5213, you can postpone the determination by the IRS as to whether or not you are engaged in an activity for profit. That is, you cannot be audited during the initial five-year test period. This may sound good, but it's not, for two reasons.

First, there is nothing automatic about the Hobby Loss Provision. If you show net losses for three or four consecutive years, you may not hear from the IRS. By filing the form you are actually informing the IRS that you are afraid that your losses will be disallowed. Why put yourself on record that you might be subject to the Hobby Loss Provision? Let the IRS discover your losses on its own. If you don't file Form 5213, you still retain all your rights to refute the IRS that you have engaged in the activity not to make a profit.

Second, when you file Form 5213, you are also agreeing to extend the period for tax assessment (statute of limitations) for two years after the due date of the return in question for the first tax year of the five-year test period. For example, if the test period is 1998 through 2002, the IRS would normally have until April 15, 2002, to initiate an audit of the 1998 return. However, if you file a 5213, the IRS has until April 15, 2004, an extra two years. This could mean giving the IRS five years to assess you for additional tax instead of the normal three! It's better not to fill out the form.

Form 872 (Consent to Extend the Time to Assess Tax) and Form 872-A (Special Consent to Extend the Time to Assess Tax)

When an audit has been going on for six months or more and the statute of limitations, normally three years, will be up in one year or less, the auditor may ask you to sign Form 872 or 872-A. Before you even think about signing either one, you should consider that the wrong choice could hurt you badly.

For each extension request you can negotiate with the auditor to limit the extension to specific issues. Also, the IRS must notify you of your right to refuse to sign the extension. However, if you don't agree to an extension of the statute of limitations, the IRS will send you a Statutory Notice of Deficiency, which will force you to end up in Tax Court or at least have the IRS commence collection actions against you. In addition, if it looks as though you can't settle your case with the auditor at this point and you're thinking of taking your case to Appeals, signing an extension for at least one year is usually required.

So now the question is, which one do you sign? *Under no circumstances should you choose Form 872-A, which may leave the extension date open-ended.* This gives the IRS an unlimited amount of time to complete your examination. The case could end up at the bottom of the pile and the clock could tick away as interest charges mounted up. I know of cases like this that have gone on for years. The law provides a 10-year limitation and ensures other taxpayer rights. (See 1998 Tax Legislation in Chapter 12.)

Therefore, when signing an extension, choose Form 872, which defines the end of the extension period. And you absolutely want to limit this period to one additional year.

One more thing: Make sure the agent doesn't inadvertently hand you the 872-A instead. I've had that happen to me.

The Fallacy of Giving the IRS Backup Data for Deductions

Many tax preparers suggest including backup data with your return when you have taken a larger than normal deduction. For example, they suggest that if you have sustained a large casualty loss, you should include repair bills and appraisals. My advice to you is this: Do not include this data. The only thing you accomplish by including backup data is to bring the questionable items to the attention of IRS reviewers. Also, if the return is selected for a review, by the time it reaches the reviewer your backup data may be incomplete after having gone through mail and sorting machines and being handled by lots of different people.

Let the IRS carry out its audit function its way. If your return is selected for a correspondence audit to verify one glaring item, you can submit all your documentary proof at that time.

RULE 3. IF ANY INFORMATION THAT YOU ARE PUTTING ON A TAX RETURN IS A GRAY AREA, GO FOR AS CLOSE TO FULL DEDUCTIBILITY AS POSSIBLE

Often the data taxpayers are planning to include on a return is not a perfect fit for the category or line that they think it belongs on. For example, a variety of expenses can appear in more than one place on Form 1040. The secret is knowing which schedule to choose to gain the biggest tax advantage and how to support your claims. This also applies if you are filing as a partnership or an S or C corporation.

The majority of taxpayers choose to report expenses on three schedules, all used in connection with the 1040 form: Schedule C (Profit or Loss from Business), Schedule E (Supplemental Income and Loss [from rental real estate, royalties, partnerships, S corporations, estates, trusts, REMICs, etc.]), and Schedule A (Itemized Deductions).

The essential differences among these is that many expenses listed on Schedule A are subject to formulas that limit deductibility, such as percentage of adjusted gross income. In contrast, expenses listed on Schedule C and Schedule E are fully deductible, with the exception of certain restraints, such as home office expenses on Schedule C and passive loss amounts on Schedule E, both of which are sometimes not fully deductible on their respective schedules.

Form 1040, Schedule C (Profit or Loss from Business)

Form 1040, Schedule C (Profit or Loss From Business) is used to report the income from a business operated by a self-employed person, the income of someone who renders part- or full-time service as an independent contractor, or of someone who carries on a trade or business as a proprietor. In Chapter 8, taxpayers were advised to reduce their 1040 line items by eliminating Schedule C in its entirety. If you must continue to use Schedule C, there are certain flexibilities you should know about. (The following information can apply to all business entities, such as partnerships, LLCs, S corporations, and C corporations.)

Schedule C contains about 25 listed expense items and an unlimited amount of other miscellaneous expense categories, and it provides taxpayers with ample opportunities to increase business deductions. Some line items are more flexible than others.

Listed Items
    Advertising
    Car and truck expenses
    Legal and professional services
Other Expenses
    Telephone

You can use these items to your advantage.

Advertising

You're self-employed, and you decide to print up some resumes and place ads for your services in your local newspaper, at a total cost of $2,500. As a self-employed person you can report this as a business expense on Schedule C and take a full $2,500 deduction.

If these or other job-related expenses are incurred while you are an employee, they must be reported on Schedule A in a section titled "Job Expenses and Most Other Miscellaneous Deductions." Here, however, the total amount of your deductions is subject to a reduction of an amount equal to 2 percent of your adjusted gross income (AGI). If you are single with an AGI of $60,000 and in the 25 percent tax bracket, 2 percent is $1,200, so your deduction would be reduced by this amount, and would be only $1,300.

Car and Truck Expenses

No matter what type of business you are in, you probably use your car some of the time for business reasons. Taxpayers in this position have two choices for computing and reporting vehicle expenses.

The simplest and safest way to report these expenses is by using the mileage method. To do this, simply multiply business miles driven by the allowable mileage rate (currently 36 cents for 2003), add tolls and parking expenses, and you have your deduction. If you use your car for a mere 5,000 business miles during the year, this will provide you with a $1,800 deduction.

Using the alternative direct method, you simply add up all your auto expenses—gas and oil, repairs, and insurance—plus depreciation. You then must factor in the number of days per week the car is used for business purposes. If it's Monday to Friday, then you can deduct five-sevenths of the auto expenses. The remainder of the costs represent those incurred for personal use and are not deductible.

Since many business owners often use their cars on Saturdays and perhaps even on an occasional Sunday to greet an out-of-town customer or supplier, deduct six-sevenths of the total car expenses and present your position if you are audited.

To decide which works best, compare the direct-method costs with the mileage costs and go with the one that offers the largest deduction. You should also factor in one further consideration: If you are audited, with the direct method you have to document every last item of expense with receipts, and maintain a diary that shows full details of your business miles. With the mileage method, a diary that shows your business miles is all that is required. If you lease your car, you can use either the mileage or the direct method. However, once you begin using direct-method costs, you must continue using it as long as you use that particular car for business. If you used mileage costs, you can switch to direct-method, but no switching back again. (See also "Auto Expense," later in this chapter.)

Legal and Professional Services

The IRS wants you to apportion deductible legal and accounting fees to each appropriate schedule on your return: Schedules A, C, and E; or "Other Income," line 21 on page 1 of the 1040. Since a tax professional usually spends a considerable amount of time preparing the business part of your return, it is perfectly acceptable for you to request that the bill be weighted in favor of Schedule C, where it is deductible in full without limitations. If a legal fee is personal in nature and doesn't relate to the business, exclude it. For example, preparation of a will is personal, but tax advice that was part of a discussion with the attorney is deductible. The tax and investment planning portions of a bill from a financial planner would likewise be deductible. Speak to the attorney or the financial planner before the bill arrives, explain that you're tax-savvy, and insist that the tax advice be clearly shown on the bill.

The greatest advantage for taxpayers is achieved by including expenses for legal and professional services in a schedule that offers 100 percent deductibility. Table 11.1 shows what a detailed bill and its traceable deductions might include.

Telephone Expenses

Generally speaking, you can take a more aggressive position if you use estimates to supplement actual receipts. For example, since there are no receipts available for coins put into public telephones, working people who spend a lot of time on the road can conceivably declare they spend as much as $50 a week on business calls from pay phones. Even if you have a telephone credit card or a cellular phone, it is more economical to use coins for calls under one dollar. Because items such as telephone calls

TABLE 11.1   Where to List Legal and Professional Services for Maximum Deductibility

Item	Schedule
Professional fees in pursuit of back alimony	Line 21, page 1 of 1040
Audit fees to uncover hidden assets of ex-spouse relating to alimony	Line 21, page 1 of 1040
Attorney's fees on purchase of a new home	Add to cost basis of home
Legal fees in attempt to keep your job or to secure rights when leaving a job	Schedule A (Miscellaneous Deductions) subject to 2 percent of AGI limitation
Legal fees to secure ownership interest in a property*	Add to cost basis of property
Legal fees to collect back rent*	Schedule E, Part 1
Tax preparer's fees for preparation of business payroll tax returns	Schedule C
Attorney's fees for setting up a new business	Schedule C
Planning advice in reference to a new business venture	Schedule C
Professional fees for representation at tax audits	Schedule C or Schedule A (Miscellaneous Deductions), if personal
Preparation of tax returns	Same
Financial planning	Same

*The last eight items are also generally deductible by partnerships, LLCs, and corporations.

are not a major expense, IRS auditors spend little time in this area, so reasonable estimates are usually accepted.

If you have a dedicated business phone, most IRS auditors will accept your deduction as a 100 percent business cost. Don't worry, auditors generally will not test your honesty by calling specific telephone numbers.

For a smaller business, where your previously personal telephone has been switched over to both business and personal use, you have to determine which portion is now business-related and which long-distance calls are to your Aunt Sylvia. However, an auditor will not usually compare your usage of the telephone now that you are in business to the time when your phone was strictly personal. So estimate generously in favor of business use.

Expenses for Business Use of Your Home

As you learned in the chapter on the underground economy, this is still a hot topic. Taxpayers were once able to deduct home-office expenses directly on Schedule C. Now all of this is done on Form 8829, a clever IRS device/weapon. (For a full discussion of how to obtain the maximum benefit from Form 8829, see Chapter 7.)

Form 1040, Schedule E (Supplemental Income and Loss)

Another useful schedule that allows taxpayers flexibility regarding the gray areas of deductions is Schedule E, Part 1. This schedule is used to report income or loss from real estate rentals and royalties.

Bear in mind that many of the considerations concerning expenses that taxpayers can place on Schedule C are also appropriate for Schedule E. An expense on Part 1 of Schedule E is fully deductible against rental income. So the IRS is on the lookout for expenses that may be more personal than business and that should rightly be placed on Schedule A (Itemized Deductions) or some other schedule that, because of the threshold of the deductible, will reduce the expense to a meaningless amount. (See "Legal and Other Professional Fees," later in this section.)

Direct expenses that are deductible against rental income are easy to identify. These include cleaning, maintenance, utilities, commissions, insurance, mortgage interest, and real estate taxes. To give owners of rental property the greatest advantage, the following discussion focuses on items that are subject to interpretation, and how an aggressive position regarding these expenses may be possible.

Auto Expenses

To arrive at the maximum amount that you can deduct as a proper business-related auto expense on Schedule E, you have to ask yourself some questions that an IRS auditor would ask: Do you use your car to visit your properties? How often? How far is the round trip? Even if you do not run the day-to-day operations, do you drive to a specific location to meet with the managing agent, or sign new leases, or collect rents directly from tenants? Certainly, you would make a personal visit if one of the properties was sold or if you were purchasing a new rental property.

If you answer yes to some of these questions, you can deduct your auto expenses on Schedule E. You can determine how much to deduct by using the mileage method—total up the business miles and multiply by the allowable mileage rate. As usual, to back up your figures, keep a diary of trips associated with the rental property. (See also "Car and Truck Expenses," earlier in this chapter.)

Travel Expenses

Is your rental property in another state? Many residents of one state have rental properties in another and have to travel there periodically by air to buy or sell a property, or to take care of an existing problem. If you decide to stay a little longer and vacation for a few days, your air travel plus the cost of hotels and 50 percent of meals while you are involved in the business-related activities are still fully deductible against rental income. If your spouse is a co-owner of the property, then his or her expenses are also deductible if he or she accompanies you.

Keep an accurate diary of your business activities so that you have clear and convincing evidence that the trip was not solely personal in nature. Since a deduction like this is usually substantial, have all expenditures fully documented. Estimates are not appropriate in this situation.

Legal and Other Professional Fees

Sometimes it's hard to differentiate between a fee for ordinary legal services, which is deductible in one year, and a fee for legal services in connection with a purchase of property, which must be added to the cost basis of the property and depreciated over a period of years, or in connection with a sale of property when a legal fee decreases the capital gain generated from the sale.

Your attorney may be performing services for you on an ongoing basis, and your bill may not provide an adequate explanation of the services rendered. If this is the case, ask your attorney for a bill with the services listed. If you can't obtain a more descriptive bill, take an aggressive position by deducting a reasonable part of the entire bill as being applicable toward your business activities.

Most taxpayers are aware that the charge for local Internet service is fully deductible if it is substantially incurred for business purposes. However, what if a person located outside the United States performs services for your business and transmits the work to you via the Internet? Not only are your payments fully deductible business expenses, but you will also not owe any employment taxes or be required to withhold federal income tax.

Repairs

The cost of repairs to a property used in a trade or business is deductible as an ordinary and necessary business expense. Capital expenditures must be depreciated over a period of years. Generally, improvements, additions, or replacements that extend the property's life or increase its value must be capitalized. How do you determine whether the property value increased or if the property's useful life was extended? You should approach your local real estate appraiser, who may provide you with an appraisal that indicates no change in the property's value, which allows you to write off the entire repair in the current year.

A client of mine owns a large commercial building that needs $400,000 of routine repairs and maintenance on the outside walls every four years, which is required by local law. Although you would expect that a job that expensive would normally extend the property's useful life and be capitalized, the expense is deductible ratably over each of the four years ($100,000 per year) as an ordinary, recurring business expense.

YOUR TAX-SAVING STRATEGY

If you do not need additional write-offs, the best approach is to capitalize the expenditure (add to the property's cost basis), and depreciate it over $27\frac{1}{2}$ years (residential) or 39 years (nonresidential). That way you avoid a potential argument with an IRS auditor, since a common IRS position is to push for capitalization of large items rather than expense the items in their entirety in the current year.

Form 1040, Schedule A (Itemized Deductions)

If you're not sure about what and how much to deduct on Schedules C and E, a more appropriate place for your expenses may be Schedule A. Relocating expenses from Schedule C or E to Schedule A will probably reduce the items' deductibility because of the many limitations. However, the trade-off is greater peace of mind and a decreased chance that you'll be audited.

Table 11.2 lists the most common expenses taken on Schedule A and explains their limitations.

TABLE 11.2   Typical Expenses on Schedule A Subject to Limitations

Description of Expenses	Location on Schedule A	How It Works
Medical and dental	Lines 1–4	Otherwise deductible medical and dental expenses must be decreased by $7\frac{1}{2}$ percent of Adjusted Gross Income (AGI).*
Investment interest	Line 13	Deductible only to the extent of net investment income. Unused portion can be carried over to future years.
Contributions by cash or check	Line 15	Donations to public charities are limited to 50 percent of AGI. Unused portion can be carried over for five years. A detailed receipt is required for items $250 or higher.*
Contributions other than by cash or check	Line 16	Form 8283 (Noncash Charitable Contributions). If you make noncash charitable contributions in excess of $500, you must include Form 8283 with your return. If the noncash deduction exceeds $5,000, you will also have to include a separate appraisal on the item donated.
Casualty and theft losses	Line 19	Must be reduced by 10 percent of AGI plus $100.
Job expenses and most other miscellaneous deductions, including unreimbursed employee business expenses	Lines 20, 21, 22	The total of lines 20 through 22 must be reduced by 2 percent of AGI and the net amount entered on line 26.

*See tax-saving strategy in text.

YOUR TAX-SAVING STRATEGY

Self-employed people are allowed to deduct 100 percent of their health insurance premiums from their adjusted gross income (70 percent for 2002).

If you offer group health insurance to all of your employees, and your spouse is one of them, your spouse can elect family coverage, which will include you. This translates into a 100 percent health insurance deduction for your business as compared to the partial deductibility when you pay personally, because of the 7.5 percent of AGI deductible.

These are obvious pluses for anyone owning a business. They also make for a sweeter package of incentives currently available to the dramatically growing number of small business owners as well as to those who work at home.

YOUR TAX-SAVING STRATEGY

Cash contributions of $250 or more require a detailed receipt from the charitable organization. Because of this rule, taxpayers are making these two mistakes: (1) After obtaining the detailed receipt, they are attaching it to the 1040. The only requirement is that you actually have it when the return is filed. (2) Taxpayers are obtaining detailed receipts if their total cash contributions are $250 or higher. You need the detailed receipt only for single cash contributions of $250 or higher.

YOUR TAX-SAVINGS STRATEGY

Donating your old car to a charity can produce a contribution deduction of several thousand dollars or more. However, don't go overboard when assigning a fair market value to the old vehicle. The IRS may not know if the car was damaged but it can recognize inflated values that might be higher than what you could get by selling it, times your tax bracket rate.

What Wage Earners Can Do

Attention everyone out there who earns W-2 income from a salary: You can receive some of the financial benefits that come from loopholes in our tax laws by relocating income and expense items to Schedules E and C.

To do this, you should try to find a way to create self-employment income. As you know from the Hobby Loss Rule, the IRS is constantly monitoring businesses that don't have a profit motive and are carried on as a hobby. So there's no point in creating something that looks like a hobby. What I am suggesting here is the creation of a bona fide business that stems from a personal interest.

Some taxpayers actively pursue a hobby that can easily be turned into a business venture. For example, someone I know, Carl Jennings, a high school teacher, loved to tinker with clocks. He decided to put his free time to better use by beginning a clock-repair service. He began to visit local stores that both sold and repaired clocks and informed the store owners that he was open for business. Three months later, he was so busy he had to turn down new work.

There's no reason why you can't do it too. Follow these guidelines:

- Develop a new source of income, something you always wanted to do but never did. The tax benefits you will gain should give you plenty of motivation and incentive to pull this together.

- Set up your new business so you can work when you want to.
- If the business mushrooms, incorporate as an S corporation.
- Make your home your full-time place of business where most of your relevant business activities occur, and follow the suggestions in this book, which allow you the complete array of home office deductions.
- Take out-of-pocket costs, such as supplies and tools that were previously considered personal items, as items fully deductible against your self-employment income.
- When traveling to suppliers or customers, take deductions for the business use of your auto.
- If possible, make contributions to a self-employed retirement plan, which will eventually supplement your retirement pay from your nine-to-five pension plan.

Before we leave this discussion of how to achieve full deductibility by using Schedules C, E, or A, there's something you need to be warned about: The IRS is constantly on the lookout for taxpayers who use Schedules C and E to load up on expenses that are not fully deductible elsewhere or not deductible at all. Because expenses listed on these two schedules are fully deductible against income, taxpayers tend to abuse this capability. As a result, Schedules C and E have become popular audit triggers (C more so than E). Going too far can get you into trouble. The IRS generally allows reasonable leeway when taxpayers estimate expenses, but you need to avoid crossing the line between a generous estimate of a deduction and downright abuse. Always be prepared with some reasonable explanation for why you have chosen to place your expenses on Schedule C.

Knowing when to be aggressive, especially regarding the opportunities available to taxpayers on Schedules C, E, and A, can save you money and hold up against IRS scrutiny.

RULE 4. FILE YOUR PERSONAL TAX RETURN BY APRIL 15— USE AN EXTENSION ONLY IF ABSOLUTELY NECESSARY

The idea that your return will slip by unnoticed because you file later than April 15 is no longer valid.

Computers are slaves. On April 10, they will process 100,000 returns each day at the same rate as on August 10, when they may process only 5,000 returns.

Some tax professionals argue that workloads are set and returns are selected for audit by the end of August, so if you file in September or October, your return will not be selected for audit. This is a fallacy. A return can be selected for audit at any time. Furthermore, if your return contains some unusually large deductions, the chances of it being selected for audit will not diminish simply because you wait until October to file.

Another theory suggests that the IRS likes to review a return for audit potential when it has leisure time. Therefore, if you file four or five months after April 15, you are giving the IRS what it wants—more time to make up its mind about your return.

There are other, more substantial reasons why you are not well served by delaying the filing of your return. For one thing, hiring a tax professional anytime in April or later is expensive: no doubt 25 to 30 percent higher than normal. This is because the taxpayer must still make a good-faith effort to compute and pay all taxes by April 15 even with the extension form in hand. For the tax professional, the extension requires an unavoidable duplication of effort. The tax professional must first go through all items of income and expense to prepare a reasonable guesstimate. Then, weeks or months later, the same job must be repeated in even greater detail.

Furthermore, for those who pay estimated quarterly taxes, filing late complicates the following year's payments. If you file on August 1, you have already missed the following year's estimated tax due dates of April 15 and June 15. Since you did not have accurate figures to work with, based on the previous year's return, you may have underpaid these estimates and may be subject to underpayment penalties.

RULE 5. DON'T WORRY ABOUT BEING UNABLE TO INTERPRET OR DECIPHER THE COMPLEX IRS TAX FORMS— MANY IRS AUDITORS DON'T UNDERSTAND THEM EITHER

A great deal has been said in this book about the complexity of our tax laws. It is no surprise, therefore, that this same complexity characterizes many of our tax forms. Here are the most complex ones and what to do about them.

Schedule D (Form 1040—Capital Gains and Losses)

Who would have ever thought that a basic 1040 form like Schedule D would be so complicated that the thought of preparing it manually would be unimaginable. The confusion is widespread and includes sophisticated as well as ordinary investors. Tax preparers are blaming Congress for the complexity of Schedule D, which includes 10 different tax rates for capital gains, depending on the type of asset, length of time held, and when it was sold. Although there have been some positive adjustments in the capital gains areas, there are still going to be 40 lines on the Schedule D. The IRS estimates that it will take the average taxpayer four hours, 19 minutes, to complete the schedule without professional help.[1]

Adding to the confusion is the failure of some small mutual funds to provide adequate or timely information. Oftentimes taxpayers receive revised 1099s for the same transaction much later than the original report. Given the changes that have to be included because of ever-changing tax legislation, plus the tight time constraints handed out by Congress, the IRS did a great job of rewriting Schedule D. It encompasses all the aspects of the overly complex capital gains law.

Good luck on this one, but if you are one of the 21 million taxpayers who files this form, I recommend that you do not try Schedule D without a computerized tax program.

Form 6251 (Alternative Minimum Tax—Individuals)

Computing taxable income is based on either the IRS tax table or the alternative minimum tax (AMT) method. The higher of the two is the tax you pay. All taxpayers are supposed to compute their taxes on the basis of these two methods. Determining who is subject to the AMT and who is less likely to be affected by it gets extremely complicated. But if you don't compute AMT, you're placing yourself at risk of being audited.

To complete Form 6251 using the AMT method, you start with your regular taxable income, then make adjustments on the basis of approximately 20 items that Congress has added on over the years. The more common add-ons are personal exemptions, standard deduction (if used), state and local taxes, certain interest expense, part of medical expenses, certain income from exercising incentive stock options, and passive-activity losses. Then you add on "tax preference" items (about 10 in all), special tax deductions given to a select group of taxpayers, many of whom are partners in oil and gas enterprises and real estate investments, whose tax information is passed through via K-1s. If the resulting "Alternative Minimum Taxable Income" (AMTI) exceeds $58,000 for a joint return ($40,250 for single or head of household), then the AMTI is subject to tax at a rate of 26 percent on the first $175,000 and 28 percent on AMTI greater than $175,000. (See newest MSSP Guides in Chapter 7). Nowadays the computer does the work for the IRS, so if you are subject to the AMT and it consists of routine add-ons that can be extracted directly from your tax return (e.g., from itemized deductions), and you fail to file Form 6251, you can be sure the IRS will recompute your tax as submitted on your 1040 and send you a bill for the difference. (See Misconception 6 in Chapter 9.)

Form 8582 (Passive Activity Loss Limitations)

Form 8582 is another terribly complex form—10 pages of instructions—that affects hundreds of thousands of taxpayers. This form is used by people who have investments in any passive activity, such as oil and gas or real estate. The form measures available passive losses for the current year and the amount to be carried over to future years.

The process of filling out this form is a nightmare. First, data must be gathered from your current year and prior year's returns and grouped into two broad categories: "rental real estate activities with active participation" and "all other passive activities." Then activities with net income must be segregated from those with net losses.

Before reporting the information, you must first complete up to six preliminary worksheets preprinted by the IRS that accompany the form. You see, unless the losses described on Form 8582 stem from unincorporated real estate activities that you operate yourself, much of the input for these worksheets originates from K-1s that taxpayers receive from partnership and S corporation investments. Remember that the IRS recently admitted that it has difficulty matching this part of the K-1 to taxpayer returns.

The form determines the amount of passive losses you can deduct this year and how much has to be deferred to future years. So no matter what, if you are a passive investor, you really must go through this exercise and determine whether you are entitled to any current deductions.

Form 8615 (Tax for Children Under Age 14 Who Have Investment Income of More Than $1,500)

The complexity of this form begins with the task of first determining if you are required to file it. (The answer is in Misconception #16, in Chapter 9.) If you do, the plot thickens if your child has capital gain income, which mandates the use of a 54-line two-column monstrosity, part of Form 8615 called Capital Gains Rates Tax Calculation Worksheet. Finally, if you have more than one child under 14 years old with investment income, you have to apportion the extra tax to each child by filling out up to five additional worksheets under one heading, also part of Form 8615—Net Capital Gain Worksheets.

The only plus side to complex forms such as these is this: If you attempt to complete them, you can be confident that an IRS auditor will understand only a little more than you do.

RULE 6. STRIVE TO BE NEAT

I have been telling my clients for years that neat returns, especially computerized ones, are less likely to be audited than handwritten or sloppy ones. Even the IRS has gone on record stating that computerized returns are preferable and, as I see it, less likely to be selected for audit than hand-prepared returns, which often contain errors or are illegible, causing them to be selected for further review. Accordingly, a whole new industry now supplies computer software specifically designed for nonprofessional use, allowing taxpayers to produce extremely complicated schedules (e.g., passive losses).

There are several other areas where neatness and good organization can and should be applied.

When you have been asked to submit material to a tax auditor, the auditor should be handed well-organized records pertaining only to the matter being questioned, with an adding machine tape on the top. The more time an auditor spends on your case, the more pressure he or she is under to collect additional taxes.

Also, when submitting a diary intended to show a detailed log of your travels, be sure that the entries are as neat as possible. In most cases, where a diary is being used as evidence, adequate information contained in the diary will, for IRS purposes, support deductions for entertainment, auto expenses, airline travel, auto rentals, hotels, taxicabs, and local travel.

Records should be in perfect order for corporate audits as well. The IRS revenue agent usually reviews corporate records such as minutes, capital stock certificates, stockholder loan agreements, and related promissory notes. When the corporation has made loans, each disbursement should be covered by a separate promissory note and a set of corporate minutes of the meeting in which the loan was authorized, as well as complete details as to the rate of interest and repayment dates.

RULE 7. WHEN ALL ELSE FAILS, FOLLOW ONE OR MORE OF THESE FOUR STEPS

1. If you haven't already done so, schedule a face-to-face problem-solving meeting with IRS personnel at a Taxpayer Assistance Center. For locations and hours listed by individual states, go to the IRS web site at www.irs.gov under "Individuals/Local IRS Taxpayer Assistance/Contact my Local Office." Make an appointment or just walk in and you can:

- File Innocent Spouse claims.
- Make an Installment Agreement.

- Prepare an Offer in Compromise.
- Request a Release of Federal Tax Lien or Levy.
- Review IRS account or notice issues.

2. If 30 days have gone by with no action, your next step is to contact a Taxpayer Advocate (TA) at 1-877-777-4778. Also obtain a copy of IRS Publication 1546, "The Taxpayer Advocate Service of the IRS." They were formerly called the Problem Resolution Office, and their job is to assist you in resolving problems with the IRS. I have repeatedly said this is the best-kept secret in the IRS because the TA reports directly to Congress, not to the IRS, and also has the discretion *not* to inform the IRS of any contact with you or of any information you provided to a local IRS office.

For urgent matters, you may need Form 911 (Application for Taxpayer Assistance Order to Relieve Hardship) (TAO). It is designed, as the instructions indicate, "for a significant hardship situation that may have already occurred or is about to occur if the IRS takes or fails to take certain actions. A significant hardship normally means not being able to provide the necessities for you or your family." Because of newly broadened powers, you can get the TA to issue a TAO if there is:

- An immediate threat of adverse action.
- A delay of more than 30 days in resolving a taxpayer problem.
- An incurring by the taxpayer of significant costs (attorney's or accountant's fees) if relief is not granted.
- Irreparable injury or long-term adverse impact on the taxpayer if relief is not granted.

*Benefits to taxpayers:*A TAO can be a tremendous help if a taxpayer, or the tax pro or attorney handling the hardship case, is able to secure one. I have had clients whose lives, along with their homes and possessions, have literally been saved by a timely TAO. If the law is applied as intended, hundreds or thousands of TAOs will be authorized, saving taxpayers who desperately need this level of help. If you are in an emergency situation, call the Taxpayer Advocate office directly and someone there will help you fill out Form 911.

3. If you are using a tax professional, tell him that he can receive preferred treatment at the Practitioner Priority Service national hot line, 1-866-860-4259, on weekdays from 7:30 A.M. until 5:30 P.M. local time (Alaska and Hawaii are Pacific time). Account-related inquiries on individual and business tax accounts will be accepted from tax practitioners when representing a client. A valid authorization must first be faxed to the IRS for the taxpayer, type of tax, and tax period involved. From a

professional viewpoint, I have found the personnel covering these phones to be the most helpful and task-oriented in the entire IRS. This service is a *must* for any tax professional.

4. When all else fails, write to your congressperson.

Almost every congressperson has a contact in the IRS who is dedicated to being responsive to taxpayers. If you have been involved with an IRS issue that just isn't getting resolved, try writing to your congressperson. I have recommended this many times with good results. Typically, someone in the congressperson's office calls, followed by someone in the IRS, and in a matter of weeks the issue gets resolved.

Taking this route, however, has its pitfalls. In your first letter, you must fully document the case so that it is clear and accurate. The congressperson will forward your letter to his or her contact in the IRS.

After this the IRS will treat you strictly according to the letter of the law. The IRS is not particularly fond of this approach because it is both a pressure tactic and leaves them no way to wiggle out. However, this should get you the response you've been waiting for.

To learn the name or phone number of your member of Congress, call the U.S. Capitol switchboard: (202) 224-3121 for Senate inquiries; (202) 225-3121 for House inquiries. Tell the operator your zip code and she can give you the phone number of your senator or representative. Give your name, city, and state, and ask for the caseworker on staff.[2] Many representatives can be contacted via the Internet through the House of Representatives home page at www.house.gov/ and selecting "Member Offices." To know who your representative is, go to the Write Your Representative web site at www.house.gov/writerep/. By entering your state and ZIP+4 code, you will be connected to the e-mail system of your member of Congress. You can also reach the Senate and senators from your state at www.senate.gov.

RULE 8. MAKE IT YOUR BUSINESS TO KNOW WHICH TAX LOOPHOLES APPLY TO YOUR PERSONAL TAX SITUATION

By now you know that hundreds of loopholes exist in our tax laws. Creating a complete list of these is impossible. Tax newsletters, sent by subscription only, are full of them. Here are some loopholes that one doesn't often see elsewhere. They are arranged by general subject, and if any apply to you, take advantage of them.

Proceeds from a Lawsuit

What you are receiving from the proceeds of a lawsuit, such as awards due to age discrimination, emotional distress, harassment, physical injuries, or punitive damages, determines whether the award is taxable income. Sometimes an award can be allocated among several categories and reduce your tax bill.

If you receive money that is taxable income to you, the arrangement with your attorney must be planned in advance for the best tax results. Most cases like this are taken on a contingency basis, that is, the attorney's share is tied into the eventual outcome of the case. Have a formal agreement prepared up front that assigns a portion of the legal action to the attorney (assignment of both income and rights to the claim), and have it state that the attorney's fee can be paid only from his share of the gross proceeds. If you follow these instructions, you will have no legal rights to his portion, and the attorney's fee is excluded from your income.[3]

Family Limited Partnerships

The use of Family Limited Partnerships (FLPs) or, as an alternative, Family Limited Liability Companies (FLLCs) has increased recently due to a softening of IRS opposition to FLPs. An FLP is most often used as a tool to reduce estate and gift taxes. An FLP consists of general partners (Mom and Dad) who control the assets of the FLP, plus limited partners (their children) who have no role in managing the assets. Participants in a FLLC are called members.

After Mom and Dad set up the FLP, they transfer personal assets to the FLP, typically including real estate, marketable securities, and shares of family businesses. The children are then given limited partner interests in the FLP, usually 95 to 99 percent of the total FLP pie. Effectively, the assets are held by the children, but Mom and Dad are still in control. Result? Most of the future appreciation of the assets will be excluded from Mom and Dad's estate.

Even better, you can discount the value of assets being transferred, because the children have no control over the assets and would have a tough time selling their FLP interests. The result is that Mom and Dad's gifts of FLP interests to the children are reduced to a discounted value that will use up a smaller chunk of Mom and Dad's $1 million (each) lifetime gift tax exclusion. In recent cases, valuation discounts of 20 to 30 percent have been commonplace.[4]

YOUR TAX-SAVING STRATEGY

Mom and Dad must make tangible current gifts to the children (not future interests) in order to validate the transfers of property. No gift tax return is required as long as Mom and Dad's combined annual gifts do not exceed $22,000 per child. However, you may still want to file gift tax returns to start the running of the three-year statute of limitations, after which the IRS cannot question the returns.

Foreign Income

U.S. citizens and resident aliens who live and work in foreign countries are eligible to exclude from their income up to $80,000 of wages and moving expenses beginning in 2002. To qualify, you must be a resident of the foreign country for an uninterrupted period that includes a full tax year. However, short business trips or vacations are allowed.

If you do not meet these requirements, you may still qualify by meeting the physical presence test. This is achieved if 330 full days out of any 12 consecutive months are spent in a foreign country (or countries—no limit). For example, an engineer working for a company that sends him to work in five different countries during a 12-month period will qualify for the exclusion, even though his 330 days are not consecutive.[5]

Note: For wages that are eligible for the foreign income exclusion, you are not required to pay Social Security taxes. Also, the foreign income exclusion is not automatic and must be elected on Form 2555, Foreign Earned Income, and attached to your Form 1040.

You Want to Eliminate IRS Penalties

There are approximately 150 penalties that the IRS can impose on you, the most common ones being for late payment of taxes or late filing of tax returns. Before you try to get the penalties abated, complete the filing of past due returns and try to pay the amounts of tax and interest that are due. Interest charges cannot be waived. This will, it's hoped, put the IRS employee into a conciliatory frame of mind.

Although the IRS does not publicly disclose a list of acceptable reasons for lowering a taxpayer's penalties, you have to show that you acted reasonably and in good faith. Here's the scoop on what the IRS may be moved by.

In my experience, health- and age-related reasons are accepted a majority of the time. This includes physical or emotional illness (including drug and alcohol abuse); health problems of family members, especially if you are a care provider; your advanced age; emotional problems caused by a divorce; and nonfiling or nonpayment caused by your ex-spouse, which, in turn, has prompted you to file for Innocent Spouse Relief (see "Innocent Spouse" Relief, Chapter 12). Another excuse that has recently prompted the IRS to reduce a taxpayer's penalties involved a business owner who was having unusual business problems that kept him at the office an unreasonable amount of time—for example, more than 14 hours a day, seven days a week.

Surprisingly, the IRS will not lower penalties if your tax preparer was sick, or even passed away. In this case, the IRS says you should have taken precautions to avoid late filing or late payments. Furthermore, someone with a chronically unreliable filing history would have diminished chances of having these excuses being accepted. On the other hand, the IRS frequently grants waivers for penalties incurred by first-time offenders.

You're Facing Bankruptcy

According to bankruptcy law, taxpayers can file a bankruptcy petition, which must be done with the help of a professional. Although this can be expensive and complicated to execute, here's what it can do for you: It can bring collection activities to a halt. The government cannot issue a notice of intent to levy, nor can the government seize your property and sell it for the payment of taxes.

In our current environment of easy credit, many taxpayers have been falling behind in paying their bills. Ultimately many file for personal and/or business bankruptcy. Since one of the ultimate creditors is bound to be the IRS, there are steps taxpayers can take to ease their burden if they fall on financially hard times. Even if your tax liability is insurmountable, be sure to file your return on time. In a federal bankruptcy court proceeding, filing in a timely manner could result in your tax liability being discharged in as little as three years. Even newly assessed tax liabilities, such as those caused by a tax audit, are dischargeable only 40 days after they have been assessed.

For Married Couples

If you are married and either of you is involved in a bankruptcy, you and your spouse should file separate returns. With separate returns, each spouse is responsible only for his or her own tax liability. This allows at least one spouse to remain debt-free.

The disadvantages in this are that separate return rates are higher, and itemized deductions such as mortgage interest and real estate tax can be deducted only by the spouse who pays for them. But with a little forethought and planning, you can end up in a better place if the spouse who earns the highest income pays for these kinds of major deductions.

If you file jointly, the IRS can go after either spouse to collect any unpaid tax assessments, although relief is given to the innocent spouse if the innocent spouse can prove he or she had no knowledge or limited knowledge of the other spouse's misdeeds. (See Chapter 12.)

YOUR TAX-SAVINGS STRATEGY
If you expect a refund upon filing your return, and your spouse has unpaid assessments to the IRS, you could attach Form 8379, Injured Spouse

Claim and Allocation, to your return. This *should* result in your receiving a timely refund. In some cases, the IRS has disregarded the instructions on Form 8379 and has attempted to apply the refund of the innocent spouse against the assessment of the other spouse. It generally takes many months before the error is corrected and your money is returned. If you are counting on a prompt receipt of the refund that you are rightfully entitled to, file a separate tax return.

If you cannot pay your taxes promptly and cannot work out an installment agreement with the IRS, your IRA can be levied upon and seized. Furthermore, when the financial institution holding your IRA pays over the money to the IRS, it is considered a taxable distribution to the taxpayer. However, the 10 percent early distribution penalty for taxpayers under $59\frac{1}{2}$ years of age does not apply to distributions made on account of an IRS levy.

If you feel that the seizure of your IRA by the IRS is imminent, withdraw the money immediately and send in an estimated tax payment representing the income tax and penalty on the withdrawal. You then at least have control over the balance of the proceeds.

For Divorcing Couples: Who's Entitled to Exemptions for the Children?

If you are separated or divorced, and you wish to claim a child as an exemption, one of the five dependency tests you must meet is that more than one-half of the support must be furnished by the parent, or by both parents combined in the case of divorced or separated parents. Even if the noncustodial parent actually provides up to 100 percent of the dependent's support, the custodial parent is deemed to have provided more than half of the dependent's support and, accordingly, is entitled to the exemption. However, the custodial parent can release the exemption to the noncustodial parent by using Form 8332 (Release of Claim to Exemption for Child of Divorced or Separated Parents).

Exception: If a couple with a child have never been married to each other, only the parent who has provided more than half of the child's support can take the dependency exemption. The qualifying parent cannot release the exemption to anyone else.

Alimony and Child Support

Alimony is generally deductible by the person who pays it and is taxable income to the person who receives it. Child support is not deductible nor is it taxable income.

A well-planned divorce agreement will allow the higher earner, who is usually making the payments, to have as much as possible treated as alimony, which is tax-deductible. Even if the higher-earning spouse covers the tax liability of the lower-earning spouse, the savings could be substantial. For example, a husband is in a combined federal and state tax bracket of 45 percent and his wife is in a 20 percent bracket. If $10,000 of child support is relabeled alimony, the wife incurs taxes of 20 percent of $10,000, or $2,000, for which she is reimbursed by her ex-husband. The husband saves 45 percent of $12,000 of payments, or $5,400, a net savings of $3,400.

Tax Basis of Assets

Not all assets are alike, especially with respect to their cost basis for tax purposes. During divorce negotiations, try to retain assets that have a high cost basis. This will result in smaller capital gains when you ultimately dispose of the assets. Also, benefits in qualified retirement plans must be payable pursuant to a qualified domestic relations order (QDRO) so that the transferring spouse will not be taxed on any benefits transferred to the other spouse. The QDRO must specify the exact amount of benefits payable to the other spouse and be delivered in writing to the plan administrator.

You Are Incorporated as a C Corporation, and the Corporation Is Discontinued because of Heavy Losses

A shareholder can take the loss of his capital investment on his 1040 as an ordinary loss and not as a capital loss by using Section 1244 of the Internal Revenue Code. On a joint return, you can deduct losses from the sale or worthlessness of Section 1244 stock up to $100,000 ($50,000 on separate returns). Any excess above the threshold is a capital loss. This provision is limited to companies whose original capitalization is under $1 million and covers only regular operating businesses, not tax shelters or real estate. *Note:* There are no disadvantages to using this provision. If your business does well, Section 1244 will be forgotten.

You Have a Highly Appreciated Business Asset, But You Don't Want to Pay Capital Gains

Use Like-Kind Exchanges

You could merely want to acquire a property that requires less time and effort to manage than your current one, or you are looking for more rental income.

This is the time to use the flexibility of like-kind exchanges, commonly known as Section 1031 property. If investment or business property is exchanged solely for like-kind property, no gain or loss is recognized on the swap, and the new replacement property that you own assumes the cost basis of the old property that you gave up. The type of property most often used here is appreciated real estate. Some assets that are excluded from this section are foreign real estate, publicly traded securities, and inventory of the business. If cash accompanies the swap, gain must be recognized by the recipient equal to the amount of cash received, commonly called "boot." If one party assumes liabilities in an amount greater than the other party, the excess is also deemed to be boot.

Since it is often difficult to put both parties together to do a simultaneous transfer, a delayed exchange is possible with a few conditions. After the transfer, the replacement property must be identified within 45 days and the deal must be completed within 180 days of the transfer. In a delayed exchange, the recommended method is to have the original sales proceeds held by a qualified intermediary (usually a financial institution) in order to conform to several administrative details. The rules may seem complex, but the reduced tax bill will simplify the process for all participants. Also, you can hold on to the property indefinitely or exchange it for other properties by using Section 1031 repeatedly. An added benefit is that at your death your heirs will receive the property with a stepped-up cost basis, which will result in the deferred capital gains tax never being paid.

You Operate as a Sole Proprietorship or S Corporation, and You Want to Hire Your Dependent Child

The major advantage to hiring your dependent child (under 18 years of age) to work in your sole proprietorship is that you don't have to pay FICA and Medicare taxes. (Of course the salary must be paid for actual services rendered.) Remember that the first $4,750 of wages paid is not subject to income tax because that is the standard deduction for single taxpayers. The next $7,000 is taxed at 10 percent, and the next $21,400 is taxed at 15 percent.

The Tax Court has allowed deductible salaries for children as young as 7 years old. See *James A. Moriarty*, T.C. Memorandum 1984–249.

You and your child can save some additional money if he or she contributes up to $3,000 to a traditional IRA—for example, to save for college. (Even though taxes and a penalty would have to be paid when the money is withdrawn early—before your child reaches retirement age—the benefit of the current deduction still makes it worthwhile.) Assuming the child's taxable income is not more than $28,400, you will be able to save about $450 on federal taxes, because no tax will have to be paid on the $3,000 in the IRA. You can also put $2,000 annually into a Coverdell

Education Savings Account, or a Roth IRA may be a better solution. (see Chapter 12.)

This discussion concerns wages, or earned income, of a dependent. Don't confuse this scenario with the so-called kiddie tax, which is a tax on the investment income (interest and dividends) of children under age 14 and is based on the parents' tax rates. (See Chapter 9.)

If you pay wages to your children from an S corporation, you must pay FICA and Medicare taxes, because all corporate wages are subject to these taxes. But there is another advantage with an S corporation: You can reduce your tax bill by splitting income with other members of your family. This is accomplished by allowing each family member to own stock in the corporation. Each person reports his or her share of income on the 1040, including children, who will probably be in the lowest tax bracket.

Warning: This arrangement works best with children over 14 years of age, who are not subject to the "kiddie tax."

Warning: In this situation, parents/owners cannot take an unreasonably low salary to reduce personal taxable income, because if this is discovered during an audit, the IRS can reallocate income among family members.

You Operate a Business, and You are Thinking of Buying Your Own Building

A common mistake is to form a regular C corporation to acquire the real estate. When the company disposes of the property, a double tax will generally result. The first tax is at the corporate level upon sale, and then the shareholders are taxed on the proceeds received in liquidation of the business.

Better way: Take ownership of the property through an LLC or partnership and then lease it to the operating business. In this way, there will be only one tax at the personal level, and lease payments will be deductible by the business and will probably be at least partially tax sheltered to the property owners by depreciation deductions that they can take on their personal returns for the leased property. Moreover, they retain greater flexibility to finance or sell the property for their own account with the funds raised in the process being locked in the business. And if an owner dies while still owning the property, his heirs will inherit the property at fair-market value, effectively eliminating taxable gain on the appreciation in the property's value to that point.

Even better: Transfer gift shares of the LLC or partnership to your children who are over age 13 and who are probably in a much lower tax bracket than you. Gifts can qualify for minority interest" and "lack of marketability" valuation discounts for gift tax purposes, which together may amount to as much as 40 percent. This can enable a series of gifts to transfer much more than their gift-tax valuation in terms of value of the gift property. For instance, with a 33 percent valuation discount, a tax-free $11,000 gift can transfer ownership of $16,500 of assets.

Choosing the Best Pension Plan

If you are a business owner who has few or no employees, you might want to forget about the more cumbersome profit-sharing, Keogh, or de-fined benefit pension plans and take a good, hard look at a Simplified Employee Pension (SEP) plan or Solo 401(k) plan.

SEP Advantages:
- To set up a plan, you need to fill out only a one-page form.
- No additional reports or annual tax returns need to be filed.
- Setup of the plan can be done and deductible contributions can be made up until the extended due date of your return, say, October 15, 2004. Most other plans have to be in place by year's end.
- You can skip a contribution altogether if you have a bad year.
- Beginning in 2002, you can contribute up to 25 percent of salary or self-employed earnings ($200,000 maximum) or $40,000, whichever is less.
- Even though you have a SEP, you can still contribute another $3,000 to a traditional or Roth IRA if you qualify.

Disadvantages: If you have employees, you'll have to contribute the same percentage of their pay that you do for yourself. Also, if your earn-ings are under $50,000, you will probably achieve a higher deduction by setting up a SIMPLE pension plan (see Chapter 12).[6]

If you are a business owner who wants to maximize contributions to your retirement plan and have no employees except your spouse, the Solo 401(k) might be your best choice.

Solo 401(k) Advantages
- Deductible contributions have two parts: (1) Beginning in 2002, you can contribute up to 25 percent of salary or self-employed earnings ($200,000 maximum) or $40,000; and/or (2) up to $12,000 ($1,000 more if age 50 or older) not exceeding 100 percent of com-pensation; the total of (1) and (2) must not exceed $40,000. If your spouse is employed by you, he or she is entitled to receive the same generous contributions. Businesses with multiple owners can set up this plan as long as there are no employees beyond the owners and their spouses.
- You can skip a contribution altogether if you have a bad year.

- To set up a plan, minimal paper work is required and setup charges are minimal.
- Income from a sideline business is eligible. However, your total contributions to this and other 401(k) plans cannot exceed the 2003 limit of $12,000.

Disadvantages: If you have employees, you'll have to contribute the same percentage of their pay that you do for yourself. Setup of the plan must be completed by December 31 even though contributions can be completed as late as the employer's tax-filing due date, including extensions. Once the plan assets exceed $100,000, a Form 5500-EZ will have to be filed annually.

The Best Pension Plan for Business Owners Over 50

If you are older than 50 and the majority of your employees are 20 years or more younger than you, you can contribute much larger amounts if you adopt a defined benefit plan, which provides for specified benefits, typically in the form of a monthly retirement pension based on levels of compensation and years of service. Plan contributions are actuarially calculated to provide the promised benefit and are not allocated to individual accounts for the participants. Since you are closer to retirement than your younger workers and will require a larger pension, your annual contribution can be $50,000 or more in many cases, while your younger employees receive considerably smaller amounts. If they leave before they are fully vested, their contributions revert to the plan, leaving you with reduced future contributions.

TAX-SAVINGS STRATEGY

If you are short on cash, fund your retirement plan contribution with a refund. Deductible contributions to qualified retirement plans, including SEPs, can generally be made until the extended due date of the tax return, even if the return is actually filed before then. File an extension, then immediately file the tax return to claim a refund, deducting plan contributions on the return to help generate the refund. When the refund arrives, use it to help finance the retirement plan contributions.

You Want to Lease an Automobile for Business Purposes Instead of Buying One

Over the years the IRS has set up special tables for the annual depreciation of an auto used for business. In 2001 and 2002, an automobile costing more than $15,500 was considered to be a luxury car. For luxury cars placed in service in 2001 and 2002 (any automobile used for business purposes), you could take maximum depreciation of $3,060 for the first year, $4,900 for the second year, $2,950 for the third year, and $1,775 for each succeeding year. *Caution:* These dollar caps are applicable if the automobile is used 100 percent for business.

The Job Creation and Worker Assistance Act passed in 2002 increased first-year depreciation on luxury vehicles to $7,660, a $4,600 increase. The increase is effective for vehicles acquired from September 11, 2001, to December 31, 2004, and placed in service by December 31, 2004. The Tax Act of 2003 increased first-year depreciation on luxury vehicles to $10,710, a $7,650 increase, for vehicles placed in service after May 5, 2003. If you are eligible for both, you can elect either one, or neither one; it's up to you.

YOUR TAX-SAVINGS STRATEGY

If you bought an auto for work between September 11, 2001 and December 31, 2002 and did not take the extra depreciation on your 2001 or 2002 returns, you can file an amended return to claim the extra deduction of up to $4,600 now, and obtain a corresponding tax refund.

If you lease a luxury car that has a fair market value in excess of $15,500, you are required to include in your W-2 income an amount specified for that market value. You can find these values in IRS Publication 463, "Travel, Entertainment, Gift, and Car Expenses," or call 1-800-TAX-FORM, or go to the IRS web site at www.irs.gov.

Theoretically this additional W-2 income treats leased autos the same as purchased autos for tax purposes. In actual practice, though, you obtain a much greater tax savings when you lease an auto, especially if the lease is for at least four years. For example, if you leased a car in 2002 valued at $32,000 for four years at a rate of $475 per month, over four years you'd pay a total of $22,800. According to the IRS's "leasing inclusion table," assuming the car could be claimed as 100 percent business use, you would have to add back to your income $779 over the four-year period. Therefore, your net tax deduction for the four years is $22,021.

If, instead, you purchased the car for $32,000, your monthly payments would be considerably higher and the depreciation deductions on your business tax return would be only $17,285. The extra write-off ($22,021 − $17,285) is $4,736, and if you are in the 33 percent tax bracket, this is a tax savings of $1,562.88.

One downside to leasing is that if you put on high mileage, you will have to pay a hefty 10 to 20 cents per mile for excess mileage over the typically allowable 15,000 miles per year. On the other hand, buying a high-priced car usually requires a substantial down payment, while leasing requires only a deposit equal to one or two monthly payments. Also, a leased car cannot be taken by creditors, whereas an owned car can. If you buy a new car, you can probably use it for seven or eight years, but the paramount advantage of leasing is that you get the luxury of driving a new car every four years, along with a substantial business lease deduction that is more advantageous than if you bought a vehicle.

If the auto is used 100 percent for personal use, leasing and buying end up costing about the same, assuming you sell the auto just after you finish paying the last installment. But if you keep the personal-use auto for a long time, leasing is more expensive. Also, if you drive a luxury vehicle such as a sports car, those vehicles often depreciate very quickly in the first few years, which means a purchase would make more economic sense.

You Want to Lease a Sport Utility Vehicle

Much larger depreciation deductions are available for some sports utility vehicles (SUVs) than for other cars—and the JCWA and the Tax Act of 2003 made these deductions larger still. The reason is that vehicles weighing more than 6,000 pounds are not subject to the depreciation limits that apply to autos generally. Therefore full depreciation is allowed as follows:

Year 1	20.00 percent	Year 4	11.52 percent
Year 2	32.00 percent	Year 5	11.52 percent
Year 3	19.20 percent	Year 6	5.76 percent

Moreover, like most other business equipment, a heavy luxury business car is eligible for additional first-year depreciation—Section 179 depreciation—and also for the 30 percent bonus first-year depreciation that is provided by the JCWA or the 50 percent bonus provided by the Tax Act of 2003. Combined, regular depreciation, Section 179, and bonus depreciation can provide tremendous first-year deductions for a vehicle. As an example, take a $50,000 luxury SUV weighing over 6,000 pounds, purchased in 2002 and used 100 percent for business.

First, $24,000 of its cost could be deducted immediately using a Section 179 election, reducing its undeducted basis to $26,000.

Second, 30 percent bonus depreciation could be claimed on the remaining basis of $26,000, giving another deduction of $7,800, and reducing the undeducted basis in the SUV to $18,200.

Third, the regular first-year 20 percent depreciation for vehicles can be claimed for the remaining basis, giving an additional depreciation deduction of $3,640.

All together, $35,440 ($24,000 + $7,800 + $3,640) of the SUV's price is deductible in the first year—more than 70 percent of its cost—compared to only $7,660 for a lighter luxury auto. The first year deduction for the SUV was more than *4.5 times larger* than for a lighter luxury car with the same price.

For 2003, the Tax Act of 2003 increased the allowable Section 179 amount to $100,000. Accordingly, if you bought a new eligible SUV in 2003 for up to $100,000, you can write-off the entire amount in the first year.

You Want to Trade in a Car Used for Business Purposes

When an old car that has been used for business purposes is traded in for a new business car, no gain or loss is recognized. The basis of the old car (generally cost less accumulated depreciation) is added to the net cost of the new car, and a new depreciation period begins. This can produce positive results if you would have ended up with a gain on the sale of the old car, since no gain will be recognized for tax purposes until the vehicle is sold. But if your old car was expensive and its sale would result in a recognized tax loss if sold outright, what you can do is sell the car for cash and buy a new car with the proceeds. In that way, you will have a deductible business loss that you can use on this year's return.

RULE 9. USE TO YOUR ADVANTAGE THE FACT THAT THE IRS SYSTEM FOR DOCUMENT RETRIEVAL IS ARCHAIC

Given what you already know about the massive failure of the IRS's Tax Systems Modernization, if should be no surprise that the IRS still faces grave problems when it comes to retrieving tax returns.

The negative implications of these problems continue to be far-reaching. Hundreds of thousands of individual taxpayers, as well as IRS staffs from Examination, Collection, and CID who work directly with taxpayers, are all stymied by the situation. But probably the most visible person who has to deal with this embarrassing mess, aside from the taxpayer and the taxpayer's representative, is the IRS auditor who is preparing for an audit, or who is in the midst of one. Not being able to locate a specific tax return consistently affects an auditor's role, behavior, and performance.

Mrs. Raymond hired me as her accountant in 1994 and asked whether I could assist her in obtaining a home equity loan. This was not an easy task, since the IRS had placed a lien on her house and I have not yet come across a mortgage lender who will provide a borrower with any funds if the IRS has a lien on that person's property.

I discovered that the IRS had disallowed a tax shelter deduction from Mrs. Raymond's 1985 tax return. After the tax was assessed, the IRS filed the lien in October 1990.

Further investigation made me increasingly suspicious. Each time I phoned the IRS, all I got were indirect answers. I also wondered why the IRS had not sent

Mrs. Raymond even one collection letter during the past three years. I did find out that the tax Mrs. Raymond owed, including penalties and interest, amounted to over $100,000.

I finally reached an auditor at the IRS office in Mrs. Raymond's hometown who had been assigned to the case and who admitted to me that Mrs. Raymond's entire file had been lost! He had turned the situation over to his supervisor because it was "too hot to handle." The supervisor delayed for another three months while he insisted on a thorough search of the storage warehouse where Mrs. Raymond's file might have been sent in error—a warehouse in Passaic, New Jersey.

When the search proved fruitless, the supervisor would not take the responsibility of excusing a $100,000 case simply because a file had been misplaced. He forwarded the case to the regional Problem Resolution Office (PRO), obviously hoping for a miracle. Nothing was solved, but at least the matter was out of his hands.

Everyone I dealt with at the IRS tried to hide this information trail from me as long as they could.

After only 30 days—PRO is the most efficient unit in the entire IRS—a credit was put through for the entire $100,000. A short while later, Mrs. Raymond's equity loan cleared.

Auditors like to have some independent corroboration of items of income so they can verify what the taxpayer has previously included on the tax return being examined. After all, they are trained to look for information that may be missing, altered, or omitted intentionally, and part of their job is not to accept automatically what the taxpayer or the taxpayer's representative is handing over.

But any IRS auditor knows that when a request for a copy of a tax return is made, the return may not be received until after the audit is completed, or too late in the audit process for it to be useful.

A successful self-employed sales rep, Mr. Joseph, was being audited for 1996. His business operations were filed on Form 1040, Schedule C, and an 1120S (Income Tax Return for an S Corporation), since he also owned part of an S corporation in a separate business.

During the audit, the agent requested copies of Mr. Joseph's 1040s for 1995 and 1997 and the 1120Ss for 1995 and 1996. I gave the auditor Mr. Joseph's 1040 for 1997 and the 1120S for 1996 (which was the final return filed for this corporation), and said we didn't have copies of the 1040 or 1120S for 1995. The returns were destroyed in a flood that Mr. Joseph had at his former office. The auditor naturally said he'd try to retrieve them from the IRS system.

Expecting that the IRS would take a minimum of 45 days to get the copies, if they ever got them, I made my next and final date with the auditor less than 30 days later. At that meeting, the auditor still had not received the requested tax returns, so he proceeded with the audit, disallowing $9,500 of items on Mr. Joseph's Schedule C business return (specifically insurance and entertainment), and then closed the case. If the missing returns contained any information that could have been damaging to Mr. Joseph, the IRS will never know.

How to Take Advantage of the IRS's Ancient Retrieval System

The implications of this situation for taxpayers are particularly important if you are facing or involved in an audit. Take your time locating a copy of an earlier return if you think that a prior return will

- Contradict any information on the return being audited.
- Provide reasons for the auditor to examine additional areas for which you have less than adequate proof.

You are playing for time here, because time is most likely on your side, as we just discussed. For example, you may know that something on a past or current return will show up as an inconsistency—a K-1 from a rental property that no longer appears, or dividend income on an investment for which the dividend is no longer reported and there is no reported sale of the investment. There may be adequate explanations for these inconsistencies, but you should conclude the audit as soon as possible before the auditor receives the requested information from the IRS.

RULE 10. IF YOU ARE INVOLVED WITH IRS PERSONNEL IN ANY WAY, BEHAVE DECENTLY

When dealing with revenue officers in particular, do not make them angry by complaining about the IRS in general terms, by treating them rudely, lying to them, or insisting that you're being treated unfairly. If you do, they will be more prone to use their arsenal of weapons—liens, levies, seizures, and sales of property—in an arbitrary and capricious manner.

If you receive any correspondence from the IRS, answer it promptly. If you have received a notice of tax due and you do not agree with it, or if you know for a fact that the IRS is wrong, do not disregard the notice or the IRS. Send a letter to the IRS with the notice, explaining why you feel the tax is incorrect. If you can't pay the tax, send in a token payment and say that more money will be coming shortly.

This way you are appealing to the human side of the person who reads your response. You can appease that person for a while as long as he or she does not think that you are a renegade. You also have ample opportunity to restate your case to his or her supervisor or to an appeals officer, if you choose.

This is the perfect place for me to reinforce one of the major themes of this book: learning about the IRS personality. Don't forget, with an IRS auditor you're usually dealing with a civil service employee who is just trying to get through the day without making waves. Most often, these IRS staff members are not ambitious enough to go through the extra effort required to make life miserable for you. But if you anger them with a poor attitude, they will probably try harder to get the added proof needed to show that you are not telling the truth.

12

The Latest Tax Legislation:
What to Watch Out For,
How to Benefit

In June 2001, the long-awaited Economic Growth and Tax Relief Reconciliation Act of 2001 was signed by President Bush as the Tax Act of 2001. Some of the changes began in 2002, but most of the changes were scheduled to go into effect in 2003 and later. At the urging of the President, Congress subsequently passed an economic stimulus package in June 2003 entitled the Job and Growth Tax Relief Reconciliation Act of 2003, (the Tax Act of 2003) which accelerates the effective dates of many of the provisions contained in the Tax Act of 2001. Other new provisions of the Tax Act of 2003 affect the tax rates on capital gains and dividend income and contain additional benefits for corporations, large and small. The 2001 and 2003 acts affect almost every part of an individual's return, and corporate returns as well. There are new, reduced income tax rates, and changes in such areas as retirement savings, education savings and deductions, the marriage penalty, tax breaks for children, estate and gift taxes, and others. Many have been noted throughout this book in the pertinent subject areas.

The discussion of the provisions of the 2001 and 2003 tax acts within this book is not intended to be all-inclusive. However, all important changes that affect the average individual taxpayer for 2001 and beyond are here. Not included are numerous administrative changes to pension and retirement plans that pertain mainly to big companies and governmental organizations, and certain estate tax provisions that pertain only to the very wealthy.

This chapter begins with a discussion of the Jobs and Growth Tax Relief Reconciliation Act of 2003, which is followed by a discussion of the other important tax legislation of the past five years, grouped by subject.

This comprehensive analysis includes the most important far-reaching provisions of the Tax Act of 2001.

THE JOBS AND GROWTH TAX RELIEF RECONCILIATION ACT OF 2003

Capital Gains Legislation

The maximum tax on net long-term capital gains has generally been lowered to 15 percent (5 percent for those whose incomes are in the 10 or 15 percent tax bracket). To qualify, you must hold the asset for more than 12 months. If you hold the asset for one year or less, you will be subject to tax at your ordinary income tax rate, ranging up to 35 percent.

While these changes are positive, there continue to be two unfavorable exceptions:

1. The maximum tax on net long-term capital gains of collectibles such as artwork, stamps, and coins will continue to be 28 percent even though they need only be held for more than 12 months.
2. Net long-term capital gains attributable to real property will be taxed at two rates. To the extent depreciation has generally been taken on the property, the maximum tax rate will be 25 percent. The balance of capital gain, if any, will be taxed at the lower, favorable rate of 15 percent.

Capital Losses
The Tax Act of 2003 does not change the $3,000 annual capital loss limitation. Capital losses will also not be available for offset against qualifying dividends even though such dividends are subject to the same rates at capital gains. Thus, $3,000 of available capital losses will be applied against ordinary income; dividends will be taxed separately at capital gains rates.

IRAs and Qualified Pension Plans
The benefit of the lower tax rates on capital gains will not apply to gains generated within qualified plans, such as 401(k) plans and IRAs. Distributions from these accounts will still be taxed as ordinary income regardless of the source of income.

Effective Date
The new capital gains rates generally apply to capital assets sold after May 5, 2003, and installment payments received after May 5, 2003. Mutual funds, as well as individuals, will have to segregate sales by date, which will add eight new lines to the much more complicated Sched-

ule D. In addition, the IRS estimates that up to six million individuals who could file Form 1040A when reporting capital gains distributions from mutual funds will now be required to file Form 1040 and attach Schedule D.

Dividend Income Legislation

The top federal tax rate for dividends received by individuals is reduced to 15 percent (5 percent for those whose incomes are in the 10 or 15 percent tax bracket). These are the same rates that are applicable to capital gains.

The lower tax rates apply to dividends received from a domestic corporation or a qualified foreign corporation on or after January 1, 2003. This includes dividends passed through to investors by mutual funds, real estate investment trusts, partnerships, and so on.

IRAs and Qualified Pension Plans

Investments in retirement plans such as 401(k) plans and traditional IRAs receive no benefit from the rate reduction. Distributions from these accounts will still be taxed as ordinary income even if the funds represent dividends paid on stocks held in the account.

Holding Period Qualification for Reduced-Rate Dividends

For a dividend to be eligible for the reduced rates, the recipient must hold the stock for at least 61 days during the 120-day period surrounding the ex-dividend date. There is a separate 61-day holding period requirement for each dividend.

Interest Income

Interest earned on savings accounts, certificates of deposit and government bonds is still taxed at ordinary tax rates. The new low tax rates apply only to stock dividends.

Depreciation

JCWAA created a 30 percent additional first-year bonus depreciation allowance for qualifying property acquired between September 11, 2002, and September 10, 2004, and placed in service by December 31, 2004. The allowance is generally available for new business property that has a recovery period of 20 years or less.

For assets acquired after May 5, 2003, the Tax Act of 2003 increased the first-year bonus depreciation to 50 percent and extended the period that you have to acquire the property until December 31, 2004. Also increased by the Tax Act of 2003 is the maximum dollar amount that may be deducted under Section 179 (additional first-year depreciation). It has been increased from $25,000 to $100,000 for qualifying property placed in service from January 1, 2003, to December 31, 2005 (see Form 8829, Chapter 7 and "Depreciation of Assets," Chapter 8). The $100,000 limit is phased out dollar-for-dollar for any qualifying property placed in service during the year that exceeds $400,000. Here's a comprehensive example for a qualifying business asset that was acquired on June 15, 2003 for $150,000:

Original cost	$150,000
Section 179 deduction	−100,000
Balance	$ 50,000
Bonus deduction—50%	− 25,000
Balance	$ 25,000
Regular first year deduction—20%	− 5,000
Balance	$ 20,000

The result is that the taxpayer received an immediate depreciation deduction in the amount of $130,000 in the first year.

Your Tax Savings Strategy

If assets purchased in the same year have different useful lives for depreciation purposes and you want to use Section 179, take the deduction on the longest-lived assets first. Also, if you are in a tax bracket of 15 percent of less, it may be better not to take any of the Section 179 deduction if you expect to be in a higher income tax bracket in later years. Depreciation may provide a more valuable tax benefit to reduce taxable income in the following years.

Your Tax Savings Strategy

Small business off-the-shelf software previously had to be depreciated and deducted on a straight-line basis over 36 months. It can be expensed immediately as part of Section 179.

The Marriage Tax Penalty Legislation

Here's the story: Do you believe that the "married-joint" filing status allows you to pay less in taxes than a "single" filing status, or that the "married-joint" tax rates and exemptions are double those of the "single" filer? Wrong. The marriage penalty kicks in whenever both spouses work and end up paying more taxes as a couple than they would if each of them were single. This generally happens when both spouses have relatively equal incomes. For example, using the 2003 tax tables that were in use prior to the Tax Act of 2003, if Bruce and Nancy each earned $35,000, and each filed as a single taxpayer without other income such as interest, dividends, and capital gains, and each used the standard deduction of $4,750 for a single filer instead of itemizing deductions, each would have to pay federal tax in the amount of $3,780. That means their total tax bill together, using the single filing status, would amount to $7,560. If Bruce and Nancy had the exact same income but they were married and filed a "married-joint" tax return in 2003, their tax bill would amount to $8,812.50. In other words, as a married couple, they would have to pay $1,252.50 in additional taxes, about 16 percent more.

How did this come into being? First, the standard deduction for a single taxpayer is $4,750 in 2003, while the standard deduction on a joint return is $7,950. Shouldn't the deduction on the joint return be at least double that of the single return, or $9,500? The fact is, it's not, and therein lies the penalty for married folks. Second, federal tax brackets, which delineate taxable income ranges and the percent they are taxed at, are not set up in a logical fashion. For example, in 2003, using the old tables, if a single person has taxable income of $25,350 and files a single return, he or she is taxed at a rate of 15 percent on taxable income above $6,000 ($19,350). Wouldn't you expect that the taxable income of a married couple subject to the 15 percent rate would be double the $19,350, or $38,700? As before, it simply doesn't work that way, because the top end of the 15 percent rate for a joint return is only $47,450 in 2003, significantly less than twice the single top end amount of $28,400. As a result, some of the joint-return taxable income is taxed at the next highest rate of 27 percent, while the two single returns are not taxed above the 15 percent rate.

The situation becomes more complex the more you examine it. There are other penalties that affect married people besides the standard deduction and the bias in tax rates. For example, couples generally face a quicker phaseout of itemized deductions and personal exemptions, and lower deductions regarding rental property and capital losses. But in a more favorable light, a tax "bonus" (reduction in taxes) might be realized by couples who file jointly but have a wide discrepancy in their earnings, or couples with only one working spouse.

For any married person who thinks it's possible to avoid the marriage penalty by filing "married-separate" tax returns, think again. When married couples file separately, they cannot use the "single" tax rates used for unmarried people; they must use the "married, filing separate" rates. True, these rates are exactly half of those for the "married, filing joint" tax brackets, but they are still less favorable than the "single" rates. So the marriage penalty is generally not eliminated. As with every tax situation, there are upsides and downsides regarding possible options available for couples who want to avoid the marriage penalty.

The Tax Acts of 2001 and 2003 finally provide tax relief from the marriage penalty. There are three basic areas in which the legislation provides relief from the marriage penalty: increases to the standard deduction for joint filers that will double that for single filers; increases in the size of the 15 percent tax bracket for joint filers that is twice that for single filers; and increases in the phaseout range for joint filers relating to the Earned Income Credit.

For the 2003 tax year, the standard deduction for single filers is 200 percent of the standard deduction for married taxpayers filing jointly. Effective for the 2005 tax year, the gap between two single standard deductions and one married-filing-joint standard deduction will flip back to 174 percent and then gradually increase again to 200 percent in 2009. The following is a summary showing the standard deduction for married couples filing a joint return as a percentage of the standard deduction for single individuals during the next seven years:

2003 and 2004	200%
2005	174%
2006	184%
2007	187%
2008	190%
2009 and beyond	200%

The second area of modification relating to the marriage penalty involves the increase in the 15 percent tax bracket. For the 2003 tax year, tax bracket ranges for single filers are 200 percent of those for married couples filing joint returns (similar in concept to the standard deduction). Effective for the 2005 year, the percentage of 15 percent bracket sizes for single filers will flip back to 180 percent and then gradually increase again to 200 percent in 2008. The following is a summary of the planned increases and decreases to the 15 percent tax bracket for married couples filing joint returns over the next six years:

2003 and 2004	200%
2005	180%
2006	187%
2007	193%
2008 and beyond	200%

The third area of modification relates to the Earned Income Credit. A married individual must file a joint return in order to claim the EIC, which is then based on the couple's combined income. The credit is phased out for taxpayers whose earned income exceeds a phaseout amount. The Tax Act of 2001 increased the phaseout amounts starting in 2002 and will complete it in 2008. Due to the increased phaseout amounts, the EIC will be more attainable for married couples filing joint returns. The Earned Income Credit is discussed in Chapter 2.

Lower Income Tax Rates

There is a new 10 percent rate, which is applied to the first $14,000 of taxable income on a joint return, $10,000 for a head of household, and $7,000 for singles. In 2005 through 2007, the 10 percent rate will revert to the old law and will apply to the first $12,000 of taxable income on a joint return, $10,000 for a head of household (no change), and $6,000 for singles. The "bonus" or "refund" that you received in the third and fourth quarters of 2003 is nothing more than an advance resulting from the new 10 percent tax rate that you probably would have received anyway when you file your 2003 return. There is no reduction in rates for the 15 percent tax bracket, although the bracket will be widened as a part of the marriage penalty relief (see preceding section). The reduced rates for the other tax brackets will phase in as shown in Table 12.1.

Child Tax Credit

Updates in 2003 now allow a parent to take a $1,000 tax credit for each qualifying child under the age of 17. A child qualifies if the taxpayer can claim a dependency exemption for that person, and if that person is a son or daughter, stepson or stepdaughter, or a foster child. The credit begins to phase out at AGI of $110,000 for married taxpayers filing joint returns. For taxpayers filing single or as head of household, the threshold is $75,000. For married taxpayers filing separate returns, the threshold is $55,000. Any unused Child Tax Credit cannot be carried forward to future years.

TABLE 12.1   Reduced Rates for Individual Income Taxes

	Third Bracket	Fourth Bracket	Fifth Bracket	Top Bracket
2002	27	30	35	38.6
2003 to 2010	25	28	33	35
2011 and beyond	28	31	36	39.6

The maximum credit *is scheduled to change* as follows:

Year	Child Tax Credit
2005–2008	$700
2009	$800
2010	$1,000
2011	$500

If you exceed the AGI thresholds, determining partial credit is a nightmare without a computer program.

2001 TAX LEGISLATION

Most of the provisions of the Tax Act of 2001 became effective in 2002 and later, but the effective dates of many provisions have been accelerated by the Tax Act of 2003 (see previous sections in this chapter). Some are basic changes, such as income tax reductions. And some are complex, such as the estate and gift tax areas. Because many provisions are complicated, confusing, and change every few years, it's best to do frequent and careful reading and planning to stay on top of your financial situation.

Here are the major changes that affect the average American taxpayer:

- Individual tax rate reductions.
- Itemized deduction phaseout repealed.
- Personal exemption phaseout repealed.
- Alternative Minimum Tax.
- IRA contribution increases.
- IRA catch-up contributions for people over 50.
- Deemed IRAs under employer plans.
- 401(k), 403(b), and 457 contribution increases.
- 401(k), 403(b), and 457 catch-up contributions for people over 50.
- Roth IRA contributions for 401(k) and 403(b) plans.
- SIMPLE IRAs.
- Retirement savings contribution credit.
- Small-business credit for pension plan expenses.
- Required minimum distribution rules liberalized.
- Child Tax Credit increases.
- Dependent Care Credit increases.
- Adoption tax benefits.
- Modification of Education IRAs.
- Qualified tuition programs (Section 529 plans).
- Employer-provided educational assistance.
- Student loan interest deduction.

- Deduction for higher education expenses.
- Marriage penalty.
- Estate and gift taxes.[1]

Now let's take an in-depth look at some of the major changes not previously discussed in this book. These are changes made in the Tax Act of 2001 and also by other legislation in the past five years.

Child and Dependent Care Credit

This is unrelated to the Child Tax Credit discussed earlier in this chapter.

A taxpayer who maintains a household that includes one or more qualifying individuals (generally, a dependent under 13 years old) can receive a maximum credit of up to 35 percent for expenses paid for the care of the qualifying individual while the taxpayer is gainfully employed. Expenses are limited to $3,000 for one individual and $6,000 for two or more. The credit of 35 percent gradually decreases after AGI exceeds $15,000, but not below 20 percent. Thus, a taxpayer with $3,000 of expenses who has an AGI over $43,000 is still entitled to a credit of $600 (20 percent of $3,000).

Education Tax Incentives

There is now in effect a range of tax relief in the form of credits and educational savings accounts modeled after IRAs. These are provided for students and their families from the first year of college onward, making higher education somewhat more affordable. There are also opportunities for self-employed taxpayers and employees who want to take courses to improve job skills or simply to learn more about their job or occupation.

HOPE Scholarship Credit

A nonrefundable HOPE scholarship tax credit can be taken against federal income taxes for qualified tuition and related expenses for a taxpayer, a spouse, and any dependents, up to $1,500 for each of the first two years of college if the student attends on at least a half-time basis. The $1,500 credit can be taken as follows: 100 percent of the first $1,000 of tuition and fees required for enrollment or attendance, or $1,000; and 50 percent of the next $1,000, or $500, paid for each of the first two years. These credits can be taken by families with AGI up to $83,000 a year and are gradually phased out for families with AGI up to $103,000 ($41,000 to $51,000 for single filers). The HOPE credit is indexed for inflation. Any unused HOPE credit cannot be carried forward to future years.

YOUR TAX-SAVING STRATEGY

The HOPE credit is computed on a per-student basis—that is, a separate credit is allowed for each eligible student in a taxpayer's family.

Lifetime Learning Credit

Individuals are allowed to claim a nonrefundable Lifetime Learning Credit (LLC) against federal income taxes equal to 20 percent of up to $10,000 (i.e., $2,000) of qualified tuition and fees paid during the taxable year on behalf of the taxpayer, the taxpayer's spouse, or any dependent (or up to a maximum credit per taxpayer return of $2,000). In other words, the LLC does not vary based on the number of students in the taxpayer's family. The student can be enrolled in an undergraduate or graduate degree program on at least a half-time basis, or take courses at an eligible institution to acquire or improve job skills even if enrolled on a less-than-half-time basis.

The credit is phased out according to the same income ranges that apply to the HOPE credit, but, in contrast to the HOPE credit, the Lifetime Learning Credit may be claimed for an unlimited number of taxable years. Any unused LLC cannot be carried forward to future years.

If you take the HOPE Scholarship or Lifetime Learning Credit, that amount must be reduced by certain other tax-free educational benefits you may also receive, such as scholarships, fellowships, and any employer-provided educational assistance. In other words, cheating the government by taking double tax benefits simultaneously is a no-no.

YOUR TAX-SAVING STRATEGY

Taxpayers who have more than one student in college should elect the HOPE credit over the Lifetime Learning Credit. Each family should spend some time to determine which credit benefits it the most.

Note: Two forms are needed when applying for the Child Tax Credit, the HOPE Scholarship Credit, and the Lifetime Learning Credit. These are Form 8812 for the Child Tax Credit and Form 8863 for the other two. See IRS Publication 970, "Tax Benefits for Higher Education," for more details about these credits and other tax benefits for taxpayers who paid higher education costs.

Coverdell Education Savings Accounts (ESAs)

An Education Savings Account allows parents to shelter earnings on college savings. The ESA was created exclusively for the purpose of saving tax-free dollars that will eventually be used toward a child's education expenses. Parents can contribute $2,000 per child annually until each child reaches the age of 18. The deduction is phased out at certain AGI levels—between $190,000 and $220,000 for couples filing jointly, and between $95,000 and $110,000 for other filers. If your AGI exceeds the thresholds, gift the contribution to another family member, such as a grandparent, who can then make the deposit.

Coverdell ESA contributions are not tax-deductible, but accumulated earnings are tax-free; so are withdrawals if the money is used for qualified education expenses. Qualified education expenses include undergraduate- or graduate-level room, board, books, or tuition, and also include elementary and secondary school expenses plus related computer equipment and software. If the beneficiary doesn't attend college, or if a remainder of the earnings is left, the money must be withdrawn, generally subject to a tax and a 10 percent penalty, within 30 days after the child turns 30. However, before the beneficiary reaches 30, the account balance can be rolled over or transferred tax-free to another ESA for another member of the family who is under 30 years old.

Note: The contribution deadline is April 15 of the following year. Generally, if in 2003 you exclude from your income a distribution from an ESA to pay education expenses, no HOPE Scholarship Credit, LLC, or any business-related education deduction is allowed. However, the HOPE credit and LLC may be claimed in the same year when distributions are made from an ESA as long as credits are not claimed for amounts paid with tax-free distributions.

Qualified State Tuition Programs (QSTP) (529 Plans)
To save for a family member's college education, you can participate in a qualified state tuition program. This is how it works: You can contribute to two types of state plans and make cash contributions to an account for a designated beneficiary that are earmarked to cover that person's costs of higher education. When the student begins post-secondary education, you can take distributions from the account to cover the qualified education expenses. Almost all the states now offer tax-favored tuition savings plans, although program features vary considerably. All plans fall into one of three categories: prepaid tuition plans, savings plans, or educational institution plans.

1. Prepaid tuition plan: A state-operated trust offers residents a hedge against tuition inflation by agreeing to pay future tuition at a public university or college pegged to current tuition levels. The state's contractual promises may or may not be guaranteed.
2. College savings plan: Here, the basic idea is that contributions will grow over time in a state-sponsored mutual fund, hopefully keeping pace with rising tuition costs. Since this is not guaranteed, there is the possibility that there will be a shortfall when college time rolls around. Most new QSTPs are savings plans because they are more flexible than prepaid tuition plans and have upside potential from their investments in the stock market.
3. Educational institution plan: Beginning in 2002, eligible public and private institutions also offer QSTPs.

Several states have plans that are open to both residents and nonresidents, and in some states the student can attend college anywhere in the world. There are no income restrictions to these plans for the donor; contributions can be made by parents, grandparents, or anyone else. Some states have maximum limits on total contributions, but they are generous, well over $100,000 per student in several states. Many states allow a current deduction for state income tax purposes for part of the contributions, and most states exempt the amounts from state income tax. Distributions are not federally taxable to the extent they are used to pay for qualified higher education expenses. Balances are transferable to another child in the family, but if you withdraw the money for other uses, you will be subject to taxes, penalties, and withdrawal fees. Transfers can be made between qualified tuition plans for the same designated beneficiary. The definition of a family member for purposes of beneficiary has changed, and rollovers may include first cousins of the individual beneficiary. *Note:* You can claim a HOPE or LLC and exclude amounts distributed from a QSTP in the same year for the same student as long as the distribution is not used for the same expenses for which a credit will be claimed.

If someone in your family plans to attend college, check this out so you can start saving now. For further information, visit the College Savings Plans Network web site at www.collegesavings.org or www.saving forcollege.com.

YOUR TAX-SAVING STRATEGY

QSTPs and Coverdell ESAs offer very similar income tax benefits. The contrast is that an ESA can be used for elementary and secondary school and college costs but is limited to a $2,000 annual contribution and is subject to AGI phaseouts. On the other hand, much higher amounts can be put into a QSTP, but it can be used only for higher education. Also, with an ESA you make your own investment decisions. In QSTPs, the state hires the money managers.

Note: You can contribute to both a QSTP and an ESA

Deductions for Interest on Student Loans

For interest due and paid on qualified education loans, individuals may claim a deduction up to a maximum of $2,500 per year. The deduction is phased out at certain AGI levels—between $100,000 and $130,000 for couples filing jointly, and between $50,000 and $65,000 for other filers. A deduction cannot be taken if you are a dependent of another taxpayer or if your filing status is married filing separately.

The deduction is allowed for interest paid on a qualified education loan and is deductible for all years during the loan repayment period The deduction is allowed whether or not the taxpayer itemizes other deductions on Schedule A, Form 1040. Expenses paid with the loan proceeds generally include tuition, fees, room and board, and related expenses. The indebtedness must be incurred exclusively to pay for higher education expenses, and the student must be enrolled at least half-time.

One option to maximize the new education benefits is to take the HOPE credit for the first two years, the Lifetime Learning Credit for the next two years, followed by the student loan interest deduction after graduation.

YOUR TAX-SAVING STRATEGY

Parents who take out a student loan to pay education expenses are entitled to the interest deduction. However, if your AGI exceeds the limits, here's a better plan: If possible, use the proceeds of a home equity loan for the education expenses. This will provide you with a full mortgage interest deduction on Schedule A (1040).

Employer Educational Assistance Exclusion

The educational assistance exclusion is available to employees who receive reimbursements from their employers for undergraduate education costs, including tuition, fees, books, and related expenses. Beginning in 2002, the exclusion includes graduate education costs. Up to $5,250 per year can be deducted on the employer's business return yet is not taxable income to the employee. This is a substantial tax-free benefit for the estimated 800,000 people who receive educational assistance from their employers. Interestingly, shareholders of an S corporation who own 2 percent or more of the corporation are generally subject to income tax on fringe benefits, but they can receive educational assistance tax-free.

Tuition and Fees Deduction

For 2002 to 2005 only, a new deduction is available for higher education expenses, defined the same way as for HOPE credit purposes. The deduction is allowed whether or not the taxpayer itemizes other deductions on Schedule A, Form 1040, though you must file Form 1040 or 1040A to use this deduction. Couples filing jointly whose AGI does not exceed $130,000 ($65,000 for single filers) can claim up to $3,000 per year in 2003 and up to $4,000 in 2004 and 2005. In 2004 and 2005 only, couples filing jointly whose AGI does not exceed $160,000 ($80,000 for single filers) can claim up to $2,000.

None of the income limits have phaseout rules. For example, if in 2003 you are single and your AGI is $65,001, you receive no deduction. Also, this deduction cannot be taken in the same year as a HOPE credit or LLC for the same individual. See IRS Publication 970 for full details.

Educational Business Expenses

If your employer does not have an educational assistance exclusion plan, you have two remaining choices if you are taking a business-related course: Take the Lifetime Learning Credit (LLC), which is available even if you enroll on a less-than-half-time basis, or, as under prior law, take a miscellaneous itemized deduction on Schedule A (1040). Remember, if you choose the latter, you must first reduce the total of your miscellaneous deductions by 2 percent of your AGI.

If you are self-employed, you will take your deduction on Schedule C and it will be fully deductible. To be eligible for either of these deductions, the expenses must be used to maintain or improve your skills in your current line of business or be required to maintain your job status. Both the HOPE credit and interest on student loans would normally not be available for business purposes because of the requirement that attendance be on at least a half-time basis.

YOUR TAX-SAVING STRATEGY

Here is a possible sequence of educational benefits to consider. Of all the programs, the best is the employer educational assistance because nothing beats a course you can take for free. For the self-employed, unless the HOPE credit is available, which is unlikely, a deduction on Schedule C would provide the greatest benefit, since self-employment tax as well as federal and state taxable income are reduced. Next in line, for those who can take a full itemized deduction on Schedule A, the benefit is greater than taking the LLC because the LLC is limited to 20 percent of $10,000 of educational expenses, or $2,000, while the Schedule A deduction has no upper limit for expenses. Just as significant is that if this itemized deduction reduces income subject to a 25 percent or higher rate, the minimum savings would be 25 percent of $10,000, or $2,500, which is $500 more than the LLC.

Penalty-Free Withdrawals from Traditional IRAs for Higher Education Expenses

In addition to the educational incentives just described, taxpayers can withdraw money penalty-free from an existing IRA if the money is to be used for higher education expenses (including graduate-level) for a taxpayer, a spouse, or any child or grandchild. (See also "Roth IRA," later in this chapter.) A child does not have to live with you or qualify as your dependent for you to receive the tax break.

YOUR TAX-SAVING STRATEGY

Penalty-free educational distributions are not allowed to be taken from a qualified retirement plan. So you might want to consider transferring funds to an IRA and then making a penalty-free education distribution.

Pension and Retirement Incentives

Individual Retirement Accounts (IRAs)—401(k) Plans, 403(b) Plans, Allowing Full IRA Deduction for Nonworking Spouses

It used to be especially difficult for active participants in employer-sponsored retirement plans to make tax-deductible contributions to IRAs. The active participation of one spouse in an employer-sponsored plan triggered possible limitations on IRA deductions for both spouses if certain AGI limits were exceeded—in other words, the deduction was phased out for married taxpayers with a joint income of $40,000 to $50,000 ($25,000 to $35,000 for singles and heads of households).

These AGI ranges were increased in 2003 to $60,000 to $70,000 for married couples, and $40,000 to $50,000 for single and head-of-household taxpayers. Furthermore, these limits increase each year until the phaseout range is $80,000 to $100,000 for married taxpayers and $50,000 to $60,000 for single taxpayers.

Even if the other spouse participates in a retirement plan at work, the law allows a nonworking or nonparticipating (but working) spouse to contribute a fully deductible $3,000. This is subject to phaseout at a joint AGI level of between $150,000 and $160,000, far greater than previous levels.

This obviously represents significant changes to the old law. The previous income limits were in place for more than 10 years without allowing indexing for inflation, and lawmakers seemed not to consider the severity of limiting contributions when only one spouse was a member of a pension plan.

IRAs: Changes Effective in 2002

Maximum annual contributions for all IRAs have been increased, and individuals who are age 50 or older can make additional catch-up contributions to their IRAs, in increments of $500 or $1,000. Their maximum annual IRA contributions will increase to the levels shown in Table 12.2.

401(k) Plans, 403(b) Annuities, and Other Plans: Changes Effective in 2002

There are also increases in the contribution amounts to 401(k) salary deferral plans, 403(b) tax-sheltered annuity plans, salary reduction Simplified Employee Pensions (SAR-SEPs), 457 deferred compensation plans, and SIMPLE retirement plans, as shown in Table 12.3.

Individuals who are age 50 or older and who have already made the maximum allowable pre-tax contribution can make additional catch-up contributions to 401(k), 403(b), SAR-SEP, 457, and SIMPLE plans, as shown in Table 12.4.

An employer is permitted to make matching contributions with respect to catch-up contributions but is not required to do so.

TABLE 12.2   Maximum Annual Contributions to IRAs (2002)

Tax Years	Normal Maximum	Age 50 or Older
2002 to 2004	$3,000	$3,500
2005	$3,000	$4,500
2006 to 2007	$4,000	$5,000
2008 and beyond	$5,000	$6,000

TABLE 12.3   Maximum Annual Contributions to Other Retirement Plans

Year	401(k)/403(b) Plans, SAR-SEPs, and 457 Plans	Simple Plans
2002	$11,000	$7,000
2003	$12,000	$8,000
2004	$13,000	$9,000
2005	$14,000	$10,000
2006	$15,000	$10,000

TABLE 12.4   Additional Retirement Plan Contributions for Persons Age 50 and Older

Tax Year	401(k)/403(b)/SEP/457	SIMPLE
2002	$1,000	$500
2003	$2,000	$1,000
2004	$3,000	$1,500
2005	$4,000	$2,000
2006 and beyond	$5,000	$2,500

Also, beginning in 2006, a 401(k) or 403(b) plan may include contributions to a "Roth contribution program." Subject to certain conditions, this provision acts just like a regular Roth IRA. A designated Roth contribution would not be excluded from the participant's income when made, but later distributions from the plan would be tax-free. More will be said about Roth IRAs later in this chapter.

Compensation Limits

According to Congress, the previous compensation limits for most qualified pension plans did not allow workers to accumulate adequate retirement benefits. Beginning in 2002, for 401(k), 403(b), and 457 pension plans, there is an increase of the percentage of compensation limit (on which deferrals are based) from 25 percent to 100 percent of compensation.

YOUR TAX-SAVING STRATEGY

Low-paid spouses of high earners who want to defer a large percentage of their income in a 401(k), 403(b), or 457 plan could use this provision. For example, say a spouse who works part-time earns $12,000 in 2003. Under prior law, the maximum amount of elective deferrals and other contributions was $3,000 (25 percent of $12,000). In 2003, the spouse can defer up to $12,000, the new deferral limit for 2003. Also, if the spouse elects to defer less than $12,000, the spouse could receive employer-matching contributions that bring the 2003 total contribution up to $12,000 (100 percent of compensation).

Deemed IRAs Under Employer Plans

Beginning in 2003, if an eligible retirement plan, such as a 401(k) or 403(b) plan, allows employees to make voluntary employee contributions to a separate account that is established within the plan and meets the requirements of either a traditional IRA or a Roth IRA, then the account is deemed a traditional or Roth IRA. The contributions are covered by the tax laws for the type of IRA chosen.

Greater Pension Portability

Workers now have greater control over their retirement funds. It is easier to roll over or transfer money from one retirement plan to another, as well as between IRAs and employer-sponsored retirement plans. You can roll over most types of employer-sponsored plans into another plan or an IRA, and can roll over an IRA into your new employer's plan, if your employer allows such moves. This is good news for government workers with 457 plans who, prior to 2002, could transfer money only from one 457 plan to another 457 plan.

Special Pension Credit for Low-Income Taxpayers

For years 2002 to 2006 only, the Tax Act of 2001 creates a nonrefundable tax credit ranging from 10 to 50 percent of the first $2,000 contributed to IRAs, 401(k), 403(b), SIMPLEs, or 457 government plans. The credit will be available to joint filers with AGI of $50,000 or less, heads of household with $37,500 or less, and all others with $25,000 or less. The credits are as shown in Table 12.5.

This credit requires no recordkeeping by the taxpayer and serves as a powerful incentive for low-income workers to make contributions to their employers' plan. Participation by low-income employees also helps with nondiscrimination testing, which increases amounts that can be contributed by more highly paid employees.

Full-time students and individuals who are dependents of others are not eligible for this credit, and you must be age 18 or older. The credit is in addition to any deduction or exclusion allowed for the contributions.

TABLE 12.5   Special Pension Credit for Low-Income Taxpayers

Adjusted Gross Income			
Joint	Head of Household	All Others	Allowable Credit
$30,000 or less	$22,500 or less	$15,000 or less	50%
$30,001 to $32,500	$22,501 to $24,375	$15,001 to $16,250	20%
$32,501 to $50,000	$24,376 to $37,500	$16,251 to $25,000	10%

You must file Form 1040 or 1040A with Form 8880 to receive the credit. See IRS Publication 590 for full details.

Roth IRA

The objective of the Roth IRA is to shelter earnings from federal taxes. In a sense it is the opposite of the traditional IRA. In the latter, investors deduct annual IRA contributions from their taxable income, and the taxes on IRA earnings are deferred. When the money is withdrawn, generally after age 59 $\frac{1}{2}$, taxes are paid at the ordinary income tax rates. However, with the Roth IRA, investors are not given an upfront deduction, but all earnings from contributions made are exempt from federal taxes—with some exceptions. The earnings can be withdrawn after a five-year period beginning with the first tax year in which a contribution was made. A subsequent conversion from a traditional IRA will not start the running of a new five-year period. In general, qualified distributions include any money taken after age 59 $\frac{1}{2}$, upon death or disability, for purchasing a first home up to a lifetime limit of $10,000, and to pay for college expenses.

There is a full deduction for AGIs under $150,000 for joint filers and $95,000 for singles. The phaseout range for joint filers is from $150,000 to $160,000 and from $95,000 to $110,000 for singles.

The Roth IRA is a boon to middle-income and upper-income taxpayers who thus far have been unable to make deductible IRA contributions because they participate in a company retirement plan and have income above certain levels. The Roth IRA also gives married couples earning less than $160,000 and individual taxpayers with incomes below $110,000 the chance to invest $3,000 a year in stock funds or other investments and avoid all federal tax as long as the money is used as directed.

The biggest benefits are the following:

- People who earned too much to qualify for deductible IRAs can now qualify for a Roth IRA.
- Tax benefits remain intact in later years even if the holder's income rises way above contribution limits.

- There are no requirements, as with a deductible IRA, for distributions to begin at age 70½.
- Although you pay regular income tax when you roll over money from a traditional IRA into a Roth IRA, you escape the 10 percent tax imposed on withdrawals before 59½. (Rollovers are allowed only for taxpayers with an AGI of $100,000 or less, either single or married.) The taxable portion of the conversion is not taken into account when calculating the $100,000 AGI limit. However any rollover to a Roth IRA raises your income tax bill because you will be incurring taxes on the transferred amounts. But you have choices for how to minimize paying taxes on the additional income resulting from the rollover. You could transfer just enough each year so that you do not push yourself into a higher tax bracket. The lower your other taxable income is for a given year, the more you can transfer without jumping into a higher tax bracket. Or you can increase your withholding from wages or estimated taxes to cover the shortfalls.

Keep in mind that you must take a distribution from your traditional IRA by December 31, 2003, to start the conversion process, and you must complete the transfer into the Roth IRA within 60 days.

YOUR TAX-SAVING STRATEGY

Let's say you converted $50,000 from a traditional IRA to a Roth IRA in July 2003 but the investment has dropped in value to $25,000. You now decide the tax bill is too steep. Assuming you have already filed your 2003 return, you have until October 15, 2004, to *recharacterize* the conversion (a new term which means to change the character or type of your IRA) back to your traditional IRA by filing an amended return, Form 1040X (Amended U.S. Individual Income Tax Return). You will also need to attach Form 8606 (Nondeductible IRAs) to the amended return to claim your refund. This method is also available if you have not yet filed but have requested an extension of time to file until August 15 or October 15, 2004. And here's an added bonus: After the recharacterization, if you wait at least 30 days, you have the option to convert your traditional IRA back into a Roth IRA. Do this only if you expect your 2004 AGI to be under $100,000.

YOUR TAX-SAVING STRATEGY

If you make a conversion of a traditional IRA into a Roth IRA and then discover you made some sort of mistake (e.g., your AGI was too high to allow the conversion), you may correct the error without penalty. If the value of your traditional IRA dropped significantly during the last bear market, consider converting part or all to a Roth IRA at new, lower tax rates. *Note:* Your AGI must be $100,000 or less.

Here is a deduction strategy if you have investment losses in your Roth IRAs: If you liquidate all your Roth accounts and incur a net loss from your investments, the loss is deductible on Schedule A, Form 1040, as a miscellaneous deduction, to the extent it exceeds 2 percent of AGI.

Note: For 2003, the most anyone can contribute to any type of IRA is $3,000 a year (plus an additional $500 if age 50 or older), plus another $2,000 per year to a Coverdell ESA (See "Education Tax Incentives" earlier in this chapter.) The new option to pull out money early for education and first-home buying without penalty applies to all retirement IRAs.

When you make withdrawals from a Roth IRA, the first money withdrawn is considered to come from annual contributions, which will be free of tax and penalties. The next will be considered converted amounts, which are generally free of tax and penalties; and finally, you'll tap earnings that may be subject to tax and penalties if they are taken before you reach 59½.

How do you decide which IRA is for you? It may appear that a tax-free growth in the future can be more valuable than getting a tax deduction today and withdrawing money at a later date at ordinary income tax rates. But the determining factor is the tax bracket you are in. If you expect to be in a lower tax bracket in retirement, it probably makes better sense to take the deduction now using a traditional IRA, because you will get more of a tax break. If your desire is to lower your tax bite, the deductible IRA is also preferable since you can take the tax write-off, reducing the cost of funding the account.

Changing When to Begin Withdrawals from Tax-Deferred Retirement Accounts

Prior to 1997, anyone participating in a qualified tax-deferred retirement plan had to begin to withdraw the money by age 70½. Now, you can begin to withdraw the money at that age or you can keep your money in the account as long as you're employed—that is, until you retire. The only exception is for someone who is at least a 5 percent owner of the company, in which case the money must begin to be distributed no later than April 1 of the calendar year following the year in which that person reaches age 70½. *Note:* You are still required to begin distributions from traditional IRAs by age 70½.

This is clearly a boon for those tens of thousands still earning salaries who don't need their pension money. Now their money can remain untouched, tax-deferred, and growing.

Note: If you have already elected to begin taking pension money and now want to make a change, your pension plan will be permitted to stop your distributions until required to do otherwise. If you continue to withdraw money, be aware that the minimum required distribution for participants who have started taking distributions has been greatly reduced.

Minimum Distributions from Retirement Plans—Recent Regulations

If you are fortunate enough to have the means to fund your retirement without tapping into your qualified retirement plans, final regulations issued by the IRS in 2002 allow you to keep more of the funds in your account for the use of your heirs and beneficiaries. The tax breaks assigned to IRAs and most qualified pension plans are specifically designed to provide a source of income during a participant's retirement years. The tax law penalizes you if you take the funds out prior to retirement, generally prior to age 59 $\frac{1}{2}$, while also providing penalties if you don't take out enough during retirement.

The new regulations simplify the rules for minimum required distributions (MRDs) and, for most taxpayers, reduce the amount of the minimum distribution they must receive. The MRD will now be computed under a single uniform period table for all participants of the same age (see Table 12.6). Most participants will be able to calculate their MRD for each year based on just two variables: their current age and their account balance as of the end of the prior year. If your spouse is more than 10 years younger than you are, a different table must be used, which will slightly increase the amount of the MRD. There is also a table for use by beneficiaries. All the tables are included in IRS Supplement to Publication 590 (IRAs).

Other good news: It will no longer be necessary to determine your beneficiary by the required starting date, usually age 70 $\frac{1}{2}$. If the participant dies on or after the required starting date, the distribution period will generally be based on the life expectancy of the designated beneficiary, or over the remaining life of the plan participant if there is no designated beneficiary. However, the beneficiary will not have to be designated until September 30 of the year following the year of the participant's death. Therefore, beneficiaries can be changed without any impact on the amount of the MRD—that is, an IRA with multiple beneficiaries can be divided into separate accounts, or a beneficiary can disclaim rights to the funds in favor of someone else after the participant's death. For example, a surviving spouse is the primary beneficiary of 100 percent of the participant's IRA, and her two children are the secondary beneficiaries. By disclaiming her right to the IRA soon after her spouse's death, she ensures that the IRA will transfer to her two children.

If the participant dies before the required starting date, the distribution period will generally be based on the life expectancy of the designated beneficiary, or over a period of five years if there is no designated beneficiary. After the participant's death, as under prior law, a spouse who is the sole beneficiary can roll over the IRA into her own IRA and

**TABLE 12.6   Applicable Divisors for MDIB
(Minimum Distribution Incidental Benefit)**

Age	Applicable Divisor	Age	Applicable Divisor
70	27.4	93	9.6
71	26.5	94	9.1
72	25.6	95	8.6
73	24.7	96 & older—	
74	23.8	See IRS Supp. to Publ. 590	
75	22.9		
76	22.0		
77	21.2		
78	20.3		
79	19.5		
80	18.7		
81	17.9		
82	17.1		
83	16.3		
84	15.5		
85	14.8		
86	14.1		
87	13.4		
88	12.7		
89	12.0		
90	11.4		
91	10.8		
92	10.2		

Source: Tax Hotline, Dec. 12, 2002, p. 14.

has several choices as to when to begin taking distributions. She can also name new beneficiaries (e.g., children) and begin her own new schedule of MRDs.

IRA Beneficiaries

Make sure that you have named both a primary beneficiary and a contingent beneficiary for each IRA. For multiple beneficiaries of a single IRA, each beneficiary's share should be specified in a fraction, percentage, or using the word *equally*. Then, by September 30 of the year following the year of the participant's death, each beneficiary can establish a separate account and use his or her individual life expectancy for a withdrawal rate.

Do not take for granted that the financial institution that holds your IRA also holds your beneficiary designations. Because there has been such a large number of bank and brokerage mergers over the years, many beneficiary forms have been misplaced or lost completely. So you must keep a copy of all IRA beneficiary designations with your other important papers, and give copies to your attorney or financial adviser

If the form cannot be found and you were not yet receiving distributions, your estate will receive the proceeds and be required to pay out the entire amount within a relatively short five years. This is why you should never name your estate as any kind of beneficiary. However, if distributions had already begun, the IRA balance would have to be paid out over the remaining life of the plan participant.

If there have been changes in your family circumstances, such as the birth of children, marriage, divorce, or a death, you may want to change beneficiary selections. When making these changes, other pitfalls arise if you name minor children, or multiple or contingent beneficiaries. It is important to seek professional help with your IRAs especially regarding this issue.

Penalty-Free Withdrawals from IRAs and Corporate Pension Plans

Generally, withdrawals from corporate pension plans and traditional IRAs, and earnings from Roth IRAs, before age 59 1/2 are subject to income tax and a 10 percent penalty.

However, under the following seven circumstances, you can take an early distribution from a traditional or Roth IRA without the penalty:

1. For medical expenses that exceed 7.5 percent of the taxpayer's adjusted gross income and are used for the taxpayer, the taxpayer's spouse, or dependents. The withdrawn money can be used to hire a nurse, to pay for prescription drugs, and even to purchase eyeglasses, hearing aids, and dentures. *Note:* The amount withdrawn will be subject to income tax that can be offset by taking a corresponding medical expense deduction if it is itemized on Schedule A (Itemized Deductions).

    Early distributions can also be made from IRAs penalty-free to pay for medical insurance for the taxpayer, the taxpayer's spouse, or dependents without regard to the 7.5 percent minimum of adjusted gross income, if the individual has received federal or state unemployment compensation for at least 12 weeks and the withdrawal is made in the year the unemployment compensation is received or in the following year. Although self-employed taxpayers generally do not receive unemployment benefits, they do qualify for this penalty-free tax break. All those who qualify can continue to withdraw from their IRAs to pay for health insurance for up to 60 days after they find a new job.

2. If you make a series of equal annual payments that must continue for the longer of five years or until you reach age 59 1/2. After that age, you can withdraw differing amounts without the 10 percent

penalty. If you violate the payment schedule, all payments, past and present, generally will be subject to the 10 percent penalty. However, because of the recent stock market downturns, you can now make a one-time switch to a payment method that bases annual distributions on the value of your account each year (per IRS Revenue Ruling 2002-62).

3. If you have a physical or mental disability expected to last indefinitely (or until death) that stops you from performing the type of work you were doing before your condition arose.

4. If the distribution is tax-free and you never used it as a deduction against your income. This includes distributions from nondeductible traditional IRAs and distributions of annual contributions from Roth IRAs.

5. If the distribution is for higher education expenses of the account's owner, a spouse, a child, or a grandchild (see "Education Tax Incentives" earlier in this chapter).

6. If the distribution, up to $10,000, is used to buy a first home for the account owner, a spouse, a child, or a grandchild.*

7. For distributions of converted rollover amounts that have been in a Roth IRA for at least five years.

Concerning the corporate or Keogh pension plan, you can take early distributions from either of these without the 10 percent penalty in certain cases:

a. For certain medical expenses (see point 1 above).

b. For certain annual payments (see point 2 above), except that the payments must begin after you leave the company.

c. For a physical or mental disability (see point 3 above).

d. If the distribution is taken after you leave the company and you are at least 55 years of age at that time.

YOUR TAX-SAVING STRATEGY

Before incurring additional income tax and a 10 percent penalty by taking any distributions from your corporate pension or self-employed

---

*A "first-time home buyer" is someone who hasn't owned a home in the past two years. Also, you have only 120 days to buy the home or return the money to the IRA without penalty.

Keogh plan, it is a good idea to check with your employer regarding the possibility of borrowing from your pension plan account balance. The rates of interest are usually reasonable.

YOUR TAX-SAVING STRATEGY

A couple who buys a home jointly can increase the lifetime $10,000 limit to $20,000 if each one withdraws $10,000 from his or her own IRAs. To receive this break, both spouses must qualify as first-time home buyers. *Note:* You do not owe income tax on money withdrawn from a Roth IRA to buy the first home as long as the money has been in the Roth account for at least five years. If less than five years, you are taxed on the earnings from the Roth IRA

A summary of the phaseout ranges for the credits and exemptions considered thus far are given in Table 12.7.

SIMPLE

The Savings Incentive Match Plan for Employees (SIMPLE) is a simplified IRA or 401(k) plan. SIMPLE plans can be adopted by self-employed individuals, and by employers having 100 or fewer employees who received at least $5,000 in compensation for the preceding year and who do not maintain another employer-sponsored retirement plan. Employees who earned at least $5,000 from the employer in any two preceding years before the SIMPLE plan was offered and who also are expected to receive at least $5,000 in compensation for the current year are eligible to participate. Employees' contributions, which are generally matched by the employer up to 3 percent of compensation, cannot exceed the contribution limit of $8,000 for 2003 plus another $1,000 if you are age 50 or older.

The SIMPLE can be adopted as an IRA or as part of a 401(k) salary-deferral plan. As such, it involves typically intricate and sometimes confusing rules for employers matching specific sums, vesting, and how contributions and distributions are made, including associated tax implications.

It is important to review the fine print for this plan, but generally it is a good incentive for small businesses and their employees. Some benefits for both employees and employers are as follows:

- SIMPLE plans are not subject to the nondiscrimination rules that other qualified pension plans are. This means that the amount of money an individual earns or a person's ownership percentage of a company does not control or limit the amount that person can contribute to the plan.

TABLE 12.7   2003 Income Tax Phaseout Ranges

Provision	Single[1]	Married Filing Jointly[1]
Child Tax Credit[2]	$75,000–$87,000	$110,000–$120,000
Adoption Credit	$152,390–$192,390 AGI	Same as single
Itemized Deductions	Deductions reduced by 3% of AGI in excess of $139,500	Same as single
Interest on Education Loans	$50,000–$65,000 AGI	$100,000–$130,000 AGI
HOPE and Lifetime Learning Education Credits	$41,000–$51,000 AGI	$83,000–$103,000 AGI
Coverdell ESA	$95,000–$110,000 AGI	$190,000–$220,000 AGI
Education Savings Bonds	$57,600–$72,600 AGI	$86,400–$116,400 AGI
Personal and Dependency Exemptions	$139,500–$262,000 AGI[3]	$209,250- $331,750 (AGI)[3]
Individual Retirement Accounts (IRAs)		
a) Active participant in another plan	$40,000–$50,000 AGI	$60,000–$70,000 AGI[4]
b) Not an active plan participant	No limitations apply	$150,000–$160,000 AGI[5]
Contributory Roth IRAs	$95,000–$110,000 AGI	$150,000–$160,000 AGI
AMT Exemptions	$112,500–$255,500 tentative alternative minimum taxable income	$150,000–$346,000 tentative alternative minimum taxable income

1. AGI is adjusted gross income. Different modifications may apply depending on the specific provision that applies.

2. Based on one child. The credit is reduced by $50 for each $1,000, or fraction thereof, of AGI above the lower threshold.

3. $104,625-$165,875 for married filing separately and $174,400-$296,900 for head of household. Exemptions are reduced by 2% for each $2,500 increment ($1,250 for married filing separately) in AGI in excess of these amounts.

4. Applies when both spouses are active plan participants or only the participant spouse contributes.

5. Applies if at least one spouse is not an active participant.

- Contributions are deductible by the employer and are excludable from the employee's income.
- Contributions are immediately vested—that is, the money is yours to keep even if your employment is terminated.

Note: Unlike other Keogh and 401(k) plans, a required percentage of all eligible employees do not have to elect to participate. An employer may establish a SIMPLE even if no employees wish to participate, but the employer must notify employees of their right to do so. Generally speaking, this is an easier plan for employers to adopt and administer, and less expensive as well.

A significant drawback for employees is that if you withdraw money in the first two years, you are subject to a 25 percent withdrawal penalty (on SIMPLE IRAs only), which is 15 percent more than normal IRAs.

For employers, a major drawback is that they must continue to match at least 1 percent of employees' compensation even if the business is doing poorly. In my experience, the SIMPLE has proven itself to be somewhat unpopular with employers, particularly those having smaller companies, because of their reluctance to offer the amount of matching contributions necessary to establish the plan. Though these employers receive a deduction off their corporate taxes, when the numbers are added up, the difference in opening the SIMPLE even with the amount subsidized by the government doesn't seem to be enough of an incentive. For self-employed individuals and partners in partnerships, see Chapter 11 Choosing the Best Pension Plan for a discussion of a Simplified Employee Pension (SEP) and Solo 401(k) plans.

Use Form 5304—SIMPLE, or Form 5305—SIMPLE: the first if all contributions go to a financial institution designated by the employer; the second if eligible employees are permitted to choose their own financial institution.

SIMPLE plans must have been set up by October 1, 2003, for 2003 contributions to be deductible on your 2003 tax return.

Tax Credit to Offset Cost of Pension Plan for Small Businesses

Beginning in 2002, small-business employers are eligible for a nonrefundable credit for costs incurred in setting up a qualified pension plan, limited to 50 percent of the administrative expenses of the plan for each of the first three plan years, subject to a maximum of $500 for each year. Eligibility is restricted to employers who had 100 or fewer employees who earned at least $5,000 in the preceding year, and the plan must include at least one employee who is not highly compensated. In other words, a one-person owner plan is not eligible.

Tax-Planning Opportunities for Selling Your Home

Here are a few tax-planning strategies for homeowners whose primary residences have substantially increased in value.

Capital Gains Provisions—Home Sale

Under prior law, a homeowner paid no tax on profits from the sale of a home if within two years of the sale those profits were "rolled over" by buying another home costing at least as much as the one that was sold. Now, a married couple can exempt up to $500,000 of profit on the sale of a home if the house or apartment has been the primary residence of one spouse for at least two of the last five years; a single homeowner can exempt up to $250,000; and even if two or more unmarried people own the home, each owner is eligible for a $250,000 exclusion on his or her share of the gain. In effect, the new law means most homeowners (certainly those with homes selling for under $500,000) will now be able to avoid paying taxes when selling their primary residence.

Note: The tax exemption on profits of a home sale can be used repeatedly, so long as the seller lives in the home for at least two years.

The real estate industry is generally positive about the new capital gains law because it has stimulated business, especially in the lower price ranges, and brought product into the market by those who want to sell their homes but don't plan to buy more expensive ones. It also helps that mortgage rates are at historically low levels.

As with the previous law, when a home is sold at a loss, no deductions or other tax benefits are available to the seller.

YOUR TAX-SAVINGS STRATEGY

If you and your spouse own your home jointly, and one spouse dies, be aware that the survivor will inherit half the house at its current fair market value. Taxable profit would be reduced on a subsequent sale of the house. For example, you originally bought the house for $100,000 and at your wife's death it is valued at $500,000. Your total cost basis upon sale of the house is now stepped up to $300,000, which consists of one-half of $500,000, or $250,000 of her stepped-up cost, plus $50,000 of your original cost. If you sell the house for $550,000, the $250,000 profit will be entirely eliminated by your $250,000 exclusion.

Vacation Homes Versus Primary Residences

People who own a vacation home often declare it as their primary residence to gain the tax advantage of living in a new state, such as Florida or Texas, which has no personal income tax. However, there may be bigger benefits available if you can arrange your affairs so that your former primary residence is your tax home when it comes time to sell. The tendency is to sell an original primary home before the vacation home. This could mean having to pay the full capital gains tax and losing the exemption, $500,000 for married couples and $250,000 for singles. The solution: At your first inclination to sell your home, switch your permanent residence back to the original home, the sooner the better. The requirement is to live there at least 183 days a year. Other means of acquiring proof of residency are to change your voting address, get a driver's license in the state where you want to demonstrate a principal residence, and file your federal and state returns from that location. True, you may lose the savings of living in a tax-free state, but after two years you can move back to the vacation home and you have up to three years to sell your original primary residence and take the exemption. If your home doesn't sell after the fifth year, switch your permanent residence back and start over. This works no matter what state your second home is in.

If Marriage or Divorce Is in the Picture
If you intend to marry and are facing a home sale with a large built-in gain, don't sell before the wedding. From a tax perspective, it's really best if you marry and have your spouse move in with you, live in that house for two years, then sell the home and take the $500,000 exemption for married couples.

If you are lucky enough to have a spouse who also owns a home, after you've lived in your home and sold it, move into your spouse's home, making that your primary residence for the next two years, then sell it and take the exemption. If this sounds somewhat calculating, just think of how much you'll be calculating into your bank account.

Divorcing couples should decide what to do with the marital residence before the divorce is finalized. If one spouse remains in the house after the divorce, the home sale exclusion is limited to $250,000 for singles. In other instances, one or both spouses have a new partner who wants to live elsewhere. In both cases, the best move would be to sell the house while still married in order to obtain the full $500,000 tax exclusion.

Can the spouse who is moving out buy another principal residence and qualify for the exemption? Yes, but the new home must be sold at least two years before or two years after the one involved in the divorce is sold. Remember, you can take the exemption repeatedly so long as the seller lives in the home for at least two years, or in this case, one exemption to a homeowner every two years.[2]

Renting Counts
Something that might make the above situation and others like it more feasible is to rent one of the houses. The law allows you to move into your next home before you sell the one you own and rent it out while

you're waiting for a buyer. To take the exemption on the old home when it's sold, you must prove to the IRS that you were actively trying to sell the home at the time you moved out. Sound proof would be having the home listed with a broker.

This scenario also works well for anyone who owns a principal residence and a rental property. Assume that a single person has lived in the current house for at least two of the previous five years at the time of the sale. He uses the capital gain exclusion of $250,000 and then moves into the rental unit, which is now his principal residence. After two years, he sells the rental unit at a substantial gain, of which $250,000 can be excluded under the law. It makes no difference that most of the appreciation on the second property was realized when it was a rental unit and that he had been taking depreciation for the entire time it was rented. The only part of the gain subject to tax, at a maximum rate of 25 percent, is any depreciation taken after May 6, 1997.

Falling Short of the Two-Year Requirement

Here's a feature that helps you pay less tax when selling your home. If, for certain reasons such as a job relocation, divorce, illness, death, or some other unforseen circumstance, you are unable to stay the required two years, you can still receive a partial exemption to apply against the profits from the sale of the home. To figure this out, take the number of months you used the home as a principal residence and divide by 24 months. For example, if you are married and lived in the home for 18 months and then you had a job transfer, you could take $^{18}/_{24}$ of the $500,000, or $375,000. Even if the same taxpayer lived in the primary residence for as little as one year, he or she would qualify for a $250,000 exemption, which, in most cases, would probably be sufficient to cover any taxable gain.

Repeal of Social Security Limit on Earnings

People who have reached full retirement age—65 or over—may earn unlimited amounts of income without having their Social Security benefits cut. As a result, this group now joins retirees 70 and older who, since 1983, have not had earnings limitations tied to their Social Security benefits. If you are receiving benefits and are under 65, you may still earn up to $10,680 and keep your benefits.

Although there is no longer a cap on earnings for retired people who are 65 or over, this group is still subject to paying federal income tax on part of their Social Security benefits. Retirees with an income over $25,000 for an individual, and $32,000 for a married couple filing jointly, will owe federal income tax on up to half of their Social Security retirement benefits. Single taxpayers with income over $34,000 and married couples filing jointly with income over $44,000 owe tax on as much as 85 percent of Social Security retirement benefits.[3]

Estate and Gift Taxes/Lifetime Exclusions and Tax Rates

Due to the increasing number of taxpayers subjected to federal estate/gift taxes, this area of tax law has had its share of modification in the past several years. Until 2001, estate/gift tax laws had allowed individuals to exempt from federal taxes an equivalent of $675,000 of value relating to the taxpayer's estate upon death, and/or to utilize the equivalent value on gifts made during the taxpayer's lifetime. The Tax Act of 2001 calls for separate tax treatment relating to estate taxes and gift taxes. Estate tax exempt amounts are increased to $1 million in 2002 and 2003 and reach $3,500,000 in 2009, with a repeal of estate taxes for individuals dying after 2009. Gift tax–exempt amounts are increased to $1,000,000 in 2002 and years thereafter, with no repeal for years after 2009.

In addition to changes in lifetime exclusion amounts, estate/gift tax rates were also modified under the Tax Act of 2001. Up until 2001 the maximum federal estate/gift tax rate was 55 percent, with a 5 percent surtax on cumulative transfers between $10,000,000 and $17,184,000 to phase out the benefit of the lower rates. Effective for years after 2001, the 5 percent surtax is repealed.

Table 12.8 gives a revised summary of lifetime exclusion amounts exempted from federal estate taxes, and the maximum estate/gift tax rates:

Additional information about estate and gift taxes is available in IRS Publication 950, "Introduction to Estate and Gift Taxes," at a toll-free number, 866-699-4083; and at the IRS web site, www.irs.gov, under the section called "Small Business/Self Employed."

Note: It is a good idea to review your existing will so you can make changes wherever the former $675,000 exemption amount is mentioned.

TABLE 12.8   Lifetime Exclusion and Maximum Estate/Gift Tax Rates

	Lifetime Exclusion	Maximum Estate/Gift Tax Rate
2002	$1,000,000	50%
2003	$1,000,000	49%
2004	$1,500,000	48%
2005	$1,500,000	47%
2006	$2,000,000	46%
2007 and 2008	$2,000,000	45%
2009	$3,500,000	45%
2010 and beyond (gift taxes only)		35%

Many wills contain trusts that are designed to fully utilize the exemption amount in the estate of the first spouse to die. It may also be wise to use percentages of assets rather than exemption amounts (dollar amounts) so that the will won't have to be rewritten every year, saving time and money. Even people whose assets are not large enough to require the filing of an estate tax return should have a will so their assets are disposed of correctly.

YOUR TAX-SAVING STRATEGY
Since it takes until 2009 for the full estate and gift tax exemption to take effect, eat a healthy diet, exercise accordingly, and plan to be around until 2009 to maximize your bequest to your heirs.

Adoption Tax Benefits

In 2003, taxpayers can claim a tax credit for qualified adoption expenses of up to $10,160 per child on their individual tax returns. Qualified expenses include adoption fees and attorney and court costs, and generally cover children who are under 18 years old. The credit for adoption of a special-needs child is also $10,160, regardless of the extent to which the taxpayer has qualified adoption expenses. The credit is phased out for taxpayers with $152,390 to $192,390 of adjusted gross income.

Some large companies are providing adoption assistance to their employees by establishing an adoption assistance plan that meets the requirements of Section 137 of the IR Code. Employees with modified adjusted gross income up to $151,940 can receive up to $10,160 not subject to income tax but still subject to FICA and federal unemployment taxes. The attractive part is that the cost is tax-deductible by the company.

THE TAX ACTS OF 2001 AND 2003: CONCLUSIONS

When the Economic Growth and Tax Relief Reconciliation Act of 2001 was in its early discussion phase, there was a great deal of clarity. For the most part, anyone following the talks readily noted there were some healthy signals that this could all work toward benefiting taxpayers at large. Lobbyists were told to keep a distance and corporations were told to hang on for a bit—other cuts appeared to be more important. The Republicans indicated that this new tax cut—the nation's largest in two decades—would focus on the individual taxpayer. And, equally important, this tax cut would make a good deal of sense. The filing process was to be simplified and long-term economic growth would be promoted through tax savings.

However, these conclusions were adversely affected by the economic downturn that continued at full strength during 2001 and 2002, forcing our political leaders to pass the Tax Act of 2003. This legislation accelerates the implementation of the major provisions of the Tax Act of 2001, including the doubling of the tax credit for children, new benefits for married couples, and the reduction of individual income rates to a level not seen in many years. Other benefits of the Tax Act of 2003 were heavily frontloaded in the early years resulting in an overall cost of $320 billion. Many of the major provisions are effective only for 2003 and 2004, except for the individual tax rate reductions, which will be in effect until 2010, and the reduction in the capital gains and dividend rates, which are good until 2008. Table 12.9 summarizes recent tax changes and their dates of implementation.

In 2003, no further changes were made to the estate tax, and it will not be fully repealed until 2010. Without further changes, tens of millions of middle-class taxpayers will have most of their tax reductions eaten away by an outdated set of rules that governs the Alternative Minimum Tax.

The bottom line, sadly, is this: By 2010, the very same tax laws that applied before will come back into play, a so-called sunset provision. But long before 2010, surely many of the deep tax cuts contained in this legislation will be changed. Just as President Reagan's huge 1981 tax cut was rolled back within a few years after passage, you can be sure that retirement and estate tax planning will be more complicated until 2010. We will do our best in this publication to help you sort things out.

TAXPAYER PROTECTIONS AND RIGHTS

Many of the new laws set forth in RRA '98 deal with one extremely important issue, essentially what all the recent hullabaloo has been about—taxpayer protections and rights. These are intended not only to help those already caught in the IRS audit and collections process, but also to help taxpayers avoid having problems with the IRS in the first place. The most significant provisions discussed in this section include a shift in the burden of proof from the taxpayer to the IRS; adjustments in awards, costs, and civil damages granted to taxpayers; taxpayer confidentiality privileges; innocent spouse relief; and a variety of audit and collections safeguards designed to impede heavy-handed IRS tactics.

Shift in Burden of Proof

Do you think that the burden of proving who is right in a tax dispute with the IRS can make the difference between winning and losing? One

TABLE 12.9   10-Year Tax Forecast

The chart below provides important amounts and percentages for 2002 through 2011. Changes made by the Jobs and Growth Tax Relief Reconciliation Act of 2003 are indicated in the shaded portion of the chart. Additional limitations, inflation adjustments, effective dates and transitional rules may apply. See the Explanations in CCH's *2003 Tax Legislation: Law, Explanation and Analysis* or *2003 Tax Legislation: Explanation and Analysis* for complete discussions of the changes.

	2002	2003	2004	2005	2006	2007	2008	2009	2010	2011
Capital Gains										
Capital gains rate	20%	15%*	15%	15%	15%	15%	15%	20%	20%	20%
Capital gains rate for taxpayers in 10% or 15% bracket	10%	5%*	5%	5%	5%	5%	0%	10%	10%	10%
Dividends										
Dividends rate (taxed as capital gains)	Did not apply	15%	15%	15%	15%	15%	15%	Will not apply	Will not apply	Will not apply
Dividends rate for taxpayers in 10% or 15% bracket (taxed as capital gains)	Did not apply	5%	5%	5%	5%	5%	0%	Will not apply	Will not apply	Will not apply
Income Tax Rate Reductions										
Top bracket	38.6%	35%	35%	35%	35%	35%	35%	35%	35%	39.6%
Fifth bracket	35%	33%	33%	33%	33%	33%	33%	33%	33%	36%
Fourth bracket	30%	28%	28%	28%	28%	28%	28%	28%	28%	31%
Third bracket	27%	25%	25%	25%	25%	25%	25%	25%	25%	28%
Second bracket	15%	15%	15%	15%	15%	15%	15%	15%	15%	15%
Initial bracket	10%	10%	10%	10%	10%	10%	10%	10%	10%	No 10% bracket

Expansion of 10% Bracket

Taxable income limit —joint filers	$12,000	$14,000	$14,000	$12,000	$12,000	$12,000	$14,000	$14,000	$14,000	No 10% bracket
Taxable income limit —single filers	$6,000	$7,000	$7,000	$6,000	$6,000	$6,000	$7,000	$7,000	$7,000	No 10% bracket

Marriage Penalty Relief

Basic standard deduction for joint filers —percentage of single filer amount	Did not apply	200%	200%	174%	184%	187%	190%	200%	200%	Will not apply
15% bracket size for joint filers—percentage of 15% bracket size for single filers	Did not apply	200%	200%	180%	187%	193%	200%	200%	200%	Will not apply

Child Tax Credit

Amount per child	$600	$1,000	$1,000	$700	$700	$700	$700	$800	$1,000	$ 500

AMT Exemption

Joint filers	$49,000	$58,000	$58,000	$45,000	$45,000	$45,000	$45,000	$45,000	$45,000	$45,000
Single filers	$35,750	$40,250	$40,250	$33,750	$33,750	$33,750	$33,750	$33,750	$33,750	$33,750

Code Sec. 179 Expensing

Deduction amount	$24,000	$100,000	$100,000	$25,000	$25,000	$25,000	$25,000	$25,000	$25,000	$25,000
Investment limitation (on cost of property)	$200,000	$400,000	$400,000	$200,000	$200,000	$200,000	$200,000	$200,000	$200,000	$200,000

*post-5/5/03

would think so. In the past, if you went to court to fight the IRS about the amount of taxes you owed, the IRS was presumed correct until you proved otherwise. The new law shifts the burden of proof from the taxpayer to the IRS in noncriminal cases that reach the U.S. Tax Court. However, once taxpayers get their day in court, they must comply by doing the following:

- Substantiating any item of income, deduction, or tax credit, or other tax items.
- Keeping appropriate records as required by law or regulation. (Both of these existed before the 1998 act.)
- Meeting net worth limitations (i.e., the burden of proof remains on corporations, trusts, and partnerships whose net worth exceeds $7 million).
- Cooperating with reasonable IRS requests for meetings, interviews, witnesses, information, and documents, even if these are not under the taxpayer's control.

YOUR TAX-SAVING STRATEGY

Do not go too far as you cooperate with the IRS requests for information. Inadvertently, you may provide the IRS with enough ammunition to prove its facts and overcome the burden of proof in upcoming court proceedings against you.

The burden of proof rules apply to court proceedings arising in connection with examinations after the July 22, 1998, date of enactment.

Awards, Costs, and Civil Damages

If the IRS takes a position against you that is not substantially justified, this is what you can recover: reasonable administrative and litigation costs, including fees and expenses you incur from the date on which the first letter of proposed deficiency was issued; plus expenses, costs, and fees related to persons who represent you if you win your contest with the IRS.

To determine if the IRS position is unreasonable, the court must take into account whether the IRS has lost on this point in other U.S. Courts of Appeal.

If you make a qualified offer to settle and the IRS turns you down, and then obtains a judgment against you, you can still collect reasonable costs and attorneys' fees if the IRS wins an amount that is equal to or less than your offer (not counting interest accrued). This provision is to encourage taxpayers to offer a reasonable amount for settlement of taxes owed and for the IRS to act reasonably in accepting such offers.

Civil damages may be awarded for the unauthorized inspection or disclosure of your tax returns or any information on your return. If this occurs, you are entitled to collect attorneys' fees.

If an IRS employee negligently disregards the law in connection with collecting your income tax, you can collect up to $100,000 in civil damages, and up to $1 million if an IRS employee willfully violates the law governing collections.

Impact

Now that the much-sought-after burden-of-proof switch has been made, there are questions as to how it will play out. Taxpayers, will you get the measure of relief and control from IRS collection and court officials who knew they, not you, were always in the right? Will you become bogged down complying with IRS administrative requests to prove their case? Will the law encourage the IRS to be more aggressive and intrusive, which will directly lead to more extensive costs, or will the IRS be more understanding and sympathetic, as former Commissioner Charles Rossotti has proposed? More time will have to be spent on cases to ensure full cooperation, as set down in the new law. What this means is that taxpayers must comply fully with IRS requests for information if they expect the burden of proof to shift to the IRS. Because of this, you can expect more stringent IRS audit procedures that will include many more requests for documents in the hope that taxpayers will not respond, in an effort to prevent the burden of proof from shifting. This could easily increase litigation costs. Perhaps taxpayers who have control of information will fare better by awaiting trial before disclosing that information. Or perhaps where they do not have control of information and the IRS cannot obtain that information on its own, these taxpayers may do better by doing nothing, even though the burden of proof is on their side. Be sure to get good representation—someone who has experience trying cases before the IRS.

Confidentiality Privilege

Whereas a taxpayer always enjoyed the privilege of confidentiality between him- or herself and his or her attorney, you are now entitled to the same protection of confidentiality with respect to tax advice received from any "federally authorized tax practitioner," such as a CPA or enrolled agent. The privilege applies in any noncriminal tax proceeding before the IRS or federal courts. Interestingly enough, it does not extend to written communication between a tax practitioner and a corporation in connection with the promotion of any tax shelter.

Impact

CPAs and enrolled agents should be diligent in reviewing the rules regarding this law because there are limits to the privilege. For example, the privilege usually does not apply to the preparation of tax returns, giving accounting or business advice, or tax accrual work papers.

If your civil, noncriminal case becomes a criminal case, the IRS could use a summons to compel your tax adviser to reveal details of past conversations he had with you that you would prefer left unsaid. It is also known that the IRS has threatened to implicate the tax adviser as a co-conspirator in tax evasion cases if the adviser refuses to cooperate. Despite this, the new law should prove a great help to taxpayers and CPAs working together in a tax audit situation.

Innocent Spouse Relief

Anyone who signs his or her name to a joint return immediately becomes liable for possible tax misdeeds of the other filer. Innocent spouse relief is intended to help spouses caught in IRS collection actions because of all understatements of tax attributed to the other spouse. To avoid this situation entirely, of course, married people always have the choice of filing separate returns. But once that joint return is filed, it was very difficult until recently for an innocent spouse to become free of tax liabilities unlawfully incurred by the erring spouse. Even if a divorce decree states that a former spouse will be responsible for any amounts due on previously filed tax returns, both spouses are still liable.

Both the Treasury Department and the General Accounting Office reported on what has come to be called the "joint and several liability standard," wherein joint filers are liable for one another regarding the information they submit on their 1040. Their objective was to assess how the existing law protected the rights of innocent spouses, particularly if they were separated or divorced. In early 1997, the GAO recommended no changes, but IRS former Commissioner Rossotti did the opposite. He pushed for new legislation to help innocent spouses and for a new form, Form 8857 (Request for Innocent Spouse Relief). These changes, in much stronger language, were incorporated into RRA '98.

At last, married taxpayers who file a joint return are protected from wrongful tax liabilities of their spouses under certain conditions. Innocent spouses will be liable for tax on only their own income if, in signing the joint return, they did not know, and had no reason to know, that there was an understatement of tax. Even partial relief is available, based on this same criterion.

Separate Liability Election or Separation of Liability

In addition to choosing innocent spouse relief, if you filed a joint return and became divorced, widowed, legally separated, or simply have not lived in the same household with your spouse for the past 12 months, you can still limit your tax liability through a separate liability election. This election would limit your liability only to the items on the return that specifically pertain to you. In other words, for those items, the innocent spouse would be treated as if he or she had filed a separate return.

This election may be partially or completely invalid if the electing spouse had actual knowledge of incorrect items on the joint return or if there was a fraudulent transfer of assets between spouses with the intention to avoid payment of taxes. If it can be shown that you had knowledge of your spouse's misstatement of tax liability, you will be held responsible unless you can prove you signed it under duress.

Both innocent spouse and separate liability elections are available up to two years after the IRS begins collection activities, and the two-year period will not begin until collection activities alert the spouse that the IRS intends to collect the joint liability from each spouse.

YOUR TAX-SAVING STRATEGY

The criteria in a separate liability election are based on the standard of "actual knowledge." This means that taxpayers electing separate liability could do so if they did not have actual knowledge of the specific event that created the liability. For the IRS to prove this claim, they must establish actual knowledge based on the evidence. Accordingly, the separate liability election, though offering more narrow relief, might be easier for the taxpayer to prove. In contrast, the innocent spouse election, where the criterion is that the taxpayer "knew or should have known," may offer broader relief but be easier for the IRS to disclaim. If the IRS claims that your spouse had unreported income, you can try to prove that you had no knowledge of the omission by showing that your standard of living did not change by some mysterious infusion of newfound money. To prove your case you will need to gather at least two years' worth of bank deposits and check and credit card expenditures, which you'll have to show to the IRS. Hopefully, this should do it.

Equitable Relief

In drawing up the legislation, it became obvious that other circumstances not included in the first two sections of the innocent spouse provision would prevent taxpayers from obtaining relief. To deny these people help resulting from the wrongdoing of spouses is unfair. Therefore, the equitable relief provision was born. Accordingly, you may be relieved of responsibility for taxes, penalties, and interest if you fit into these categories:

- Your circumstances make you ineligible for innocent spouse relief or separation of liability. For example, you file a joint return with your spouse where the liability is $12,000, and you pay $7,000 when you file the return. To meet your obligations, you then borrow $5,000 to pay the balance, but without your knowledge, your spouse spends the $5,000 on him- or herself.
- It would be unfair to hold you liable for an understatement or underpayment of tax given all the facts and circumstances of your situation. To decide if it is unfair, the IRS would, for example, try to determine if you received any significant benefit from the understatement of tax. Another reason deemed to be unfair circumstances would be if you were later divorced or deserted by your spouse.

There is a second new IRS form that indirectly relates to the innocent spouse situation. By filing Form 8379 (Injured Spouse Claim and Allocation), you may prevent the IRS from taking your share of any refunds on a joint return. This form is specifically designed to help when the injured spouse was not even married to the delinquent spouse at the time the tax liabilities were incurred.

All of the innocent spouse provisions apply to any tax liability arising after July 22, 1998, and to any tax liability arising before that date that is unpaid as of July 22, 1998.

Impact
The IRS is also required to

- Alert married taxpayers to the legal consequences of filing a joint return.
- Send any deficiency notice relating to a joint return separately to each name on the return.
- Establish procedures to notify taxpayers of their innocent spouse relief and/or separate liability options.

Telephone representatives specifically trained in the innocent spouse provision are available through the IRS's toll-free numbers.

By easing the former restrictions on innocent spouse relief, which were completely arbitrary and had a disproportionate effect on low-income taxpayers, determining eligibility for such relief should be simpler and more just. The impact of this law is expected to save a lot of headaches for a great number of taxpayers innocently burdened with debts they had nothing to do with and, often, didn't even know existed. Complete information is contained in IRS Publication 971, "Innocent Spouse Relief." Also see the IRS web site, www.irs.gov Individuals/ Innocent Spouse.

Collection and Audit Safeguards

New lien, levy, and collection safeguards have been legislated to protect taxpayers from unscrupulous treatment by the IRS.

Seizures of Residences and Businesses

The greatest power revenue officers have had is their ability to file federal liens and levies and to seize property belonging to taxpayers without obtaining prior approval. (See "What Collection Really Does," Chapter 3.) This is where the IRS gets you. RRA '98 strikes at the core of this power, and the changes here are dramatic.

Now, not only is supervisory approval generally required before any lien or levy action can be taken, but the supervisor must completely review the case, taking into consideration all the facts and circumstances, including the value of the asset subject to the seizure as it relates to the tax debt due. If the revenue officers and/or supervisors fail to follow the prescribed procedures, both are subject to disciplinary action. As taxpayers, you need to be informed of these steps:

- A seizure of a residence requires the written approval of a U.S. District Court judge or magistrate.
- A seizure of a residence generally cannot take place to satisfy a liability, including penalties and interest, of $5,000 or less.
- A seizure of personal or real property used in a taxpayer's trade or business generally requires the written approval of an IRS district or assistant district director, after it is determined that no other assets are available to pay the amount due.
- The IRS cannot sell any seized property for less than a previously agreed-upon minimum bid price. If sold for less, the taxpayer can sue for civil damages.
- For all sales of seized property, the IRS must provide to the taxpayer full details of the sales, including seizure and sale dates, expenses of sale, and how the net proceeds were applied to the taxpayer's tax liabilities.
- The revenue officer who is recommending the collection action has to verify your liability, determine that you will have sufficient equity in the property to yield net proceeds to apply against that liability, and give thorough consideration to other collection methods available, such as an offer in compromise or installment agreement.

Collection "Due Process"—Liens and Levies

This part of the law adds several due process safeguards in reaction to IRS collection abuses.

Within five days of filing a lien on, or at least 30 days prior to levying, a taxpayer's property, the IRS must notify the taxpayer and provide the following information in simple, nontechnical language:

- The amount of unpaid tax.
- The fact that a hearing can be requested within 35 days after receipt of the notice of lien, within 30 days for a levy.
- Available administrative appeals and procedures.
- Procedures relating to release of the lien, or alternatives that could prevent the levy on the property (e.g., installment agreements).

And in case of a levy, there are two additional notifications:

1. The proposed actions the IRS will take and the rights the taxpayer has with respect to those actions.
2. IRS provisions and procedures relating to the levy, sale, and redemption of the property.

The forms and the subsequent procedures they initiate are intended to provide taxpayers with a stronger chance for due process if they are in the difficult position of facing a lien or levy. The complete list of publications and forms sent free by the IRS regarding collection can be found in IRS Publication 594, "The IRS Collection Process."

Right of Appeal

With either a notice of lien or intent to levy, a taxpayer is entitled to a hearing conducted by an impartial person who had no prior involvement in the case. By filing Form 12153 (Request For A Collection Due Process Hearing) with the Appeals Division of the IRS within 30 days after receiving a notice, you can bring up any new appropriate issues concerning collection activity such as innocent spouse status, an offer in compromise, or an installment agreement. However, you generally cannot challenge the underlying tax liability. If you lose, you have another 30 days to appeal to the Tax Court or a higher court if appropriate.

Call the IRS at 877-457-5055 for questions related to the appeals process. You will be automatically routed to the appropriate Appeals Office site. Information is also available at www.irs.gov/prod/ind_info/appeals.

Note: Under prior law, if you lost in Appeals, your case was returned to Collection, leaving you with no alternative. Because you can now appeal to higher courts, you can expect greater consideration from the Appeals officers, who are also obligated to consider all alternative collection procedures you may make to settle your liability.

Third-Party Involvement

Another of the most damaging aspects of liens and levies occurs when the IRS notifies third parties concerning examination or collection activities targeting a taxpayer. In this book alone you have read many true stories of people whose careers and reputations have been destroyed or whose businesses and personal assets were severely weakened for years because the IRS spread the word, often without cause and almost always refusing to make amends, about a taxpayer's alleged unlawful behavior.

Now some level of safeguard has been put in place that gives taxpayers a way to fight back. Generally, in civil cases, before the IRS contacts third parties in connection with the examination of a taxpayer or the collection of any tax owed, the taxpayer must be notified of the service of a summons on a third party within a reasonable time before the date of service. This at least gives taxpayers the chance to resolve issues and volunteer information to the persons about to be contacted before the IRS gets to them.

Impact

The audit and collection safeguards combine to form some very serious protections against what has been unfair and often brutal treatment imposed by the IRS. Beginning with the first letter a taxpayer receives informing him or her of an audit or collection problem, all the way—possibly through the federal courts—the taxpayer is informed of his or her rights and should be able to make informed decisions. Revenue officers are now very cautious before arbitrarily and capriciously slapping an unwarranted lien or levy on an unsuspecting taxpayer without following prescribed protocol. Though some may continue to try these tactics, the fear of reprisals, now part of the law, has reduced unwarranted and erratic behavior considerably.

The guidelines aimed at the IRS Collection Department to maintain flexibility when negotiating a taxpayer's installment agreement or offer in compromise has not only eased the situation from the IRS's perspective but also eased the minds of thousands of taxpayers who want to unburden themselves of their tax debts. For the first time, taxpayers are given specific statutory protections against enforcement action by the IRS while they are attempting to settle their tax obligations. Read more about the impact these laws are having in Chapter 13.

13

The New IRS: What Are Its Goals?

NEW IRS MISSION

First, there's a new mission statement: "Provide America's taxpayers with top-quality service by helping them understand and meet their tax responsibilities and by applying the tax law with integrity and fairness to all."

This contrasts with the former mission, which began: "The purpose of the IRS is to collect the proper amount of tax revenue at the least cost."

It is easy to spot the difference in intent between the two. The first emphasizes fairness, the second, collecting revenue. Ponder that.

SERVING FOUR GROUPS OF TAXPAYERS

For almost fifty years, the IRS was organized as a geographically based structure where each taxpayer is served by at least one service center and a district office, with the entire operation driven by the function it performs—examination, collection, tax return processing.

In comparison, the backbone of the new IRS is built upon serving four distinct groups of taxpayers who have similar needs:

- Wage and investment income taxpayers who file 1040A, 1040EZ, and simple 1040's.
- Small business, self-employed, and supplemental income taxpayers who file C, E, F, or 2106 schedules; some, if not all, partnerships and S corporations; and corporations with assets under $10 million.
- Midsize and large corporate taxpayers, defined as corporations with assets between $10 million and $250 million. Large corporations are defined as having assets greater than $250 million.
- Tax-exempt, including employee plans, exempt organizations, and state and local governments. (See the new IRS organization chart in Appendix E.)

The shift is a dramatic one. The four groups or business units replace the IRS's four regional offices and much of the national office, leaving the remaining national office structure to focus on overseeing the IRS and broad policy concerns rather than operations. According to the IRS, regions and districts, in their old format, will no longer exist. However, the service centers continue much as they did previously. The work that goes on there, from processing to customer service, is considered crucial, though some of the service center work may be realigned to the individual business units. The service centers, along with the toll-free IRS sites and the Automated Collection System sites, are being customized to better deal with segments of customers and their questions.

The overall concept for this new subdivision is based on proven established practice throughout most of the private sector. Instead of one institution doing everything for everybody, now, within that organization, there will be different operating divisions working for different kinds of customers.

The IRS expects that by reorganizing by type of taxpayer, rather than by geographical area, the organization will have a greater ability to develop technical and industry expertise. As these changes become operational, remember that when you fill out your return, the IRS will have increasing industry expertise. In a way, the agency is extending its existing Market Segment Specialization approach.

OBSTACLES TO OVERCOME

Quotas Versus Customer Service

Do quotas exist at the IRS? Many believe they always did, though the IRS has consistently denied it, stating that at least as far back as 1988, collection quotas were outlawed.

However, during the Senate Finance Committee hearings, it appeared that IRS agents levied unwarranted tax assessments and unfairly seized property to prove they were doing their jobs. Furthermore, IRS agents struggling to meet collection quotas were targeting lower- and middle-income taxpayers who couldn't afford to fight back. In a six-month study, it was also found that tax assessments were being levied to raise the individual statistics of an IRS employee, and that there was a commonplace use of tax collection quotas to rate agents or officers.[1]

As a result of these findings, the 33 IRS district offices are no longer ranked on the basis of how closely they meet their goal of tax collections. Goals related to revenue production in the field have been suspended. Enforcement results are no longer used to evaluate employees, and penalty amounts and revenue collected are included in statistical results only on a national level.

Whistle-Blowers and Reprisals

Amidst the hard work and genuine effort going into the creation of new ways to evaluate an employee's performance comes news of the backlash directed at IRS employees who spoke up before the congressional investigation that led to RRA '98. It appears that these whistle-blowers are suffering on the job. How far, really, can the IRS possibly advance into the new millennium, with all of its defined goals and initiatives, if this kind of Stone Age attitude still surfaces within its ranks? In spite of IRS assurances that there would be no retaliation against employees, the jobs of most of the agents who testified before the Senate Finance Committee in 1997 are being threatened, according to Senator William Roth, Jr. (R-Del.) and William Nixon in their book, *The Power to Destroy.*

According to Roth, a vast majority of employees report that the agency has a "kill the messenger" attitude, and more than 70 percent of the almost 100,000 employees polled said that there are not adequate protections against retaliation for employees who come forward with reports of abuses against taxpayers or fellow employees. The IRS commissioner promised to get to the bottom of the reprisal issue.[2]

IRS Collections Are on the Way Back

From the passage of RRA '98 until now, the news regarding the results of the IRS Collection Department has been quite astonishing. The IRS says it seized taxpayer property for overdue taxes 255 times in 2001 and 364 times in 2002. This represents a sharp decrease from the same period in 1998, when there were more than 2,307 seizures, and a dramatic drop from 10,090 only five years ago. "The outlook for the last 10 years showed a drop of 96 percent, from about 10,000 seizures annually to 364 in 2002."[3] Liens on property and levies appear to be an exception to the IRS slowdown trend. Liens and levies are a reliable means for the IRS to collect delinquent taxes. It's no surprise, then, that liens showed a 71 percent increase in 2002, up from 2000; and levies show a 203 percent increase in 2002, up from 2000.

The IRS continues to say that these sorts of changes are partially due to a reallocation of IRS staff to implement new RRA '98 provisions, and to use its existing budget—somewhere around $8.1 billion—for new computers and training. In sum, the IRS has shifted large portions of its employees, about 21,000 people, including those in collection and examination, to temporarily bolster customer service efforts—answering phones, working at counters in walk-in centers, and participating in Saturday Problem-Solving

Days—and with the agencywide training effort, time usually spent on regular assignments is further eaten away.

But IRS officers in six states said in interviews with the *New York Times* that the biggest reason for the retreat was their fear of being dismissed for running afoul of the new law intended to protect taxpayers from overzealous collectors. The IRS Restructuring and Reform Act of 1998 states that agency employees must be dismissed if, following an administrative inquiry, they are found to have committed any of 10 acts, among them violating a taxpayer's constitutional or civil rights, threatening an audit for personal gain, making a false statement under oath, or falsifying or destroying documents to conceal mistakes. Employees terminated under the law have no right to appeal. It is a genuine cultural revolution, with many employees struggling to shift from an adversarial approach to the new customer service mind-set. The result, current and former IRS officials said, is near paralysis in the agency's enforcement apparatus.[4] "Seizing property, for example, now requires a 54-step process that more than two dozen revenue officers have described as virtually impossible to navigate."[5]

The culprit is allegedly what has come to be called the 10 deadly sins for which collection agents can be fired. For the benefit of all taxpayers, here they are:

1. Willfully seizing taxpayer assets without authorization.
2. Making false statements under oath about a taxpayer or taxpayer representative.
3. Violating the constitutional or civil rights of a taxpayer or taxpayer representative.
4. Falsifying or destroying documents to conceal mistakes.
5. Committing assault or battery on a taxpayer or taxpayer representative.
6. Retaliating against or harassing a taxpayer or taxpayer representative, in violation of the Tax Code or IRS rules.
7. Willfully misusing confidentiality rules to conceal information from a congressional inquiry.
8. Willfully failing to file tax returns.
9. Willfully understating tax liabilities.
10. Threatening to audit a taxpayer for personal gain.[6]

Add to this a substantial decrease in the number of tax collectors (to 5,407) and an increase in the number of tax returns being filed (to 171 million) for 2001. Former Commissioner Rossotti went on record expressing his concern, and well he should. It seems that in the collection area, things can't get much worse. The IRS is currently facing a situation where the number of tax delinquents going without paying their tax bill is so huge, billions of dollars are being left uncollected.

Is this just a sudden-death reaction to the change, and will the IRS response calm down in time? I see it as a period of adjustment. No doubt enforcement efforts will taper off during this time, but once the momentum of the new laws kicks in, there should be a leveling off. Remember, these IRS agents have been doing it their way for 15 years or more. The new law threatens those ways. Some in the agency believe that all a taxpayer has to do is say, "I'm not paying," or offer $10 a week toward an installment agreement in lieu of thousands of tax dollars owed, or say the magic word, "harassment," and that will be the end of that. But that's probably just a front, the propaganda of resistance made more real by some IRS employees relaxing their efforts. What's worse—collection agents following new rules for seizing property, or a taxpayer being unfairly harassed by having a lien placed on his house?

Here's another victory for taxpayers, and a direct hit at the IRS Collection Division: Now people with overdue taxes will be able to keep their securities (stocks and bonds), businesses, and homes if they can show that they need these assets to pay for medical care or basic living expenses. This is a real change from previous IRS collection methods of seizing a taxpayer's assets and selling them, usually at a great discount, in return for taxes owed, often with no questions asked—or allowed. Now a taxpayer with a stock portfolio and a history of paying taxes on time until trouble struck might be able to wipe out or significantly reduce a tax bill if he or she can show that the assets are needed, for example, to pay medical bills.[7] It's another step toward taxpayers receiving greater due process under the law.

If collections and enforcement continue to drop, it will be interesting to see the steps the IRS and Congress will take. Some switch—creating a balance between fair and adequate collections and fair and decent treatment of taxpayers—is in the works!

Innocent Spouse Relief—Huge Backlog of Requests

From April 1998 until the passage of RRA '98, there were 3,000 innocent spouse claims waiting to be handled at the IRS. From 1999 to 2001, the IRS received 123,753 relief requests. Of those claims, there were 52,093 relief requests still pending as of September 2001. Of the claims that met the requirements for being considered, about 36 percent were allowed in full, and 9 percent were partially allowed.[8] The IRS expects the backlog to decrease by 40 percent by the end of 2003. The IRS says that "this growth in claims is a good sign that America's taxpayers are learning about the innocent spouse provision from many sources, including our aggressive outreach program and the Taxpayer Advocates."[9] It seems that the current pileup is due to several factors: Thousands of taxpayers are becoming aware of the new law and how they can be helped by it, and IRS employees are needing more time to interpret the new law and to develop procedures to put the provisions into effect. Again, IRS staff from Examination have been borrowed from auditing assignments to help reduce the backlog and to weed out ineligible taxpayers. "In fact, the IRS has pulled about 500 auditors, more than 3 percent of its auditing force, to help with the huge backlog of innocent spouse requests. This represents at least one audit group of 10 to 15 auditors in each of the 33 IRS districts."[10]

A total of 60,272 requests filed between March 1999 and September 2001 were determined not to meet basic requirements for processing. A GAO report included the top five reasons for the delays in processing Form 8857 (Request for Innocent Spouse Relief):[11]

1. The requesting spouse did not file a joint federal tax return for the year relief was requested.
2. The collection statute of limitations had already expired and there was no longer a balance due.
3. Tax was paid in full—no refund was requested
4. No return was filed.
5. Incomplete information was submitted, and the requesting spouse did not respond to IRS requests for additional data.

For anyone wishing to check eligibility for innocent spouse relief, try going online at www.irs.gov/ind_info/s_tree/index.html. In addition, the "Spousal Tax Relief Eligibility Explorer" is available as a link from the "Tax Info for You" page of the IRS web site at www.irs.gov. This program offers an interactive prompt to help taxpayers determine whether they qualify for relief from a joint tax liability with their current or former spouse. If it appears that you qualify, the program offers to download the appropriate application form.[12]

In addition, IRS Publication 971, "Innocent Spouse Relief," outlines eligibility for innocent spouse relief, gives information about the forms needed to be filed, and tells who to contact at the IRS.

Victims of domestic violence who apply for innocent spouse relief can now be helped by the IRS. Some 80,000 people sought this protection in the last three years. If an individual is a victim of domestic violence and fears that a claim for innocent spouse relief will result in retaliation, the individual should alert the IRS by writing "Potential Domestic Abuse Case" at the top of Form 8857. Additional information explaining his or her concerns should be attached to the form. The IRS is taking extra precautions so that the other spouse cannot learn the address of the domestic abuse victim.[13]

During an address to the American Institute of CPAs Tax Division, former Commissioner Rossotti said that it's not just "innocent" spouses who are petitioning for a rollback in federal tax assessments, interest, and penalties. The requests are coming in from battered wives, individuals separated from their spouses because of military duty, and even the spouses of prison inmates. In some cases the IRS is receiving petitions for spousal relief from both parties in a failed marriage.

The innocent spouse provision is filling a tremendous need for spouses who have been wrongly accused and made responsible for tax misdeeds not their own simply because they filed a joint return. It is obvious that the situation has been pent up for years.

Note: For those filing these claims, make sure you select the correct form, either 8857 or 8379, and fill in the information as requested. Like all IRS forms, it may be confusing, so consider asking a tax pro for help.

IRS ON TRACK—DIRECTION: ELECTRONIC FILING OF INDIVIDUAL RETURNS

What follows are the primary directions that the IRS is heading.

Electronic filing, which began in 1986, has developed to the point where taxpayers can have their preapproved tax preparer e-file their returns to the IRS; or they can sit in front of a computer in their home or office, type in numbers on a 1040 on their screen, make one telephone call, then transmit their 1040 via a modem and tax preparation software directly to the IRS computers. Initially, returns were filed not by taxpayers themselves, but by tax professionals whose equipment and software have been certified by the IRS for performing electronic filing for clients. But the IRS currently accepts several formats for e-filing, as it is now called.

Electronic filing allows taxpayers' federal and state returns to be filed in one transmission to the IRS, which in turn relays the relevant data to state tax collectors.

What to Do about Electronic Filing

Lower Error Rate

The greatest benefit for taxpayers who file electronically is a dramatically lower error rate. Computer-assisted returns are generally far more accurate than those prepared by hand. The accuracy shows up in the mathematics and through general neatness. As a result, the error rate on electronic returns is less than 1 percent compared with 18 percent for paper returns.

This is what error reduction does for the average taxpayer:

- It ensures your anonymity.
- It helps you avoid a mismatch and subsequent flagging of your return for review.
- It eliminates the possibility of having your refund check delayed or of your being charged penalties that later have to be rectified.

Faster Refunds

Another benefit for people who file electronically is that a refund will arrive faster, in about three weeks or less. If your file by February 10 your refund will likely hit your bank account in as little as 10 days. The reason for the time saved is not that an electronically filed return is processed more quickly than a paper 1040, but that the refund may be deposited in a taxpayer's bank account electronically, similarly to the way many Social Security payments are made.[14] A check sent through the mail may take six or eight weeks, according to the IRS. In 2001, 34 million returns used direct deposits for refunds, up 10 percent from the previous year.[15]

Barrier to E-Filing

Tax preparers who do a high volume of returns are offering electronic filing for an extra fee. For some clients the extra fee is worth it. However, a major barrier to converting people to e-filing *is* the extra fees. During the 2003 filing season (for 2002 returns), the IRS introduced a partnership with more than a dozen online tax preparers, which allows free e-filing for mainly lower-income taxpayers. To take advantage of the free filing, taxpayers must go to the IRS web site at www.irs.gov and click on "Free Online Filing" to access the companies.

Another big reason why taxpayers shy away from e-filing is their concern over security and privacy of personal and financial information. The IRS e-file regulations prohibit the sharing of data with anyone other than the IRS, and only dedicated computer lines are used. The IRS claims that more than 250 million returns have been processed without a breach since the inception of e-filing more than 15 years ago.

Finally, there are those taxpayers who simply have a continued preference for paper filing—that is, they need to see a hard copy of the filed return or they just lack a general awareness of e-filing and how to do it.

Nationally, the number of electronic returns has increased steadily and dramatically, from 19.1 million in 1997 to 47 million returns in 2002. The IRS's prediction of 65 percent of all returns being filed electronically by the year 2002 was not met. However, the IRS has set an even more ambitious goal of having 80 percent of returns filed electronically by 2007. That leaves 20 percent for paper returns!

The present strategy has resulted in a program that primarily attracts individuals who file simple returns, are due refunds, and are willing to pay fees, now only minimal, associated with electronic filing to get those refunds sooner. The innovation of free filing should accelerate the growth of e-filing over the next few years.

DIRECTION: E-FILING ON PERSONAL COMPUTERS

In 1996, a pilot program for filing tax returns on a personal computer proved such a success, the IRS has become more gung ho for a completely paperless way to file. Meanwhile, here's how you too can get in on the act: First, complete your tax return using IRS-accepted software, found at computer stores or downloaded from participating web sites. Transmit the return to an online filing company or designated provider, such as Nelco or Turbotax, which converts the file to IRS specifications. The online company transmits the file to the IRS, and within 48 hours, you are supposed to be notified by the filing company if the return is accepted or, if it's not, which items you need to correct. After the return is accepted, you mail to the IRS a signed Form 8453-OL (U.S. Individual Income Tax Declaration for On-Line Service Electronic Filing), which is provided by either the tax preparation software or the online filing company.[16]

You no longer have to include W-2 forms with your mailing to the IRS, but the e-file provider is required to hold copies until the end of the calendar year.

Payment Methods for Online Filers

Once you submit your return using IRS e-file, various payment methods are available for the payment of federal income tax. Payment can be made using the following:

- Form 1040V (Payment Voucher). This form automatically prints out and will be sent to you when the IRS determines that you owe money based on the e-return you submitted. Simply follow the directions and return it with your payment.
- Debiting your checking or savings account.
- A credit card. See "Direction: Paying with Plastic" section later in this chapter.

What to Do about Electronic Filing for Personal Computers

There is no cost to use this capability, though the filing company may charge a small transmission fee. This is a viable alternative to filing a paper return, especially for computer-knowledgeable people. For the

2002 filing season, 9.4 million taxpayers prepared their own returns and e-filed from their home computers, a 38 percent increase over the prior year.

Paperless Electronic Filing Programs

In working toward paperless filing, the IRS has two signature programs where a number can be used as the taxpayer's electronic signature. The number can be used in place of the paper signature documents, Forms 8453/8453-OL, and you don't even have to mail in your W-2 forms as is required in the usual online filing.[17]

In the online signature program, the IRS distributed e-file customer numbers to taxpayers who used personal computers to prepare their returns in the past. These taxpayers prepared their own returns using tax preparation software and filed from their home computers.

In the practitioner signature program, taxpayers chose a personal identification number (PIN) when filing through participating practitioners. Taxpayers who participate in this program do not have to mail in the cumbersome paper signature form 8453. More than 24.8 million taxpayers signed their returns electronically in 2001 under the two signature programs.

DIRECTION: TELEPHONE FILING (TELEFILING)

In 2002, 4.2 million taxpayers filed their return via telephone. Many of these taxpayers are computer users who received the more than 21 million invitations sent to taxpayers authorizing the use of the TeleFile option. Those eligible must meet all nine requirements for filing form 1040EZ. In general, you must be single, have no dependents, be under 65 years of age and have a taxable income of less than $50,000. Go to www.irs.gov for a list of the other five filing requirements.

Taxpayers are limited to the standard deduction that is based on filing status (single or head of household): $4,750 for most single people and $7,000 for head of household. Therefore, if you have higher itemized deductions, it may be wiser to use Form 1040 unless you prefer the ease of filing offered through TeleFiling.

What to Do about TeleFiling

It's quick—about 10 minutes. Using your Touch-Tone phone, you simply enter your Social Security number, your employer's identification number (from your W-2 form), your wages, federal tax withheld, taxable interest, and unemployment compensation, if any. In seconds a voice tells you your federal adjusted gross income, taxable income, and refund due or balance owed, followed by a confirmation number. You should receive a refund within three weeks or less (versus 40 days for mailed-in returns), which can be deposited directly into your bank account. The service is free. Try it.

If you don't own a computer, TeleFiling would be a logical choice. In 2003, you can file your federal and state returns via TeleFile in most states and the District of Columbia. Taxpayers who file using TeleFiling can now also use a charge card to pay their taxes. (See "Payment Methods" earlier in this chapter.)

DIRECTION: ELECTRONIC FILING FOR BUSINESSES— ELECTRONIC FEDERAL TAX PAYMENT SYSTEM

The Electronic Federal Tax Payment System (EFTPS) was enacted as part of the North American Free Trade Agreement of 1993 (NAFTA). Designed to speed the flow of funds to the U.S. Treasury, EFTPS allows employers to deposit federal payroll taxes electronically.

It is best to enroll in the program immediately, since the process takes at least 10 weeks. Once you become part of the system, you can electronically pay business taxes owed not only on Form 941 (Employer's Quarterly Federal Tax Return) but also on Form 1120 (U.S. Corporate Income Tax Return), Form 940 (Employer's Annual Federal Unemployment—FUTA—Tax Return), and eight other infrequently used federal business tax returns.

You have four payment options:

1. Call your bank, which debits your account.
2. Call the IRS, which debits your bank account, 1-800-555-4477.
3. Use Fedwire, especially for companies required to make large deposits; it offers same-day debits.
4. Transmit from your own PC.

What to Do about EFTPS

My clients are extremely satisfied with the ease and simplicity of the system as well as with the reduced error rate and fewer penalties paid each year. EFTPS can save business taxpayers millions of dollars annually. Why? It eliminates all of the time and energy offices like mine spend answering IRS queries regarding inadequate or untimely deposits made with Form 941. We receive more questions from the IRS about this than in any other business-tax area. The number of taxpayers currently enrolling in the system continues at a rate of about 6,000 per week, now totaling more than 3.6 million taxpayers. During 2001, EFTPS processed more than 64 million federal tax payments, a total of $40 billion

E-Filing of Business and Payroll Returns

The IRS's program for electronically filing Form 941 (Employer's Quarterly Tax Return) is now completely operational. (Employers are generally required to report both the federal income tax withheld and the employer and employee portions of the FICA tax on a quarterly return, Form 941.) Go to the IRS web site, www.irs.gov, then to Businesss/Small Bus/Self-Employed/Businesses with Employees/Employment Taxes for Small Businesses /Employment Tax E-File Programs.

The Social Security Administration has developed the Business Services online web page, where small to medium-size businesses can electronically file up to 20 W-2s and conduct other related business such as the verification of Social Security numbers. The W-2 forms can be completed on your computer and then are electronically submitted to SSA before printing copies suitable for distribution to your employees. You can reach the site at www.ssa.gov/Services for Businesses/E-File Your W-2 Report. If help is needed, you can call 1-800-325-0778 Monday through Friday, 7:00 A.M. to 7:00 P.M.

Another IRS project allows almost one million small businesses that meet certain qualifications to file their Form 941 by telephone, using a toll-free number. If you receive the special TeleFile package, give it a try. I did, and it's as easy as following a few instructions, calling the number, then going through the voice prompts. This free, fast, paperless method automatically calculates the tax and any refund due or balance owed. Filers receive a confirmation number as verification of filing.[18]

Electronic filing is gradually being expanded into other business areas. Form 1041 (U.S. Income Tax Return for Estates and Trusts) can be filed electronically or via magnetic media; Form 1065 (U.S. Partnership Return of Income) and Schedule K-1s can be filed electronically, via magnetic media, or through a remote bulletin board system using modem-to-modem transmission; and Employee Benefit Plan 5500 series returns can be filed using magnetic media or electronically using a modem over telephone lines directly into IRS computers.

Using a CD-ROM

A CD-ROM is now available from the IRS entitled *The Small Business Resource Guide*. It contains all IRS business forms and publications as well as instructions for preparing a business plan and obtaining business financing. One CD-ROM per person is being made available for free and can be ordered by calling 1-800-TAX-FORM or by visiting the IRS web site at www.irs.gov.

For questions and comments about print publications or CD-ROM sales, you can also contact the U.S. Government Printing Office, Superintendent of Documents, Box 371954, Pittsburgh, PA 15250, or call 202-512-1800.

DIRECTION: INCREASING COMPLIANCE

In a genuine attempt to meet its goal of producing a more compliant taxpayer, the IRS has taken several initiatives. It has:

- Put in place revised approaches for negotiating monies owed.
- Tried to ease the taxpayer's burden through education and tax simplification.

HOW TO PAY WHAT YOU OWE—YOU CHOOSE

The essence of tax amnesty legislation is to encourage nonfilers to come forward and negotiate a means to pay or begin to pay what they owe over a period of time without being criminally prosecuted.

About six years ago the IRS finally took a good look at this situation and came up with some genuine amnesty-type measures for nonfilers, based on the philosophy that it is more sensible to encourage taxpayers to come forward and offer some payment than to threaten them and receive nothing.

Payment Vehicles—Offer in Compromise (Form 656)

An offer in compromise (OIC) is used when the IRS agrees to settle for less than the amount owed because it seems unlikely that any more can be collected from the taxpayer. Since 1992, offers in compromise that were accepted increased in astounding numbers, from 4,356 to a record 27,673 in fiscal 1996. Only about $287 million was taken in to settle debts totaling about $2.23 billion.[19] For 2001, 39,000 OICs were accepted out of 125,000 submitted (31 percent), and in 2002, 29,000 were accepted out of 124,000 submitted (23 percent). What has helped to accelerate the acceptance rate is that IRS attorneys are getting involved only if the amount owed is $50,000 or more, compared with $500 previously.

What to Do about an Offer in Compromise

- The IRS wants to get paid what it is owed.
- To realize this, it must encourage nonfilers to come in out of the cold.

Acceptance rates for offers in compromise had been slowed down because the IRS faced a growing backlog. The source of the problem seems to have been the national and local standards developed by the IRS to help revenue officers make decisions regarding allowances for living expenses—costs of housing, utilities, transportation, and such. Generally, assets or income above these standard amounts were used to satisfy paying off the taxes owed. However, in basing a decision on these criteria, individual circumstances were being overlooked, making settlements more difficult and harder to come by.

The IRS now uses a new, simplified approach to offers in compromise, made possible by a combination of new tax regulations that expand the grounds under which the IRS can accept an offer in compromise to include a determination that collecting the taxes owed would create an economic hardship for the taxpayer. The regulations also add provisions on

- Expanding the definition of basic living expenses.
- Allowing for evaluation of offers from low-income taxpayers.
- Reviewing rejected offers without requiring the taxpayer to go through Appeals (as done previously).
- Suspending examination and collection activities while offers in compromise are pending.
- Prohibiting notification of third parties when a taxpayer is targeted by the IRS. (See "Third-Party Involvement," Chapter 12.)

Taxpayers are eligible if their liability is greater than their assets and if they do not have earnings potential to pay off the amount owed over time. In the past, such offers were routinely denied if a taxpayer had certain assets such as equity in a home or a 401(k) plan, even if those assets couldn't be readily cashed in. Under this new approach, taxpayers do not necessarily have to liquidate such assets if doing so would create significant economic hardship, and are eligible for the new fixed monthly payment options. The new fixed payment combines all debts, including interest, owed by the taxpayer under the OIC into a single payment that reflects the maximum the taxpayer can pay after covering basic living expenses.

The IRS has established standards to determine appropriate essential living costs for different family sizes (food, clothing, shelter, and transportation costs). Generally, the IRS considers income in excess of these standard amounts to be available to pay tax. For additional information go to www.irs.gov/Businesses/Small Business/Self-Employed/More Topics/Offer In Compromise.

All instructions for an offer in compromise are contained in a Form 656 (Offer in Compromise) package. To apply, file Form 656 along with a financial statement on Form 433-A (Collection Information Statement for Individuals), and if you are self-employed, use Form 433-B (Collection Information Statement for Business.)

It is important to prepare your application carefully. More than half of the offers submitted in 1999 were too flawed to process, and it may take up to six months for the IRS to review your application.[20] The trend continued in 2002. Taxpayers need to make sure that they properly identify themselves on Form 656, that they state their tax liability correctly, that some amount of money is offered, and that their request includes the latest Form 656 along with Form 433-A or 433-B. Any offer in compromise that is submitted by a taxpayer and rejected by the IRS will first go through an independent administrative review before the taxpayer is notified.

Note: These new provisions are tailored for taxpayers entangled in very severe circumstances and are not designed to be a sweeping program for everyone with financial difficulties.

Disadvantages of Filing an Offer in Compromise

The key disadvantage is that when you file, the statute of limitations for the IRS to collect the tax you owe will automatically be extended from the usual 10-year collection period by as much as two additional years. If the statute of limitations is close to expiring before you submit, it is probably better if you simply wait for it to expire, at which point the IRS cannot legally collect the debt. For example, if your tax debt was assessed on June 15, 1994, the IRS is unable to collect after June 15, 2004. Generally, however, most taxpayers have several years left on the collection statute when they consider filing an offer in compromise.

YOUR TAX-SAVING STRATEGY
Though the IRS has gone on record as being more sympathetic to taxpayers who owe back taxes, IRS specialists who accept or deny compromise offers seem to insist on one thing: If your income varies from year to year, which often happens to self-employed people, the IRS will average the past three or four years to obtain an average cash flow. This may inadvertently make it appear as if you are earning more than you actually are, which, in turn, will affect your OIC payments. You can oppose this averaging method by documenting that a higher income earned in a prior

year is not likely to recur, giving a reason such as having lost your best customer or having moved on to other clients.[21]

Reminder: Once an offer is signed and accepted, the IRS will retain any refunds or credits that you may be entitled to receive for 2003 or for earlier years. This includes refunds you receive in 2004 for any overpayments you made in 2003 or in earlier years. Also, you must stay up-to-date in filing and paying all required taxes for five years from the date of the offer, or the IRS can (and probably will) rescind the offer and go after you for the entire unpaid balance of the offer. Last, if you signed a joint offer with your spouse and you made all your payments in a timely fashion, but your spouse (or former spouse) fails to comply with the requirements (e.g., he or she didn't make payments on time), your offer will not be forfeited.

For 2002, the IRS made 29,000 compromise agreements, in which it wrote off $1.7 billion of $2.1 billion in overdue taxes, collecting $301 million, or 14 percent, of the tax bills.[22]

YOUR TAX-SAVING STRATEGY

When evaluating an offer in compromise, for which you are solely responsible, the IRS takes into consideration your spouse's earnings. In so doing, more of your money, as they see it, is freed up to pay your obligation. If your spouse is female, it is up to you to argue that her earnings may not continue (e.g., because of having a child) and have her earnings eliminated from the computations. If your spouse is male, think of a different reason.

IRS lawyers who review offers in compromise are always on the lookout for taxpayers who transfer assets from one spouse to another in an attempt to hide these assets from a tax settlement. Be ready for your spouse to prove that her wealth came from her own earnings or inheritance, or was transferred from the other spouse long before the tax problems began.

Payment Vehicles—Installment Agreement Request (Form 9465)

In the last few years, the IRS has also accepted an increasing number of 9465 forms to create an installment agreement between the IRS and taxpayers who have balances due on their 1040s. Taxpayers can attach Form 9465 to the 1040 and specify the amount of the proposed monthly payment. A response from the IRS to accept, deny, or request more information regarding the terms is supposed to arrive within 30 days. The terms of the agreement are negotiated between the IRS and the taxpayer.

Form 9465 actually offers an enormous advantage. The old form required taxpayers to disclose their current financial status to the IRS, about four pages of it, including a full list of all assets and liabilities. The new form omits this requirement for tax liabilities under $10,000 as long as you are current on all previous tax obligations. Here are the advantages: Taxpayers can pay their bills without disclosing their ready assets to the IRS, which could implicate them if they have sufficient means to pay their obligation in full; a revenue officer can accept the terms of the agreement without going through a chain of command; and if taxpayers adhere to the terms of the payment schedule, no tax liens will be filed against the taxpayers' property.

The IRS says it has decided to take this approach to reduce the number of taxpayers who do not file at all because of money owed, and in the hope that taxpayers will file returns even if they cannot pay the balance due immediately.

Disadvantages of Filing an Installment Agreement

First, they are binding. Second, penalties and interest are due on the unpaid balance. Essentially, taxpayers who file Form 9465 are locked into a late-payment penalty of one quarter of one percent a month plus interest on unpaid amounts. Taken together, the cost comes to about 10 percent a year. This is less interest than on many credit cards, but you still need to think it through before you sign. You may end up owing more than you expect, and if you don't meet your monthly payment, the IRS will come after you. In addition, if your income goes up, the IRS can insist that monthly payments be increased. However, if your income drops, you must submit new financial information before the IRS will, at its discretion, consider lowering your payments, though the IRS is now required to notify taxpayers before changing the terms of an installment agreement. Finally, there is a $43 fee for setting up the installment agreement.

With the IRS's emphasis on customer service, you may stand a better chance these days of negotiating such an agreement where previously, despite laws and guidelines, the outcomes remained unknown. If you request an installment agreement, you will generally be guaranteed one if the balance you owe is $10,000 or less and if you are up-to-date on filing your returns and paying your taxes. If more than $10,000 is unpaid, some negotiation will be necessary. The IRS will look at your past record of tax compliance as well as your assets. However, with businesses, there are still many revenue officers who are hell-bent on forcing the sale of business assets to achieve some payment, even if the taxpayer is put out of business.

A few years ago only the Collection Division could work with accounts over $5,000. Now all functions within the IRS have the authority to grant installment agreements up to $25,000. That means employees in Appeals, Employee Plans and Exempt Organizations, Examination, Taxpayer Advocate, Returns Processing (in the service centers), and Taxpayer Services can help in resolving accounts.[23] Now, if you owe up to

$25,000 and the IRS believes you can pay the amount within five years, your agreement has a good chance of being accepted. If the IRS refuses to grant your installment request, investigate the possibility of making an offer in compromise. You can go to the IRS web site for an online calculator to figure a reasonable monthly installment payment and to obtain the necessary forms. Learn more at www.irs.gov under Individuals/ More Topics/ Interactive Installment Agreement Process.

During the period of negotiating for either an offer in compromise or an installment agreement, the IRS must cease all collection activities (i.e., a levy may not be placed on that person's property). This prohibition extends for 30 days after an offer in compromise is rejected or an installment agreement is terminated, and during the pending of any appeal, provided the appeal is filed within 30 days of the rejection. Neither can any levy be made when an installment agreement is in effect.

In another area, the IRS has 10 years to collect a properly assessed tax by levy, or in a court proceeding. Generally, effective after 1999, it will be very difficult for the IRS to obtain an agreement from a taxpayer to extend the 10-year limitation period on collections except in connection with an installment agreement.

How to Pay Off the IRS on Your Terms without Using IRS Installment Agreements

Rather than locking yourself into a 9465 installment agreement, I recommend the following short-term fix to ease out of tax money due:

- Send in some money as soon as you receive your first notice of tax due.
- Follow the payment up with some more money each time you receive another collection notice.
- With each notice, include a short note explaining why you cannot pay the full balance right now, such as illness or loss of your job.
- Be sure to tell the IRS that you will continue to try your best to pay as much as you can.

Using this method, you could get away with paying a fairly small amount for three to four months. If you file a 9465, you will soon be strapped with a strict payment schedule that will be fraught with penalties if you don't make all the payments on time. Hopefully, after the first few months you'll be in better shape to pay off the balance.

In 1997, $10.8 billion was collected in installment agreements, representing 2.8 million agreements struck. Those figures dropped slightly for 1998 and fell even more in the first six months of 1999 to only about $3.5 billion collected, or 778,000 installment agreements made.[24]

DIRECTION: PAYING TAXES WITH PLASTIC

You can now use a credit or charge card for the payment of federal income taxes. Taxpayers who file Form 1040, 1040A, or 1040EZ on paper or electronically can call U.S. Audiotex at 1-888-2PAY-TAX, where they will be prompted for their credit card information, Social Security number, and verification of address. American Express, MasterCard, and Discover are all accepted. The fee is roughly 2.5 percent of your tax due, which you can determine in advance by going to www.usaudiotex.com. For 2001, 313,385 taxpayers charged their taxes, a 212 percent increase in just two years.

Although taxpayers using IRS e-file can use their credit card for the payment of federal income tax, take note: Don't even think about charging your tax bill and then not paying the credit card company. The U.S. Treasury is still responsible for such bad debts, which translates into the probability of an IRS revenue officer knocking at your front door demanding payment.

If you're the least bit tempted to have less federal tax withheld from your wages during the year so you'll be able to add up the sums and subsequently charge a large amount of tax due using your credit, debit, or charge card on April 15, this is unwise. The penalty for underpaying tax during the year will outweigh any frequent flier miles you receive.

Latest Trends Reducing Penalties over the Internet

About one in seven payroll and income tax filings by employers are assessed penalties by the IRS due to late payments or underpayments. Though the average penalty is $900, the IRS often proposes a larger penalty than is required because of the complex rules involved in making the payments in a timely fashion.

New software developed by Time Value Software of Irvine, California, provides online calculation of penalties due. The software company claims that "91 percent of their users have had their penalties reduced or eliminated with an average reduction of 44 percent."[25] Service is available at www.taxpenalty.com, and the cost is $49 if penalty reduction is $500 or more. There is no fee if the penalty reduction is under $500.

If you were expecting your return to be audited but it wasn't, next year might be a different story. Congress authorized the hiring of 2,000 new IRS employees in 2001 and 2002, and the modernization of IRS computer capabilities is proceeding at a brisk pace. Former Commissioner Rossotti warned that "audit rates are down, but audits are not the only way we identify taxpayers. We get more than a billion pieces of information that come in from third parties and even though we are slow, our computers eventually do their job." As to playing audit roulette, Rossotti stated that "you have better odds going to Las Vegas." The IRS also plans to reduce the number of auditors who are assigned to divorce cases and other routine compliance work, such as answering telephone inquiries from the public.[26] At this point, there's a glimmer of hope that the IRS stands a good chance of becoming an agency that will work effectively and efficiently, and serve American taxpayers fairly, at least down the line. The IRS is trying to train its staff so that they are prepared to be emissaries, not adversaries.

IRS Customer Services continues to emphasize the agency's more civil and equitable responses to taxpayers' questions and concerns. While there has been an overall drop in audits and strong-arm agency tactics, IRS levies and liens on property—homes, boats, cars, and business property—have increased considerably in the past year.

The agency survives and continues to collect needed tax revenues, and it is going where it should—in a direction that emphasizes customer service and compliance.

APPENDIX A

Most Important Tax Forms
Discussed in This Book

| Form **SS-8**
(Rev. January 2001)
Department of the Treasury
Internal Revenue Service | **Determination of Worker Status
for Purposes of Federal Employment Taxes
and Income Tax Withholding** | OMB No. 1545-0004 |

| Name of firm (or person) for whom the worker performed services | Worker's name |

| Firm's address (include street address, apt. or suite no., city, state, and ZIP code) | Worker's address (include street address, apt. or suite no., city, state, and ZIP code) |

| Trade name | Telephone number (include area code)
(   ) | Worker's social security number |

| Telephone number (include area code)
(   ) | Firm's employer identification number | Worker's employer identification number (if any) |

Important Information Needed To Process Your Request

If this form is being completed by the worker, the IRS must have your permission to disclose your name to the firm. Do you object to disclosing your name and the information on this form to the firm? . . . . ☐ **Yes** ☐ **No**

If you answered "Yes" or did not check a box, stop here. The IRS cannot act on your request and a determination will not be issued.

You must answer ALL items OR mark them "Unknown" or "Does not apply." If you need more space, attach another sheet.

A This form is being completed by: ☐ Firm ☐ Worker; for services performed _____ to _____

(beginning date)   (ending date)

B Explain your reason(s) for filing this form (e.g., you received a bill from the IRS, you believe you received a Form 1099 or Form W-2 erroneously, you are unable to get worker's compensation benefits, you were audited or are being audited by the IRS). ....

C Total number of workers who performed or are performing the same or similar services _____

D How did the worker obtain the job? ☐ Application   ☐ Bid   ☐ Employment Agency   ☐ Other (specify) _____

E Attach copies of all supporting documentation (contracts, invoices, memos, Forms W-2, Forms 1099, IRS closing agreements, IRS rulings, etc.). In addition, please inform us of any current or past litigation concerning the worker's status. If no income reporting forms (Form 1099-MISC or W-2) were furnished to the worker, enter the amount of income earned for the year(s) at issue $ _____ .

F Describe the firm's business. ....

G Describe the work done by the worker and provide the worker's job title. ....

H Explain why you believe the worker is an employee or an independent contractor. ....

I Did the worker perform services for the firm before getting this position? . . . .☐ Yes   ☐ No   ☐ N/A

If "Yes," what were the dates of the prior service? ....

If "Yes," explain the differences, if any, between the current and prior service. ....

J If the work is done under a written agreement between the firm and the worker, attach a copy (preferably signed by both parties). Describe the terms and conditions of the work arrangement. ....

For Privacy Act and Paperwork Reduction Act Notice, see page 5.   Cat. No. 16106T   Form **SS-8** (Rev. 1-2001)

Form SS-8 (Rev. 1-2001)   Page **2**

Part I   Behavioral Control

1   What specific training and/or instruction is the worker given by the firm? ....

2   How does the worker receive work assignments? ....

3   Who determines the methods by which the assignments are performed? ....
4   Who is the worker required to contact if problems or complaints arise and who is responsible for their resolution? ....

5   What types of reports are required from the worker? Attach examples. ....

6   Describe the worker's daily routine (i.e., schedule, hours, etc.). ....

7   At what location(s) does the worker perform services (e.g., firm's premises, own shop or office, home, customer's location, etc.)? ....

8   Describe any meetings the worker is required to attend and any penalties for not attending (e.g., sales meetings, monthly meetings, staff meetings, etc.). ....
9   Is the worker required to provide the services personally? . . . . ☐ Yes ☐ No
10 If substitutes or helpers are needed, who hires them? ....
11 If the worker hires the substitutes or helpers, is approval required? . . . . ☐ Yes ☐ No
    If "Yes," by whom? ....
12 Who pays the substitutes or helpers? ....
13 Is the worker reimbursed if the worker pays the substitutes or helpers? . . . . ☐ Yes ☐ No
    If "Yes," by whom? ....

Part II   Financial Control

1   List the supplies, equipment, materials, and property provided by each party:
    The firm ....
    The worker ....
    Other party ....
2   Does the worker lease equipment? . . . . ☐ Yes ☐ No
    If "Yes," what are the terms of the lease? (Attach a copy or explanatory statement.) ....

3   What expenses are incurred by the worker in the performance of services for the firm? ....

4   Specify which, if any, expenses are reimbursed by:
    The firm ....
    Other party ....
5   Type of pay the worker receives: ☐ Salary   ☐ Commission   ☐ Hourly Wage   ☐ Piece Work
    ☐ Lump Sum   ☐ Other (specify) ....
    If type of pay is commission, and the firm guarantees a minimum amount of pay, specify amount $ _____ .
6   If the worker is paid by a firm other than the one listed on this form for these services, enter name, address, and employer identification number of the payer. ....

7   Is the worker allowed a drawing account for advances? . . . . ☐ Yes ☐ No
    If "Yes," how often? ....
    Specify any restrictions. ....

8   Whom does the customer pay? . . . . , ☐ Firm   ☐ Worker
    If worker, does the worker pay the total amount to the firm? ☐ Yes ☐ No   If "No," explain. ....
9   Does the firm carry worker's compensation insurance on the worker? . . . . ☐ Yes ☐ No
10 What economic loss or financial risk, if any, can the worker incur beyond the normal loss of salary (e.g., loss or damage of equipment, material, etc.)? ....

Form **SS-8** (Rev. 1-2001)

Department of the Treasury
Internal Revenue Service

www.irs.gov

Form 656 (Rev. 5-2001)
Catalog Number 16728N

Form 656

Offer in Compromise

This Offer in Compromise package includes:

■ Information you need to know before submitting an offer in compromise

■ Instructions on the type of offers you can submit

■ Form 433-A, Collection Information Statement for Wage Earners and Self-Employed Individuals, and Form 433-B, Collection Information Statement for Businesses

■ A worksheet that wage earners and self-employed individuals can use to calculate their offer amount

■ Instructions on completing an offer in compromise form

■ Two copies of Form 656

Note: You can get forms and publications by calling 1–800–829–1040 or 1–800–829–FORM, or by visiting your local Internal Revenue Service (IRS) office or our website at *www.irs.gov*.

What You Need to Know Before Submitting an Offer in Compromise

What is an Offer in Compromise?

An *Offer in Compromise* (OIC) is an agreement between a taxpayer and the Internal Revenue Service (IRS) that resolves the taxpayer's tax liability. The IRS has the authority to settle, or *compromise*, federal tax liabilities by accepting less than full payment under certain circumstances. The IRS may legally compromise for one of the following reasons:

■ **Doubt as to Liability** — Doubt exists that the assessed tax is correct.

■ **Doubt as to Collectibility** — Doubt exists that you could ever pay the full amount of tax owed.

■ **Effective Tax Administration** — There is no doubt the tax is correct and no doubt the amount owed could be collected, but an exceptional circumstance exists that allows us to consider your offer. To be eligible for compromise on this basis, you must demonstrate that collection of the tax would create an economic hardship or would be unfair and inequitable.

Form 656, Offer in Compromise, and Substitute Forms

Form 656, *Offer in Compromise*, is the official compromise agreement. Substitute forms, whether computer-generated or photocopies, must affirm that:

1. The substitute form is a verbatim duplicate of the official Form 656, and

2. You agree to be bound by all terms and conditions set forth in the official Form 656.

You must initial and date all pages of the substitute form, in addition to signing and dating the signature page.

You can get Form 656 by calling 1–800–829–1040 or 1–800–829–FORM, by visiting your local Internal Revenue Service (IRS) office, or by accessing our website at www.irs.gov

Am I Eligible for Consideration of an Offer in Compromise?

You may be eligible for consideration of an *Offer in Compromise* if:

1. In your judgment, you don't owe the tax liability (**Doubt as to Liability**). You must submit a detailed written statement explaining why you believe you don't owe the tax liability you want to compromise. You won't be required to submit a collection information statement if you're submitting an offer on this basis alone.

2. In your judgment, you can't pay the entire tax liability in full (**Doubt as to Collectibility**). You must submit a collection information statement showing your current financial situation.

3. You agree the tax liability is correct and you're able to pay the balance due in full, but you have exceptional circumstances you'd like us to consider (**Effective Tax Administration**). To receive consideration on this basis, you must submit:

a. a collection information statement, and

b. a detailed written narrative. The narrative must explain your exceptional circumstances and why paying the tax liability in full would either create an economic hardship or would be unfair and inequitable.

We'll also consider your overall history of filing and paying taxes.

Note: If you request consideration on the basis of effective tax administration, we're first required to establish that there is no doubt as to liability and no doubt as to collectibility. We can only consider an offer on the basis of effective tax administration after we've determined the liability is correct and collectible.

When Am I Not Eligible for Consideration of an Offer in Compromise?

You are not eligible for consideration of an *Offer in Compromise* on the basis of **doubt as to collectibility** or **effective tax administration** if:

1. You haven't filed all required federal tax returns, or

2. You're involved in an open bankruptcy proceeding.

Note: If you are an in-business taxpayer, you must have filed and deposited all employment taxes on time for the two (2) quarters preceding your offer, as well as, deposit all employment taxes on time during the quarter you submit your offer.

What We Need to Process Your Offer in Compromise

For us to process your offer, you must provide a complete and correct Form 656 and:

- Form 433-A, *Collection Information Statement for Wage Earners and Self-Employed Individuals,* if you are submitting an offer as an **individual** or **self-employed taxpayer**.

- Form 433-B, *Collection Information Statement for Businesses,* if you are submitting an offer as a **corporation** or **other business** taxpayer. We may also require Forms 433-A from corporate officers or individual partners.

For a more detailed explanation of the information required to complete these forms, see the section entitled, "Financial Information" on page 3.

Note: We don't need a collection information statement for an offer based solely on doubt as to liability.

Please complete all applicable items on Form 656 and provide all required documentation. We may contact you for any missing required information. If we don't receive a response to our request or receive the required information, we won't recommend your offer for acceptance and will return your Form 656 to you by mail. We will explain our reason(s) for returning your offer in our letter. The reasons for return are:

- The pre-printed terms and conditions listed on Form 656 have changed

- A taxpayer name is missing

- A Social Security Number or Employer Identification Number is missing, incomplete, or incorrect

- An offer amount or payment term is unstated

- A signature is missing

- A collection information statement (Form 433-A or Form 433-B) is missing or incomplete, if your offer is based on doubt as to collectibility or effective tax administration

- We did not receive collection information statement verification

- Our records show you don't have a tax liability

- Your offer is submitted to delay collection or cause a delay which will jeopardize our ability to collect the tax

Note: You should personally sign your offer and any required collection information statements unless unusual circumstances prevent you from doing so. If someone with an authorized power of attorney signs your offer because of unusual circumstances, you must include a completed Form 2848, Power of Attorney and Declaration of Representative, with your offer.

What You Should Do If You Want to Submit an Offer in Compromise

Determine Your Offer Amount

All offer amounts (**doubt as to liability**, **doubt as to collectibility**, or **effective tax administration**) must exceed $0.00.

■ **Doubt as to Liability**

Complete Item 9, *Explanation of Circumstances*, on Form 656, explaining why, in your judgment, you don't owe the tax liability you want to compromise. Offer the correct tax, penalty, and interest owed based on your judgment.

■ **Doubt as to Collectibility**

Complete Form 433-A, *Collection Information Statement for Wage Earners and Self-Employed Individuals*, or Form 433-B, *Collection Information Statement for Businesses*, as appropriate, and attach to your Form 656. For assistance in determining your offer amount, visit our website at www.irs.ustreas.gov/ind_info/oic/index.html. If you are a wage earner or self-employed individual, figure your offer amount by completing the worksheet on pages 10–11.

You must offer an amount greater than or equal to the "reasonable collection potential" (RCP). The RCP equals the net equity of your assets plus the amount we could collect from your future income. Please see page 8, **Terms and Definitions**, for more detailed definitions of these and other terms.

If special circumstances cause you to offer an amount less than the RCP, you must also complete Item 9, *Explanation of Circumstances*, on Form 656, explaining your situation. Special circumstances may include factors such as advanced age, serious illness from which recovery is unlikely, or unusual circumstances that impact upon your ability to pay the total RCP and continue to provide for the necessary expenses for you and your family.

■ **Effective Tax Administration**

Complete Form 433-A or Form 433-B, as appropriate, and attach to Form 656.

Complete Item 9, *Explanation of Circumstances*, on Form 656, explaining your exceptional circumstances and why requiring payment of the tax liability in full would either create an economic hardship or would be unfair and inequitable.

Enter your offer amount on Item 7 of Form 656.

Financial Information

Note: We do not require this information if your offer is based solely on doubt as to liability.

You must provide financial information when you submit offers based on **doubt as to collectibility** and **effective tax administration**.

If you are submitting an offer as a wage earner or self-employed individual, you must file Form 433-A, *Collection Information Statement for Wage Earners and Self-Employed Individuals*, with your Form 656. If you are a corporation or other business taxpayer, you must file Form 433-B, *Collection Information Statement for Businesses*. We may also request Forms 433-A from corporate officers or individual partners.

You must send us current information that reflects your financial situation for at least the past six months. Collection information statements must show all your assets and income, even those unavailable to us through direct collection action, because you can use them to fund your offer. The offer examiner needs this information to evaluate your offer and may ask you to update it or verify certain financial information. We may also return offer packages without complete collection information statements.

When only one spouse has a tax liability but both have incomes, only the spouse responsible for the debt is required to prepare the necessary collection information statements. In states with community property laws, however, we require collection information statements from both spouses. We may also request financial information on the non-liable spouse for offer verification purposes, even when community property laws do not apply.

Determine Your Payment Terms

There are three payment plans you and the IRS may agree to:

- **Cash** (paid in 90 days or less)

- **Short-Term Deferred Payment** (more than 90 days, up to 24 months)

- **Deferred Payment** (offers with payment terms over the remaining statutory period for collecting the tax).

Cash Offer

You must pay cash offers within 90 days of acceptance.

You should offer the realizable value of your assets plus the total amount we could collect over 48 months of payments (or the remainder of the ten-year statutory period for collection, whichever is less).

Note: We require full payment of accepted doubt as to liability offers at the time of mutual agreement of the corrected liability. If you're unable to pay the corrected amount, you must also request compromise on the basis of doubt as to collectibility.

Short-Term Deferred Payment Offer

This payment plan requires you to pay the offer within two years of acceptance.

The offer must include the realizable value of your assets plus the amount we could collect over 60 months of payments (or the remainder of the ten-year statutory period for collection, whichever is less).

You can pay the short-term deferred payment plan in three ways:

Plan One

- Full payment of the realizable value of your assets within 90 days from the date we accept your offer, and

- Payment within two years of acceptance of the amount we could collect over 60 months (future income) or the remaining life of the collection statute, whichever is less.

Plan Two

- Cash payment for a portion of the realizable value of your assets within 90 days from the date we accept your offer, and

- The balance of the realizable value plus the amount we could collect over 60 months (future income) or the remaining life of the collection statute, whichever is less, within two years of acceptance.

Plan Three

- The entire offer amount in monthly payments extending over a period not to exceed two years from date of acceptance (e.g., four payments within 120 days of acceptance).

For example, on a short-term deferred payment total offer of $16,000, you might propose to pay your realizable value of assets (e.g., $13,000) within 90 days of acceptance and the amount of your future income (e.g., $50 per month for 60 months, or $3,000) over 6 monthly payments of $500 each, beginning the first month after acceptance.

We may file a Notice of Federal Tax Lien on tax liabilities compromised under short-term deferred payment offers.

Deferred Payment Offer

This payment plan requires you to pay the offer amount over the remaining statutory period for collecting the tax.

The offer must include the realizable value of your assets plus the amount we could collect through monthly payments during the remaining life of the collection statute.

For wage earners and self-employed individuals who want to submit a deferred payment offer, we will help you determine your future income amount. To compute this amount, we must calculate the remaining time left on the collection statute for each period of the tax liability.

- Call 1–800–829–1040 to assist you in this calculation.

- Using Form 433-A Worksheet, multiply the amount from Item 12, Box O, by the number of months remaining on the collection statute. Add that amount to Item 11, Box N, and use the total as the basis for your offer amount in Item 7 of Form 656.

You can pay the deferred payment plan in three ways:

Plan One

- Full payment of the realizable value of your assets within 90 days from the date we accept your offer, and

- Your "future income" in monthly payments during the remaining life of the collection statute

Plan Two

- Cash payment for a portion of the realizable value of your assets within 90 days from the date we accept your offer, and

- Monthly payments during the remaining life of the collection statute for both the balance of the realizable value and your future income

Plan Three

- The entire offer amount in monthly payments over the life of the collection statute

For example, on a deferred payment offer with 7 years (84 months) remaining on the statutory period for collection and a total offer of $25,000, you might propose to pay your realizable value of assets (e.g., $10,000) within 90 days and your future income (e.g., $179 per month for 7 years, or $15,000) in 84 monthly installments of $179. Alternately, you could also pay the same total $25,000 offer in 84 monthly installments of $298.

Just as with short-term deferred payment offers, we may file a Notice of Federal Tax Lien.

Note: The worksheet on page 10 instructs wage earners and self-employed individuals how to figure the appropriate amount for a Cash, Short-Term Deferred Payment, or Deferred Payment Offer.

How We Consider Your Offer

An offer examiner will evaluate your offer and may request additional documentation from you to verify financial or other information you provide. The examiner will then make a recommendation to accept it or reject the offer. The examiner may also return your offer if you don't provide the requested information.

The examiner may decide that a larger offer amount is necessary to justify acceptance. You will have the opportunity to amend your offer.

Additional Agreements

When you submit certain offers, we may also request that you sign an additional agreement requiring you to:

- Pay a percentage of your future earnings

- Waive certain present or future tax benefits

Withholding Collection Activities

We will withhold collection activities while we consider your offer. We will not act to collect the tax liability:

- While we investigate and evaluate your offer

- For 30 days after we reject an offer

- While you appeal an offer rejection

The above do not apply if we find any indication that you submitted your offer to delay collection or cause a delay which will jeopardize our ability to collect the tax.

If you currently have an installment agreement when you submit an offer, you must continue making the agreed upon monthly payments while we consider your offer.

If We Accept Your Offer

If we accept your offer, we will notify you by mail. When you receive your acceptance letter, you must:

- Promptly pay any unpaid amounts that become due under the terms of the offer agreement

- Comply with all the terms and conditions of the offer, along with those of any additional agreement

- Promptly notify us of any change of address until you meet the conditions of your offer. Your acceptance letter will indicate which IRS office to contact if your address changes. Your notification allows us to contact you immediately regarding the status of your offer

We will release all Notices of Federal Tax Lien when you satisfy the payment terms of the offered amount. For an immediate release of a lien, you can submit certified funds with a request letter.

In the future, not filing returns or paying taxes when due could result in the default of an accepted offer (see Form 656, Item 8(d), the *future compliance provision*). If you default your agreement, we will reinstate the unpaid amount of the original tax liability, file a Notice of Federal Tax Lien on any tax liability without a filed notice, and resume collection activities. The future compliance provision applies to offers based on **doubt as to collectibility**. In certain cases, the future compliance provision may apply to offers based on **effective tax administration**.

We won't default your offer agreement when you have filed a joint offer with your spouse or ex-spouse as long as you've kept or are keeping all the terms of the agreement, even if your spouse or ex-spouse violates the future compliance provision.

Except for offers based on **doubt as to liability**, the offer agreement requires you to forego certain refunds, and to return those refunds to us if they are issued to you by mistake. These conditions are also listed on Form 656, Items 8(g) and 8(h).

Note: The law requires us to make certain information from accepted Offers in Compromise available for public inspection and review in your local IRS Territory Office. Therefore, information regarding your Offer in Compromise may become publicly known.

If We Reject Your Offer

We'll notify you by mail if we reject your offer. In our letter, we will explain our reason for the rejection. If your offer is rejected, you have the right to:

■ Appeal our decision to the Office of Appeals within thirty days from the date of our letter. The letter will include detailed instructions on how to appeal the rejection.

■ Submit another offer. You must increase an offer we've rejected as being too low, when your financial situation remains unchanged. However, you must provide updated financial information when your financial situation has changed or when the original offer is more than six months old.

Terms and Definitions

An understanding of the following terms and conditions will help you to prepare your offer.

Fair Market Value (FMV) – The amount you could reasonably expect from the sale of an asset. Provide an accurate valuation of each asset. Determine value from realtors, used car dealers, publications, furniture dealers, or other experts on specific types of assets. Please include a copy of any written estimate with your Collection Information Statement.

Quick Sale Value (QSV) – The amount you could reasonably expect from the sale of an asset if you sold it quickly, typically in ninety days or less. This amount generally is less than fair market value, but may be equal to or higher, based on local circumstances.

Realizable Value – The quick sale value amount minus what you owe to a secured creditor. The creditor must have priority over a filed Notice of Federal Tax Lien before we allow a subtraction from the asset's value.

Future Income – We generally determine the amount we could collect from your future income by subtracting necessary living expenses from your monthly income over a set number of months. For a cash offer, you must offer what you could pay in monthly payments over forty-eight months (or the remainder of the ten-year statutory period for collection, whichever is less). For a short-term deferred offer, you must offer what you could pay in monthly payments over sixty months (or the remainder of the statutory period for collection, whichever is less). For a deferred payment offer, you must offer what you could pay in monthly payments during the remaining time we could legally receive payments.

Reasonable Collection Potential (RCP) – The total realizable value of your assets plus your future income. The total is generally your minimum offer amount.

Necessary Expenses – The allowable payments you make to support you and your family's health and welfare and/or the production of income. This expense allowance does not apply to business entities. Our Publication 1854 explains the National Standard Expenses and gives the allowable amounts. We derive these amounts from the Bureau of Labor Statistics (BLS) Consumer Expenditure Survey. We also use information from the Bureau of the Census to determine local expenses for housing, utilities, and transportation.

Note: If the IRS determines that the facts and circumstances of your situation indicate that using the scheduled allowance of necessary expenses is inadequate, we will allow you an adequate means for providing basic living expenses. However, you must provide documentation that supports a determination that using national and local expense standards leaves you an inadequate means of providing for basic living expenses.

Expenses Not Generally Allowed – We typically do not allow you to claim tuition for private schools, public or private college expenses, charitable contributions, voluntary retirement contributions, payments on unsecured debts such as credit card bills, cable television charges and other similar expenses as necessary living expenses. However, we can allow these expenses when you can prove that they are necessary for the health and welfare of you or your family or for the production of income.

IRS

Department of the Treasury
Internal Revenue Service

www.irs.gov

Form 656 (Rev. 5-2001)
Catalog Number 16728N

Form 656

Offer in Compromise

IRS RECEIVED DATE

Item 1 — Taxpayer's Name and Home or Business Address

Name

Name

Street Address

City   State   ZIP Code

Mailing Address (if different from above)

Street Address

DATE RETURNED

City   State   ZIP Code

Item 2 — Social Security Numbers

(a) Primary _____

(b) Secondary _____

Item 3 — Employer Identification Number (included in offer)

_____

Item 4 — Other Employer Identification Numbers (not included in offer) _____

_____

Item 5 — To: Commissioner of Internal Revenue Service

I/We (includes all types of taxpayers) submit this offer to compromise the tax liabilities plus any interest, penalties, additions to tax, and additional amounts required by law (tax liability) for the tax type and period marked below: (Please mark an "X" in the box for the correct description and fill-in the correct tax period(s), adding additional periods if needed).

❑ **1040/1120 Income Tax** — Year(s) _____

❑ **941 Employer's Quarterly Federal Tax Return** — Quarterly period(s) _____

❑ **940 Employer's Annual Federal Unemployment (FUTA) Tax Return** — Year(s) _____

❑ **Trust Fund Recovery Penalty** as a responsible person of (enter corporation name) _____

for failure to pay withholding and Federal Insurance Contributions Act Taxes (Social Security taxes), for period(s) ending _____ .

❑ **Other Federal Tax(es)** [specify type(s) and period(s)] _____

_____

Note: If you need more space, use another sheet titled "Attachment to Form 656 Dated_____ ." Sign and date the attachment following the listing of the tax periods.

Item 6 — I/We submit this offer for the reason(s) checked below:

❑ **Doubt as to Liability** — "I do not believe I owe this amount." You must include a detailed explanation of the reason(s) why you believe you do not owe the tax in Item 9.

❑ **Doubt as to Collectibility** — "I have insufficient assets and income to pay the full amount." You must include a complete Collection Information Statement, Form 433-A and/or Form 433-B.

❑ **Effective Tax Administration** — "I owe this amount and have sufficient assets to pay the full amount, but due to my exceptional circumstances, requiring full payment would cause an economic hardship or would be unfair and inequitable." You must include a complete Collection Information Statement, Form 433-A and/or Form 433B and complete Item 9.

Item 7

I/We offer to pay $ _____ (must be more than zero). Complete item 10 to explain where you will obtain the funds to make this offer.

Check one of the following:

❑ **Cash Offer (Offered amount will be paid in 90 days or less.)**

Balance to be paid in: ❑ 10; ❑ 30; ❑ 60; or ❑ 90 days from written notice of acceptance of the offer.

❑ **Short-Term Deferred Payment Offer (Offered amount will be paid in MORE than 90 days but within 24 months from written notice of acceptance of the offer.)**

$_____ within_____ days (not more than 90 — See Instructions Section, **Determine Your Payment Terms**) from written notice of acceptance of the offer; and

beginning in the _____ month after written notice of acceptance of the offer, $_____ on the _____ day of each month for a total of _____ months. (Cannot extend more than 24 months from written notice of acceptance of the offer.)

❑ **Deferred Payment Offer (Offered amount will be paid over the life of the collection statute.)**

$_____ within_____ days (not more than 90 — See Instructions Section, **Determine Your Payment Terms**) from written notice of acceptance of the offer; and

beginning in the first month after written notice of acceptance of the offer, $_____ on the _____ day of each month for a total of _____ months.

NOTE: Signature(s) of taxpayer required on last page of Form 656

Item 8 — By submitting this offer, I/we understand and agree to the following conditions:

(a) I/We voluntarily submit all payments made on this offer.

(b) The IRS will apply payments made under the terms of this offer in the best interest of the government.

(c) If the IRS rejects or returns the offer or I/we withdraw the offer, the IRS will return any amount paid with the offer. If I/we agree in writing, IRS will apply the amount paid with the offer to the amount owed. If I/we agree to apply the payment, the date the IRS received the offer remittance will be considered the date of payment. I/We understand that the IRS will not pay interest on any amount I/we submit with the offer.

(d) **I/We will comply with all provisions of the Internal Revenue Code relating to filing my/our returns and paying my/our required taxes for 5 years or until the offered amount is paid in full, whichever is longer. In the case of a jointly submitted offer to compromise joint tax liabilities, I/we understand that default with respect to the compliance provisions described in this paragraph by one party to this agreement will not result in the default of the entire agreement. The default provisions described in Item 8(n) of this agreement will be applied only to the party failing to comply with the requirements of this paragraph. This provision does not apply to offers based on Doubt as to Liability.**

(e) I/We waive and agree to the suspension of any statutory periods of limitation (time limits provided for by law) for the IRS assessment of the tax liability for the periods identified in Item 5. I/We understand that I/we have the right not to waive these statutory periods or to limit the waiver to a certain length or to certain issues. I/We understand, however, that the IRS may not consider this offer if I/we refuse to waive the statutory periods for assessment or if we provide only a limited waiver. The amount of any Federal tax due for the periods described in Item 5 may be assessed at any time prior to the acceptance of this offer or within one year of the rejection of this offer.

(f) The IRS will keep all payments and credits made, received or applied to the total original tax liability before submission of this offer. The IRS may keep any proceeds from a levy served prior to submission of the offer, but not received at the time the offer is submitted. If I/we have an installment agreement prior to submitting the offer, I/we must continue to make the payments as agreed while this offer is pending. Installment agreement payments will not be applied against the amount offered.

(g) **As additional consideration beyond the amount of my/our offer, the IRS will keep any refund, including interest, due to me/us because of overpayment of any tax or other liability, for tax periods extending through the calendar year that the IRS accepts the offer. I/We may not designate an overpayment ordinarily subject to refund, to which the IRS is entitled, to be applied to estimated tax payments for the following year. This condition does not apply if the offer is based on Doubt as to Liability.**

(h) I/We will return to the IRS any refund identified in (g) received after submission of this offer. This condition does not apply to offers based on Doubt as to Liability.

(i) The IRS cannot collect more than the full amount of the tax liability under this offer.

(j) I/We understand that I/we remain responsible for the full amount of the tax liability, unless and until the IRS accepts the offer in writing and I/we have met all the terms and conditions of the offer. The IRS will not remove the original amount of the tax liability from its records until I/we have met all the terms of the offer.

NOTE: Signature(s) of taxpayer required on last page of Form 656

(k) I/We understand that the tax I/we offer to compromise is and will remain a tax liability until I/we meet all the terms and conditions of this offer. If I/we file bankruptcy before the terms and conditions of this offer are completed, any claim the IRS files in the bankruptcy proceedings will be a tax claim.

(l) Once the IRS accepts the offer in writing, I/we have no right to contest, in court or otherwise, the amount of the tax liability.

(m) The offer is pending starting with the date an authorized IRS official signs this form. The offer remains pending until an authorized IRS official accepts, rejects, returns or acknowledges withdrawal of the offer in writing. If I/we appeal an IRS rejection decision on the offer, the IRS will continue to treat the offer as pending until the Appeals Office accepts or rejects the offer in writing. If I/we don't file a protest within 30 days of the date the IRS notifies me/us of the right to protest the decision, I/we waive the right to a hearing before the Appeals Office about the offer in compromise.

(n) If I/We fail to meet any of the terms and conditions of the offer and the offer defaults, then the IRS may:

- immediately file suit to collect the entire unpaid balance of the offer

- immediately file suit to collect an amount equal to the original amount of the tax liability as liquidating damages, minus any payment already received under the terms of this offer

- disregard the amount of the offer and apply all amounts already paid under the offer against the original amount of the tax liability

- file suit or levy to collect the original amount of the tax liability, without further notice of any kind.

The IRS will continue to add interest, as Section 6601 of the Internal Revenue Code requires, on the amount the IRS determines is due after default. The IRS will add interest from the date the offer is defaulted until I/we completely satisfy the amount owed.

(o) The IRS generally files a Notice of Federal Tax Lien to protect the Government's interest on deferred payment offers. This tax lien will be released when the payment terms of the offer agreement have been satisfied.

(p) **I/We understand that the IRS employees may contact third parties in order to respond to this request and I authorize the IRS to make such contacts. Further, by authorizing the Internal Revenue Service to contact third parties, I understand that I will not receive notice, pursuant to section 7602(c) of the Internal Revenue Code, of third parties contacted in connection with this request.**

NOTE: Signature(s) of taxpayer required on last page of Form 656

Item 9 — Explanation of Circumstances

I am requesting an offer in compromise for the reason(s) listed below:

Note: If you are requesting compromise based on doubt as to liability, explain why you don't believe you owe the tax.
If you believe you have special circumstances affecting your ability to fully pay the amount due, explain your situation.
You may attach additional sheets if necessary.

Item 10 — Source of Funds

I/we shall obtain the funds to make this offer from the following source(s):

Item 11

If I/we submit this offer on a substitute form, I/we affirm that this form is a verbatim duplicate of the official Form 656, and I/we agree to be bound by all the terms and conditions set forth in the official Form 656.

Under penalties of perjury, I declare that I have examined this offer, including accompanying schedules and statements, and to the best of my knowledge and belief, it is true, correct and complete.

11(a) Signature of Taxpayer

Date

11(b) Signature of Taxpayer

Date

For Official Use Only

I accept the waiver of the statutory period of limitations for the Internal Revenue Service.

Signature of Authorized Internal Revenue Service Official

Title

Date

NOTE: Signature(s) of taxpayer required on last page of Form 656

Completing Form 656, Offer in Compromise

We have included two Offer in Compromise forms. Use one form to submit your offer in compromise. You may use the other form as a worksheet and retain it for your personal records.

Note: If you have any questions about completing this form, you may call 1–800–829–1040 or visit your local IRS office or our website at www.irs.ustreas.gov/ind_info/oic/index.html. We may return your offer if you don't follow these instructions.

Item 1: Enter your name and home or business address. You should also include a mailing address, if it is different from your street address.

Show both names on joint offers for joint liabilities. If you owe one liability by yourself (such as employment taxes), and other liabilities jointly (such as income taxes), but only you are submitting an offer, list all tax liabilities on one Form 656. If you owe one liability yourself and another jointly, and both parties submit an offer, **complete two Forms 656**, one for the individual liability and one for the joint liability.

Item 2: Enter the social security number(s) for the person(s) submitting the offer. For example, enter the social security number of both spouses when submitting a joint offer for a joint tax liability. However, when only one spouse submits an offer, enter only that spouse's social security number.

Item 3: Enter the employer identification number for offers from businesses.

Item 4: Show the employer identification numbers for all other businesses (excluding corporate entities) that you own or in which you have an ownership interest.

Item 5: Identify your tax liability and enter the tax year or period. Letters and notices from us and Notices of Federal Tax Lien show the tax periods for trust fund recovery penalties.

Item 6: Check the appropriate box (es) describing the basis for your offer.

Doubt as to Liability offers require a statement describing in detail why you think you do not owe the liability. Complete Item 9, "Explanation of Circumstances," explaining your situation.

Doubt as to Collectibility offers require you to complete a Form 433-A, *Collection Information Statement for Wage Earners and Self-Employed Individuals*, if you are an individual taxpayer, or a Form 433-B, *Collection Information Statement for Businesses*, if you are a corporation or other business taxpayer.

Effective Tax Administration offers require you to complete a Form 433-A, *Collection Information Statement for Wage Earners and Self-Employed Individuals*, if you are an individual taxpayer, or a Form 433-B, *Collection Information Statement for Businesses*, if you are a corporation or other business taxpayer. Complete Item 9, "Explanation of Circumstances."

Note: Staple in the upper left corner the six (6) pages of the collection information statement before you send it to us.

Item 7:

Enter the total amount of your offer (see page 3, "Determine Your Offer Amount"). Your offer amount cannot include a refund we owe you or amounts you have already paid.

Check the appropriate payment box (cash, short-term deferred payment or deferred payment — see page 4, "Determine Your Payment Terms") and describe your payment plan in the spaces provided.

Item 8:

It is important that you understand the requirements listed in this section. Pay particular attention to Items 8(d)

and 8(g), as they address the future compliance provision and refunds.

Item 9:

Explain your reason(s) for submitting your offer in the "Explanation of

Circumstances." You may attach additional sheets if necessary.

Item 10:

Explain where you will get the funds to pay the amount you are offering.

Item 11:

All persons submitting the offer must sign and date Form 656. Include titles of authorized corporate officers, executors, trustees, Powers of Attorney, etc. where applicable.

Note: Staple in the upper left corner the four (4) pages of Form 656 before you send it to us.

Where to File

IF YOU RESIDE IN

the states of Alaska, Alabama, Arizona, California, Colorado, Hawaii, Idaho, Kentucky, Louisiana, Mississippi, Montana, Nevada, New Mexico, Oregon, Tennessee, Texas, Utah, Washington, Wisconsin or Wyoming,

AND

You are a wage earner or a self-employed individual without employees,

THEN MAIL

Form 656 and attachments to:
Memphis Internal Revenue Service
Center COIC Unit
PO Box 30803, AMC
Memphis, TN 38130-0803

AND

You are **OTHER** than wage earner or a self-employed individual without employees,

THEN MAIL

Form 656 and attachments to:
Memphis Internal Revenue Service
Center COIC Unit
PO Box 30804, AMC
Memphis, TN 38130-0804

IF YOU RESIDE IN

Arkansas, Connecticut, Delaware, District of Columbia, Florida, Georgia, Illinois, Indiana, Iowa, Kansas, Maine, Maryland, Massachusetts, Michigan, Minnesota, Missouri, Nebraska, New Hampshire, New Jersey, New York, North Carolina, North Dakota, Ohio, Oklahoma, Pennsylvania, Puerto Rico, Rhode Island, South Carolina, South Dakota, Vermont, Virginia, West Virginia or have a foreign address,

AND

You are a wage earner or a self-employed individual without employees,

THEN MAIL

Form 656 and attachments to:

Brookhaven Internal Revenue Service
Center COIC Unit
PO Box 9007
Holtsville, NY 11742-9007

AND

You are **OTHER** than wage earner or a self-employed individual without employees,

THEN MAIL

Form 656 and attachments to:

Brookhaven Internal Revenue Service
Center COIC Unit
PO Box 9008
Holtsville, NY 11742-9008

Form **872** (Rev. January 2001)	Department of the Treasury-Internal Revenue Service **Consent to Extend the Time to Assess Tax**	In reply refer to: Taxpayer Identification Number

taxpayer(s) of _____
(Name(s))

_____
(Number, Street, City or Town, State, ZIP Code)

and the Commissioner of Internal Revenue consent and agree to the following:

(1) The amount of any Federal _____ tax due on any return(s) made by or
(Kind of tax)

for the above taxpayer(s) for the period(s) ended _____

_____

may be assessed at any time on or before _____ . However, if
(Expiration date)

a notice of deficiency in tax for any such period(s) is sent to the taxpayer(s) on or before that date, then the time for assessing the tax will be further extended by the number of days the assessment was previously prohibited, plus 60 days.

(2) The taxpayer(s) may file a claim for credit or refund and the Service may credit or refund the tax within 6 months after this agreement ends.

MAKING THIS CONSENT WILL NOT DEPRIVE THE TAXPAYER(S) OF ANY APPEAL RIGHTS TO WHICH THEY WOULD OTHERWISE BE ENTITLED.

YOUR SIGNATURE HERE ➤ _____
(Date signed)

SPOUSE'S SIGNATURE ➤ _____
(Date signed)

TAXPAYER'S REPRESENTATIVE
SIGN HERE ➤ _____
(Date signed)

CORPORATE
NAME ➤ _____

CORPORATE
OFFICER(S)
SIGN HERE ➤ _____   *(Title)*   *(Date signed)*

_____   *(Title)*   *(Date signed)*

INTERNAL REVENUE SERVICE SIGNATURE AND TITLE

_____   _____
(Division Executive Name - see instructions)   *(Division Executive Title - see instructions)*

BY _____
(Authorized Official Signature and Title - see instructions)   *(Date signed)*

(Signature instructions are on the back of this form)   www.irs.gov   Catalog Number 20755I   Form **872** (Rev. 1-2001)

Instructions

If this consent is for income tax, self-employment tax, or FICA tax on tips and is made for any year(s) for which a joint return was filed, both husband and wife must sign the original and copy of this form unless one, acting under a power of attorney, signs as agent for the other. The signatures must match the names as they appear on the front of this form.

If this consent is for gift tax and the donor and the donor's spouse elected to have gifts to third persons considered as made one-half by each, both husband and wife must sign the original and copy of this form unless one, acting under a power of attorney, signs as agent for the other. The signatures must match the names as they appear on the front of this form.

If this consent is for Chapter 41, 42, or 43 taxes involving a partnership or is for a partnership return, only one authorized partner need sign.

If this consent is for Chapter 42 taxes, a separate Form 872 should be completed for each potential disqualified person, entity, or foundation manager that may be involved in a taxable transaction during the related tax year. See Revenue Ruling 75-391, 1975-2 C.B. 446.

If you are an attorney or agent of the taxpayer(s), you may sign this consent provided the action is specifically authorized by a power of attorney. If the power of attorney was not previously filed, you must include it with this form.

If you are acting as a fiduciary (such as executor, administrator, trustee, etc.) and you sign this consent, attach Form 56, Notice Concerning Fiduciary Relationship, unless it was previously filed. If the taxpayer is a corporation, sign this consent with the corporate name followed by the signature and title of the officer(s) authorized to sign.

Instructions for Internal Revenue Service Employees

Complete the Division Executive's name and title depending upon your division.

If you are in the Small Business /Self-Employed Division, enter the name and title for the appropriate division executive for your business unit (e.g., Area Director for your area; Director, Compliance Policy; Director, Compliance Services).

If you are in the Wage and Investment Division, enter the name and title for the appropriate division executive for your business unit (e.g., Area Director for your area; Director, Field Compliance Services).

If you are in the Large and Mid-Size Business Division, enter the name and title of the Director, Field Operations for your industry.

If you are in the Tax Exempt and Government Entities Division, enter the name and title for the appropriate division executive for your business unit (e.g., Director, Exempt Organizations; Director, Employee Plans; Director, Federal, State and Local Governments; Director, Indian Tribal Governments; Director, Tax Exempt Bonds).

If you are in Appeals, enter the name and title of the appropriate Director, Appeals Operating Unit.

The signature and title line will be signed and dated by the appropriate authorized official within your division.

OMB No. 1545-1504

Department of the Treasury – Internal Revenue Service

TAXPAYER ADVOCATE *SERVICE*

Application for Taxpayer Assistance Order (ATAO)

Form **911**
(Rev. 3-2000)

Section I.	Taxpayer Information		
1. Name(s) as shown on tax return		4. Your Social Security Number	6. Tax Form(s)
		5. Social Security No. of Spouse	7. Tax Period(s)
2. Current mailing address (Number, Street & Apartment Number)		8. Employer Identification Number (if applicable)	
		9. E-Mail address	
3. City, Town or Post Office, State and ZIP Code		10. Fax number	
11. Person to contact		12. Daytime telephone number	13. Best time to call

14. Please describe the problem and the significant hardship it is creating. *(If more space is needed, attach additional sheets.)*

15. Please describe the relief you are requesting. *(If more space is needed, attach additional sheets.)*

I understand that Taxpayer Advocate employees may contact third parties in order to respond to this request and I authorize such contacts to be made. Further, by authorizing the Taxpayer Advocate Service to contact third parties, I understand that I will not receive notice, pursuant to section 7602(c) of the Internal Revenue Code, of third parties contacted in connection with this request.

16. Signature of taxpayer or corporate officer	17. Date	18. Signature of spouse	19. Date

Section II.   Representative Information (if applicable)

1. Name of Authorized Representative	3. Centralized Authorization File Number (CAF)
2. Mailing Address	4. Daytime telephone number
	5. Fax number
6. Signature of Representative	7. Date

Cat. No. 16965S

Form **911** (Rev. 3-2000)

Section III.   (For Internal Revenue Service only)

Taxpayer Name	Taxpayer Identification Number (TIN)

1. Name of Initiating Employee	2. Employee Telephone Number	3. Operating Division or Function	4. Office

5. How Identified & Received (Check the appropriate box)   **6. IRS Received Date**

IRS Function Identified Issue as Meeting TAS Criteria
- ❑ (r) Functional referral (Functional area identified TP/Rep issue as meeting TAS criteria)
- ❑ (x) Congressional correspondence/inquiry not addressed to TAS but referred for TAS handling

Taxpayer or Representative Requested TAS Assistance
- ❑ (c) Taxpayer or representative filed Form 911 or sent other correspondence to TAS
- ❑ (n) Taxpayer or representative called into a National Taxpayer Advocate (NTA) Toll-Free site
- ❑ (p) Taxpayer or representative called TAS (other than NTA Toll-Free)
- ❑ (s) Functional referral (Taxpayer or representative specifically requested TAS assistance)
- ❑ (w) Taxpayer or representative sought TAS assistance in a TAS walk-in area
- ❑ (y) Congressional corresp/inquiry addressed to TAS or any Congressional specifically requesting TAS assistance

7. TAS Criteria (Check the appropriate box)
- ❑ (1) Taxpayer is suffering or about to suffer a significant hardship
- ❑ (2) Taxpayer is facing an immediate threat of adverse action
- ❑ (3) Taxpayer will incur significant costs, including fees for professional representation, if relief is not granted
- ❑ (4) Taxpayer will suffer irreparable injury or long-term adverse impact if relief is not granted
- ❑ (5) Taxpayer experienced an IRS delay of more than 30 calendar days in resolving an account-related problem or inquiry
- ❑ (6) Taxpayer did not receive a response or resolution to their problem by the date promised
- ❑ (7) A system or procedure has either failed to operate as intended or failed to resolve a taxpayer problem or dispute with the IRS
- ❑ (8) Congressional Duplicate of any criteria or non-criteria case already in TAS or on TAMIS
- ❑ (9) Any issue/problem not meeting the above TAS criteria but kept in TAS for handling and resolution

8. Initiating Employee: What actions did you take to help resolve the problem?

9. Initiating Employee: State reason(s) why relief was not provided.

Section III Instructions (For Internal Revenue Service only)
1. Enter your name.
2. Enter your telephone number.
3. Enter your function (i.e.; ACS, Collection, Examination, Customer Service, etc.). If you are now part of one of the new Business Operating Divisions (Wage & Investment Income, Small Business/Self-Employed, Large/Mid-Size Business, Tax-Exempt/Govt Entity), enter the name of the division.
4. Enter the number/Organization Code for your office. (e.g.; 18 for AUSC, 95 for Los Angeles).
5. Check the appropriate box that best reflects how the taxpayer informed us of the problem. For example, did TP call or write an IRS function or TAS? Did TP specifically request TAS assistance/handling or did the function identify the issue as meeting TAS criteria?
6. The IRS Received Date is the date TP/Rep first informed the IRS of the problem. Enter the date the TP/Rep first called, walked in or wrote the IRS to seek assistance with getting the problem resolved.
7. Check the box that best describes the reason/justification for Taxpayer Advocate Service (TAS) assistance and handling.
8. Indicate the actions you took to help resolve taxpayer's problem.
9. State the reason(s) that prevented you from resolving taxpayer's problem and from providing relief. For example, levy proceeds cannot be returned since they were already applied to a valid liability; an overpayment cannot be refunded since the refund statute expired; or current law precludes a specific interest abatement.

Section IV.   (For Taxpayer Advocate Service only)

1. TAMIS CF#	2. BOD/Client	3. How Recd Code	4. Criteria Code	5. IRS Recd Date	6. TAS Recd Date
7. Reopen Ind	8. Func/Unit Assigned	9. Employee Assigned	10. Major Issue Code	11. ATAO Code/Subcode	12. PSD Code
13. Special Case Code	14. Complexity Code	15. Outreach	16. Local Use Code ❑ TP _|_|_|_|_|_| ❑ Case _|	17. Relief Date	18. TAS Clsd Date
19. Cust Satisfact Cde	20. Root Cause Code				

Hardship ❑ Yes ❑ No	Taxpayer Advocate Signature	Date

Cat. No. 16965S   Form **911** (Rev. 3-2000)

Instructions

When to use this form: Use this form to request relief if any of the following apply to you:

1. You are suffering or about to suffer a significant hardship;
2. You are facing an immediate threat of adverse action;
3. You will incur significant costs, including fees for professional representation, if relief is not granted;
4. You will suffer irreparable injury or long-term adverse impact if relief is not granted;
5. You experienced an IRS delay of more than 30 calendar days in resolving an account-related problem or inquiry;
6. You did not receive a response or resolution to your problem by the date promised;
7. A system or procedure has either failed to operate as intended or failed to resolve your problem or dispute with the IRS.

If an IRS office will not grant the relief requested or will not grant the relief in time to avoid the significant hardship, you may submit this form. No enforcement action will be taken while we are reviewing your application.

Where to Submit This Form: Submit this application to the Taxpayer Advocate office located in the state or city where you reside. For the address of the Taxpayer Advocate in your state or city or for additional information call the National Taxpayer Advocate Toll-Free Number 1-877-777-4778.

Third Party Contact: You should understand that in order to respond to this request you are also authorizing the Taxpayer Advocate Service to contact third parties when necessary and that you will not receive further notice regarding contacted parties. See IRC 7602(c).

Overseas Taxpayers: Taxpayers residing overseas can submit this application by mail to the Taxpayer Advocate, Internal Revenue Service, PO Box 193479, San Juan, Puerto Rico 00919 or in person at 2 Ponce de Leon Avenue, Mercantil Plaza Building, Room GF05A, Hato Rey PR 00918. The application can also be faxed to (787) 759-4535.

Caution: Incomplete applications or applications submitted to an Advocate office outside of your geographical location may result in delays. If you do not hear from us within one week of submitting Form 911, please contact the Taxpayer Advocate office where you originally submitted your application.

Section I Instructions--Taxpayer Information

1. Enter your name(s) as shown on the tax return that relates to this application for relief.
2. Enter your current mailing address, including street number and name and apartment number.
3. Enter your city, town or post office, state and ZIP code.
4. Enter your Social Security Number.
5. Enter the Social Security Number of your spouse if this application relates to a jointly filed return.
6. Enter the number of the Federal tax return or form that relates to this application. For example, an individual taxpayer with an income tax issue would enter Form 1040.
7. Enter the quarterly, annual or other tax period that relates to this application. For example, if this request involves an income tax issue, enter the calendar or fiscal year; if an employment tax issue, enter the calendar quarter.
8. Enter your Employer Identification Number if this relief request involves a business or non-individual entity (e.g.; a partnership, corporation, trust, self-employed individual with employees).
9. Enter your E-mail address.
10. Enter your fax number including the area code.
11. Enter the name of the individual we should contact. For partnerships, corporations, trusts, etc., enter the name of the individual authorized to act on the entity's behalf.
12. Enter your daytime telephone number including the area code.
13. Indicate the best time to call you. Please specify a.m. or p.m. hours.
14. Describe the problem and the significant hardship it is creating for you. Specify the actions that the IRS has taken (or not taken) to cause the problem and ensuing hardship. **If the problem involves an IRS delay of more than 30 days in resolving your issue, indicate the date you first contacted the IRS for assistance in resolving your problem.**
15. Describe the relief you are seeking. Specify the actions that you want taken and that you believe necessary to relieve the significant hardship. Furnish if applicable any relevant proof and corroboration as to why relief is warranted or why you cannot or should not meet current IRS demands to satisfy your tax obligations.
16.&18. If this application is a joint relief request relating to a joint tax liability, both spouses should sign in the appropriate blocks. If only one spouse is requesting relief relating to a joint tax liability, only the requesting spouse has to sign the application. If this application is being submitted for another individual, only a person authorized and empowered to act on that individual's behalf should sign the application.
       NOTE: The signing of this application allows the IRS by law to suspend, for the period of time it takes the Advocate to review and decide upon your request, any applicable statutory periods of limitation relating to the assessment or collection of taxes..
17.&19. Enter the date the application was signed.

Section II Instructions--Representative Information

Taxpayers: If you wish to have a representative act on your behalf, you must give him/her power of attorney or tax information authorization for the tax return(s) and period(s) involved. For additional information see Form 2848, Power of Attorney and Declaration of Representative or Form 8821, Tax Information Authorization, and the accompanying instructions.

Representatives: If you are an authorized representative submitting this request on behalf of the taxpayer identified in Section I, complete Blocks 1 through 7 of Section II. Attach a copy of Form 2848, Form 8821 or other power of attorney. Enter your Centralized Authorization File (CAF) number in Block 3 of Section II. The CAF number is the unique number that the IRS assigns to a representative after Form 2848 or Form 8821 is filed with an IRS office.

Paperwork Reduction Act Notice: We ask for the information on this form to carry out the Internal Revenue laws of the United States. Your response is voluntary. You are not required to provide the information requested on a form that is subject to the Paperwork Reduction Act unless the form displays a valid OMB control number. Books or records relating to a form or its instructions must be retained as long as their contents may become material in the administration of any Internal Revenue law. Generally, tax returns and return information are confidential, as required by Code section 6103. Although the time needed to complete this form may vary depending on individual circumstances, the estimated average time is 30 minutes. Should you have comments concerning the accuracy of this time estimate or suggestions for making this form simpler, please write to the Internal Revenue Service, Attention: Tax Forms Committee, Western Area Distribution Center, Rancho Cordova, CA 95743-0001.

Cat. No. 16965S

Form **911** (Rev. 3-2000)

Form **2553**
(Rev. December 2002)

Department of the Treasury
Internal Revenue Service

Election by a Small Business Corporation
(Under section 1362 of the Internal Revenue Code)
▶ See Parts II and III on back and the separate instructions.
▶ The corporation may either send or fax this form to the IRS. See page 2 of the instructions.

OMB No. 1545-0146

Notes:
1. *Do not file Form 1120S, U.S. Income Tax Return for an S Corporation, for any tax year before the year the election takes effect.*
2. *This election to be an S corporation can be accepted only if all the tests are met under **Who May Elect** on page 1 of the instructions; all shareholders have signed the consent statement; and the exact name and address of the corporation and other required form information are provided.*
3. *If the corporation was in existence before the effective date of this election, see **Taxes an S Corporation May Owe** on page 1 of the instructions.*

Part I	**Election Information**	

Please Type or Print

Name of corporation (see instructions)	**A** Employer identification number
Number, street, and room or suite no. (If a P.O. box, see instructions.)	**B** Date incorporated
City or town, state, and ZIP code	**C** State of incorporation

D Check the applicable box(es) if the corporation, after applying for the EIN shown in **A** above, changed its name ☐ or address ☐

E Election is to be effective for tax year beginning (month, day, year) . . . . ▶   /   /

F Name and title of officer or legal representative who the IRS may call for more information

G Telephone number of officer or legal representative ( )

H If this election takes effect for the first tax year the corporation exists, enter month, day, and year of the **earliest** of the following: (1) date the corporation first had shareholders, (2) date the corporation first had assets, or (3) date the corporation began doing business . . . . ▶   /   /

I Selected tax year: Annual return will be filed for tax year ending (month and day) ▶ ....

If the tax year ends on any date other than December 31, except for a 52–53-week tax year ending with reference to the month of December, you **must** complete Part II on the back. If the date you enter is the ending date of a 52–53-week tax year, write "52–53-week year" to the right of the date.

J Name and address of each shareholder; shareholder's spouse having a community property interest in the corporation's stock; and each tenant in common, joint tenant, and tenant by the entirety. (A husband and wife (and their estates) are counted as one shareholder in determining the number of shareholders without regard to the manner in which the stock is owned.)	K Shareholders' Consent Statement. Under penalties of perjury, we declare that we consent to the election of the above-named corporation to be an S corporation under section 1362(a) and that we have examined this consent statement, including accompanying schedules and statements, and to the best of our knowledge and belief, it is true, correct, and complete. We understand our consent is binding and may not be withdrawn after the corporation has made a valid election. (Shareholders sign and date below.)		L Stock owned		M Social security number or employer identification number (see instructions)	N Share-holder's tax year ends (month and day)
	Signature	Date	Number of shares	Dates acquired		

Under penalties of perjury, I declare that I have examined this election, including accompanying schedules and statements, and to the best of my knowledge and belief, it is true, correct, and complete.

Signature of officer ▶   Title ▶   Date ▶

For Paperwork Reduction Act Notice, see page 4 of the instructions.   Cat. No. 18629R   Form **2553** (Rev. 12-2002)

Form 2553 (Rev. 12-2002)   Page **2**

Part II   Selection of Fiscal Tax Year (All corporations using this part must complete item O and item P, Q, or R.)

O   Check the applicable box to indicate whether the corporation is:
   1. ☐ A new corporation adopting the tax year entered in item I, Part I.
   2. ☐ An existing corporation retaining the tax year entered in item I, Part I.
   3. ☐ An existing corporation changing to the tax year entered in item I, Part I.

P   Complete item P if the corporation is using the automatic approval provisions of Rev. Proc. 2002-38, 2002-22 I.R.B. 1037, to request **(1)** a natural business year (as defined in section 5.05 of Rev. Proc. 2002-38) or **(2)** a year that satisfies the ownership tax year test (as defined in section 5.06 of Rev. Proc. 2002-38). Check the applicable box below to indicate the representation statement the corporation is making.

   1. Natural Business Year ► ☐ I represent that the corporation is adopting, retaining, or changing to a tax year that qualifies as its natural business year as defined in section 5.05 of Rev. Proc. 2002-38 and has attached a statement verifying that it satisfies the 25% gross receipts test (see instructions for content of statement). I also represent that the corporation is not precluded by section 4.02 of Rev. Proc. 2002-38 from obtaining automatic approval of such adoption, retention, or change in tax year.

   2. Ownership Tax Year ► ☐ I represent that shareholders (as described in section 5.06 of Rev. Proc. 2002-38) holding more than half of the shares of the stock (as of the first day of the tax year to which the request relates) of the corporation have the same tax year or are concurrently changing to the tax year that the corporation adopts, retains, or changes to per item I, Part I, and that such tax year satisfies the requirement of section 4.01(3) of Rev. Proc. 2002-38. I also represent that the corporation is not precluded by section 4.02 of Rev. Proc. 2002-38 from obtaining automatic approval of such adoption, retention, or change in tax year.

Note: *If you do not use item P and the corporation wants a fiscal tax year, complete either item Q or R below. Item Q is used to request a fiscal tax year based on a business purpose and to make a back-up section 444 election. Item R is used to make a regular section 444 election.*

Q   Business Purpose—To request a fiscal tax year based on a business purpose, you must check box Q1. See instructions for details including payment of a user fee. You may also check box Q2 and/or box Q3.

   1. Check here ► ☐ if the fiscal year entered in item I, Part I, is requested under the prior approval provisions of Rev. Proc. 2002-39, 2002-22 I.R.B. 1046. Attach to Form 2553 a statement describing the relevant facts and circumstances and, if applicable, the gross receipts from sales and services necessary to establish a business purpose. See the instructions for details regarding the gross receipts from sales and services. If the IRS proposes to disapprove the requested fiscal year, do you want a conference with the IRS National Office?
   ☐ Yes   ☐ No

   2. Check here ► ☐ to show that the corporation intends to make a back-up section 444 election in the event the corporation's business purpose request is not approved by the IRS. (See instructions for more information.)

   3. Check here ► ☐ to show that the corporation agrees to adopt or change to a tax year ending December 31 if necessary for the IRS to accept this election for S corporation status in the event (1) the corporation's business purpose request is not approved and the corporation makes a back-up section 444 election, but is ultimately not qualified to make a section 444 election, or (2) the corporation's business purpose request is not approved and the corporation did not make a back-up section 444 election.

R   Section 444 Election—To make a section 444 election, you must check box R1 and you may also check box R2.

   1. Check here ► ☐ to show the corporation will make, if qualified, a section 444 election to have the fiscal tax year shown in item I, Part I. To make the election, you must complete **Form 8716**, Election To Have a Tax Year Other Than a Required Tax Year, and either attach it to Form 2553 or file it separately.

   2. Check here ► ☐ to show that the corporation agrees to adopt or change to a tax year ending December 31 if necessary for the IRS to accept this election for S corporation status in the event the corporation is ultimately not qualified to make a section 444 election.

Part III   Qualified Subchapter S Trust (QSST) Election Under Section 1361(d)(2)*

Income beneficiary's name and address	Social security number
Trust's name and address	Employer identification number

Date on which stock of the corporation was transferred to the trust (month, day, year) . . . . ►   /   /

In order for the trust named above to be a QSST and thus a qualifying shareholder of the S corporation for which this Form 2553 is filed, I hereby make the election under section 1361(d)(2). Under penalties of perjury, I certify that the trust meets the definitional requirements of section 1361(d)(3) and that all other information provided in Part III is true, correct, and complete.

_____   _____
Signature of income beneficiary or signature and title of legal representative or other qualified person making the election   Date

*Use Part III to make the QSST election only if stock of the corporation has been transferred to the trust on or before the date on which the corporation makes its election to be an S corporation. The QSST election must be made and filed separately if stock of the corporation is transferred to the trust after the date on which the corporation makes the S election.

✪   Form **2553** (Rev. 12-2002)

Form **4822** (Rev. 6-83)	Department of the Treasury - Internal Revenue Service **STATEMENT OF ANNUAL ESTIMATED PERSONAL AND FAMILY EXPENSES**

TAXPAYER'S NAME AND ADDRESS	TAX YEAR ENDED

	ITEM	BY CASH	BY CHECK	TOTAL	REMARKS
1. PERSONAL EXPENSES	Groceries and outside meals				
	Clothing				
	Laundry and dry cleaning				
	Barber, beauty shop, and cosmetics				
	Education *(tuition, room, board, books, etc.)*				
	Recreation, entertainment, vacations				
	Dues *(clubs, lodge, etc.)*				
	Gifts and allowances				
	Life and accident insurance				
	Federal taxes *(income, FICA, etc.)*				
2. HOUSEHOLD EXPENSES	Rent				
	Mortgage payments *(including interest)*				
	Utilities *(electricity, gas, telephone, water, etc.)*				
	Domestic help				
	Home insurance				
	Repairs and improvements				
	Child care				
3. AUTO EXPENSES	Gasoline, oil, grease, wash				
	Tires, batteries, repairs, tags				
	Insurance				
	Auto payments *(including interest)*				
	Lease of auto				
4. DEDUCTIBLE ITEMS	Contributions				
	Medical Expenses — Insurance				
	Medical Expenses — Drugs				
	Medical Expenses — Doctors, hospitals, etc.				
	Taxes — Real estate *(not included in 2. above)*				
	Taxes — Personal property				
	Taxes — Income *(State and local)*				
	Interest *(not included in 2. and 3. above)*				
	Miscellaneous — Alimony				
	Miscellaneous — Union dues				
5. PERSONAL ASSETS, ETC.	Stocks and bonds				
	Furniture, appliances, jewelry				
	Loans to others				
	Boat				
	TOTALS ▶				

Cat. No. 23460C

*U.S. Government Printing Office: 1996 - 405-506/33726

Form 4822 (Rev. 6-83)

Form **5213**
(Rev. July 2000)
Department of the Treasury
Internal Revenue Service

**Election To Postpone Determination
as To Whether the Presumption Applies That an
Activity Is Engaged in for Profit**
▶ To be filed by individuals, estates, trusts, partnerships, and S corporations.

OMB No. 1545-0195

Name(s) as shown on tax return | Identifying number as shown on tax return

Address (number and street, apt. no., rural route) (or P.O. box number if mail is not delivered to street address)

City, town or post office, state, and ZIP code

The taxpayer named above elects to postpone a determination as to whether the presumption applies that the activity described below is engaged in for profit. The determination is postponed until the close of:
- The 6th tax year, for an activity that consists mainly of breeding, training, showing, or racing horses or
- The 4th tax year for any other activity,
after the tax year in which the taxpayer first engaged in the activity.

1   Type of taxpayer engaged in the activity (check the box that applies):

☐ Individual   ☐ Partnership   ☐ S corporation   ☐ Estate or trust

2a Description of activity for which you elect to postpone a determination

2b First tax year you engaged in activity described in 2a

Under penalties of perjury, I declare that I have examined this election, including accompanying schedules, and to the best of my knowledge and belief, it is true, correct, and complete.

(Signature of taxpayer or fiduciary) | (Date)

(Signature of taxpayer's spouse, if joint return was filed) | (Date)

(Signature of general partner authorized to sign partnership return) | (Date)

(Signature and title of officer, if an S corporation) | (Date)

For Privacy Act and Paperwork Reduction Act Notice, see instructions on back.   Cat. No. 42361U   Form **5213** (Rev. 7-2000)

General Instructions

Purpose of Form

Use Form 5213 to elect to postpone an IRS determination as to whether the presumption applies that an activity is engaged in for profit.

General Information

Generally, if you are an individual, estate, trust, partnership, or S corporation in an activity not engaged in for profit, some of your deductions may not be allowed. However, an activity is presumed to be engaged in for profit (and, therefore, deductions are not limited) if the gross income exceeds the deductions:

● From an activity that consists mainly of breeding, training, showing, or racing horses for each of 2 or more of the tax years in the period of 7 consecutive tax years ending with the tax year in question or

● From any other activity for each of 3 or more of the tax years in the period of 5 consecutive tax years ending with the tax year in question.

For information on the limits on deductions in not-for-profit activities, see **Pub. 535,** Business Expenses.

Who Should File

Individuals, estates, trusts, partnerships (including limited liability companies or other entities that are treated as partnerships for Federal tax purposes), and S corporations should use this form if they want to postpone an IRS determination as to whether the presumption applies that they are engaged in an activity for profit. An election made by a partnership or an S corporation is binding on all persons who were partners or shareholders at any time during the presumption period.

You may not use this form if you have been engaged in:

● Breeding, training, showing, or racing horses for more than 7 years or

● Any other activity for more than 5 years.

If you elect a postponement and file this form on time, the IRS will generally postpone the determination until after the end of the 4th consecutive tax year (6th tax year for an activity that consists mainly of breeding, training, showing, or racing horses) after the tax year in which you first engaged in the activity. This period of 5 (or 7) tax years is called the "presumption period." The election to postpone covers the entire presumption period.

Joint Returns

If you and your spouse filed a joint return, both of you must elect to postpone the determination even if only one of you is engaged in the activity.

How Many Forms To File

Generally, if you want a postponement for more than one activity, you must file a separate Form 5213 for each activity. However, you may file one form for more than one activity if all of the activities have the same presumption period. Be sure to describe each activity in detail and list the first tax year in which you were engaged in the activities.

Generally, in determining whether you are engaged in more than one activity, you must consider all of the following:

● The similarity of the activities,

● The business purpose that is (or might be) served by carrying on the activities separately or together in a trade or business or investment setting, and

● The organizational and economic interrelationship of the activities.

When To File

File this form within 3 years after the due date of your return (determined without extensions) for the first tax year in which you engaged in the activity. However, if you received a written notice that the IRS proposes to disallow deductions attributable to an activity not engaged in for profit (under Internal Revenue Code section 183) and you want a postponement of the determination, you must file this form within 60 days of receiving the notice. This 60-day period does not extend the 3-year period referred to above.

Where To File

File this form with the Internal Revenue Service Center where you are required to file your return. Do not send it in with any other return because that will delay processing the election to postpone. However, if the IRS notifies you about proposing to disallow deductions for an activity not engaged in for profit, file the form with the IRS office that sent you the notification.

Automatic Extension of Period of Limitations

Generally, filing this form automatically extends the period of limitations for assessing any income tax deficiency specifically attributable to the activity during any year in the presumption period. The extension also applies to partners or shareholders in the activity.

The period is extended until 2 years after the due date for filing the return (determined without extensions) for the last tax year in the presumption period. For example, for an activity subject to a 5-year presumption period that began in 1998 and ends in 2002, the period of limitations automatically extends to April 15, 2005, for all tax years in the presumption period that would otherwise expire before that date. Periods of limitations for tax years in the 5-year period expiring after April 15, 2005, would remain open until their normal expiration date. However, early termination of the presumption period does not terminate the automatic extension of the period of limitations.

The automatic extension applies only to those deductions attributable to the activity and to any deductions (such as medical expenses or charitable contribution deductions) that are affected by changes made to adjusted gross income.

The automatic extension does not affect general waivers of the statute of limitations that may be executed.

Specific Instructions

Name and Identifying Number as Shown on Tax Return

Enter your name(s) and identifying number as shown on your tax return for the first tax year in which you engaged in the activity. If you are an individual, your identifying number is your social security number (SSN). If you are other than an individual, your identifying number is your employer identification number (EIN).

If you and your spouse filed a joint return, enter both your name and your spouse's name as they were shown on your tax return. Enter the SSN that was shown first on your return as your identifying number.

Signature and Date

Be sure to sign and date the form on the appropriate line or lines. Keep a copy for your records.

Privacy Act and Paperwork Reduction Act Notice. We ask for the information on this form to carry out the Internal Revenue laws of the United States. We need this information to determine your eligibility for making the election to postpone determination as to whether the presumption applies that an activity is engaged in for profit. If you make this election, you are required by Internal Revenue Code section 183 to provide the information requested on this form. Under section 6109, you must disclose your SSN, individual taxpayer identification number (ITIN), or EIN. Routine uses of this information include giving it to the Department of Justice for civil and criminal litigation, and to cities, states, and the District of Columbia for use in administering their tax laws. If you fail to provide this information in a timely manner, or provide incomplete or false information, you may be liable for interest and penalties.

You are not required to provide the information requested on a form that is subject to the Paperwork Reduction Act unless the form displays a valid OMB control number. Books or records relating to a form or its instructions must be retained as long as their contents may become material in the administration of any Internal Revenue law. Generally, tax returns and return information are confidential, as required by Code section 6103.

The time needed to complete and file this form will vary depending on individual circumstances. The estimated average time is:

Recordkeeping	7 min.
Learning about the law or the form	10 min.
Preparing the form	10 min.
Copying, assembling, and sending the form to the IRS . .	20 min.

If you have comments concerning the accuracy of these time estimates or suggestions for making this form simpler, we would be happy to hear from you. You can write to the Tax Forms Committee, Western Area Distribution Center, Rancho Cordova, CA 95743-0001. **Do not** send the form to this address. Instead, see **Where To File** on this page.

Form **8275** (Rev. May 2001) Department of the Treasury Internal Revenue Service	**Disclosure Statement** Do not use this form to disclose items or positions that are contrary to Treasury regulations. Instead, use Form 8275-R, Regulation Disclosure Statement. See separate instructions. ▶ **Attach to your tax return.**	OMB No. 1545-0889 Attachment Sequence No. **92**
Name(s) shown on return		Identifying number shown on return

Part I General Information (see instructions)

(a) Rev. Rul., Rev. Proc., etc.	(b) Item or Group of Items	(c) Detailed Description of Items	(d) Form or Schedule	(e) Line No.	(f) Amount
1					
2					
3					

Part II Detailed Explanation (see instructions)

1

2

3

Part III Information About Pass-Through Entity. To be completed by partners, shareholders, beneficiaries, or residual interest holders.

Complete this part only if you are making adequate disclosure for a pass-through item.

Note: *A pass-through entity is a partnership, S corporation, estate, trust, regulated investment company (RIC), real estate investment trust (REIT), or real estate mortgage investment conduit (REMIC).*

1 Name, address, and ZIP code of pass-through entity	2 Identifying number of pass-through entity
	3 Tax year of pass-through entity / / to / /
	4 Internal Revenue Service Center where the pass-through entity filed its return

For Paperwork Reduction Act Notice, see separate instructions.   Cat. No. 61935M   Form **8275** (Rev. 5-2001)

Form **8275-R**	**Regulation Disclosure Statement**	OMB No. 1545-0889

Form **8275-R**
(Rev. February 2002)
Department of the Treasury
Internal Revenue Service

Regulation Disclosure Statement
Use this form only to disclose items or positions that are contrary to Treasury regulations.
For other disclosures, use Form 8275, Disclosure Statement. See separate instructions.
▶ **Attach to your tax return.**

OMB No. 1545-0889

Attachment
Sequence No. **92A**

Name(s) shown on return	Identifying number shown on return

Part I **General Information** (See instructions.)

(a) Regulation Section	(b) Item or Group of Items	(c) Detailed Description of Items	(d) Form or Schedule	(e) Line No.	(f) Amount
1					
2					
3					

Part II **Detailed Explanation** (See instructions.)

1

2

3

Part III **Information About Pass-Through Entity.** To be completed by partners, shareholders, beneficiaries, or residual interest holders.

Complete this part only if you are making adequate disclosure for a pass-through item.

Note: *A pass-through entity is a partnership, S corporation, estate, trust, regulated investment company (RIC), real estate investment trust (REIT), or real estate mortgage investment conduit (REMIC).*

1 Name, address, and ZIP code of pass-through entity	2 Identifying number of pass-through entity
	3 Tax year of pass-through entity / / to / /
	4 Internal Revenue Service Center where the pass-through entity filed its return

For Paperwork Reduction Act Notice, see separate instructions.   Cat. No. 14594X   Form **8275-R** (Rev. 2-2002)

The Salvation Army Valuation Guide 2002

Appliance	Low	High
Air Conditioner	$20.00	$90.00
Dryer	$45.00	$90.00
Gas Stove	$50.00	$125.00
Heaters	$7.50	$22.00
Radio	$7.50	$50.00
Refrig. (wkg)	$15.00	$250.00
T.V. (B/W Working)	$25.00	$60.00
T.V. (Color Working)	$75.00	$225.00
Washing Machine (working)	$27.50	$150.00
Children	**Low**	**High**
Bicycles	$15.00	$65.00
Blouses	$2.00	$8.00
Boots	$3.00	$20.00
Coats	$4.50	$20.00
Dresses	$3.50	$12.00
Jackets	$3.00	$25.00
Jeans	$3.50	$12.00
Pants	$2.50	$12.00
Shirts	$2.00	$6.00
Shoes	$2.50	$8.75
Skirts	$1.50	$6.00
Slacks	$2.00	$8.00
Snowsuits	$4.00	$19.00
Socks	$0.50	$1.50
Sweaters	$2.50	$8.00
Underwear	$1.00	$3.50
Dry Goods	**Low**	**High**
Bedspreads	$3.00	$24.00
Blankets	$2.50	$8.00
Chair Covers	$15.00	$35.00
Curtains	$1.50	$12.00
Drapes	$6.50	$40.00
Pillows	$2.00	$8.00
Sheets	$2.00	$8.00

Throw Rugs	$1.50	$12.00
Towels	$0.50	$4.00
Furniture	**Low**	**High**
Bed Complete (dbl)	$50.00	$170.00
Bed Complete (sgl)	$35.00	$100.00
Bedroom Set (Complete)	$250.00	$1,000.00
Carriage	$5.00	$100.00
Chest	$25.00	$95.00
China Cabinet	$85.00	$300.00
Clothes Closet	$15.00	$50.00
Coffee Table	$15.00	$65.00
Convertible sofa (with mattress)	$85.00	$300.00
Crib (w/mattress)	$25.00	$100.00
Desk	$25.00	$140.00
Dining Room Set (Complete)	$150.00	$900.00
Dresser w/Mirror	$20.00	$100.00
End Tables (2)	$10.00	$50.00
Floor Lamps	$7.50	$40.00
Folding Beds	$20.00	$60.00
Hi Riser	$35.00	$75.00
High Chair	$10.00	$50.00
Kitchen Cabinets	$25.00	$75.00
Kitchen Chair	$2.50	$10.00
Kitchen Set	$35.00	$170.00
Mattress (dbl)	$12.50	$75.00
Mattress (sgl)	$15.00	$35.00
Play-Pen	$3.75	$30.00
Rugs	$20.00	$90.00
Secretary	$50.00	$140.00
Sofa	$35.00	$200.00
Trunk	$5.00	$70.00
Wardrobe	$20.00	$100.00
Men	**Low**	**High**
Jackets	$7.50	$25.00
Over Coats	$15.00	$60.00
Pajamas	$2.00	$8.00
Pants-shorts	$3.50	$10.00
Raincoat	$5.00	$20.00
Shirts	$2.50	$12.00
Shoes	$3.50	$25.00
Slacks	$5.00	$12.00
Suits	$15.00	$60.00
Sweaters	$2.50	$12.00

Swim Trunks	$2.50	$8.00
Tuxedo	$10.00	$60.00
Under-shirts	$1.00	$3.00
Under-shorts	$1.00	$3.00
Women	**Low**	**High**
Bathing Suits	$4.00	$12.00
Bathrobes	$2.50	$12.00
Blouse	$2.50	$12.00
Boots	$2.00	$5.00
Bras	$1.00	$3.00
Coats	$10.00	$40.00
Dresses	$4.00	$19.00
Evening Dresses	$10.00	$60.00
Foundation Garments	$3.00	$8.00
Fur Coats	$25.00	$400.00
Fur Hats	$7.00	$15.00
Handbags	$2.00	$20.00
Hats	$1.00	$8.00
Jackets	$4.00	$12.00
Nightgowns	$4.00	$12.00
Pants Suits	$6.50	$25.00
Shoes	$2.00	$25.00
Skirts	$3.00	$8.00
Slacks	$3.50	$12.00
Slips	$1.00	$6.00
Socks	$0.40	$1.25
Suits	$6.00	$25.00
Sweaters	$3.75	$15.00

Request for a Collection Due Process Hearing

Use this form to request a hearing with the IRS Office of Appeals only when you receive a **Notice of Federal Tax Lien Filing & Your Right To A Hearing Under IRC 6320**, a **Final Notice - Notice Of Intent to Levy & Your Notice Of a Right To A Hearing**, or a **Notice of Jeopardy Levy and Right of Appeal**. Complete this form and send it to the address shown on your lien or levy notice for expeditious handling. Include a copy of your lien or levy notice(s) to ensure proper handling of your request.

(Print) Taxpayer Name(s):_____

(Print) Address: _____

Daytime Telephone Number:_____ Type of Tax/Tax Form Number(s): _____

Taxable Period(s):_____

Social Security Number/Employer Identification Number(s):_____

Check the IRS action(s) that you do not agree with. Provide specific reasons why you don't agree. If you believe that your spouse or former spouse should be responsible for all or a portion of the tax liability from your tax return, check here [ ] and attach Form 8857, Request for Innocent Spouse Relief, to this request.

_____ **Filed Notice of Federal Tax Lien (Explain why you don't agree. Use extra sheets if necessary.)**

_____ **Notice of Levy/Seizure (Explain why you don't agree. Use extra sheets if necessary.)**

I/we understand that the statutory period of limitations for collection is suspended during the Collection Due Process Hearing and any subsequent judicial review.

Taxpayer's or Authorized Representative's Signature and Date:_____

Taxpayer's or Authorized Representative's Signature and Date:_____

IRS Use Only:

IRS Employee *(Print)*: _____ IRS Received Date:_____

Employee Telephone Number: _____

Form **12153** (01-1999)   Catalog Number 26685D   Department of the Treasury – Internal Revenue Service

(Over)

Where to File Your Request

It is important that you file your request using the address shown on your lien or levy notice. If you have been working with a specific IRS employee on your case, you should file the request with that employee.

How to Complete Form 12153

1. Enter your full name and address. If the tax liability is owed jointly by a husband and wife, and both wish to request a Collection Due Process Hearing, show both names.

2. Enter a daytime telephone number where we can contact you regarding your request for a hearing.

3. List the type(s) of tax or the number of the tax form(s) for which you are requesting a hearing (e.g. Form 1040, Form 941, Trust Fund Recovery Penalty, etc.).

4. List the taxable periods for the type(s) of tax or the tax form(s) that you listed for item 3 above (e.g., year ending 12-31-98, quarter ending 3-31-98).

5. Show the social security number of the individual(s) and/or the employer identification number of the business(s) that are requesting a hearing.

6. Check the IRS action(s) that you do not agree with (Filed Notice of Federal Tax Lien and/or Notice of Levy/Seizure). You may check both actions if applicable.

7. Provide the specific reason(s) why you do not agree with the filing of the Notice of Federal Tax Lien or the proposed Notice of Levy/Seizure action. One specific issue that you may raise at the hearing is whether income taxes should be abated because you believe that your spouse or former spouse should be responsible for all or a portion of the tax liability from your tax return. You must, however, elect such relief. You can do this by checking the indicated box and attaching Form 8857 to this request for a hearing. If you previously filed Form 8857, please indicate when and with whom you filed the Form.

8. You, or your authorized representative, must sign the Form 12153. If the tax liability is joint and both spouses are requesting a hearing, both spouses, or their authorized representative(s), must sign.

9. It is important that you understand that we are required by statute to suspend the statutory period for collection during a Collection Due Process Hearing.

APPENDIX B
State Filing Authority Telephone Numbers and Web Sites

Below is a listing of the web sites for all the states for you to order state forms and where your questions can be answered regarding your state filing requirements. Further information about electronic and fax services plus forms for all states is available at **www.1040.com/state.htm** and **taxsites.com/state.html**.

State	Information Numbers	Web Site Addresses
Alabama	334/242-1170	ADOR.STATE.AL.US
Alaska	907/465-2320	REVENUE.STATE.AK.US
Arizona	602/542-4260	REVENUE.STATE.AZ.US
Arkansas	501/682-1130	STATE.ARK.ORG
California	800/338-0505	FTB.CA.GOV
Colorado	303/232-2414	TAXCOLORADO.COM
Connecticut	860/297-5962	DRS.STATE.CT.US/
Delaware	302/577-3300	STATE.DE.US/REVENUE/
District of Columbia	202/727-4829	CFO.WASHINGTONDC.GOV/ETSC/MAIN.SHTM
Florida	904/359-6070	SUNG.DMS.STATEFL.US/DOR
Georgia	404/656-4293	2.STATE.GA.US/DEPARTMENTS/DOR
Hawaii	800/222-7572	STATE.HI.US/TAX/TAX.HTML
Idaho	208/334-7560	2.STATE.ID.US/TAXFORMS.HTM
Illinois	800/732-8866	REVENUE.STATE.IL.US
Indiana	317/232-2240	AI.ORG/DOR
Iowa	515/281-3114	STATE.IA.US/TAX/INDEX/HTML
Kansas	877/526-7738	KSREVENUE.ORG
Kentucky	502/564-4580	REVENUE.KY.GOV
Louisiana	225/925-4611	REV.STATE.LA.US
Maine	207/287-2076	STATE.ME.US/REVENUE
Maryland	410/260-7951	COMP.STATE.MD.US
Massachusetts	617/887-6367	DOR.STATE.MA.US
Michigan	800/367-6263	MICHIGAN.GOV/TREASURY
Minnesota	651/296-3781	TAXES.STATE.MN.US
Mississippi	601/923-7000	TREASURY.STATE.MS.US/
Missouri	573/751-3943	DOR.STATE.MO.US/
Montana	406/444-6900	STATE.MT.US/REVENUE/CSS/DEFAULT.ASP
Nebraska	402/471-2971	REVENUE.STATE.NE.US/INDEX.HTML
Nevada	775/687-4820	STATE.NV.US/TAXATION/
New Hampshire	603/271-2192	STATE.NH.US/REVENUE
New Jersey	609/292-6400	STATE.NJ.US/TREASURY/TAXATION/

State	Information Numbers	Web Site Addresses
New Mexico	505/827-0700	STATE.NM.US/TAX
New York City	718/935-6739	CI.NYC.NY.US/FINANCE
New York State	800/225-5829	STATE.NY.US
North Carolina	919/733-3261	DOR.STATE.NC.US
North Dakota	701/328-3450	STATE.ND.US/TAXDPT
Ohio	800/282-1780	STATE.OH.US/TAX/
Oklahoma	405/521-3108	OKTAX.STATE.OK.US
Oregon	503/378-4988	DOR.STATE.OR.US
Pennsylvania	717/787-8210	REVENUE.STATE.PA.US
Puerto Rico	787/721-2020	
Rhode Island	401/222-1040	TAX.STATE.RI.US
South Carolina	803/898-5599	SCTAX.ORG/DEFAULT.HTM
South Dakota	605/773-3311	STATE.SD.US/STATE/EXECUTIVE/ REVENUE/REVENUE.HTML
Tennessee	615/253-0600	STATE.TN.US/REVENUE
Texas	512/463-4600	CPA.STATE.TX.US/M23TAXES.HTML
Utah	801/297-2200	TXDTM01.TAX.EX.STATE.UT.US
Vermont	802/828-2515	STATE.VT.US/TAX
Virginia	804/367-8055	TAX.STATE.VA.US
Washington	800/647-7706	ACCESS.WA.GOV/ONLINESERVICES/ TAXCENTER.ASPX
West Virginia	304/558-3333	STATE.WV.US/TAXREV/
Wisconsin	608/266-1961	DOR.STATE.WI.US
Wyoming	307/777-5200	STATE.WY.US

APPENDIX C
Your Rights as a Taxpayer

Department of the Treasury
Internal Revenue Service

Publication 1
(Rev. August 2000)

Catalog Number 64731W

www.irs.gov

Your Rights as a Taxpayer

The first part of this publication explains some of your most important rights as a taxpayer. The second part explains the examination, appeal, collection, and refund processes. This publication is also available in Spanish.

Declaration of Taxpayer Rights

I. Protection of Your Rights

IRS employees will explain and protect your rights as a taxpayer throughout your contact with us.

II. Privacy and Confidentiality

The IRS will not disclose to anyone the information you give us, except as authorized by law. You have the right to know why we are asking you for information, how we will use it, and what happens if you do not provide requested information.

III. Professional and Courteous Service

If you believe that an IRS employee has not treated you in a professional, fair, and courteous manner, you should tell that employee's supervisor. If the supervisor's response is not satisfactory, you should write to the IRS director for your area or the center where you file your return.

IV. Representation

You may either represent yourself or, with proper written authorization, have someone else represent you in your place. Your representative must be a person allowed to practice before the IRS, such as an attorney, certified public accountant, or enrolled agent. If you are in an interview and ask to consult such a person, then we must stop and reschedule the interview in most cases.

You can have someone accompany you at an interview. You may make sound recordings of any meetings with our examination, appeal, or collection personnel, provided you tell us in writing 10 days before the meeting.

V. Payment of Only the Correct Amount of Tax

You are responsible for paying only the correct amount of tax due under the law—no more, no less. If you cannot pay all of your tax when it is due, you may be able to make monthly installment payments.

VI. Help With Unresolved Tax Problems

The Taxpayer Advocate Service can help you if you have tried unsuccessfully to resolve a problem with the IRS. Your local Taxpayer Advocate can offer you special help if you have a significant hardship as a result of a tax problem. For more information, call toll free 1–877–777–4778 (1–800–829–4059 for TTY/TDD) or write to the Taxpayer Advocate at the IRS office that last contacted you.

VII. Appeals and Judicial Review

If you disagree with us about the amount of your tax liability or certain collection actions, you have the right to ask the Appeals Office to review your case. You may also ask a court to review your case.

VIII. Relief From Certain Penalties and Interest

The IRS will waive penalties when allowed by law if you can show you acted reasonably and in good faith or relied on the incorrect advice of an IRS employee. We will waive interest that is the result of certain errors or delays caused by an IRS employee.

THE IRS MISSION

PROVIDE AMERICA'S TAXPAYERS TOP QUALITY SERVICE BY HELPING THEM UNDERSTAND AND MEET THEIR TAX RESPONSIBILITIES AND BY APPLYING THE TAX LAW WITH INTEGRITY AND FAIRNESS TO ALL.

Examinations, Appeals, Collections, and Refunds

Examinations (Audits)

We accept most taxpayers' returns as filed. If we inquire about your return or select it for examination, it does not suggest that you are dishonest. The inquiry or examination may or may not result in more tax. We may close your case without change; or, you may receive a refund.

The process of selecting a return for examination usually begins in one of two ways. First, we use computer programs to identify returns that may have incorrect amounts. These programs may be based on information returns, such as Forms 1099 and W-2, on studies of past examinations, or on certain issues identified by compliance projects. Second, we use information from outside sources that indicates that a return may have incorrect amounts. These sources may include newspapers, public records, and individuals. If we determine that the information is accurate and reliable, we may use it to select a return for examination.

Publication 556, *Examination of Returns, Appeal Rights, and Claims for Refund*, explains the rules and procedures that we follow in examinations. The following sections give an overview of how we conduct examinations.

By Mail

We handle many examinations and inquiries by mail. We will send you a letter with either a request for more information or a reason why we believe a change to your return may be needed. You can respond by mail or you can request a personal interview with an examiner. If you mail us the requested information or provide an explanation, we may or may not agree with you, and we will explain the reasons for any changes. Please do not hesitate to write to us about anything you do not understand.

By Interview

If we notify you that we will conduct your examination through a personal interview, or you request such an interview, you have the right to ask that the examination take place at a reasonable time and place that is convenient for both you and the IRS. If our examiner proposes any changes to your return, he or she will explain the reasons for the changes. If you do not agree with these changes, you can meet with the examiner's supervisor.

Repeat Examinations

If we examined your return for the same items in either of the 2 previous years and proposed no change to your tax liability, please contact us as soon as possible so we can see if we should discontinue the examination.

Appeals

If you do not agree with the examiner's proposed changes, you can appeal them to the Appeals Office of IRS. Most differences can be settled without expensive and time-consuming court trials. Your appeal rights are explained in detail in both Publication 5, *Your Appeal Rights and How To Prepare a Protest If You Don't Agree*, and Publication 556, *Examination of Returns, Appeal Rights, and Claims for Refund.*

If you do not wish to use the Appeals Office or disagree with its findings, you may be able to take your case to the U.S. Tax Court, U.S. Court of Federal Claims, or the U.S. District Court where you live. If you take your case to court, the IRS will have the burden of proving certain facts if you kept adequate records to show your tax liability, cooperated with the IRS, and meet certain other conditions. If the court agrees with you on most issues in your case and finds that our position was largely unjustified, you may be able to recover some of your administrative and litigation costs. You will not be eligible to recover these costs unless you tried to resolve your case administratively, including going through the appeals system, and you gave us the information necessary to resolve the case.

Collections

Publication 594, *The IRS Collection Process*, explains your rights and responsibilities regarding payment of federal taxes. It describes:

- What to do when you owe taxes. It describes what to do if you get a tax bill and what to do if you think your bill is wrong. It also covers making installment payments, delaying collection action, and submitting an offer in compromise.
- IRS collection actions. It covers liens, releasing a lien, levies, releasing a levy, seizures and sales, and release of property.

Your collection appeal rights are explained in detail in Publication 1660, *Collection Appeal Rights.*

Innocent Spouse Relief

Generally, both you and your spouse are responsible, jointly and individually, for paying the full amount of any tax, interest, or penalties due on your joint return. However, if you qualify for innocent spouse relief, you may not have to pay the tax, interest, and penalties related to your spouse (or former spouse). For information on innocent spouse relief and two other ways to get relief, see Publication 971, *Innocent Spouse Relief*, and Form 8857, *Request for Innocent Spouse Relief (And Separation of Liability and Equitable Relief).*

Refunds

You may file a claim for refund if you think you paid too much tax. You must generally file the claim within 3 years from the date you filed your original return or 2 years from the date you paid the tax, whichever is later. The law generally provides for interest on your refund if it is not paid within 45 days of the date you filed your return or claim for refund. Publication 556, *Examination of Returns, Appeal Rights, and Claims for Refund*, has more information on refunds.

If you were due a refund but you did not file a return, you must file within 3 years from the date the return was originally due to get that refund.

Tax Information

The IRS provides a great deal of free information. The following are sources for forms, publications, and additional information.

- *Tax Questions:* 1–800–829–1040 (1–800–829–4059 for TTY/TDD)
- *Forms and Publications:* 1–800–829–3676 (1–800–829–4059 for TTY/TDD)
- *Internet:* www.irs.gov
- *TaxFax Service:* From your fax machine, dial 703–368–9694.
- *Small Business Ombudsman:* If you are a small business entity, you can participate in the regulatory process and comment on enforcement actions of IRS by calling 1–888–REG–FAIR.
- *Treasury Inspector General for Tax Administration:* If you want to confidentially report misconduct, waste, fraud, or abuse by an IRS employee, you can call 1–800–366–4484 (1–800–877–8339 for TTY/TDD). You can remain anonymous.

The IRS Mission

Provide America's taxpayers top quality service by helping them understand and meet their tax responsibilities and by applying the tax law with integrity and fairness to all.

The Examination Process

Introduction

The Internal Revenue Service (IRS) accepts most federal returns as filed. Some returns, however, are examined, or audited, to determine if income, expenses, and credits are reported accurately.

This publication discusses general rules and procedures we follow in examinations. It explains what happens before, during, and after an examination. It also explains appeal and payment procedures.

As a taxpayer, you have the right to fair, professional, prompt, and courteous service from IRS employees, as outlined in the Declaration of Taxpayer Rights found on page 3.

We must follow the tax rules set forth by Congress in the Internal Revenue Code. We also follow Treasury Regulations, court decisions, and other rules and procedures written to administer the tax laws.

If the examination results in a change to your tax liability, you may ask us to reconsider your case. Some reasons why we may reconsider your case include:

- Your submitting additional information that could result in a change to the additional amount we have determined that you owe;

- Your filing an original deliquent return after we have determined that you owe an additional amount, or;

- Your identifying a mathematical or processing error we made.

You must request reconsideration in writing and submit it to your local IRS office.

Department of the Treasury
Internal Revenue Service

www.irs.gov

Publication **3498** (Rev. 1-2003)
Catalog Number 73074S

What's *Inside . . .*

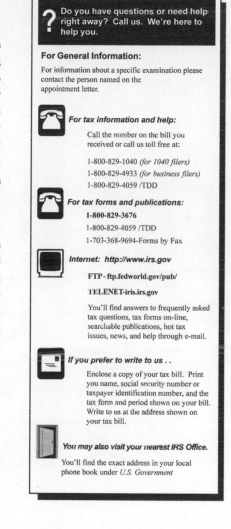

Do you have questions or need help right away? Call us. We're here to help you.

For General Information:

For information about a specific examination please contact the person named on the appointment letter.

For tax information and help:

Call the number on the bill you received or call us toll free at:

1-800-829-1040 *(for 1040 filers)*
1-800-829-4933 *(for business filers)*
1-800-829-4059 /TDD

For tax forms and publications:
1-800-829-3676
1-800-829-4059 /TDD
1-703-368-9694-Forms by Fax

Internet: http://www.irs.gov

FTP - ftp.fedworld.gov/pub/

TELENET-iris.irs.gov

You'll find answers to frequently asked tax questions, tax forms on-line, searchable publications, hot tax issues, news, and help through e-mail.

If you prefer to write to us ..

Enclose a copy of your tax bill. Print you name, social security number or taxpayer identification number, and the tax form and period shown on your bill. Write to us at the address shown on your tax bill.

You may also visit your nearest IRS Office.

You'll find the exact address in your local phone book under *U.S. Government*

Declaration of Taxpayer Rights

I. Protection of Your Rights

IRS employees will explain and protect your rights as a taxpayer throughout your contact with us.

II. Privacy and Confidentiality

The IRS will not disclose to anyone the information you give us, except as authorized by law. You have the right to know why we are asking you for information, how we will use it, and what happens if you do not provide requested information.

III. Professional and Courteous Service

If you believe that an IRS employee has not treated you in a professional , fair, and courteous manner, you should tell that employee's supervisor. If the supervisor's response is not satisfactory, you should write to the IRS Director for your Area or the Center where you file your return.

IV. Representation

You may either represent yourself or, with proper written authorization, have someone else represent you. Your representative must be a person allowed to practice before the IRS, such as an attorney, certified public accountant, or enrolled agent (a person enrolled to practice before the IRS). If you are in an interview and ask to consult such a person, then we must stop and reschedule the interview in most cases.

You can have someone accompany you at an interview. You may make sound recordings of any meetings with our examination, appeal, or collection personnel, provided you tell us in writing 10 days before the meeting.

V. Payment of Only the Correct Amount of Tax

You are responsible for paying only the correct amount of tax due under the law—no more, no less. If you cannot pay all of your tax when it is due, you may be able to make monthly payments.

VI. Help with Unresolved Tax Problems

The Taxpayer Advocate Service can help you if you have tried unsuccessfully to resolve a problem with the IRS. Your local Taxpayer Advocate can offer you special help if you have a significant hardship as a result of a tax problem. For more information, call toll-free, 1-877-777-4778 (1-800-829-4059 for TTY/TDD) or write to the Taxpayer Advocate at the IRS office that last contacted you.

VII. Appeals and Judicial Review

If you disagree with us about the amount of your tax liability or certain collection actions, you have the right to ask the Appeals Office to review your case. You may also ask a court to review your case.

VIII. Relief from Certain Penalties and Interest

The IRS will waive penalties when allowed by law if you can show you acted reasonably and in good faith or relied on the incorrect advice of an IRS employee. We will waive interest that is the result of certain errors or delays caused by an IRS employee.

Your Return Is Going To Be Examined.

Before the Examination

We accept most taxpayers' returns as filed. If we inquire about your return or select it for examination, it does not suggest that you are dishonest. The inquiry or examination may or may not result in more tax. We may close your case without change or you may receive a refund.

The process of selecting a return for examination usually begins in one of two ways. One way is to use computer programs to identify returns that may have incorrect amounts. The programs may be based on information returns, such as Forms 1099 or W-2, on studies of past examinations, or on certain issues identified by other special projects. Another way is to use information from compliance projects that indicates a return may have incorrect amounts. These sources may include newspapers, public records, and individuals. If we determine the information is accurate and reliable, we may use it to select a return for examination.

Publication 556, *Examination of Returns, Appeal Rights, and Claims for Refund,* explains the rules and procedures that we follow in examinations. The following sections give an overview of how we conduct examinations.

During the Examination

Examinations by Mail

Some examinations are conducted entirely by mail. If the examination is conducted by mail, you'll receive a letter from us asking for additional information about certain items shown on your return, such as income, expenses, and itemized deductions.

If the examination is conducted by mail, you can:

1. Act on your own behalf. *(In the case of a jointly filed return, either spouse can respond or both spouses can send a joint response.)*

2. Have someone represent you in correspondence with us. This person must be an attorney, accountant, enrolled agent, an enrolled actuary, or the person who prepared the return and signed it as the preparer. If you choose to have someone represent you, you must furnish us with written authorization. Make this authorization on Form 2848, *Power of Attorney and Declaration of Representative.*

Note: *You may obtain any of the forms and publications referenced in this publication by calling 1-800-829-3676.*

Examinations in Person

An examination conducted in person begins when we notify you by mail that your return has been selected. We'll tell you what information you need to provide at that time. If you gather the information before the examination, we may be able to complete it more easily and in a shorter time.

If the examination is conducted in person, it can take place in your home, your place of business, an IRS office, or the office of your attorney, accountant, or enrolled agent *(a person enrolled to practice before the IRS).* If the time or place is not convenient for you, the examiner will try to work out something more suitable.

Your Return Is Going To Be Examined. (cont.)

If the examination is conducted in person, you can:

1. Act on your own behalf. *(In the case of a jointly filed return, either spouse or both can attend the interview.)* If you are acting on your own behalf, you may leave to consult with your representative. We will suspend the interview and reschedule the examination. We cannot suspend the interview if we are conducting it as a result of your receiving an administrative summons.

2. Have someone accompany you, either to support your position or to witness to the proceedings.

3. Accompany someone who will represent you. This person must be an attorney, accountant, enrolled agent, an enrolled actuary, or the person who prepared the return and signed it as the preparer.

4. Have your representative act for you and not be present at the audit yourself. If you choose to have someone represent you in your absence, you must furnish us with written authorization. Make this authorization on **Form 2848**, *Power of Attorney and Declaration of Representative.*

How to Stop Interest from Accumulating

During your examination, if you think you will owe additional tax at the end of the examination, you can stop interest from accumulating by paying all or part of the amount you think you will owe. Interest will stop accumulating on the part you pay when the IRS receives your money. Interest will only be charged on the tax, penalties, and interest that are unpaid on the date they are assessed.

Consents to Extend the Statute of Limitations

We try to examine tax returns as soon as possible after they are filed, but occasionally we may request that you extend the statute of limitations of your tax return.

A return's statute of limitation generally limits the time we have to examine it and assess tax. Assessments of tax must be made within 3 years after a return is due or filed, whichever is later. We can't assess additional tax or make a refund or credit *(unless you filed a timely claim)* after the statute of limitations has expired. Also, if you disagree with the results of the examination, you can't appeal the items you disagree with unless sufficient time remains on the statute. Because of these restrictions, if there isn't much time remaining to examine your return, assess additional taxes, and/or exercise your appeal rights, you have the opportunity to extend the statute of limitations. This will allow you additional time to provide further documentation to support your position, request an appeal if you do not agree with our findings, or to claim a tax refund or credit. It also allows the Service time to complete the examination, make any additional assessment, if necessary, and provide sufficient time for processing.

A written agreement between you and the Service to extend the statutory period of a tax return is called a "consent." Consents can be used for all types of tax except estate tax.

There are two basic kinds of consent forms. One sets a specific expiration date for the extension, and the other for an indefinite period of time. Either type of consent may be limited by restrictive conditions. The use of a restricted consent is to allow the statute to expire with regard to all items on the return except those covered by the restrictive language.

If the statute of limitations for your tax return is approaching, you may be asked to sign a consent. You may:

1. Refuse to extend the statute of limitations;

2. Limit or restrict the consent to particular issues, or

3. Limit the extension to a particular period of time.

The consent will be sent or presented to you with a letter explaining this process and **Publication 1035**, *Extending the Tax Assessment Period.* For further information, refer to this publication.

Results of the Examination

If we accept your return as filed, you will receive a letter stating that the examiner proposed no changes to your return. You should keep this letter with your tax records.

If we don't accept your return as filed, we will explain any proposed changes to you and your authorized representative. It is important that you understand the reasons for any proposed changes; don't hesitate to ask about anything that is unclear to you.

What to Do When You Receive a Bill from the IRS

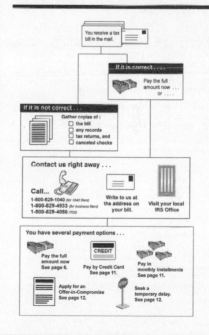

What To Do If You Agree or Disagree with the Examination Results

If You Agree

If you agree with a proposed *increase* to tax, you can sign an agreement form and pay any additional tax you may owe. You must pay interest and applicable penalties on any additional balance due. If you pay when you sign the agreement, interest is generally figured from the due date of your return to the date of your payment.

If you do not pay the additional tax and interest, you will receive a bill *(See "What To do When You Receive a Bill from the IRS" on page 10.)* If the amount due *(including interest and applicable penalties)* is less than $100,000 and you pay it within 21 business days, we will not charge more interest or penalties. If the amount is $100,000 or more, the period is reduced to 10 calendar days. If you can't pay the tax due at the end of the examination, you may pay whatever amount you can and request an installment agreement for the balance. *(See "Setting up an Installment Agreement" on page 11.)*

If you are entitled to a refund, you will receive it sooner if you sign the agreement form at the end of the examination. You will also be paid interest on the refund.

If You Do Not Agree

If you do not agree with the proposed changes, the examiner will explain your appeal rights. If your examination takes place in an IRS office, you may request an immediate meeting with the examiner's supervisor to explain your situation. You may also enter into an *Agreement to Mediate* to help resolve disputes through Fast Track Mediation services. *(See page 7.)* Mediation can take place at this meeting or afterwards. If an agreement is reached, your case will be closed.

If you cannot reach an agreement with the supervisor at this meeting, or if the examination took place outside an IRS office or was conducted through correspondence with an IRS Center employee, the examiner will prepare a report explaining your position and ours. The examiner will forward your case to the Area office for processing .

You will receive:

- A letter (know as a 30-day letter) notifying you of your rights to appeal the proposed changes within 30 days,

- A copy of the examiner's report explaining the proposed changes, and

- An agreement or a waiver form.

You generally have 30 days from the date of the 30-day letter to tell us whether you will accept the proposed changes or appeal them. The letter will explain what steps you should take, depending on what action you choose. Be sure to follow the instructions carefully. Appeal rights are explained following this section.

Caution

If you do not respond to the 30-day letter, or if you respond but do not reach an agreement with an appeals officer, we will send you a 90-day letter, also known as a *Notice of Deficiency*. This is a legal document that explains the proposed changes and the amount of the proposed tax increase. You will have 90 days (150 days if it is addressed to you outside the United States) from the date of this notice to file a petition with the Tax Court. If you do not petition the Tax Court you will receive a bill for the amount due.

Fast Track Mediation Services

If you do not agree with any or all of the IRS findings, you may request Fast Track Mediation services to help you resolve disputes resulting from the examination (audit). Fast Track Mediation offers an expedited process with a trained mediator, who will help facilitate communication, in a neutral setting. The mediator will work with you and the IRS to understand the nature of the dispute. The purpose is to help the two of you reach a mutually satisfactory resolution that is consistent with the applicable law. The mediator has no authority to require either party to accept any resolution. You may withdraw from the mediation process anytime. If any issues remain unresolved you will retain all of your usual appeal rights.

Most cases qualify for Fast Track Mediation. To begin the process, you may request the examiner or IRS representative to arrange a mediation meeting. Both you and the IRS representative must sign a simple *Agreement to Mediate* form. A mediator will then be assigned. Generally, within a week, the mediator will contact you and the IRS representative to schedule a meeting. After a brief explanation of the process, the mediator will discuss with you when and where to hold the mediation session.

For additional information, refer to Publication 3605, *Fast Track Mediation-A Process for Prompt Resolution of Tax Issues.*

How Do You Appeal a Decision?

The Appeal System

Because people sometimes disagree on tax matters, the Service has an appeal system. Most differences can be settled within this system without going to court.

Your reasons for disagreeing must come within the scope of tax laws, however. For example, you cannot appeal your case based only on moral, religious, political, constitutional, conscientious, or similar grounds.

If you do not want to appeal your case within the IRS, you may take your case directly to tax court.

Appeal Within the IRS

You may appeal our tax decision to a local appeals office, which is separate and independent of the IRS Office taking the action you disagree with. An appeals office is the only level of appeal within the IRS. Conferences with Appeals Office personnel may be conducted in person, through correspondence, or by telephone with you or your authorized representative

If you want to have a conference with an appeals officer, follow the instructions in the letter you received. We will send your conference request letter to the appeals office to arrange for a conference at a convenient time and place. You or your qualified representative should be prepared to discuss all disputed issues at the conference. Most differences are settled at this level. Only attorneys, certified public accountants or enrolled agents are allowed to represent a taxpayer before Appeals. An unenrolled preparer may be a witness at the conference, but not a representative.

If you want to have a conference with an appeals officer, you may also need to file either a **small case request** or a **formal written protest** with the contact person named

in the letter you receive. Whether you file a small case request or a formal written protest depends on several factors.

Making a Small Case Request

You may make a **small case request** if the total amount of tax, penalties, and interest for *each* tax period involved is $25,000 or less, and you do not meet one of the exceptions below for which a formal protest is required. If more than one tax period is involved and *any* tax period exceeds the $25,000 threshold, you must file a formal written protest for all periods involved. The total amount includes the proposed increase or decrease in tax and penalties or claimed refund. For an *Offer -in- Compromise*, include total unpaid tax, penalty, and interest due.

To make a small case request, follow the instructions in our letter to you by sending a brief written statement requesting an appeals conference. Indicate the changes you do not agree with and the reasons you do not agree with them.

Caution

Be sure to send the protest within the time limit specified in the letter you received.

You must file a **formal written protest**:

- If the total amount of tax, penalties, and interest for any tax period is more than $25,000;

- In all partnership and S corporation cases, regardless of the dollar amount;

- In all employee plan and exempt organization cases, regardless of the dollar amount;

- In all other cases, unless you qualify for other special appeal procedures, such as requesting appeals consideration of liens, levies, seizures, or installment agreements. *(See Publication 1660, Collection Appeal Rights, for more information on special collection appeals procedures.)*

Filing a Formal Protest

When a **formal protest** is required, send it within the time limit specified in the letter you received. Include in your protest:

- Your name and address, and a daytime telephone number.

- A statement that you want to appeal the IRS findings to the Appeals Office.

- A copy of the letter showing the proposed changes and findings you do not agree with *(or the date and symbols from the letter.)*

- The tax periods or years involved.

- A list of the charges that you do not agree with, and why you do not agree.

- The facts supporting your position on any issue that you do not agree with.

- The law or authority, if any, on which you are relying.

- You must sign the written protest, stating that it is true, under the penalties of perjury as follows:

"Under the penalties of perjury, I declare that I examined the facts stated in this protest, including any accompanying documents, and, to the best of my knowledge and belief, they are true, correct, and complete."

If your representative prepares and signs the protest for you, he or she must substitute a declaration stating:

- That he or she submitted the protest and accompanying documents and;

- Whether he or she knows personally that the facts stated in the protest and accompanying documents are true and correct.

We urge you to provide as much information as you can, as this will help us speed up your appeal. This will save you both time and money.

Additional information about the Appeals process may be found in Publication 5, *Your Appeals Rights and How to Prepare a Protest if you Don't Agree.*

After the Examination

Payment Options

You can't pay all that you owe now

If you can't pay all your taxes now, pay as much as you can. By paying now, you reduce the amount of interest and penalty you owe. Then immediately call, write, or visit the nearest IRS office to explain your situation. After you explain your situation, we may ask you to fill out a Collection Information Statement. If you are contacting us by mail or by telephone, we will mail the statement to you to complete and return to us. This will help us compare your monthly income with your expenses so we can figure the amount you can pay. We can then help you work out a payment plan that fits your situation. This is known as an installment agreement.

Payment by credit card

Individual taxpayers may make credit *(and debit)* card payments on tax liabilities *(including installment agreement payments)* by phone or Internet. Payments may be made to the United States Treasury by contacting:

*   Official Payments Corporation at 1-800-272-9829 or by logging on to www.officialpayments.com on the internet,

          or

*   PhoneCharge, Inc. at 1-888-255-8299 or by logging on to www.1888ALLTAXX.com

A convenience fee, based on the payment amount, will be charged. You will be informed of the convenience fee amount before the payment is authorized. This fee is in addition to any charges, such as interest, that may be assessed by the credit card issuer. For questions about making credit card payments, call toll free 1-877-754-4413 for the Official Payments Corporation, or 1-877-851-9964 for PhoneCharge, Inc.

Setting up an installment agreement

Installment agreements allow you to pay your full debt in smaller, more manageable amounts. Installment agreements generally require equal monthly payments. The amount and number of your installment payments will be based on the amount you owe

and your ability to pay that amount within the time we can legally collect payment from you.

You should be aware, however, that an installment agreement is more costly than paying all the taxes you owe now. Like revolving credit arrangements, we charge interest on the unpaid portion of the debt. Penalties also continue to accumulate on installment agreements.

Another cost associated with an installment agreement is a user fee. This is a one-time fee *(currently $43)* we charge to set up the agreement. If you do not meet the terms of the agreement throughout the life of the agreement, we charge an additional fee of $24 to reinstate it.

If you want to pay off your tax debt through an installment agreement, call the number shown on your bill. If you owe:

* $25,000 or less in tax, we will tell you what you need to do to set up the agreement;

*   More than $25,000, we may still be able to set up an installment agreement for you, but we may also ask for financial information to help us determine your ability to pay.

Even if you set up an installment agreement, we may still file a Notice of Federal Tax Lien to secure the government's interest until you make your final payment.

Note: We cannot take any collection actions affecting your property while we consider your request for an installment agreement, while your agreement is in effect, for 30 days after we reject your request for an agreement, or for any period while you appeal the rejection.

If you arrange for an installment agreement, you may pay with:

*   Personal or business checks, money orders, or certified funds *(all made payable to the U.S. Treasury)*,

*   Credit and debit cards,

*   Payroll deductions your employer takes from your salary and regularly sends to IRS, or

*   Electronic transfers from your bank account or other similar means.

Apply for an Offer-in-Compromise

In some cases, we may accept an *Offer-in-Compromise* to settle an unpaid tax account, including any penalties and interest. With this kind of arrangement, we can accept less that the full amount you owe when it is doubtful we will be able to collect the entire amount due.

Offers in compromise are also possible if collection action would create an economic hardship. You may want to discuss these options with your examiner.

Temporarily Delay the Collection Process

If we determine that you can't pay *any* of your tax debt, we may temporarily delay collection until your financial condition improves. You should know that if we delay collecting from you, your debt will increase because penalties and interest are charged until you pay the full amount. During a temporary delay, we will again review your ability to pay. We may also file a *Notice of Federal Tax Lien*, to protect the government's interest in your assets. See Publication 594, *The IRS Collection Process.*

After the Examination (cont.)

Innocent Spouse Relief

If you filed a joint tax return, you are jointly and individually responsible for the tax and any interest or penalty due on the joint return, even if you later divorce. In some cases, a spouse may be relieved of the tax, interest, and penalties on a joint return.

You can ask for relief no matter how small the liability.

Three types of relief are available.

- Innocent spouse relief - may apply to all joint filers;

- Separation of liability - may apply to joint filers who are divorced, widowed, legally separated, or have not lived together for the past 12 months;

- Equitable relief - applies to all joint filers.

Innocent spouse relief and separation of liability apply only to items incorrectly reported on the return. If a spouse does not qualify for innocent spouse relief or separation of liability, the IRS may grant equitable relief.

Each type of relief is different and each has different requirements. You must file Form 8857, *Request for Innocent Spouse Relief*, to request any of these methods of relief. Publication 971, *Innocent Spouse Relief*, explains each type of relief, who may qualify, and how to request relief.

You Must Contact Us

It is important that you contact us regarding any correspondence you receive from us. If you do not pay your bill or work out a payment plan, we are required by law to take further collection actions.

What If You Believe Your Bill is Wrong

Caution

If you believe your bill is wrong, let us know as soon as possible. Call the number on your bill, write to the IRS office that sent you the bill, call 1-800-829-1040 *(for 1040 filers)*, 1-800-829-4933 *(for business filers)*, 1-800-829-4059 */TDD*, or visit your local IRS office.

To help us correct the problem, gather a copy of the bill along with copies of any records, tax returns, and canceled checks, etc., that will help us understand why you believe your bill is wrong.

If you write to us, tell us why you believe your bill is wrong. With your letter, include copies of all the documents you gathered to explain your case. Please do not send original documents. If we find you are correct, we will adjust your account and, if necessary, send you a corrected bill.

Privacy Act Statement

The Privacy Act of 1974 says that when we ask you for information, we must first tell you our legal right to ask for the information, why we are asking for it, and how it will be used. We must also tell you what could happen if you do not provide it and whether or not you must respond under the law.

This notice applies to tax returns and any papers filed with them. It also applies to any questions we need to ask you so we can complete, correct, or process your return; figure your tax; and collect tax, interest, or penalties.

Our legal right to ask for information is found in Internal Revenue Code sections 6001, 6011, and 6012(a), and their regulations. They say that you must file a return or statement with us for any tax you are liable for. Your response is mandatory under these sections.

Code section 6109 and its regulations say that you must show your social security number or individual taxpayer identification number on what you file. You must also fill in all parts of the tax form that apply to you. This is so we know who you are, and can process your return and papers. You do not have to check the boxes for the Presidential Election Campaign Fund.

We ask for tax return information to carry out the U.S. tax laws. We need it to figure and collect the right amount of tax.

We may give the information to the Department of Justice and to other Federal agencies, as provided by law. We may also give it to cities, states, the District of Columbia, and U.S. Commonwealths or possessions to carry out their tax laws. And we may give it to certain foreign governments under tax treaties they have with the United States.

We may also disclose this information to Federal, state, or local agencies that investigate or respond to acts or threats of terrorism or participate in intelligence or counterintelligence activities concerning terrorism.

If you do not file a return, do not give us the information we ask for, or provide fraudulent information, the law says that we may have to charge you penalties and, in certain cases, subject you to criminal prosecution. We may also have to disallow the exemptions, exclusions, credits, deductions, or adjustments shown on your tax return. This could make your tax higher or delay any refund. Interest may also be charged.

Please keep this notice with your records. You may want to refer to it if we ask you for other information. If you have questions about the rules for filing and giving information, please call or visit any Internal Revenue Service office.

Useful Web Sites

IRS WEB SITE

The most useful of all tax web sites is the IRS web site. On it you can find the following helpful resources. To locate them, start on the IRS home page, www.irs.gov, then click on the links shown here in italics.

Audit Technique Guides: The very same guides that IRS auditors use during tax examinations are available for download by taxpayers. Guides exist for more than 50 different kinds of businesses and can be a great help by telling you what to expect if you ever face an IRS audit. Click on *Business/Market Segment Specialization Program*.

Compromise Agreements: To learn whether you might be able to compromise a tax bill that you can't afford to pay, and the terms that may be available to you, read the IRS's "Collection Financial Standards." Find them after clicking on *Individuals* on the IRS home page.

E-mail Newsletters: The free "Digital Dispatch," containing national tax news, and "Local News Net," containing information pertaining to your local IRS district, can be sent to your e-mail address. The IRS also has e-mail newsletters on special subjects like employee benefit plans. To subscribe go to *The Newsroom/e-News Subscriptions*.

Estate and Gift Taxes: For information on the tax rules for passing your wealth to the next generation, click on *Businesses/Estate and Gift Taxes*.

Frequently Asked Questions (FAQs): The IRS has an extensive list of commonly asked tax questions and the answers to them. Go to *Individuals/Frequently Asked Questions*.

Innocent Spouse Relief: If you think you shouldn't be liable for the tax bill of a spouse or former spouse, learn the rules for getting relief by clicking on *Individuals/Innocent Spouse*.

Installment Payments: To find out how to pay a tax bill in installments and learn the terms you may qualify for, use the IRS's Interactive Installment Payment Process. Find it by clicking on *Individuals/More Topics*.

IRS News: For all the latest IRS news releases, updates about the tax law and regulations, filing season problem reports, and other tax current events, click on *The Newsroom* on the IRS home page.

IRS Publications: These give the IRS's own explanations on almost every tax subject. To get the full list and download what you want, click on *Forms and Publications* on the IRS home page.

Local IRS Offices: You can obtain addresses, phone numbers, hours of service, and other contact information for your local IRS office, plus information about special services it provides—such as scheduled dates when "walk-in help" will be offered. Click on *Individuals* and then *Contact My Local Office*.

Mediation of Tax Disputes: To learn about the new voluntary mediation program the IRS has started to speed the resolution of what otherwise could be costly tax disputes, click on *Businesses/SmallBus Self-Employed/Fast Track Mediation*.

Questions Answered by E-mail: If you can't find an answer to your tax question on the IRS web site, you can submit it to the IRS through the site to get an answer by e-mail. Click on *Help*, then *Tax Law Questions*.

Retirement Plans: Company plans and IRAs provide valuable tax deductions and benefits but are subject to complex tax rules. For help with them, click on *Retirement Plans* on the IRS home page.

Refund Status: When your tax refund hasn't arrived yet, you can find out where it is and when you can expect it by clicking on *Individuals/Where's My Refund?*

Small Business Resources: This provides links to a wide range of other government agencies and business resources of special value to small businesses and self-employed persons. Click on *Businesses/SmallBus Self-Employed*.

Starting a Business: For help stepping through the process of starting up a business, click on *Businesses/Starting a Business*. You'll find not only tax information but links to the Small Business Administration and other sources of help with important nontax business start-up issues.

Tax Law: Instead of going to a law library, you can obtain the Tax Code, IRS regulations, the "Internal Revenue Bulletin" (which contains IRS administrative rulings), and the "Internal Revenue Manual" (detailing IRS procedures) from the IRS electronically. Click on *Individuals/More Topics/Tax Regulations*, then make your selection.

Taxpayer Advocate: Get help from within the IRS in resolving problems with the IRS bureaucracy and delaying imminent seizures and liens. Click on *Individuals/Taxpayer Advocate*.

Tax Products CD-ROM: This contains an entire library of tax forms, publications, and other tax information. Click on *Businesses* to find it.

Withholding Calculator: For help in calculating how much income tax you should have withheld from your paycheck, click on *Individuals/Withholding Calculator*.

Your Rights as a Taxpayer: Your rights during the tax audit, appeal, and collection processes are explained on the Taxpayer Advocate's web page. Click on *Individuals/Taxpayer Advocate*.

OTHER TAX-RELATED WEB SITES

Electronic Tax Discussions: Tax discussions on various subjects conducted on bulletins sent out to participants by e-mail. You can participate or read the archives of past discussions. Hosted by tax analysts. Go to www.tax.org, then click on *Cool Stuff* and *Free Bulletins*.

Essential Links: Very comprehensive listing for tax information and resources plus current tax news.
www.el.com/elinks/taxes

General Accounting Office: Overseer of the IRS. The financial operations of the IRS are reviewed in detail.
www.gao.gov

Legal Information Institute: Presents U.S. Supreme Court and Appeals Court decisions and a wide array of other legal resources.
www.law.cornell.edu

Roth IRAs: Comprehensive site is updated with Roth IRA information and has calculator utilities. Useful for both tax professionals and ordinary IRA owners.
www.rothira.com

Tax History Project: An overview of the history of taxes from the seventeenth century to now. Bonus: You can view the tax returns filed by presidents from FDR to George W. Bush.
www.taxhistory.tax.org

TaxPenalty.com: Reduce payroll tax penalties by calculating them under alternative methods permitted by the IRS.
www.taxpenalty.com

Taxsites (Federal): Gateway to a wide range of tax and accounting information. Has links to online tax services such as Commerce Clearing House and Research Institute of America.
www.taxsites.com

Taxsites (States): Comprehensive list of tax resources for all states, including links to state tax agencies.
www.taxsites.com/state.html

Taxweb: Broad collection of links to federal and state agencies, including tax discussion groups.
www.taxweb.com.

1040.COM: Good site for forms, instructions, publications, and bulletins in PDF format. Allows quick access and download, and is kept current.
www.1040.com

Transactional Records Access Clearinghouse (Syracuse University): Thousands of facts and statistics about the IRS.
www.trac.syr.edu

U.S. Tax Court: Read court decisions and learn the rules for taking a case to court, including the rules for the small case division where you don't need a lawyer.
www.ustaxcourt.gov

What the IRS Doesn't Want You to Know: The author's own web site will provide you with a wealth of information: monthly tax tips, the ability to ask Marty a tax question, and links to other sites.
www.irsmaven.com

FINANCIAL AND BUSINESS WEBSITES

American Institute of Philanthropy: How charities spend their money, plus ratings of charities.
www.charitywatch.org

Appraisers: FAQs about appraisals and contact information for appraisers.
www.appraisers.org

CNN/Money: A supermarket of financial news presented by the editors of CNN and *Money* magazine.
http://money.cnn.com

Estate Planning: Articles on estate planning are offered at this site. Titles include "Have You Done Proper Estate Planning?" and "Your Will or Trust Is Not a Complete Estate Plan." Also available are links to articles from the American Bar Association.
www.ca-probate.com/news_idx.htm

Human Resources: Human resources topics, including compensation and benefit plan issues.
www.hr-esource.com

Margin Investing: An easy-to-understand instructional guide covering investing on margin. Includes an interactive calculator that figures out the probable risk of a margin call.
www.tradeworx.com/sec/cgi-bin/tutorialmargin.cgi

Medicare: Medicare's official presence online. Users can search for health plans and nursing homes, as well as for participating physicians and prescription assistance programs. Includes a detailed list of contact phone numbers.
www.medicare.gov

Morningstar Finance: All about mutual funds.
www.morningstar.com

Motley Fool: Portfolio tracking, financial news, and lots more, written in plain, easy-to-understand language.
www.fool.com

N.Y. State College Tuition Program
www.osc.state.ny.us/college/index.htm

Prophet Finance: The place to go for conducting simple or sophisticated technical analysis of stocks.
www.prophetfinance.com

S&P Equity Investor Services
www.stockinfo.standardpoor.com

Small Business Administration: Excellent information source about starting and maintaining a business. Loaded with online tutorials, helpful software, and information about SBA applications and assistance programs.
www.sba.gov

Small Business Owners: Buying and selling a business, franchising, marketing, and more.
www.helpbizowners.com

Small Cap Center: Information about earnings and investments, as well as computer-related and telecommunications news.
www.smallcapcenter.com

Social Security Administration: All about Social Security benefits and procedures. Useful for requesting earnings and benefit statements.
www.ssa.gov

Social Security Administration—Retire: A retirement planner that walks you through the retirement application.
www.ssa.gov/retire2/index.htm

State College Savings Plan
www.collegesavings.org

Internal Revenue Service

Internal Revenue Service

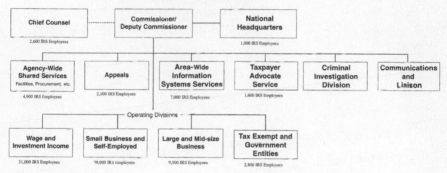

Chief Counsel	**Commissioner/ Deputy Commissioner**	**National Headquarters**
2,600 IRS Employees		1,000 IRS Employees

Agency-Wide Shared Services	Appeals	Area-Wide Information Systems Services	Taxpayer Advocate Service	Criminal Investigation Division	Communications and Liaison
Facilities, Procurement, etc.					
4,900 IRS Employees	2,100 IRS Employees	7,000 IRS Employees	1,600 IRS Employees		

— Operating Divisions —

Wage and Investment Income	Small Business and Self-Employed	Large and Mid-size Business	Tax Exempt and Government Entities
21,000 IRS Employees	30,000 IRS Employees	9,500 IRS Employees	2,800 IRS Employees

(NOTE: All numbers are approximate and subject to change.)

Notes

All IRS publications are issued by the Department of the Treasury and published by the U.S. Government Printing Office in Washington, D.C.

1 Why Every Taxpayer Must Read This Book

1. *Tax Hotline*, June 2001, p. 15.
2. David Cay Johnston, "Man Pursued by IRS Wins $75,000 to Pay His Lawyer," *The New York Times*, Feb. 9, 1999, A:12:1.

2 The IRS Personality

1. Ken Rankin, "And the Award for Tax Headache of the Year: AMT," *Accounting Today*, May 1-21, 2000, p. 5.
2. *Tax Hotline*, June 2001, p. 1.
3. Don Van Natta, Jr., "11 Officers Are Accused of Failure to Pay Taxes," *The New York Times*, July 17, 1996, B:3:5.
4. *IRS 1980 Annual Report*, pp. 10-11.
5. *IRS 1998 Data Book*, advance draft, Table 1.
6. Jerold L. Waltman, *Political Origins of the U.S. Income Tax* (Jackson, Miss.: University Press of Mississippi, 1985), p. 17.
7. Ibid., p. 113.
8. Mary A. Turville, "Treasury Proposes Crackdown on EIC Errors," *National Public Accountant*, July 1997, p. 8 ("Capital Corridors").
9. *IRS 1999 Data Book*, Table 9; *IRS 2000 Data Book*, advance draft, Table 9.
10. Lillian Doris, ed., *The American Way in Taxation: Internal Revenue, 1862-1963* (Englewood Cliffs, N.J.: Prentice-Hall, 1963), p. 39.
11. Gerald Carson, *The Golden Egg: The Personal Income Tax—Where It Came From, How It Grew* (Boston: Houghton Mifflin, 1977), p. 210.
12. Clayton Knowles, "Nunan Mentioned in Tax Cut Case," *The New York Times*, Feb. 15, 1952, 10:5.
13. Clayton Knowles, "Nunan Accused Before the Senate of Complicity in 4 New Tax Cases," *The New York Times*, Feb. 22, 1952, 1:2.

14. John C. Chommie, *The Internal Revenue Service* (New York: Praeger, 1970), p. 94.
15. *IRS 1997 Data Book*, Table 23.
16. David Cay Johnston, "IRS Workers Are Suspended in Bribery Case," *The New York Times*, July 29, 2000, A:7:6.
17. *IRS 2002 Data Book*, Table 25.
18. Ibid.

3　Who Runs the Show

1. IRS, *Tax Hints 1999*, p. 3.
2. "IRS Sets New Audit Priorities," IRS Update, *The CPA Letter/Medium Firms*, November 2002.
3. Marilyn Leibowitz, territory mgr, Taxpayer Education and Communication, National Research Program, at Fourth Annual Tax Practitioners' Institute, Presented by Queensborough Community College in partnership with IRS, November 1, 2002.
4. IRS Publication 4045, July 2002, IRS National Research Program.
5. Transactional Records Access Clearinghouse (TRAC), Syracuse University, 2001.
6. *Practical Accountant*, "IRS Briefing," August 1999, p. 17.
7. *IRS 2000 Data Book*, advance draft, Table 10.
8. Ibid., Table 21.
9. *IRS 1999 Data Book*, Table 21.
10. IRS, *Guide to the Internal Revenue Service for Congressional Staff*, p. 31.
11. Ibid., p. 33.
12. *IRS 2000 Data Book*, advance draft, Table 18.
13. IRS, *Internal Revenue Service Manual*, p. 4231-161.
14. TRAC, Syracuse University, 2002.
15. Ibid.
16. IRS, *Guide*, p. 11.
17. Ibid., pp. 11-12.

4　IRS People

1. David Burnham, *A Law Unto Itself: Power, Politics and the IRS* (New York: Random House, 1989), p. 22.
2. Eugene C. Steuerle, *Who Should Pay for Collecting Taxes?* (Washington, D.C.: American Institute for Public Policy Research, 1986), p. 15.
3. Ibid.
4. *Journal of Accountancy*, "IRS Forced to Operate With Less, to See a Decline in Service," Oct. 1996, p. 32 ("Tax Matters").
5. IRS, *Guide to the Internal Revenue Service for Congressional Staff*, p. 8.

6. *Commerce Clearing House*, 1998 Tax Legislation, IRS Restructuring and Reform Law, Explanation and Analysis, June 1998, Sec. 1316, pp. 344, 345.

5 Neutralizing the IRS's Power

1. David Burnham, *A Law Unto Itself: Power, Politics and the IRS* (New York: Random House, 1989), p. 21.
2. Jeff A. Schnepper, *Inside IRS* (New York: Stein and Day, 1987), p. 57.
3. General Accounting Office, *GAO Month in Review: April 1999*, Tax Policy and Administration, "Confidentiality of Tax Data: IRS Implementation of the Taxpayer Browsing Protection Act," GAO/GGD-99-43, March 31, 1999, p. 10.
4. Andrea Adelson, "IRS Is Getting a Look at Some Mortgage Applications," *The New York Times*, Dec. 29, 1996, 11:2.
5. Kenneth Harney, "IRS Casts High-Tech Net to Snare Mortgage Frauds," *Newsday*, Nov. 1, 1996, D:2:1.
6. Burnham, *A Law Unto Itself*, p. 313.
7. IRS, *Guide to the Internal Revenue Service for Congressional Staff*, p. 38.
8. *IRS Data Book*, 1994-1996 and 1997, Tables 31, 34.
9. Ibid.
10. IRS, *Guide*, p. 38.
11. Ibid.
12. Ibid.
13. *IRS Data Book*, 1994-1996, advance draft, Tables 31, 34.
14. IRS, *Guide*, p. 38.
15. Ibid.
16. *IRS Data Book*, 1994-1996 and 1997, Tables 31, 34.
17. As quoted in Burnham, *A Law Unto Itself*, p. 303.
18. John C. Chommie, *The Internal Revenue Service* (New York: Praeger, 1970), p. 177.
19. Seymour Hersh, "IRS Said to Balk Inquiry on Rebozo," *The New York Times*, April 21, 1974, 1:3; and "Ervin Unit to Get Rebozo Tax Data," *The New York Times*, April 24, 1974, 1:4.
20. U.S. Congress House Committee on Government Operations, fourth report, *A Citizen's Guide on Using the Freedom of Information Act and the Privacy Act of 1974 to Request Government Records*, House Report 102-146 (Washington, D.C.: GPO, 1991), p. 2.
21. Ibid., pp. 5-6.
22. *IRS 2000 Data Book*, advance draft, Table 10.
23. Joseph A. Pechman, *Federal Tax Policy*, 4th ed., Studies of Government Finance (Washington, D.C.: Brookings Institution, 1983), p. 61.

24. Internal Revenue Service. Budget in Brief, Fiscal Year 2004, page 1.
25. Burnham, *A Law Unto Itself*, p. 308.
26. Kip Dellinger, Audit and Accounting Forum, "Is Asking for Honesty Undermining the Tax System?," *Accounting Today*, Aug. 25-Sept. 7, 1997, p. 12.

6   IRS Technology

1. *IRS 1991 Annual Report*, p. 10.
2. *IRS 2002 Data Book*, Table 1.
3. *IRS 2002 Data Book*, Tables 1, 10, 25, and 26.
4. Ingrid Eisenstadter, "Insufficient Funds and the IRS," *The New York Times*, May 17, 1998, 3:12.
5. David Cay Johnston, "Leaders of IRS Panel Urge Sweeping Overhaul of Agency," *The New York Times*, Feb. 1, 1997, 8:4.
6. David Cay Johnston, "Computers Clogged, IRS Seeks to Hire Outside Processors," *The New York Times*, Jan. 31, 1997, 1:1.

7   IRS Targets and What to Do If You're One of Them

1. Arthur Fredheim, "Audits Digging Deeper Beneath the Surface," *Practical Accountant*, March 1996, p. 20; taken from IRS commissioner Margaret Milner Richardson's speech to New York State Bar Association, Albany, N.Y., January 24, 1995.
2. Marguerite T. Smith, "Who Cheats on Their Income Taxes," *Money*, April 1991, pp. 101-102.
3. Ibid., p. 104.
4. Statistics of Income Division, Individual Income Tax Returns, Analytical Table C, 1996.
5. Alan R. Sumutka and James Volpi, "Benefits and Rewards of the 'New' Home Office Deduction," *The CPA Journal*, Feb. 2000, p. 27.
6. Jan M. Rosen, "Trained on Home Offices: Secret Weapon 8829," *The New York Times*, March 1, 1992, F:21:1.
7. Randall W. Roth and Andrew R. Biebl, "How to Avoid Getting Caught in the IRS Crackdown," *Journal of Accountancy*, May 1991, p. 35.
8. Natwar M. Gandi, "Issues in Classifying Workers as Employees or Independent Contractors," Testimony before the Subcommittee on Oversight, Committee on Ways and Means, June 20, 1996, U.S. GAO, p. 3.
9. Barry H. Frank, "What You Can Do About the IRS's All-Out Attack on Independent Contractors," *Practical Accountant*, April 1991, p. 34.
10. Ibid., p. 35.

11. Commerce Clearing House, *1998 Tax Legislation, IRS Restructuring and Reform Law, Explanation and Analysis*, June 1998, Sec. 1126, p. 270.

12. Roth and Biebl, "How to Avoid," p. 35.

13. *Practical Accountant*, "IRS Briefing," June 2001, p. 18.

14. *Standard Federal Tax Reporter*, CCH Comments (Chicago: Commerce Clearing House), March 21, 1996, Sec. 79,354 and Sec. 79,355, pp. 48,725–48,726.

15. Kathy Krawczyk, Lorraine M. Wright, and Roby B. Sawyers, "Independent Contractor: The Consequences of Reclassification," *Journal of Accountancy*, Jan. 1996, p. 48.

16. Ibid.

17. *Standard Federal Tax Reporter*, CCH Comments, Aug. 1, 1996, p. 4.

18. *Tax Hotline*, "IRS Abuse Hotline," Dec. 1997, p. 13.

19. Kruse, Inc. DC ND Ind., #1-99-cv-428.

20. Richard Byllott, "Compliance 2000 and Cash Transaction Reporting," *Nassau Chapter Newsletter* (published by New York State Society of Certified Public Accountants), vol. 36, no. 4 (Dec. 1992), p. 10.

21. *Social Security Administration/IRS Reporter*, "Market Segment Specialization in the Examination Division," Summer 1995, p. 2.

22. *Practical Accountant*, "Latest IRS Audit Technique Guides," Jan. 1996, p. 52 ("Inside the IRS").

23. *Practical Accountant*, "MSSP Guides Issued on Architects and Cancellation of RTC Debt," April 1995, p. 16 ("Inside the IRS").

24. Materials handed out at IRS's Financial Status Audits Conference, presented by Donald Caterraccio, IRS Brooklyn District; Denis Bricker, IRS Brooklyn District; Jack Angel, CPA, The Tax Institute, College of Management, Long Island University/C. W. Post Campus, July 11, 1996.

25. IRS, MSSP Garment Manufacturers, Training 3147-103, April 1997, TPDS84302H, p. 1-4.

26. Ibid.

27. IRS, MSSP Bars and Restaurants, Training 3149-118, Feb. 1998, TPDS 83849L, pp. 2-1, 2-3, 2-5.

28. IRS, MSSP Business Consultants, Training 3123-012, March 2001, p. 8.

29. *Practical Accountant*, "AMT, NOL and Garden Supplies MSSPs," June 2000, p. 18 ("IRS Briefing").

30. *IRS 1992 Annual Report*, p. 10.

31. David Cay Johnston, "Corporations' Taxes Are Falling Even As Individuals' Burden Rises," *The New York Times*, Feb. 20, 2000, 1:1:1.

32. Ibid.

33. Ibid.

34. David Cay Johnston, "2 Courts Reject IRS Efforts to Limit Tax Shelters," *The New York Times*, June 22, 2001, A:1:2.

35. Robert Reno, "This Tax Evasion Was in the Cards," *Newsday*, March 31, 2002, Money & Careers, p. f8 ("Reno on Sunday").
36. David Cay Johnston, "A Smaller IRS Gives Up on Billions in Back Taxes," *The New York Times*, April 13, 2001, A:1:1.
37. David Cay Johnston, "IRS Is Allowing More Delinquents to Avoid Tax Bill," *The New York Times*, Oct. 10, 1999, 1:1:6.
38. Ibid.
39. IRS News Release IR-2002-12; *Tax Hotline*, Dec. 2002, p. 8.

8   How to Completely Avoid an Audit

1. *IRS 1980 Annual Report*, p. 52; *IRS 1991 Annual Report*, p. 26; *IRS 1997 Data Book*, advance draft, Table 11.
2. *IRS Data Book*, 1999 and 2000, advance draft, Table 11; *IRS 2001 Data Book*, Table 10.
3. *IRS 2001 Data Book*, Table 10.
4. *IRS 1976 Annual Report*, p. 99, Table 2.
5. David Cay Johnston, "The High Price of Estate-Tax Cheating," *The New York Times*, Dec. 17, 2000, 3:13.
6. *IRS 2001 Data Book*.
7. Limited liability companies initially have an option to file with the IRS as an individual, partnership, or corporation. Most choose to file as a partnership on Form 1065 (U.S. Partnership Return of Income).
8. *IRS Data Book*, 1998 and 1999, advance draft, Table 11.
9. Report by the Treasury Inspector General for Tax Administration, #2002-30-186, September 2002.
10. IRS, MSSP Garment Manufacturers, Training, 3147-103, April 1997, TPDS84302H, p. 7-13.
11. Ibid., p. 7-16.
12. Ibid., p. 7-14.

11   Ten Ground Rules Never to Break to Win with the IRS

1. Robert D. Hershey, Jr., "Taxpayers, Defeated by Schedule D, Surrender to the Experts," *The New York Times*, March 29, 1998, Bu:1:11.
2. *National Public Accountant*, "How to Communicate with Your Members of Congress," June-July 1995, p. 35 ("Client Report").
3. *Tax Hotline*, Sept. 2001, p. 1.
4. *Tax Hotline*, May 2001, p. 7.
5. *Tax Hotline*, Dec. 2000, p. 13.
6. John M. Peterson, *Tax Hotline*, January 2000, p. 9.

12 The Latest Tax Legislation

1. Research Institute of America, "RIA's Complete Analysis of the Economic Growth and Tax Relief Reconciliation Act of 2001," 2001.
2. Joe Catalano, "New Tax Laws Create Need for Fresh Thinking by Homeowners," *Newsday*, Dec. 5, 1997, C:1:1.
3. Grace W. Weinstein, "No More Income Gap for Retirees Over 65," *Investor's Business Daily*, May 19, 2000, p. 4.

13 The New IRS

1. "IRS Horror Stories Told by Senators," *Newsday*, Sept. 24, 1997, A:7:1.
2. Melissa Klein, "Roth Reports IRS Reprisals Against Whistle-blowers," *Accounting Today*, May 10-23, 1999, p. 5.
3. TRAC, Syracuse University, 2003.
4. David Cay Johnston, "Fearing for Jobs, IRS Workers Relax Effort to Get Unpaid Taxes," *The New York Times*, May 18, 1999, A:1:1.
5. Johnston, "IRS More Likely to Audit the Poor and Not the Rich," *The New York Times*, April 16,2000, A:1.32.
6. Frederick Daily, "Big Problems at the IRS," *Tax Hotline*, March 7, 2000, p. 8.
7. David Cay Johnston, "IRS May Be Slower to Seize Some Assets," *The New York Times*, July 20, 1999, C:8:3.
8. GAO, *IRS's Innocent Spouse Program Improved*, April 2002, p. 36.
9. Charles O. Rossotti, prepared testimony before the Ways and Means Oversight Committee on IRS Restructuring and Reform Act Hearing, July 22, 1999.
10. David Cay Johnston, "Innocent Spouse Claims to IRS Soar Under New Law," The New York Times, Dec. 29, 1999, C:1:2.
11. *Journal of Accountancy*, "Is the Tax Court Becoming a Divorce Court?," Feb. 2003, pp. 35-41
12. *Practical Accountant*, "Innocent Spouse Test," June 2000, p. 20 ("IRS Briefing").
13. *Practical Accountant*, "Domestic Violence and Innocent Spouse Relief," April 2001, p. 10 ("IRS Briefing").
14. Matthew L. Wald, "The Latest Pitch: 1040PC and the Promise of a Speedy Refund," *The New York Times*, Feb. 28, 1993, "Your Taxes," 17:1.
15. GAO, *IRS's 2002 Tax Filing Season*, December 2002, p. 59.
16. Standard Federal Tax Reports (Chicago: Commerce Clearing House), "Electronic Filing for Personal Computer Users," Feb. 13, 1997, p. 3 ("Taxes on Parade").

17. Michael Stroh, "Accountant in a Box," *Newsday*, Feb. 10, 1999, C:8:1.

18. *Standard Federal Tax Reports* (Chicago: Commerce Clearing House), "IRS Announces Telefile Pilot for Filing Quarterly Payroll Tax Returns," March 3, 1997, p. 3 ("Taxes on Parade").

19. Tom Herman, "A Special Summary and Forecast of Federal and State Tax Developments," *The Wall Street Journal*, March 26, 1997, A:1:5.

20. *Money*, "Tax Redemption," May 2000, p. 146.

21. *Tax Hotline*, "Offer in Compromise Strategy," June 15, 2000, p. 15.

22. *IRS Data Book*, 2002, Table 16.

23. IRS, *Taxnotes*, 1993, p. 2 ("Procedural Changes for Granting Installment Agreements").

24. George G. Jones and Mark A. Luscombe, "Do Lower IRS Collection Stats Warrant Aggressive Strategies?," *Accounting Today*, June 21-July 4, 1999, p. 8.

25. David Cay Johnston, "Compressed Data Web Site Offers Help with IRS Penalties," *The New York Times*, Jan. 10, 2000, C:4:1.

26. David Cay Johnston, "Rate of All IRS Audits Falls; Poor Face Particular Scrutiny," *The New York Times*, Feb. 16, 2001, A:1:3.

Bibliography

All IRS publications are listed under the Department of the Treasury.

Adelson, Andrea. "IRS Is Getting a Look at Some Mortgage Applications." *The New York Times*, Dec. 29, 1996, 11:2.

· *Audit and Accounting Forum*. "Is Asking for Honesty Undermining the Tax System?" Aug. 25-Sept. 7, 1997, p. 12.

Blaustein, Randy Bruce. *How to Do Business with the IRS. Taxpayer's Edition*. Englewood Cliffs, N.J.: Prentice-Hall, 1984.

(Boardroom Classics). *Tax Loopholes*. Springfield, N.J.: Boardroom Classics, 1994.

Burnham, David. "A Law Unto Itself: Power, Politics, and the IRS. New York: Random House, 1989.

Bylott, Richard. "Compliance 2000 and Cash Transaction Reporting." *Nassau Chapter Newsletter*. Published by New York State Society of Certified Public Accountants, vol. 36, no. 4 (Dec. 1992).

Carlson, Robert C., ed. *Tax Wise Money*, vol. 2, no. 6 (June 1993).

Chommie, John C. *The Internal Revenue Service*. New York: Praeger, 1970.

(Commerce Clearing House). *1998 Tax Legislation, IRS Restructuring and Reform Law, Explanation and Analysis*. June 1998. *Standard Federal Tax Reporter, Internal Revenue Code*, "Historical Note." Chicago: Commerce Clearing House, Inc., 1994.

Cozort, Larry A. "Is the Tax Court Becoming a Divorce Court?" *Journal of Accountancy*, February 2002, p. 35.

Daily, Frederick W. *Stand Up to the IRS: How to Handle Audits, Tax Bills and Tax Court*. Berkeley: Nolo Press, 1992.

Davis Shelley, L. *IRS Historical Fact Book: A Chronology, 1646-1992*. Washington, D.C.: U.S. Government Printing Office, 1993.

Department of the Treasury, Internal Revenue Service. *1998 Tax Hints*. Brookhaven Service Center. Washington, D.C.: GPO, 1999.

———. *Guide to the Internal Revenue Service for Congressional Staff*. Legislative Affairs Division 1272. Washington, D.C.: GPO, 1991.

———. *Internal Revenue Service Manual*. Sections 912, 913, 940. Washington, D.C.: GPO, 1981.

———. *IRS 1997 Data Book* (advance report). Washington, D.C.: GPO, 1997.

———. *IRS 1998 Data Book*. Washington, D.C.: GPO, 1998.

———. *IRS 1999 Data Book*. Washington, D.C.: GPO, 1999.

———. *IRS 2000 Data Book* (advance report). Washington, D.C.: GPO, 2000.

———. *IRS Data Book*, 2001, Bulletin 55B. Washington, D.C.: GPO, 2002.

———. *IRS Data Book*, 2002, Bulletin 55B, Washington, D.C.: GPO, 2003.

———. *IRS 1976 Annual Report, IRS 1980 Annual Report, IRS 1990 Annual Report, IRS 1991 Annual Report, IRS 1992 Annual Report, IRS 1993 Annual Report (advance draft)*. Washington, D.C.: GPO, 1977, 1981, 1991, 1992, 1993.

———. IRS Market Segment Specialization Program. Garment Manufacturers, Training 3147-1093, TPDS84302H. Washington, D.C.: GPO, 1997.

———. Bars and Restaurants, Training 3149-118, TPDS83849L. Washington, D.C.: GPO, 1998.

———. *IRS Service*. Washington, D.C.: GPO, 1990.

———. Statistics of Income Division, Individual Tax Returns, Analytical Table C, 2002. Washington, D.C.: GPO, 2002.

Doris, Lillian, ed. *The American Way in Taxation: Internal Revenue, 1862-1963*. Englewood Cliffs, N.J.: Prentice-Hall, 1963.

Eisenstadter, Ingrid. "Insufficient Funds and the IRS." *The New York Times*, May 17, 1998, 3:12:4.

Electronic Tax Administration Advisory Committee. "Annual Report to Congress," 2001.

Fairly, Juliette, and Peter D. Fleming. "The Single-Participant 401(k). *Journal of Accountancy*, March 2003, p. 49.

Frank, Barry H. "What You Can Do About the IRS's All-Out Attack on Independent Contractors." *Practical Accountant*, April 1991, pp. 36-37.

Gandi, Natwar M. "Issues in Classifying Workers as Employees or Independent Contractors." Testimony before the Subcommittee on Oversight, Committee on Ways and Means, June 20, 1996. Washington, D.C.: GPO, 1996.

Gee, Edgar, Jr., Michael J. Knight, and Willis Jackson. "Independent Contractor or Employee: How the Process Works Today." *The CPA Journal*, December 1999, p. 27.

General Accounting Office, *GAO Month in Review:* April 1999, Tax Policy Administration, "Confidentiality of Tax Data: IRS Implementation of the Taxpayer Browsing Protection Act," GAO/GGD-99-43, March 31, 1999, p. 10.

Hershey, Robert D., Jr. "Taxpayers, Defeated by Schedule D, Surrender to Experts," *The New York Times*, March 29, 1998, Bu:1:1.

———. "A Technological Overhaul of IRS Is Called a Fiasco." *The New York Times*," April 15, 1996, 8:5.

Hitt, Greg. *"Favored Companies Get 11th-Hour Tax Breaks."* The Wall Street Journal, July 30, 1997, A:2.

Investor's Business Daily. "Gap for Retirees Over 65," May 19, 2000, p. 4. irs.gov web site.

Jobs and Growth Tax Relief Reconciliation Act of 2003, Law, Explanation and Analysis. Chicago: CCH Inc., 2003.

Johnston, David Cay. "Affluent Avoid Scrutiny on Taxes Even As IRS Warns of Cheating." *The New York Times*, April 7, 2002, 1:1:1.

———. "Big Accounting Firm's Tax Plans Help the Wealthy Conceal Income." *The New York Times*, June 20, 2002, C:1:3.

———. "Compressed Data Web Site Offers Help with IRS Penalties." *The New York Times*, Jan. 10, 2000, C:4:1.

———. "Computers Clogged, IRS Seeks to Hire Outside Processors." *The New York Times*, Jan. 31, 1997, 1:1.

———. "Corporations' Taxes Are Falling Even as Individuals' Burden Rises." *The New York Times*, Feb. 20, 2000, 1:1:1.

———. "Death Still Certain, But Taxes May Be Subject to a Loophole." *The New York Times*, July 28, 2002, A:1:5.

———. "Fearing for Jobs, IRS Workers Relax Efforts to Get Unpaid Taxes." *The New York Times*, May 18, 1999, A:1:1.

———. "Government Sues Accountant, Saying He Helped Clients Try to Dodge Millions in Taxes." *The New York Times*, March 15, 2002, A:19:1.

———. "The High Price of Estate-Tax Cheating." *The New York Times*, Dec. 17, 2000, 3:13.

———. "Hunting Tax Cheats, IRS Vows to Focus More Effort on the Rich." *The New York Times*, Sept. 13, 2002, A:1:1.

———. "Innocent Spouse Claims to IRS Soar Under New Law." *The New York Times*, Dec. 29, 1999, C:1:2.

———. "IRS Audits of Working Poor Increase." *The New York Times*, March 1, 2002, C:2:1.

———. "IRS Bolstering Efforts to Curb Cheating on Taxes." *The New York Times*, Feb. 13, 2000, A:6:1.

———. "IRS Is Allowing More Delinquents to Avoid Tax Bills." *The New York Times*, Oct. 10, 1999, 1:1:6.

———. "IRS May Be Slower to Seize Some Assets." *The New York Times*, July 20, 1999, C:8:3.

———. "IRS More Likely to Audit the Poor and Not the Rich." *The New York Times*, April 16, 2000, A:1:32.

———. "IRS Paid Millions in False Claims for Slavery Credit." *The New York Times*, April 14, 2002, 1:22:1.

———. "IRS Workers Are Suspended in Bribery Case." *The New York Times*, July 29, 2000, A:7:6.

———. "Key Questions on Tax Breaks: How Big? Who Gets Them?" *The New York Times*, Dec. 16, 2002, C:4:1.

————. "Leaders of IRS Panel Urge Sweeping Overhaul of Agency." *The New York Times*, Feb. 1, 1997, 8:4.

————. "Man Pursued by IRS Wins $75,000 to Pay His Lawyers." *The New York Times*, Feb. 9, 1999, A:12:1.

————. "Moving Tax Simplification Toward Front Burner." "The New York Times, April 26, 2001, C:1:2.

————. "New Tools for the IRS to Sniff Out Tax Cheats." *The New York Times*, Jan. 3, 2000, C:1:15.

————. "Officers May Gain More Than Investor in Move to Bermuda." *The New York Times*, May 20, 2002, A:1:1.

————. "Rate of All IRS Audits Falls; Poor Face Particular Scrutiny." *The New York Times*, Feb. 16, 2001, A:1:3.

————. "A Smaller IRS Gives Up on Billions in Back Taxes." *The New York Times*, April 30, 2001, A:1:1.

————. "Socking It Away Amid Red Tape." *The New York Times*, March 12, 2002, G:4:1.

————. "Taking Aim at Tax Mavens, IRS Seeks Credit Card Slips." *The New York Times*, Oct. 20, 2000, A:1:5.

————. "A Tax Break for the Rich Who Can Keep a Secret." *The New York Times*, Sept. 10, 2002, 1:1:1.

————. "A Tax That's Often Ignored Suddenly Attracts Attention." *The New York Times*, June 5, 2002, C:1:3.

————. "2 Courts Reject IRS Efforts to Limit Tax Shelters." *The New York Times*, June 22, 2001, A:1:2.

————. "White House Seeks to Ease Rules Put on IRS Workers." *The New York Times*, Feb. 12, 2002, C:4:3.

————. "Your Taxes: A 'Stealth Tax' is Creeping Up on Growing Numbers of Americans." *The New York Times*, Feb. 17, 2002, 3:17:1.

Jones, George G., and Mark A. Luscombe. "Do Lower IRS Collection Stats Warrant Aggressive Strategies?" *Accounting Today*, June 21-July 4, 1999, p. 8.

Journal of Accountancy. "CPAs Recommend Simplifying Earned Income Tax Credit ("Tax Matters"), July 1995, p. 36; "IRS Audits Focus on Market Segments" ("Tax Matters"), Aug. 1995, p.21; "Independent Contractor: The Consequences of Reclassification," Jan. 1996, p. 47.

Klein, Melissa. "Roth Reports IRS Reprisals Against Whistle-blowers." *Accounting Today*, May 10-23, 1999, p. 5.

Knowles, Clayton. "Nunan Accused Before the Senate of Complicity in 4 New Tax Cases." *The New York Times*, Feb. 22, 1952, 1:2.

————. "Nunan Mentioned in Tax Cut Case." *The New York Times*, Feb. 15, 1952, 10:5.

The Leader-Herald (Johnstown, N.Y.). "Clinton Signs New Law Ending Earnings Limits for 60-somethings," April 1, 2000, p. 1.

McCormally, Kevin. "How a Dumb Idea Became a Law." *Kiplinger's Personal Finance*, July 1993, pp. 44-47.

Miller-Segarra, Tracey. "IRS Gets Down to Business with Rossotti." *Accounting Today*, July 13-26, 1998, p. 45.

Money. "Tax Redemption," May 2000, p. 146.

National Public Accountant. "How to Communicate with Your Members of Congress" ("Client Report"), June/July 1995, p. 35; "Treasury Proposes Crackdown on EITC Errors" ("Capital Corridors"), July 1997, p. 8.

(New York State Society of Certified Public Accountants). "New IRS Audit Approach Sending Tremors Through the CPA Profession." *Tax and Regulatory Bulletin*, vol. 5, no. 2 (Aug./Sept. 1995), p.1.

Newsday. "Audit Says Employees for IRS Stole $5.3 Million," Nov. 17, 1998, C:8:1; "The Ease of E-Filing," Feb. 16, 2003, F:2:4; "IRS Casts High-Tech Net to Snare Mortgage Frauds," Nov. 1, 1996, D:2:1; "IRS Horror Stories Told by Senators," Sept. 24, 1997, A:7:1; "Roth: The Kind of IRA That Keeps on Giving," April 14, 2002, F:2; "This Tax Evasion Was in the Cards," March 31, 2002, F:8.

NPA Journal. "SSA Develops Electronic Filing Option for Employees" ("Practitioner Communiqué"), July 1997, p. 10.

Pechman, Joseph A. *Federal Tax Policy.* 4th ed. Studies of Government Finance. Washington, D.C.: Brookings Institution, 1983.

Practical Accountant. "Audits Digging Deeper Beneath the Surface," March 1996, p. 20; "Latest IRS Audit Technique Guides," Jan. 1996, p. 62; "MSSP Guides Issued on Architects and Cancellation of RTC Debt," April 1995, p. 16; "IRS Briefing," August 1999, p. 17; "AMT, NOL, and Garden Supplies MSSPs," June 2000, p. 18; "IRS Briefing," June 2000, p. 20; "IRS Briefing," April 2001, p. 10; "IRS Briefing," June 2001, p. 18.

Queensborough Community College, Fourth Annual Tax Practitioners' Institute, November 1, 2002, Queensborough Community College in Partnership with IRS—Taxpayer Education and Communication.

Rankin, Ken. "And the Award for Tax Headache of the Year: AMT." *Accounting Today*, May 1-21, 2000, p. 5.

―――. "GAO Auditors Expose IRS's 'Pervasive Weaknesses.' " *Accounting Today.* April 26-May 9, 1999, p. 5.

(Research Institute of America). *A Guide for Securing Independent Contractor Status for Workers.* New York: Research Institute of America, 1991.

―――. "RIA's Complete Analysis of the Economic Growth and Tax Relief Reconciliation Act of 2001," New York: Research Institute of America, 2001.

Rosen, Jan M. "Trained on Home Offices: Secret Weapon 8829." *the New York Times*, March 1, 1992, F:21:1.

Rossotti, Charles O. Prepared testimony before the Ways and Means Oversight Committee on IRS Restructuring and Reform Act Hearing, July 22, 1999.

Roth, Randall W., and Andrew R. Biebl. "How to Avoid Getting Caught in the IRS Crackdown." *Journal of Accountancy*, May 1991, pp. 35-37.

Schmeckebier, Lawrence F., and Francis X. A. Eble. *The Bureau of Internal Revenue: Its History, Activities and Organization*. Baltimore: John Hopkins Press, 1923.

Schnepper, Jeff A. *Inside IRS*. New York: Stein and Day, 1987.

Smith, Marguerite T. "Who Cheats on Their Income Taxes." *Money*, April 1991, pp. 101-108.

Social Security Administration/IRS Reporter. Market Segment Specialization in the Examination Division," Summer 1995, p. 2; Market Segment Understanding Program Provides Guidelines," Fall 1995, p. 2.

Standard Federal Tax Reporter; CCH Comments. March 21, 1996, Sec. 79:354 and Sec. 79:355, pp. 48,725-726; Aug. 1, 1996, p. 4; March 3, 1997, p. 3.

Standard Federal Tax Reports. "Electronic Filing for Personal Computer Users" (Chicago: Commerce Clearing House), p. 3 ("Taxes on Parade").

Stern, Philip M. *The Best Congress Money Can Buy*. New York: Pantheon, 1988.

———. *The Rape of the Taxpayer*. New York: Random House, 1972.

Steuerle, Eugene C. *Who Should Pay for Collecting Taxes?* Washington, D.C.: American Institute for Public Policy Research, 1986.

Stevenson, William D. "The Middle Class Predator." *National Public Accountant*, Dec. 2, 2002, p. 42.

Strassels, Paul N., with Robert Wool. *All You Need to Know About the IRS: A Taxpayer's Guide*. New York: Random House, 1979.

Stroh, Michael. "Accountant in a Box." *Newsday*, Feb. 10, 1999, C:8:1.

Tax Hotline. David Ellis and James Glass, eds. Published by Boardroom Reports, Inc., New York, N.Y. March 1999, May 1999, March 7, 2000, June 15, 2000, Dec. 2000, May 2001, June 2001, July 2001, Sept. 2001, Nov. 2001, March 2002, April 2002, July 2002, Aug. 2002, Oct. 2002, Nov. 2002, Jan. 2003, March 2003.

Tax Points. "The IRS Audit Rate Still Falling," Sept. 2000, p. 1; "Offer in Compromise Strategy," June 15, 2000, p. 15; John M. Peterson, Jan. 2000, p. 9.

U.S. Congress. House Committee on Government Operation. *A Citizen's Guide on Using the Freedom of Information Act and the Privacy Act of 1974 to Request Government Records*. Fourth Report. House Report 102-140.

Van Natta, Don, Jr. "11 Officers Are Accused of Failure to Pay Taxes." *The New York Times*, July 17, 1996, B:3:5.

Walker, Jack L. *Mobilizing Interest Groups in America: Patrons, Professions, and Social Movements*. Ann Arbor: University of Michigan Press, 1991.

The Wall Street Journal. "A Special Summary and Forecast of Federal and State Tax Developments," March 26, 1997, A:1:5; "Favored Companies Get 11th-Hour Tax Breaks," July 30, 1997, A:2; "Tax Report," July 21, 2000, p. 1; "Tax Report," July 25, 2001, p.1.

Waltman, Jerold L. *Political Origins of the U.S. Income Tax.* Jackson, Miss.: University Press of Mississippi, 1985.

Washington, D.C.: GPO, 1991.

————. *The Public Statutes at Large of the United States of America from the Organization of the Government in 1789 to March 3, 1845.* Ed. Richard Peters. Vol. 1. Boston: Charles C. Little and James Brown, 1850.

The Washington Post. "Computer Problems Taxing IRS," March 15, 1996, 1:5.

Weiner, Alan E. *All About Limited Liability Companies & Partnerships.* Melville, N.Y.: Holtz Rubenstein & Co., 1994.

Winograd, Jeffrey L. "Washington Alert." *Federal Taxes Weekly*, Jan. 6, 2000, p. 23.

Witnah, Donald R., ed. *The Greenwood Encyclopedia of American Institutions.* S. V. "Government Agencies." Westport, Conn., and London: Greenwood Press, 1983.

Zorack, John L. *The Lobbying Handbook.* Washington, D.C.: Professional Lobbying and Consulting Center, 1990.

Index